George S. Odiorne is professor of management at the University of Massachusetts.

GEORGE S. ODIORNE

# THE
# CHANGE
# RESISTERS

How They Prevent
Progress and What
Managers Can Do
about Them

A SPECTRUM BOOK

PRENTICE-HALL, INC.   Englewood Cliffs, New Jersey 07632

190671

*Library of Congress Cataloging in Publication Data*

Odiorne, George S.
  The change resisters.

  (A Spectrum Book)
  Includes index.
  1. Organizational change.  I.  Title.
HD58.8.34     658.4'06     80-28341
ISBN  0-13-127902-5
ISBN  0-13-127894-0 (pbk.)

658.406
0 24

© 1981 by Prentice-Hall, Inc., Englewood Cliffs, New Jersey 07632

A SPECTRUM BOOK

10  9  8  7  6  5  4  3  2  1

Printed in the United States of America

Editorial/production supervision and interior design by Cyndy Lyle
Manufacturing buyer Cathie Lenard
Cover design by Honi Werner

Prentice-Hall International, Inc., *London*
Prentice-Hall of Australia Pty. Limited, *Sydney*
Prentice-Hall of Canada, Ltd., *Toronto*
Prentice-Hall of India Private Limited, *New Delhi*
Prentice-Hall of Japan, Inc., *Tokyo*
Prentice-Hall of Southeast Asia Pte. Ltd., *Singapore*
Whitehall Books Limited, *Wellington, New Zealand*

# Contents

# Preface

This book tells about the troubles we have fallen into because we can't manage change in modern society. Managers, administrators, politicians, parents, and institutional readers as well as professionals all are troubled by resistance to change. The book is organized along the following lines:

1. The various ways resistance to change appears are outlined in separate chapters. This book is more than just a tome on resistance to change at the psychological level; every influence producing resistance to planned change is detailed. The mental set of the change resister, the ways systems get locked into activity traps, the growth of professions—all these have produced resistance to planned change. There are changes we like and changes we don't like, and those changes, together with how we can deal with them, are detailed separately.

2. In some ways resistance to change is the effect of a special kind of adaptation of formal logic. The best minds of our society often seem bent upon criticism and resistance rather than creation and innovation. How these powers of logic get turned around into opposition is detailed in some length.

3. At the end of each chapter (most chapters are made up of a detailed chronicle of how the change resisters work) I list some antidotes or ways of dealing with the particular kind of resistance. The idea thus isn't merely to spell out how terrible things have become in the change area, but also to suggest some ways you can respond if you would produce managed change.

4. Chapters 16 through 19 of the book are all antidote! They describe a system for introducing change in the light of all the forces for change resistance that have been spelled out in exhaustive and appalling detail in the prior chapters.

5. There are some underlying assumptions that should be noted before you start reading. For example, it is assumed that change is occurring faster than before, and that this rate of change is causing us problems. This has been spelled out in Alvin Toffler's *Future Shock*. It also assumed that our problem in dealing with this accelerated rate of change is more one of management than of slowing it down. There is no way we can learn to adapt to change without learning how to manage it; our central nervous systems aren't equipped for accepting the kind of change we now produce.

The kind of change needed is *managed change* or *planned change,* which is a form of *management by anticipation.* This contrasts with our present methods of unplanned, unmanaged, and chaotic change.

Some notes of appreciation are due to many who read the manuscript and made critical and invaluable comments on it. Professor Sidney Sufrin drew liberally on his ample experience to give me the benefits of his generous wisdom. Many graduate students pierced the veil of nonsense and illogic that appeared in earlier versions. My patient wife Janet provided boundless support, including hours that could have been spent in less boring and onerous tasks, while this was being written. Judy Rose and Elaine Fydenkevez performed admirably in typing and proofing the pages. To all of them my deepest thanks.

# one

# The anti-planning mentality

Just imagine that you are president of a giant public utility that provides light and gas to one of America's largest cities and its surrounding region. Here are a few of your problems:

- You own most of a nuclear power-generating plant that was intended to produce a new, clean, pollution-free source of energy, but now you are tied up in lawsuits by environmentalists, the government, and the fishing industry (which declares you are causing thermal pollution), and student activists picket the site month on end while the broadcast media treat their picket line as if it were the latest American Revolution. They ignore your sober statements of fact.

- You have just learned that the people in New York who rate your corporate bonds with letters such as AAA or AAa, for example, have just reduced your bonds by one letter. This will add about five million dollars to your company's interest costs.

- You cannot get a rate increase from the state board that sets the rates you charge your customers because the board is catching too much pressure from unions and consumer groups, including a group whose legal expense is paid for by a government supported legal group.

- Twenty-one percent of the people in your service area are members of an ethnic minority group, but only one half of one percent of your employees are from that group, and most of them are janitors. The federal, state, and local equal employment officials are suing you for action. Meanwhile your middle managers go through the procedures of complying with the rules for equal employment opportunity but no results come forth in improving your ratios of minorities hired. "No qualified minorities are applying for jobs, and we cannot hire unqualified help and keep the power and gas flowing," the middle managers will tell you.

- There is a lawsuit in court for twenty-three million dollars filed against your company under a 1964 law; it charges your firm with discriminating in the wages,

1

hiring, and promotion of women employees. The plaintiffs have subpoenaed all of your records and declare they will press their suit if you do not settle now.

• Labor Department inspectors have been making regular visits under the Occupational Safety and Health Act (OSHA), and a steady stream of small complaints are coming forth from them.

• You have a coal-fired generating plant. Just four years ago you spent ten million dollars putting scrubbers on your smokestacks, coming up to the standards for that time, but there is a suit to require that the smoke be scrubbed even cleaner. Now the clean-air people are back and it looks like twenty million dollars more, according to your engineers, to come up to the new standards.

That is just the beginning. The first page in fact.

• You have been plagued with some minor power failures (called *brownouts*), which in the past would have been barely noticed. But the recent large New York City power outages have heightened everyone's attention to such outages, and now if you lose only ten blocks, a headline appears in the local press.

• You have tried to keep up with the most modern computer technology, but recently one employee working in a computerized branch of the accounting department was discovered with a defalcation of $150,000. Your controller and auditor tell you that there is no such thing as a computer totally secure from such sophisticated rip-offs. You protest, "You mean it is possible that even now we are being stolen blind by some clever computer thieves?" They look you soberly in the eye and reply, "We hope not, but nothing is one hundred percent sure in computer auditing."

All of these worries to be resolved and problems to be remedied keep you awake at night sometimes. But there is one thing that keeps you even more concerned:

*What is next, and who else besides me is worrying about the future, and how can I prevent even worse things than the headaches we have today?*

That question is the essence of this book: how to *manage by anticipation.* While in the example you imagined you were a president and thus sat in the position described by President Harry Truman's motto "The buck stops here," the same kind of pressure—to do a better job of anticipating the future—faces every manager at every level. In fact, it does not face just utility company presidents, or just business managers; it faces people at every level of living.

Governmental officials need to shape public policy to prevent disasters from fossil-fuel shortages, to find jobs for all who want them, and to stop inflation. We need to conserve our available land space and natural resources. Water will be in short supply, not just in time of drought, but every year, wet or dry. Population is exploding in certain parts of the world and pressing against the food supply, while at the same time the expectations people have of more food and better standards of living are growing rapidly. Institutions such as the church, the family, the university, and the hospital are becoming increasingly afflicted with the problems of the past that are ganging up on them.

To cope with this change, it is not enough simply to describe it while it is happening, or even to explain it after it has happened. We need a more compelling style of managing our affairs that can improve our life in the future. That is what this book is all about.

The utility company president undoubtedly suffers at times from a sense of inability to control what is happening. The feeling that one is being managed by events rather than managing them would be inescapable by a normal person in such a position. Yet, how much more is the sense of futility about trying to control their own destiny among ordinary people, middle managers, professionals, administrators, teachers, and workers! To be a president or a supervisor affords a person certain limited areas of power and influence. The boss can, within prescribed limits, move things around within his or her own responsibility areas. The homemaker can make numerous independent decisions within one household. But it is an increasingly prevalent condition for people in today's world to suffer from a sense of powerlessness, and furthermore to be uneasy or discontented with that powerlessness. It seems to an increasing number of people that all of the important decisions in their lives are being made for them rather than by them.

The population of the world increases at an alarming rate, the size of organizations grows, and bureaucratic systems of control seem to engulf us. This makes the world more depersonalized: we are governed mechanically by procedures and regulations and are more apt to be known as a number, such as our social security number, ZIP code, area code, or credit card number, than by our qualities as human beings.

All this has some redeeming features: we have a high standard of living, and more security for our old age, or for illnesses or unemployment; but being reduced to something less than our full human capacities makes us frustrated and angry. The world seems to many a giant absurdity, and some become angry or alienated. For while the world becomes more impersonal and permits less individual difference and self-realization, the desire for those ego ideals rises. Not only do the ruling people want to be somebody, but many previously left behind because of their race, color, religion, sex, national origin, or physical handicaps also want to realize their highest potentialities. They face a world that increasingly denies them those ego desires that only more power can bring.

Accordingly, people rush to the bookstands to buy books on power, how to attain it, how to use it, and how to manipulate and control other people and the environment. Hints for developing a piercing stare, or for sitting or standing around in ways that exude power over others, are avidly devoured by people suffering from a sense of powerlessness.

In this book we will deal with a different approach to self-actualization of yourself, your organization, your career. Rather than attack the situation as unfair, or even castigate those in charge of things—who really don't have all that power themselves these days—we will look at a rational but *situational* method of gaining power to attain your own goals.

If there is a single theme for this book, it would be a saying attributed to Lincoln: "If we know where we are, and perhaps a bit about how we got there, we might be able to see where we are trending, and thereby affect our destiny." This idea can affect your business, your organization, your career, or your life. No single book can honestly promise to remake your personality. It might, however, change your behavior in such a way that your condition is better, your sense of personal control over your own affairs increased. That, too, is the purpose of this book.

## IS LIFE'S BUSINESS A JOY RIDE OR A PLANNED GRAND TOUR?

To understand how we get into many of the jams we get into, we need some explanation of how planning has gotten itself off on the wrong foot and stayed there. There are, we propose here, two kinds of planning:

1. *Implicit planning* is the kind you do when you are heading out on a Sunday afternoon for what all passengers understand as *not really going anywhere special.* This is a "joy ride." *Let's get out the old bus and go for a ride* is a long-standing American pastime. We may go to the park, out into the country, up to the mountains, or down to the seashore. Who really cares? The end sought is understood by all to be joyous, and if when we get back we can agree it was all a ball, nobody cares whether or not we got sidetracked and didn't get where we originally thought we would go.

This kind of planning is close to the "American way." It is winging it, and getting there is all of the fun. You fly now and pay later. People who don't understand the joy-ride theory of planning are considered stuffy old fuddy-duddies, longhairs, pointy heads, and party-pooping wet blankets. This is the traditional American way, not only for Sunday afternoon rides in the old bus, but also for running the country or a corporation, taming the West, building a city, or covering the countryside with highways.

The thesis here is that joy-ride planning, which really isn't planning at all, is outmoded. It's a kind of freewheeling, open-dealing way of life that has fallen by the wayside in the modern world. It increasingly gets us into deeper trouble and more painful crises. The price we pay is too high for the momentary pleasure it brings.

2. *Explicit planning* is a far less romantic and fun-filled way of living. It includes setting out clearly in advance where we are going, what the final destination will be, when we will arrive, what intermediate stations are along the way and when each will be passed, and what the average speed and mileage will be. It also includes a clear calculation of what the trip will cost, what the terms of payment will be, where the money is coming from, and who will be responsible for every job in every detail, with some standards of performance for everyone. Every planned stop is covered with a reservation and guarantee, and provisions for the unexpected are thought out in advance and protective actions then taken to avert surprises.

Obviously the second kind of planning isn't all that fun-filled for people who have become hooked on joy rides, or, as we shall put it, are still in the JR frame of mind. Americans are in the throes of changing from the joy ride to the planned grand tour (PGT), and they aren't sure they are enjoying the change. The first kind of planning (which isn't planning at all) means we live for the present. The second, explicit planning (PGT), means we live more in the past and the future than in the present. Much of our waking hours is spent in studying the past to find meanings and the future to predict and control events. (Even our formal and explicit planning [PGT] hasn't been perfected that much. The highly touted, perhaps reverential, use of the computer is more for toy value than planning except in statistics courses in universities.)

It is also obvious that unless we can manage this transition from JR to PGT we will be in deeper and deeper trouble as time goes by. That's why we need to understand the anti-planning mentality which is so pervasive, and perhaps some antidotes for it. We shall look at the roots of the JR mentality and see how deeply it is embedded in the minds of many citizens, managers, and leaders.

## PLANNING: THE AMERICAN TRADITION

Americans, unlike the Russians, have been suspicious of and resistant to explicit planning. The explanation may lie in their past successes. Americans have been models of what success should look like. The opposite has been true of the Russians. From days of the czar through modern Soviet planning systems, the Russians have often done things the hard way. Their climate is harsh, their crops fail more often than others', and even when they win—as they did in World War II—it is the hard way.

The nineteenth century in America, on the other hand, was a fountainhead of optimism and individualism that embedded itself in the American character. It has only been in the Depression of the thirties and the turbulence of the seventh and eighth decades of the twentieth century—with Vietnam, Watergate, and the counterculture—that we have begun to act like chronic self-doubters. Along with this self-doubt came the first attention to planning at the national and corporate levels on any kind of serious scale. Yet even now, there are substantial streaks of optimism and cheery reliance on luck, pluck, and energy to make everything look rosy, and to make planning a kind of exercise in which bureaucrats and pointy heads are playing games with themselves. It does not really have much effect upon the future; it is just an exercise. Even in the most serious and solemn planning departments, the annual plan is often referred to as a "planning exercise."

## THE PERVASIVE NINETEENTH-CENTURY MENTALITY

There were few if any explicit national goals or corporate planning departments in the nineteenth century. No Office of Management and Budget did cost-effectiveness analysis to determine that we should make the Louisiana or the Gadsden purchase.

Andrew Carnegie built his steel company into a near billion-dollar business without Harvard Business School methods.

The American character of the nineteenth century has been described by Henry Steel Commager as one shared by a culture where success was in the air.[1] Nature had been generous and her riches were available to all, especially those who had the wisdom to have been born white and male. Incurably optimistic, the American knew that life would be successful and prosperous and that the future of everyone could easily be better than that of his or her parents. The son of the laborer could become a merchant or a banker. The poor bootblack could become a statesman. This optimism led to a sense of power. The models of Daniel Boone, Davy Crockett, and the Oregon Trail pioneers were all part of every child's education, and the mythology of never-ending growth and attainment was dealt out daily with breakfast. American culture was materialistic, and Americans attained a level of material success and wealth that no people had ever attained before. Hard work and ingenuity would carry the day, and shiftlessness was the major vice, for it could lead to poverty, which ranked as one of the major immoralities. The world was big, and distances of several hundred miles became a trifle. The Mississippi, the Great Lakes, the Grand Canyon were embedded in the American consciousness in such a way that size became a fixation. Great prairies and mountains produced a sweep of imagination and ambition the old world never knew. Crèvecoeur said this attitude was in the American climate and the immigrant "no sooner breathes our air than he forms schemes and embarks upon designs that he never would have thought of in his own country."

All of this led to a profound mistrust of the abstract and such things as theories and speculations. Things that were cultured were to be viewed with suspicion and skepticism. These circumstances opened the way to talent or to luck, and a democratic cast of mind led to the conclusion that big shots and smart people were somehow effete and objects of ridicule.

The nineteenth-century American was good-natured, generous, hospitable, and sociable. This led to a kind of hearty carelessness, which has been described as the most pervasive and persistent quality in the American. The American could afford to be careless in work and in trade, preferring versatility to pride in quality of craftsmanship. Things were done in grandiose fashion rather than with meticulousness. The American attitude toward authority—bureaucrats, experts, and stuffed shirts—was heartily contemptuous. Discipline was self-imposed and imposed by nature and by the situation, rather than by the authority of rank or organizational status. Success was *implicit* in the system, in the air, in the land, in the people, so why bother to write down the future? Just enjoy it.[2] While early depressions had been painful and frightening, they never shook the basic confidence of Americans in the system.

---

[1] H. S. Commager, *The American Mind* (New Haven, Conn.: Yale University Press, 1950).
[2] M. Lerner, *America as a Civilization* (New York: Simon & Schuster, 1957). A basic picture must also include Tocqueville, *Democracy in America* (New York, 1954), 2, and Charles Dickens, *American Notes,* (London, 1842).

# THE GROWTH OF PLANNING
# AFTER THE DEPRESSION

Two decades in the twentieth century produced a series of events that changed eternal and persistent optimism into some lingering periods of self-doubt. The first followed the crash of 1929.

During the twenties the self-esteem of Americans ran high, since they were firm in the belief that it was they who had won World War I. Even if the geographical frontiers were mainly ended, the mentality of expansionism continued relatively unfettered. The spirit of the pioneer ran in the American personality, and the chronic habit of chasing visions and pipe dreams remained a way of life for most. The ultimate in this pot-of-gold psychology was the great bull market of 1928 that was to lead to the crash of 1929 and the following decade-long depression.[3] This speculative fever caught up not only bankers and financiers, but the middle class and ordinary workers as well. Buying on margin, plunging with hard-earned savings, they bought and bought as the market surged up. The speculative fever infected everyone across the nation. The volume of shares traded went up, and after the election of Herbert Hoover as president of the United States, a new upward spurt made old gains seem paltry.

Some eary warning signals by the Federal Reserve Board and conservative commercial bankers alike were ignored. Even the sharp drop in selected issues did not faze the fanatical investors. One estimate was that 300 million shares were held on margin. From September to October, the market began to slide, with louder and louder assurances from forecasters on Wall Street and in academia that all was well. On Black Tuesday, October 29, 1929, the market collapsed, undoing the great American pipe dream that every man could become a millionaire, and that things could grow upward and onward without interruption. General Motors dropped from 72 to 36 and Union Carbide from 137 to 59. Former paper millionaires were pressed for margin calls and unloaded everything to pay their loans, only to cause the drop to go down even faster. By the time the run was made, suicides, bankruptcies, and disillusionment were a nationwide epidemic.

The effect of the crash was far more than economic and monetary. It produced a general decline in business, and the economy sloped off steadily through 1932, with great unemployment. Mutters of rebellion and the need for "an American Mussolini" were bruited about by the end of 1932. People who openly cried that the problem was not temporary and could not be overcome called for systemic changes in the entire way in which business and government were organized and planned. The idea of a planned economy, which had been considered tantamount to Bolshevism, was now an open matter for debate, and advocates became stronger and more confident.

The long recovery from the Depression came under the political leadership of Franklin D. Roosevelt, who restored confidence at the same time he moved the

---

[3] A. M. Schlesinger, Jr., *The Crisis of the Old Order 1919-1933* (Boston: Houghton Mifflin Company, 1957); and C. W. Wright, *Economic History of the United States* (New York: McGraw-Hill, 1949).

country a quantum leap forward toward a centrally planned society. The use of fiscal policy to affect prosperity and the rise of the government bureaucracy to control banking, securities, and other aspects of the private economy were never to be reversed. The old freewheeling private enterprise system now came under a *modified* form of capitalism, more tightly controlled and policed than would have been thought possible during the optimistic, untrammeled business climate of the nineteenth century.

The coming of World War II went a long way to restore confidence in business. The conduct of a victorious war on two fronts, and the resurgence of private initiative to raise production to unimagined levels, not only for guns but for butter as well, did something to blunt the pain of the Great Depression. The planned economy, however, never really went away, but grew. As the end of World War II appeared, documents suggesting new levels and forms of national planning were common. American power and prestige in the world were never greater, and Americans touring abroad were like visiting conquerers. The dollar was the basis for fiscal security and stability in the world, and our possession of the H-bomb and the technology of mass production made it clear once more to Americans that they were well founded in their optimism and visionary style of operating.

A second move toward a planned society occurred during the sixties, when the Vietnam war, which started as a minor incursion to fulfill a political commitment to a minor nation, turned into a horrible war, with heavy deaths and casualties, and a debilitating inflationary drain upon the economy. Young people in colleges and high schools openly rebelled against the draft, and in the process wracked the country with demonstration, strife, and open rioting. At the same time, long oppressed blacks began the first of what proved to be a revolution of the left-behind, and shook people's confidence in their essential happiness and belief that we were indeed the chosen people of the world. Major attacks upon major institutions, including government, the press, the universities, and corporations, merged into a new movement. The *London Economist* in 1978 said the period was made up of three weird evangelical spasms: The great society that drew too many bright people into anti-productive government jobs plus strong anti-discrimination programs which meant promoting the least suitable people and third, the econut spasm that favored the rights of snail darters over productive dams. All of this, the *Economist* proposed, produced a drift away from productivity, which led in turn to a decline in the value of the dollar, inflation, and unemployment.

The sheer power of the American colossus was noted by J. J. Servan-Schreiber in his book *The American Challenge* in 1968.[4] The giant economy that was America dominated the world economy at that time, producing twice the goods and services of all European industry combined, including that of both Britain and the Common Market—and two and one half times as much as that of

---

[4] J. J. Servan-Schreiber, *The American Challenge* (New York: Atheneum, 1968); *see also U.S.A.: The Permanent Revolution,* by the editors of *Fortune, Time,* and *Life* (New York. 1951).

the Soviet Union. America generated one third of all the production of all countries of the world while having only six percent of the world's population and seven percent of the earth's surface. Its per capita productivity was forty percent higher than the next highest, with corresponding levels of profits and family income. In machinery, autos, electronics, and chemicals, its production was more than two thirds of the total world production level. At the same time, in high-technology areas such as chemicals and computers, it was gaining rapidly even from the position of leadership. The percentage of the population between the ages of 20 and 24 enrolled in colleges and universities was nearly double that of the next highest, Russia, and higher than that of all others by appreciably larger margins.

What may have been missed in these booster-like statistics about American productivity and growth is that they were based largely upon the achievements of a few large corporations such as General Motors, American Telephone & Telegraph, DuPont, IBM, and similar blue-chip organizations. *All of these large corporations had grown beyond the nineteenth-century image of America and had been built soundly upon sophisticated and immensely complicated systems of corporate strategic planning, in collaboration and uneasy partnership with a government that planned for the entire economy.* All of them were sophisticated users of computers in analytical techniques, applied scientific management and modern behavioral sciences in their marketing and employee relations, and reinvested substantial amounts of their revenues into training and development of their human resources and into physical and scientific research and engineering development. For the most part they were divisionalized companies, financially complex and sophisticated, managed by objectives, and employing larger and larger amounts of capital with ever-increasing skills at forecasting and shaping their own future through strategic management systems.

## THE PERSISTENT ANTI-PLANNING MENTALITY

Early in the seventies it was a fair bet that we would continue into the planned society. The growth of expanding government programs to conduct wars on poverty, bad neighborhoods, and poor health care, and similar programs designed to allay the ills of society from Washington, continued apace. Republicans and Democrats alike had come to adopt the dominant role of planning in our lives. Revenue sharing by the federal government with towns and cities was a means of funneling federal taxation back to municipalities to provide some property tax relief. Its true effect was to produce a great leap in local planning. While many local planners were nothing more than proposal writers seeking federal funds, they also engaged in all sorts of projects and schemes to overhaul the traffic flow on Main Street, to build new housing for the elderly, and to beef up local police forces. New agencies and bureaus of government sprang up like mushrooms, all designed to plan and control some aspect of American Life.

Any assumption that the old, nineteenth-century mentality that opposed planning was dead was not an accurate one, however. Nothing demonstrated this more clearly than the response of the American public to the energy crisis. When in the early 1970's and again in 1979 the oil-producing nations of the Middle East suddenly quadrupled the price of crude oil, it threw the planners in government and corporations into a giant tailspin. Congress blamed the oil companies, and the oil companies hauled out numerous early warnings they had issued to an unheeding public showing that the shortage was predictable. It was now apparent that not only was the supply of oil finite, but the end of existing reserves was in sight. All of those automobiles, factories, and homes that were dependent upon fossil fuels were vulnerable. Furthermore, the people who controlled the largest known reserves were now prepared to exploit their power to withhold oil.

Long lines of cars at gas stations, sharp rises in home heating-oil bills, and breathtaking rises in electrical costs all made an immediate impression upon the public at large. But it was to prove a passing spook, and a hearty skepticism was observed that somehow this was a trick by corporations and politicians to dupe the average person.

*The response of the public at large to the energy crisis, in contrast to that of corporations and government, was clear-cut evidence of a strong anti-planning mentality at large.* Confronted with real and present fuel shortages for their own gas-guzzling cars, Americans *could* now picture an energy shortage. But gradually, whenever the lines ended, so did the urgency of planned conservation. The 55-mile-an-hour speed limit, which became a national law, was blithely ignored by a majority of drivers once the shortage passed. The end of the long lines for gas meant a return to a more profligate consumption of energy. When President Carter founded his energy program upon its being "the moral equivalent of war," he found few volunteers to join up and a remarkable reluctance in Congress to support new laws to eliminate gas guzzlers and to demand a more austere life style to conserve energy.

Each year, substantial numbers of Americans who can afford to do so do not buy insurance on their lives. They die intestate—without wills—and have no disability insurance beyond that provided by law under social security. Of the hundreds of thousands of businesses, only the major corporations have seemed willing to commit resources to planning. The rate of business failures is such that the average length of life of a business is reported to be seven years. The reason for the failures, reports Dun & Bradstreet, a master scorekeeper in such matters, is bad management, which includes a lack of planning.

Consultant Jack Bologna in 1978 reported on a study of 308 bankers, farmers, and middle and upper managers that revealed some of the reasons given by them for not planning. "Planning consumes too much time" was the most frequent reason given.[5] While planning indeed consumes time, it has a high yield in time itself, to say nothing of the yield in survival and other deferred payoffs.

Professor Sidney Sufrin offers still another reason why Americans at large and small business in particular do not plan. The planning that Americans have learned to rely upon from the nineteenth century, he proposes, was a form of *implicit planning.* What they avoid and resist is *explicit planning.* The implicit plan-

---

[5] J. Bologna, *Planning Commandments* (Westfield, Mass.: MBO Inc., 1978).

ning is that which presumes that the free enterprise system with its "invisible hand" serves in such a way as to implicitly govern things. If all persons and small businesses will merely go forth daily and seek their own self-interest, the balance of competition with supply and demand will take care of planning. The competent will do well and the incompetent will not. Few people go into business with the assumption that failure is possible; most presume that their own self-reliance and ingenuity will help them survive, and the overall plan is the system itself. People following their instincts are in accord with natural law. What more planning could be asked? To outplan God?

The Russian experience with a planned society offers some more worldly and tangible evidence to bolster the case of the anti-planners. The Russians are a prime case of explicit planning and its limitations. For decades they issued somber five-year plans that were regularly missed. Often the failures were due to risks of nature, such as the harsh climate and unpredictable weather of the land, which resulted in failures in wheat, cattle, and industrial production. More often, the plans went sour because they themselves were defective; failure often grew out of the lack of skilled or imaginative execution, or from the pressures of individual ingenuity among self-dealing subpopulations that thwarted the planners. Bureaucratic organizations, which treated plans as though they were self-executing, were often far removed from the people who would be required to quell their own interests in behalf of the state. If sixty years of commitment to explicit planning has not worked successfully, suggest the anti-planners, then how can it be proposed as a panacea to replace individual ingenuity and self-reliance? Planning, it thus seems, might easily be equated with anti-American attitudes, if not downright subversion.

C. West Churchman, writing in *The Systems Approach,* concedes that the idea of using behavioral scientists and planners to assist in analysis of systems and changing them has not been a particularly popular one in the United States.[6] Far more likely is the case where the individual manager armed with experience will survey the various aspects of the system, obtain some data and reports from underlings, and make up his or her own mind what should be done. If this is followed up by some motivational or even inspiring leadership, things will be done satisfactorily. This is illustrated in a 1978 report in *Omega* magazine, a journal of management science published in England. It reported on the practices of top executives in fifty firms that owned and operated expensive and complex computer facilities. A majority reported that when they had calculations to do, they used the back of an envelope. Fifty-seven percent stated that such calculations usually took less than five minutes. Thus, an important form of anti-planning is founded on a faith in intuition, experienced leadership, and an occasional dash of brilliance, and perhaps an old envelope.

One form of anti-planner confronted by the systematic planner and analyst is the chronic skeptic. The movie *No Time for Sergeants* depicted a hillbilly who thwarted the most detailed and meticulous plans of his leaders by his innocence and native ingenuity. The rube overcoming the system has been a long-time favorite

---

[6] C. W. Churchman, *The Systems Approach* (New York: Dell Pub. Co., Inc., 1968).

of American moviegoers. To the skeptic, the real nature of the world is an enigma, a puzzle and a mystery, and that so-called progress is not really progress at all. One wag has pointed out that the popular song "Forty-five Minutes from Broadway," written by George M. Cohan in 1904, referred to the town of New Rochelle, New York. After the ensuing seventy-five years since that musical was written, with all of the planning and scientific advances that have taken place, it takes about fifty minutes from New Rochelle to Broadway, or longer if ordinary train and commuting schedules are measured. "Muddling Through" was the label applied by skeptic Charles Lindblom to the laughable effects of attempting to plan matters in government.

Determinism is still another basis for anti-planning, says Churchman. Nothing really can be changed, for social forces produce unpredictable influences and the only viable operating method is to develop an attitude of acceptance of much that will happen, matched perhaps by some ability to respond quickly when things go wrong. Certainly they will go wrong. A cardinal rule of the skeptic and the determinist is the widely known washroom rubric called *Murphy's Law:* Anything that can go wrong, will. The field of business publication is replete with periodic humorous books that skewer the foolishness of planners. For there seem to be certain deterministic rules, such as Parkinson's Law and the Peter Principle, which make all formal planning seem futile, if not downright ridiculous.

Religious determinism is likewise a source of anti-planning. The outcomes of the future cannot be fathomed, for they require that mortals probe the mind of God, which is unfathomable and mysterious. Revelations and unremitting faith, usually in the goodness of God, make it apparent to religious anti-planners that it is possible only to help oneself and hope for the best. The planners and systems analysts then have merely substituted faith in progress, objectives, and approximations for true faith and can hardly hope to improve on the eternal verities by their foolish behavior.

In education, the humanist becomes an anti-planner, seeing all systematic games as essentially opposed to the self. The dignity of humanity, they propose, is achieved not in pursuing progress, bigness, and goals, but in the pursuit of one's own inner life, in understanding one's inner being, and in developing its potential. Much of the resistance of the counterculture and the student radical movement, and of humanistic psychology, adheres to this form of anti-planning.

For the planner, then, anti-planning must be considered as fundamental to sound planning, for it must be dealt with and faced as a realistic aspect and complement of the planning process.

## LARGE-SCALE BUREAUCRACY AS A SOURCE OF THE ANTI-PLANNING MENTALITY

For large corporations or government agencies, the very size of the organization produces an environment that can produce anti-planners in sizable numbers. Large organizations are based upon the division of labor, into ever-increasing numbers of tiny, fragmented tasks, all of which require a person or staff to execute. It is among this large population of specialists in small bits that the anti-planning is prone to appear. While the corporation itself engages in central planning, strategic marketing, and financial planning especially, among the people who must do the daily chores of carrying out those plans a countermovement in opposition to planning seems to be prevalent. While the division of labor has a proven effect of enhancing the total yield from resources employed by the corporation, it also depersonalizes things for people engaged in the finely honed, specialized jobs. Procedures, policies, and regulations abound in such organizations, with the consequence that the overall plan becomes less and less meaningful to each individual at lower levels. Middle managers become specialized in refinements of the master plan and in turn further refine their segments into more narrowly defined specialties.

Employees caught in such a web of activity quite understandably lose the sense that they are directly contributing to master schemes, and in turn lose their sense of commitment to them. They become apathetic and in some instances, sullen, if not mutinous, at the impersonality of the system that has turned them into instrumental devices of the larger organization. In this state, they have no involvement in the planning process and feel no ownership of it. This produces a lack of urgency in its implementation, and considerable energy is expended in seeking personal discretion and freedom from constraint. Thus, a paradox emerges. The organization that succeeds admirably at the top in devising explicit plans and strategies must employ thousands of workers for whom daily tasks are defined generally but who have no apparent connection to anything visible except the job description that surrounds their work. Alan Harrington describes this as "people going to work and disappearing into their job descriptions." They are not seen again as real people until quitting time.[7]

The idea that these thousands of workers, too, should devise subplans and perhaps amend and change the explicit instructions they have received to adapt to new directions and goals is quite foreign to their style and manner of working. That the company may be engaged in a giant strategy of capturing a new market or of radically reducing costs to save itself from bankruptcy is lost upon them. They implicitly assume that somewhere in the upper reaches of the firm, somebody knows what is right and wrong but they need not be concerned, for they are there simply to do their jobs. Never having been consulted about the larger plans, they feel no compulsion or even desire to innovate or to propose changes that might be more or less responsive to changes in the direction so heartily desired and sought at the top. Far removed from important decision making, they proceed upon the implicit assumption that competence at one's duties, acquired through years of repetition, will suffice to preserve their jobs and the organization as well.

The factory worker putting ends into the double seamer on the production line where one-quart oil cans are filled is as remote from the energy crisis, or the social impact of energy policy, as is the aborigine of the Australian outback. Life consists not of planning, but rather of working, and any suggestion that some kind

[7] A. Harrington, *Life in the Crystal Palace* (New York: Knopf, 1959).

of planning would be beneficial, to say nothing of changing one's behavior to suit the new overall plan of the firm, is not only remote but ridiculous. Since planning is a civilized and acquired skill, the lack of opportunity to engage in planning produces great ranks of people for whom planning is both foreign and impractical. Natural laws which purportedly governed the scheme of economic affairs through an invisible hand in a capitalist society take on a new form for the worker, far removed from the councils where directional changes are created. Natural law for many workers is simply doing a good job, without variation. Tight technical organization and tight discipline of the organization, in however kindly a style it is administered, produces generations of workers and supervisors who live in a world where planning is implicit rather than explicit. Sadly, when the time comes to choose from among the lesser-ranking people who might rise to a post where they would be responsible for explicit planning, most are likely to be totally devoid of any experience that could serve them in that more elevated role.

## ANTIDOTES TO ANTI-PLANNING

Decentralization as a major modification of the original division of labor described by Adam Smith helps to alleviate this condition somewhat, for it makes the decision makers more visible by localizing decisions at lower ranks. The management system known as *management by objectives* (MBO) has further extended this planning down even further into supervisory and professional ranks. At the beginning of each year every manager and subordinate, under MBO, sit down and discuss hoped-for targets and goals of subordinates and obtains commitments to those individual goals on the job. These goals then become standards for judging individual performance. They also help train people in planning at their own level, and in that sense they ease the impact of the anti-planner.

# two

# The activity trap:
## why we do not manage change very well

Some of the largest and most affluent corporations are caught in an insidious trap. It is called the *activity trap,* and it afflicts small and large corporations alike. It extends beyond the business world, to governments, schools, hospitals, churches, and even families.

Unless victims are aware of it, the activity trap will ensnare the wisest, most experienced old hands.

What is the activity trap?

It is the abysmal situation people find themselves in when they start out for what once was an important and clear, perhaps even noble, objective, but in an amazingly short time become so enmeshed in the activity of getting there that they forget where they are going.[1]

Every business starts out to achieve some objective, usually an increasing profit. Resources are assembled from stockholders, loans, or savings and are poured into the enterprise. Everyone gets busy, engaging in *activity* designed to carry the organization toward its objectives. Once-clear goals may evolve into other goals even though the activity remains the same—and becomes an end in itself. In other words, the goal moves, but the activity persists and becomes a false goal. This false goal becomes a criterion for making decisions, and the decisions get progressively worse.

If this seems complicated, look at some examples of the activity trap:

- Quality-control directors act as if the enterprise were created for them to shut it down and hold up everything produced yesterday.
- Accountants act as if the business were created for them to keep the books on it. No longer do they keep books so the boss can run it better.

[1] G. S. Odiorne, *Management and the Activity Trap* (New York: Harper & Row, Pub., 1974).

- The sales manager acts as if there were no problems that couldn't be solved by more volume. Sales go up, but profits fall.
- Production bosses get tonnage out the back gate by shipping junk, or using wrong labels and faulty addresses, then ride the backs of the help to get more production out tomorrow.
- Personnel managers behave as if the entire purpose of hiring all those people, providing them with tools and equipment, and building a plant were for the personnel department to make them happy.
- The labor relations director acts as if the company were formed so that he or she could fight with union officers.

Meanwhile, the stockholders and the president sit atop the mess wondering where the profits have gone.

The activity trap is a self-feeding mechanism if you do not turn it around. Everybody becomes emotionally attached to some irrelevancy and does his or her job *too well*. Its ultimate stage is reached when the president himself loses sight of why the company's in business, and demands more and more activity, rather than results. Orders follow to add layers of professionals to help control the activity. Large corporations have acres of lawyers, each outstripping the other in preventing everybody from producing anything. Profits decline and the president adds a battery of accountants. So what happens? Considerable accounting is produced; costs go up. Engineers fight engineering problems by hiring more engineers, each with a technical opinion designed to prevent something from happening someplace else in the firm. Many professionals spend their entire working life taking in each other's administrative laundry, creating jobs and administrative hierarchies to generate more activity that is increasingly unrelated to the purpose of the company's existence.

Churches, too, become enmeshed in covered-dish suppers and basketball leagues—activities generating little other than indigestion and flat feet.

Families get so entangled in the mechanical process of living that they forget what families were started for. A story is told of the perfect housewife whose son got up at night to go to the bathroom; when he came back, his bed had been made. Service clubs spend more and more time exhorting the members to "support this activity," with no hint of a worthwhile payoff.

Meanwhile, all this activity eats up resources, money, space, budgets, savings, and human energy like a mammoth tapeworm.

While it is apparent that the activity trap cuts profits, loses ball games, and fails to achieve missions, it has an equally dangerous side effect on people: They *shrink* personally and professionally.

Take any boss and one of his or her subordinates. Ask the employee to write down what specific results he or she thinks the boss wants produced in the next quarter. Now ask the boss, "What results would you like to see that subordinate produce next quarter?" The average manager and subordinate won't agree on results sought, but they may be reasonably close on the activities to be conducted.[2] Answers will differ, and the existence of the differences, as we shall see, will cause the subordinate to shrink essentially in potential. Research shows that:

1. On regular, ongoing responsibilities, the average boss and subordinate, caught in the activity trap, will fail to agree on expected outputs at a level of 25 percent.
2. At the same time, as a result of this failure to agree on regular responsibilities, they will disagree on what the subordinate's major problems are at a level of 50 percent.
3. The worst gap of all is the failure of boss and subordinate to agree on how the subordinate's job should be improved. On this latter count, they fail to agree at a level of 90 percent.

As a result, nothing really changes in the way things are done. The environment changes, the customers' tastes change, the values of employees change. But the methods remain static and the organization is crippled by the outdated acts of its own employees.

The human consequence is that employees *shrink*. The organization drains its people of their zap, and finds itself employing pygmies. They look like real people, wear neckties, drive cars, and pay taxes, but they are performance midgets. They nod their heads when the boss chastises them but know they have been cheated. They are stabbed daily in duels they did not know were under way. Trees fall upon them, and *then* somebody yells "timber." Their defensive recourse? Keep *active*.

They redouble their energy when they have lost sight of their goal. They may be chastised, or even fired, for doing something wrong when they did not know what "right" was to begin with. They run a race without knowing how long the track is. They wonder if it is time to sprint for the wire, but they cannot guess when, because it might be a 100-yard dash or the Boston Marathon.

The effect is cumulative. Because they do not know the ordinary objectives of their job, they are hit for failures growing out of not knowing what spells success. This produces a reluctance to discover shortcomings. Suggesting something new in such an environment is risky. Better to stick with the old activity. Looking busy becomes safer than being productive.

This tendency toward activity is not inevitable, if top people try to circumvent it. The law of gravity is always with us, but some people build bridges.

In America's best-managed organizations, the management has leadership systems that concentrate on output and results. In such organizations, every manager sits down with every subordinate manager periodically and asks, "What are you going to produce for me next quarter or next year?" The two talk about objectives, outputs, results, and indicators until they agree on what the future should hold. One

[2] Odiorne, *MBO II: A System of Management Leadership for the Eighties* (Belmont, Calif.: Fearon, 1979).

of the parties then confirms the agreement with a memo. Now when the curtain goes up, both actors have the same script; this improves the quality of the acting considerably.

- The emphasis is on outputs, not activities.
- All persons know what is expected of them, and can tell immediately how well they are doing.
- Each is responsible for explicit results and has made a commitment to someone else to try to achieve them.
- Each employee feels free to make necessary decisions and take necessary actions to achieve the objectives.
- At the end of the period, the manager and subordinate sit down once more and talk again. "Here is what you said you were going to produce. How well did you do, and what are you going to do next quarter?"

The key person in this type of productive organization is the top executive. He or she determines that the organization will be managed by objectives, not activity. The top person determines the corporate objectives and strategic goals. The subordinate managers define their operational objectives to fit those top-level goals and strategies. Top management should not be involved in day-to-day operations, but should manage them by the agreed-upon objectives.

Nonbusiness organizations need explicit objectives, too. Families with defined objectives can get off the backs of their offspring, permitting wider latitudes in activity and behavior if the end result is good. Service clubs find that definite objectives attract monetary and human resources for their achievement.

Virtually any organization can get caught in the activity trap, because the bait is so alluring. But the security of the trap is inherently false, and the rewards diminish at an accelerated rate. Organization, after all, is not an end in itself; it is a means of achieving specific objectives. To accomplish this, the participant—if they themselves are to survive—must eventually get down to business rather than the "busyness" of the activity trap.

## WHY ARE WE SO VULNERABLE TO THE ACTIVITY TRAP?

If the activity trap were not so damaging in its effects, we could simply ignore it. But the problems of the world, as well as of business, are in large part attributable to our being ensnared. What is there about us, our culture, and our education that permits us—especially the best educated and most intelligent—to be so easily caught up in the activity trap? We need to understand the roots of the activity trap if we are to escape it.

Some of our behavior is instinctive. Pain avoidance, pleasure seeking—these are things which we do by instinct and which are *innate*. We are born with them. A green plant will turn naturally toward the light, while a certain amoeba will turn away, each doing this without any brain to govern it or any central nervous system to direct it. For people and animals, some behavior is acquired through *imprinting,* or learning at a very early age. For some, this imprinting period is in the first few days of life; for larger animals and humans, it is in the first few years. The Jesuit order is said to have asserted, "Give me a youngster for the first five years and we do not care who has him for the rest of his life." Most of the behavior that creates the activity trap comes much later than the imprinting and is produced through *conditioning*—or learning. People cross the street on green lights and are conditioned to wait when the light is red, although any city dweller knows how faulty this conditioning can become. It is this conditioned behavior that produces the activity trap. The longer and more intensive the conditioning, the longer the period of time it takes to get rid of the behavior. We learn to do certain things as conditioned responses to the lights and signals we receive, but those learned responses are in turn modified by our own nature and imprinted learning. Tigers do not eat hay and grass, in part because their teeth cannot crop grass and their digestive systems would not break it down if they did, and so they eat deer, which do eat grass. Ordinarily, tigers do not eat people unless something in the environment makes it impossible to find deer or their legs go bad and they cannot catch deer, in which case they seek an easier game and may become people-eaters.

One reason for our vulnerability to the activity trap is the habit mechanism. William James once called habit the "flywheel of civilization." By this he referred to the many small actions in life which we daily engage in without conscious thought. As an organism we acquire skills which, once acquired, we use until they are extinguished. Some of our most important, life-preserving behaviors, even some of the most pleasurable, we do by habit. We rise and prepare ourselves for the day without ever making a conscious mental effort. In effect, many of our striped muscles (the heavy ones which do the work) become accustomed to routine performance once they are trained. They function for long periods of time in the same way that our smooth muscles—and our glandular system—work: involuntarily and under a kind of systematic self-control. Most of us would not function very efficiently if we had to issue orders to all of our cells and nerves. Even on those days when we suspect that some of our internal organs are goofing off (and in fact being downright insubordinate), we cannot do much about them except hope that they will get back to work and do their job properly in due time. Much of our ordinary behavior falls into this drill of acting in automatic and routinized ways. It makes the activity trap stronger.

Mental lapses likewise will tend to reinforce the activity trap some of the time. Professor James Reason, an English experimental psychologist, has studied the phenomena of absent-mindedness at some depth, acts which he calls "slips of action."[3] These are the behaviors of people that lead to events that are sometimes embarrassing, and sometimes even catastrophic. A pilot's error in a plane accident, many automobile accidents on expressways, or simply a wrong turn on the way home can naturally follow such slips in action. These slips are actions that

---

[3] "Authority on Mental Lapses," *New York Times,* Aug. 21, 1978.

deviate from intention and are sufficiently common that Professor Reason was able to record 700 of them among 37 men and women in a two-week period.

These slips of action occurred in normal people. They fell into four major categories in ordinary living. *Selection failures* are those in which we substitute a wrong action for a proper one. The telephone rings and you reply by saying "Come in" when you should say "Hello." A *discrimination failure* is one in which you face a familiar situation but it produces an inappropriate response. For example, you intend to play tennis but pack your golf shoes in your duffel bag. The third slip is a kind of *test failure* where you terminate an action too soon. You break into applause before the number is finished, or perhaps you walk out and get in your car at the half time of the game. In other words, you terminate a series of events too soon, or too late. The conferee who shows up a day early or a day late, or shows up for a party on the wrong night, is guilty of a test failure. *Storage failure* is simply general forgetfulness, such as forgetting whether or not you put salt into the soup, or whether you took your medication that day.

Usually such failures grow out of distraction. All of the competition for our attention in the workaday world produces a bemusement with the things that are foremost in our minds. Somehow the public at large has the impression that executives and government leaders should be exempt from such human imperfection. Often they can protect themselves from the possible serious effects of such slips by surrounding themselves with secretaries and aides who will catch most of their errors. But even with such systematic safeguards, there are numerous tales of well-known people making slips in action. Harold Geneen, who built International Telephone & Telegraph into one of the world's largest corporations, was renowned for his selection failures in addressing his key vice-presidents, often mispronouncing or grossly distorting their names. "He's a great man but I wish the hell after eleven years he would learn what my name is," one of them wryly reported. One major corporate executive who commuted daily to Wall Street in New York was reported to have delayed a complex merger of three large corporations when he left a briefcase with all the important papers contained in it in the back seat of his limousine, which had taken off immediately for a trip to upstate New York on a business jaunt. "I was so busy reading the *Times,* I simply folded the paper as I always do and got out of the car as I always do," he said in explaining his discrimination failure. In a case of test failure, one large corporate chairman adjourned the meeting without conducting the reelection of corporate officers until he was reminded of the necessity by a vigilant secretary, and he was required to call the board members back, much to their amusement and his chagrin. News stories of messengers who leave thousands of dollars in cash behind in trains, subways, and taxis indicate that storage failures are common. The lost-and-found departments in every kind of organization are filled with amazing examples of storage failures. Children, false teeth, trousers, and even more valuable items cram the racks of every airline, bus company, and railroad. During World War II, I can recall how busy noncommissioned officers were after a column of soldiers started hiking again after a five-minute break, finding it necessary to remind everyone to go back to pick up their gear before continuing the march into combat. They left behind gas masks, rifles, grenades, canteens, rations, and backpacks at every stop unless policed and reminded.

This evidence that humans are by nature fallible should come as no surprise to all of us, who are similarly imperfect. The foregoing pictures of our absent-mindedness and mental lapses tend to show how the activity trap is rooted in normal human behavior.

## THE CULTURAL SOURCES OF THE ACTIVITY TRAP

One of the more popular ongoing debates is whether people are shaped mainly by heredity or by environment. Some people have even proposed an argument of free will, in which a person's behavior was largely his or her own making, his or her own deliberations, decisions, and actions. If we consider a cluster of behaviors that we now call the activity trap, it is probably more reasonable to presume that such behavior is determined in small part by our genetic makeup, which is a product of our evolution as a species, but is mainly due to environmental circumstances to which we have been exposed. It is a behavior we learn and, accordingly, can unlearn.

Having been born members of the human species, we immediately begin acquiring a set of behaviors from the outside world—known as the culture—that we are exposed to as individuals. Not everyone responds the same way to identical stimuli. Two boys raised in the same home by the same parents have some common genetic features, but they may respond differently to the culture in which they are raised. The idea of imprinting is not inconsistent with this; it merely proposes that there are certain critical times in life when we are extremely sensitive to such influences. Throughout our lives we continue to acquire new repertoires of behavior, including the capacity to resist change even when it would be more consistent with our own chosen objectives to make such a change.

Employees, professionals, and managers are subjected to the cultural influences which shape their behavior, and which affect their ability to adapt to new deeds and necessary new goals. They also learn from their culture to cling to the past, to resist change.

The cultural influences affecting us include education, professionalism, and the social values or character of the society in which we grow up and live our lives. Let us look at each of these three cultural influences that produce our abilities—or incapacities—for change.

**Our book-bag minds** One explanation lies in the way we were educated. We studied in specialized classes, taking on single subjects in fifty-minute bites. From the first hour, where we studied math, we rushed to the second hour, where we studied English. Then we dashed down a corridor to a third room, where we studied chemistry. This has so compartmentalized our minds that we see knowledge and life in discrete blocks, specializations, and compartments. A student with the temerity to suggest in chemistry class that English was somehow a related subject was promptly suppressed. From this early training, we went into a compartmentalized world of specialization where engineering was different from purchasing and both were different from personnel administration. This hardening of the categories thus extended to life itself. Our homes were separated from work, our church from our life. As the popular song of the sixties put it, we separated our lives into "boxes—little boxes."

Our book-bag learning is a cause of our entrapment in professionalism. We studied something for four to six years in college and became complete masters of a series of activities, which were often obsolete by the time we were certified as professionals. The professions cluster together into tight circles which, among other things, enforce standards of behavior, called ethics, upon their members. This discipline of professional standards often produces a resistance to change, if the change conflicts with the prevailing wisdom of the profession itself. It often causes form to take precedence over performance. One large engineering department of my acquaintance is proudest of a wall covered with framed professional engineering certificates. Some wags suggested these were necessary because nobody else could tell by their output that they were professional.

The activity trap, then, is mainly a conditioned type of behavior, and the longer and more heavily it has been reinforced, the more it will persist. The conditioning comes from society and from organizations as well as from other influences, such as our own memories and our ability to reason. It is exactly this reasoning process that distinguishes human from animal and is the basis for choosing and selecting new behaviors despite past conditioning or even present instincts. The manipulation of memories into new and unusual combinations, while not an exclusive property of humans, is at least developed to a higher level in us and means that the activity trap is an escapable one. Among the things that we learn, or produce, from the recesses of our minds are *values*. These values become embedded into our language and our behavior and make us slower in changing.

**Our other-directed habits** The character of the people around us also affects the ways we adapt to change. Sociologist David Riesman once explained the American character as being rooted in one of three basic sources.[4] We are, he said, either tradition-directed, inner-directed, or other-directed. The values which produce our characteristic behavior, he said, in an older society were founded in *tradition*. People did things because their parents and grandparents did them, or because they were a respected and often repeated way of doing things in their culture, tribe, town, or organization. If it was traditional to serve hot dogs on the Fourth of July, we had hot dogs on that date every year whether we liked them or not, because tradition directed our behavior.

A strategic planner for the General Electric Company reported that pride was its most important impediment. He said there were divisions that thought appli-

[4] D. Riesman, *The Lonely Crowd* (New Haven, Conn.: Yale University Press, (1950).

ances should be produced just because it is a GE tradition, and they would stick with a loser because of the pride involved in that tradition.

On the other hand, as society changed toward more individualistic values, we were governed by these new values and became inner-directed. Thus, we were governed strongly, and knowingly, by the imprinting done by our fathers and mothers, older brothers and sisters, teachers, and early authority and model figures, not because it was a tradition, but because we had internalized those values. We had assumed them not only into our conscious minds, but into our unconscious as well. Many a firm is ruled by its founder, who has subjectively decided the kind of business the firm will be in and refuses to brook any suggestion for changing product or market structure. Scoffing at objective profit figures, the boss snorts, "I decide around here."

The modern individual, Riesman proposes, is more apt to be *other-directed*. Rather than choosing one's behavior from the dictates of an oil-painting image of grandfather or some old family tradition, or even one's own individual conscience, one is likely to be conducting a never-ending public opinion survey of what others are doing and what the world expects. This becomes the model for behavior. Modern humanity, Riesman proposes, is more apt to be steering its ship by the position of other ships in the convoy, rather than by the light of the stars (tradition) or even by the gyroscope of conscience and personal values.

It would seem, then, that the modern generation is not one whit better able to break out of the activity trap than the people of the tradition-bound middle ages, or the puritanical nineteenth century. It is more likely that modern professionals will stay within the bounds of current professional practices than deviate. The average staff person is strongly oriented toward the members of his or her professional association than toward company purposes. Conventional wisdom presses upon us to avoid deviance from accepted ways of doing things. This produces problems when the objectives change to any radical degree.

## THE CULT OF ACTIVITY
## WHICH WE JOIN AND SUPPORT

Activity is more than an ordinary trap, for most traps become recognizable to the prey as traps. The activity trap, on the other hand, is hardly recognized as a trap, but is considered a valuable asset for its owner. It has a narcotic effect, and we are addicted to our own worst habit.

When the family takes off for its summer vacation to see America from a recreational vehicle, the master of the house may immediately set a target mileage to be covered of six hundred miles a day which is often attained at the expense of the purpose of the vacation. Not only interesting byways are missed, but also the very reason for the vacation. At home we rush pell-mell toward the weekend of tennis, golf, jogging, swimming, handball, hiking, and other forms of activity that are but one symptom of the cult of activity. Even more sedentary pastimes, such as endless and joyless staring at the TV, watching boring reruns of drab entertainment in thirty-minute modules, become activities without meaning or purpose.

In the organization, the boss who desires to be a good leader is enmeshed in the activity trap and accordingly devises measures of activity which, if achieved, are rewarded and which, if missed, are deplored. The evidences of activity management are revealed in the systems used to measure the organization and its people. Time cards are punched so that people can be policed with respect to their presence rather than evaluated for their contribution. Their presence is evidence that they are on the scene and under the eye of bosses who can assure that activity is being produced. Position descriptions are written for purposes of job evaluation and determination of pay. Most such job descriptions are descriptions of activity, and perhaps of the style with which those activities are generated. Such words as *diligent, loyal,* and *trustworthy* are used to evaluate the performance of people, and the criteria which make them evidence of successful stewardship are all related to more activity rather than less.

The selection process of young people into the organization tends to reproduce on the staff those people whose background and education will best equip them for organizational activity rather than individual effectiveness and personal growth. Being a hard worker, a key element in promotability and sharing in the rewards of the organization, is a virtue which becomes self-evident in most organizations. Not that hard work is bad and sloth is good; but the reasons for and results of hard work are lost in the cult of activity.

The activity trap takes its most pervasive form when the top management of the firm is itself ensnared. For management devises systems to produce activity, and accordingly organizes the entire structure to produce more rather than less activity, regardless of its output effects. Furthermore, the style in which action ensues should conform to the higher bosses' model of pure activity. *Do it my way* becomes more important than *produce my result for a fair reward,* which is closer to the ultimate goals of hiring people to begin with. In the designation of certain approved personality tests of subordinates, those traits which meet the highest levels of approval are those which produce evidence of activity rather than output, or even the relationship between input and output. The aspects of behavioral science which receive the greatest attention and acceptance in the activity-centered world of organization are those which translate motion into *movement* rather than *sound directions.*

Because management is the custodian of success for people who labor in the organization, the organization thus becomes a conditioning influence over the values of the people in it. People who work in a hierarchy adopt the values of the people above and around them, and success means pleasing them. Being active, even if the activity is meaningless, produces rewards and success without regard for the qualitative output of the organization.[5] Morale consists of being happy in one's activity. In the novel and subsequent movie, *The Bridge Over the River Kwai* a com-

---

[5] G. E. West, "Bureau Pathology and the Failure of MBO," *Human Resource Management,* 20, no. 1, October 1977.

pany of British engineers, captives of the Japanese, are shown building a railroad bridge over a gorge. The fact that the very act of building such a structure was itself treasonable and seditious to the British cause was lost upon the colonel in charge and invisible to the men involved. Rather than lying about in despair and awaiting death as inactive prisoners, they went forth daily to practice their skills where their captors had failed. Their morale was high, their physical health improved, and they sang a lilting song, whistling a stirring air ("Colonel Bogie's March") as they went about their perfidious and treasonable acts with professional competence. Of course, the common soldiers of the company engaged in betrayal of their oaths as soldiers only under the order of their commanding officer, and it was ultimately he who saw the enormous wrongness of what he had demanded of his company. The bridge was blown up by his own countrymen.

It would be foolish to deny that successful organizations, too, are to be hard-working and active where they have chosen their goals and set the purposes clearly. But the two elements, activity and output, are lamentably not always tied together. The essence of the activity trap is not in escaping activity but in improving valuable output.

# three

# The changes we like and the changes we dislike

Longshoreman-philosopher Eric Hoffer once wrote of his experience as a migrant worker picking peas in the West in 1936. Starting in the Imperial Valley and moving north, he picked the last peas in June in Tracy, California. He then shifted to Lake County, where, for the first time, he was going to pick string beans. Many years later he recalled his hesitation as he was about to address himself to picking string beans. "Even the change from peas to string beans had in it the element of fear," he reported.[1] How much more difficult it is for us then to adapt to a world which is changing around us and requires that we adapt to something new.

Having mastered a skill or set of skills, and finding that we can enjoy a sense of adequacy in the world, the changes which are not of our own making or choosing produce uneasiness. The more radical the change, the deeper and more lasting the uneasiness. As Hoffer put it, "A population undergoing drastic change is a population of misfits, and misfits live and breathe in an atmosphere of passion." The old-time policeman who now finds that he cannot bulldoze his beat into peaceable behavior under new court rulings such as *Miranda* is a misfit, even though he has enjoyed many years of continuous success at his work. The old forest ranger who is confronted with new ecological and environmental principles and laws is a misfit in the very forests where he has performed admirably under earlier ways. The supervisor who must now employ young, college-educated women in positions that have been traditionally held by older, less-educated white males is a misfit and, accordingly, is apt to behave passionately toward the change.

The close alliance between lack of confidence and being a misfit causes us to seek a substitute, the intensity of passionate behavior, for the lost confidence. Competence is often a suitable replacement for passionate faith and intensity of feelings. The professional football player who is master of all of the required moves and feints need not be as passionate in play as the unskilled youngster. The high school

<hr>

[1] E. Hoffer, *The Ordeal of Change* (New York: Harper & Row, Pub., Perennial Library, 1952).

team often operates on high energy, which it needs as a substitute for the calm competence of the professional. When any segment of our society consists largely of misfits—those who simply cannot succeed in the environment in which they have been placed and cannot change the environment, or acquire the competence needed—it will engage in spasms of action and passionate behavior.

## THE CHANGES WE LIKE ARE
## THE ONES WE CREATE

A refined analysis of the process by which misfits are created in times of change might be useful. It is apparent from the many changes around us that not all of them are acts of God or nature, or even of a social force beyond our control; some of them are of our own making. Given the situation in which we are the *mover* rather than the *moved,* we do not become misfits, but seem to enjoy and even seek out such change.

During several months of 1978, I had occasion to meet with different groups of executives from a variety of American corporations, and employed the opportunity to solicit their views about what changes they liked and what changes they did not like. The information was obtained in a free-response type of survey. On a single sheet, each person was asked to write in the upper right-hand corner the year in which he or she was first employed for pay. Following this, the paper was divided into two columns and the groups were instructed, "In the left hand column list those changes which have occurred during your working life which you liked. In the right hand column list those changes which you disliked." One hundred ninety-two executives cooperated, providing a list of likes and dislikes which divided as follows:

- Changes I liked: 746
- Changes I disliked: 575

That means that fifty-five percent or more of the changes that they recalled and reported in the world around them and in business were changes they liked. About forty-five percent they disliked. An item analysis of the nature of the response in each category showed the following:

The highest-ranking changes that were liked:

1. Technological changes
2. The growth of business
3. Expansion of the economy
4. Rising levels of education
5. More equality among races and sexes
6. The new, easier life style
7. Our improvements in health care

Those changes that were most often mentioned as being disliked included the following:

1. The decline of the cities and urban blight
2. Wars and changes in foreign affairs

3. The rising influence of government in our lives
4. The rising power of labor unions
5. The deteriorating environment: pollution and other problems
6. General social decay and disorder
7. The behavior of modern youth and its decline in morals

Even without further data on the specific responses, it is clear that there are many aspects of life that modern managers find felicitous, at least to the extent that this respondent group was representative. But there are paradoxes in their answers. They like technology, such as better planes and cars, but they dislike pollution. They especially reported liking the computer, but they dislike the social changes that apparently can be attributed to it. They liked the rising levels of education in society, but they did not like the behavior of the young people which they attribute to the educational system. Most important, they liked those things that business itself created or produced: technological change, growth of business, and expansion of the economy. Yet many of the things they disliked are side effects, mainly unintended, of those very beneficial changes. Since the questions were seeking free responses, there was no opportunity for people to see the paradoxical character of their overall responses and quickly correct them to fit a more rational appearance. The survey in effect resembles the ambivalent way in which business leaders view change. On balance, they like changes, but there are many undesired side effects.

My conclusions?

*Most people like those changes they have caused to happen, for they are adapting as they create the changes. They become misfits, however, when other changes occur because of natural drifts and mutation, and because of unintended side effects of changes they have made happen.*

The modern automobile as a case study reveals the dilemma of changes we like and changes we do not. The modern car is by all engineering standards far superior to earlier models. Even discounting the puffery of manufacturers' advertisements, the life of the current models is considerably longer than that of their counterparts of twenty or even ten years ago. Longer life is due to superior engineering, computerized engineering and testing of components and materials, and superior testing. Objective studies in 1978 showed that the modern car, with good care, could easily be driven more than 100,000 miles before it was ready for the junk pile. Large trucks with mileages of 300,000 and more are common. The cost of maintenance as a percentage of total cost has been declining steadily; less lubrication is needed, and superior lubricants are presently in use. The modern car is more self-adjusting and -regulating as microprocessors under the hood make adjustments without the aid of the service garage.

All of this, of course, is ignored as new and more exacting statistics of performance show major and minor epidemics of defects. If 100 cars out of 300,000 of a particular model show up as bursting into flames or rolling over when rounding a particular kind of curve, all of the 300,000 will be recalled under new and more stringent auto safety laws. Amidst great waves of publicity, the minuscule percenage of defects is ignored and the reputation of all of them is tainted. The original balloon tires of the 1920's went an average of seventy-five miles before a blowout could be expected, but few complained. Today, if 300 tires out of 10 million rip apart, it is not noticed that the vast majority of steel-belted radial tires will go more than 40,000 miles before they are considered worn out.

*It is the unintended side effects which have become magnified, and by heightened overstatement of the unfavorable aspects of change we produce a resistance to change itself.*

Almost every field of technology, and especially those fields which have some impact upon people, is susceptible to this overstatement of side effects. We heighten the effect of certain insecticides upon birds and other wildlife, and in banning them, we leave the fields of Colorado open to ravages by crickets, which destroy millions of dollars in crops and destroy food while people in the world are starving. By concentrating with great mental intensity we make it easier and easier for more and more people who would plan, change, and make things happen feel the stigma of feeling like misfits, and in the process, we dampen the influences that would produce desirable and necessary change.

## THE KEENEST ABILITY OF THE HUMAN MIND

Having determined that something is true, we have at our command the most highly developed instrument of humanity: the human mind's ability to criticize. The ability or propensity to initiate or to create is far less widespread in the population, and far less likely to be produced by our educational system. Nicholas Murray Butler, once president of Columbia University, is reported to have stated that people can be classified into three categories: "the small group of people who make things happen, a little larger group who watch what goes on, and the overwhelming majority who have not the slightest idea of what is happening." To these three might be added a subset; those who watch everything that is being done and point out what is wrong with it.

Such critique in science is not a useless function, but rather is highly invaluable. In science, the researcher who submits his or her work to the scrutiny of peers through publication invites others to replicate that work, to find errors in it if they exist. In science, James B. Conant writes, "new concepts are continually developing from experiment and observation and lead to further experiment and observation." New concepts most often come out of the results of old experiments, but concepts on a grand scale may change the character and direction of the experimentation sharply. Conant goes on: "A well established concept may prove a barrier to the acceptance of a new one. If a conceptual scheme is highly satisfactory to those who use it neither a few old facts which cannot be reconciled nor a few new ones cause the concept to be abandoned."[2]

[2] J. Conant, *On Understanding Science* (New Haven, Conn.: Yale University Press, 1948); *see also* J. W. N. Sullivan, *The Limitations of Science* (New York: Mentor, NAL, 1969).

The ability to create hypotheses is an action of creation and imagination that comes to those who are both imaginative and informed, as well as trained. Lacking the imaginative and creative aspect of science and scientific thinking processes are those who are merely trained and intelligent. To them goes the vital work of testing hypotheses, which is to disprove the hypothesis, if possible. Not disproved, the new concept or hypothesis takes its place as a tentative conclusion. This process of science is widespread in our thinking. We find that most of our best thinking efforts go into disproving things, and the creation is left to a small group of people who have innate creative gifts or have been imprinted or conditioned to think imaginatively and creatively.

To be trained as a scientist means that one is ready to engage in what J. W. N. Sullivan called "a promise of a long and probably inconclusive investigation," an insistence upon evidence, and an absence of generosity in drawing conclusions from evidence.[3] Carried into the social and humanistic sphere, it proves to be the death knell of innovation and experimentation in human affairs.

The major difference between experimentation in human affairs and experiments on the inanimate lies in the *purposive* character of humanistic matters. As Whitehead put it, "There is clear evidence that certain operations of certain animal bodies depend upon the foresight of a purpose, an end, and a purpose to attain it."[4]

*Thus it is the objectives, purposes, and aims of human behavior that cause it to differ from naturalistic, scientific kinds of explanations. Objectives, then, are what distinguish human beings from objects.*

## THE LOGIC OF DEFENSIVENESS

When the activity trap bites with its cruel but pleasing jaws into a man or woman, it also narcotizes the victim to its own damaging consequences. It is a fur-lined trap. Its sharp teeth feel good, but the withdrawal pains can be unbearable. Any new objective that entails the worries of freedom produces a longing for the tried and true confines of old ways, old activities, even when the traditions are only a few days or weeks old.

Among the premier skills of the activity trappist, a priest of anti-change, is the development of a high-level art of kicking the fact under the rug (for short, KTFUR). This is no mere reflex of a knee-jerk nature; it implies a sophisticated skill in resisting innovation and new concepts, a skill that can be mastered only after long practice as a misfit and some deep study. Six major gambits of illogic stock the armory for KTFUR warfare:[5]

1. What is popular is true.
2. The Grand Canyon proof.
3. Soberly explaining that black is white.

---

[3] N. R. F. Maier and J. J. Hayes, *Creative Decision Making* (New York: John Wiley, 1962).
[4] A. N. Whitehead, *Science and the Modern World* (New York: Macmillan, 1925).
[5] W. H. White, *The Organization Man* (New York: Simon & Schuster, 1956).

4. Hypostatizing the data.
5. Misplacing literalism.
6. Using irrelevant precision.

Confronted with a new demand, a new objective, a change in the conditions that created the original demand for an activity or net of activity, the dedicated anti-planner can use each or all of these gambits in many combinations and permutations to justify avoiding changes in behavior. Let us look at what each one means, and how it might look in practice.

**1. Prevalent proof, or what's popular is true**     John Gardner has pointed out the weight of popular opinion in constraining rebellion and nonconformity. The first restraining hand clutching the arm of the rebel or the change agent is that of his or her best friend. A "proof" of fact using popular opinion often sounds like this:

*Hundreds of research studies have been conducted into the nature of supervisory behavior in creative organizations, and they all point conclusively to . . .*

Considering the astronomical improbability that hundreds of behavioral scientists would ever be all pointed in any single direction, the statement is suspect. Has its author actually studied all of the research? Can this be demonstrated against evidence to the contrary? Are there also differences that might need explaining? It might be considerably more valid to point to *one* good study if the conclusions in it serve to guide or prescribe behavior in some new and untried problem situation. A prevalent proof conclusion requires that the studies being used have enough similarities in situation, people, and time to resemble the new problem area.

Ganging up on a problem with prevalent proof takes some of the following forms:

- *All of the other kids are going.* (which proves that you are an anomaly if not a downright freak if you don't let *your* offspring go also)
- *It is a widely known fact that nuclear power is dangerous* . . . (which, of course, means that you are an uninformed hayseed if you didn't also know)

Having thus prepared you for the dire possibilities of being isolated from the wider population of the *informed,* prevalent proof also marks you as a person so dull that you could exist amid the wider group and not be aware of what everyone else is aware of. This, of course, suggests that you are *behind* them. It seldom admits that you may in fact *be ahead* of all, or have better information, or superior insights, or a better viewing site.

Ralph Waldo Emerson offered encouragement to those who would kick the activity trap. "If you would be a man," he proposed, "be a non-conformist." Not to be a stubborn rebel for its own sake, only to permit you to see the facts, if they are accessible, and to eschew kicking them under the rug simply because everyone else has not seen them.

The major vehicle for keeping things moving in the same old paths in business is the existence of a maze of committees, task forces, and boards. These, in any modern organization, are the major repository of the decision-making power. Norman R. F. Maier has clearly stated the rationale for such group decision-making systems. He notes that decisions may have varied levels of quality, or Q. They also may attain varied levels of acceptance, or A. When we presume that high levels of Q will automatically produce high levels of A, we may be falling into a major error. It would hardly be conscionable if the only output of committees were to be bad decisions, or low Q, if its only benefit was attaining high A. This would merely mean that people would be enthusiastic and competent in doing the wrong things. On the other hand, as organizations grow in complexity, they accumulate high degrees of expertise in various functions such as engineering, marketing, personnel, and accounting. Without the general acceptance of many experts, the most brilliant decision may come to nothing. When people participate in making decisions, they make their expert contribution. Thus, they often are able to prevent the kinds of errors which grow out of ignorance. They also acquire more enthusiasm for the decision, or at least have some of their more serious reservations removed, and accordingly work more diligently to make the decision work in practice. The best decisions, Maier suggests, are accommodations of Q with A.

The committee structures of Du Pont and General Motors are evidence that such group decision making is not without some efficacy. These are extremely large organizations, and making things happen in them is necessarily a ponderous process. Yet, they retain an amazing level of vitality. The annual model change in General Motors, or the constant infusion of innovative and creative new products into the ongoing stream of activity at Du Pont, is fairly persuasive evidence that committee management is not wholly unproductive or indicative of an unbreakable activity trap. At Litton Industries, the top management committee is known as the Opportunities Board, and general managers of major divisions and groups appear before it to present and test their proposals for mergers, new product lines, and new business endeavors.

This pattern of decision making has all of the potentials of being a massive veto structure, yet in highly vibrant and innovative organizations such as ITT or General Electric, it has not only persisted as the standard way of making top management decisions but also succeeded in averting an overriding culture of the activity trap in the organizations. One of the keys would seem to be the simultaneous ability of such committee-run organizations to find and maintain a steady infusion of energetic younger people who would take over the lower-level positions and who, once in them, would continue to press against the evaluative and decision-making powers with a stream of new ideas. Without such initiative from the bottom up, the committees themselves would probably be incapable of generating and implementing all of the new ideas in the firm, obtaining acceptance for them, and governing their execution. A Litton Industries general manager has described his goals: "Keep revenue growing, keep returns on assets growing, and stay out of jail."

For some, such as David Riesman, as noted in Chapter 2, this emphasis on group decision making constitutes an ominous change in the American character. In recent times, in Riesman theory, we have become an *other-directed* people. Without traditions and conscience to guide our behavior, we look to other people, the popular will, the committee opinion, for our values. As to a radar implanted inside, we turn to prevalent proofs to find our values and make our decisions. While all three of Riesman's guides to character could serve as an explanation of the activity trap, the explanation based on other-directedness seems currently to be the most widely held. The boss who answers every decision request with "refer it to a committee" is sufficiently familiar to many executives that other-directedness cannot be discounted.

Equally valuable in explaining the prevalent-proof system of group thinking is the book written by W. H. White in the 1950's, *The Organization Man*. Individual decision making, White stated, has been replaced with group decision making, and even more important, individuals are being pressed constantly to suppress their individuality to adhere more and more to the organization's values. Its values are their values. In organizations where men and women are picked because of their ability to "fit in" and their continued rise in their organization is more attributable to ability to conform than the ability to make a strong personal contribution, prevalent proof is the only sort that can exist. If the organization calls for innovation, the adaptive person is innovative. Yet, it must be the rebel against that prevalent proof who acquires the highest rungs of the ladder, for without a display of such individuality, there can be no distinctive criteria for qualification for the top.

*Prevalent proof,* or committee management, as a method of making decisions makes the activity trap more likely. Why plan for improvement if nothing comes out right? Clearly, the committee will not encourage individual creativity and nonconformity among its own members. Yet, by careful structuring of the total organization, to permit some to innovate and others to evaluate among alternatives, this method can produce a total organization that introduces change.

2. **The Grand Canyon fallacy** This possible proof fallacy is invaluable in helping us kick the facts under the rug. In this case, the facts disappear into a chasm. This strategy can use gaps in the information as proof that an event cannot have happened.

Take the case of a research project that has failed. The director and her aide, Mr. Knowles, had apparently not been clear on certain key target dates. Accordingly, the dates were missed, the contract canceled, the sponsor infuriated, and an investigation ordered. The investigator examined all of the files and reported, "No evidence was found that the Director ever briefed Mr. Knowles on the dates required, and therefore, Knowles did not know them." The chasm here? The investigator did not interview either person. Perhaps the director told Knowles but Knowles forgot or could not meet the dates for some unknown reason. Or perhaps Knowles was incompetent. In the final conclusion the true facts were probably kicked into the chasm. No files; ergo, the communication could not have taken place.

Congressional investigators (or fault finders) seeking scapegoats have often been guilty of stating possible proof as if it were conclusive. They may refer to "interesting gaps" in the chronology of a person's records; for example:

*Mr. Jones's many journeys to foreign lands show several interesting gaps of up to a week, which could have been adequate for him to surreptitiously slip behind the iron curtain and return with his nefarious purposes achieved.*

Wives and husbands have been known to leap prodigious distances in damning their spouses by bridging the chasm between known facts and probable wrongs and drawing from this gap possible proofs of misdemeanors: "You left the office at four and arrived at mother's at eight. This proves you are philandering."

Or take the case of Sam, a salesman for an oil company. One day his boss confronted him with these charges: "Sam, some of your inventory information is incomplete on your reports. This means that you aren't taking inventories. This is a very serious violation of rules, and will be entered into your record."

Sam might merely have been a poor report writer. Or the report may have been lost, or wrongly filed. Or Sam might have been preparing to file a supplement. Or perhaps the boss had misread the  report. On the other hand, Sam could have broken the rules. The possible proof had turned into a hard fact, and the true facts were swept under the rug, or into the chasm.

**3. Appositive proof** This is another convenient way of kicking the facts under the rug. Such proof establishes the existence of a quality in A by contrast with a quality in B, even though B is wrongly described, if not described in downright gibberish. The facts are hopelessly lost. A simple example is the following conclusion drawn about two brothers, one of whom squints:

"Jerry Smith has excellent eyesight because he sees things much better than his brother, Joe, who squints because he doesn't see well."

The truth may be anywhere among the following (choose one):

1. Jerry has poor eyesight.
2. Jerry has good eyesight.
3. Jerry has fair eyesight.
4. Jerry apparently does not squint.
5. Joe has excellent, good, fair, or poor eyesight, but he squints.

For another example, take the personnel reference report on a factory supervisor who is being considered for a promotion to a white-collar job: "Mr. Jones, having been in the factory, probably has cruder manners than office supervisors who have been to college."

Poor Jones is lost in appositive proof of his comparative crude manners. There is no attempt to establish whether Jones himself was a college man. There is a garbled picture of office workers as college graduates, and a perhaps even more garbled picture of all college graduates as having good manners. (A visit to a campus might have clarified this "fact.") No evidence is presented about Jones's manners to prove them crude or otherwise.

The casualty here is the facts. Brown becomes black because it is different from another color that is called white but is really gray. In the end result, the damaging truth that might require a discomforting behavior change is put off. The appositive proof is a heartening reason for hanging on to the old activity trap for a while longer.

**4. Hypostatized proof** This type of proof can likewise muddy the waters, a condition of immeasurable value in deferring the need for change. Such logic identifies some evidence about X with X itself, and modifies the rest of the available facts to fit the data.

The most common example is that of the three blind men who each examined an elephant. The first grasped the tail and declared, "An elephant resembles a rope." The second touched the elephant's side and declared, "The elephant is like a wall." The third grasped the pachyderm's giant leg and declared, "No, it is like a tree."

With such initial evidence in hand, each could then find further corroboration. All further evidence would smell, sound, and behave in a way that suited the original data. Where new facts emerged that did not fit, they would be rejected.

All further evidence is then weighed against a criterion of *fitness* to the original thesis. That which fits is cited as corroborative. That which refutes the original case is, of course, a special case, an exception, or, as the economists call it, a *friction*.

The Ad Hoc Committee on the Triple Revolution, an august group of thinkers of the early sixties, displayed such thinking. Two legs of their predicted revolution were an impending decline in the rate of population growth and a rising level of unemployment caused by automation. The immediate rise in the rate of population growth, and the coming of inflationary overemployment and labor shortages in many places, were quickly explained away as "short term and temporary counter-trends to the long run; inevitable secular movements."

Similarly, economists for the United States Chamber of Commerce predicted that the enactment of a minimum wage law would be inescapably tied to rising unemployment. When hard data to the contrary began to emerge following the law's adoption, it was explained as "a last spurt which is natural before a long downtrend."

The boss wonders how a new employee-benefit program is being received by the employees and asks the personnel manager to look into the matter. The personnel manager is standing in line at the cafeteria and inquires of an old-time male employee what he thinks of the new benefit plan. This employee, who will benefit greatly, is delighted and states his approval. This sample is reported to the boss: "From what I hear the boys are quite happy about the whole thing." From then on, all evidence to the contrary will be judged according to its contribution to the theory that everyone is happy. It all checks out nicely, for after all, the purpose of the program was to produce pleasure and satisfaction among the large majority of employees. Any dissident who grumbles that the hundred-dollar deductible is a bad feature will be rejected, because that feeling does not corroborate the theory.

**5. Misplaced literalism** Misplaced literalism is still another means of kicking the facts under the rug and coming forth with a distortion that will be accepted as the truth. This fallacy occurs when somebody makes a humorous, figurative, or offhand remark that is then taken literally and becomes in the telling a bit of hard evidence of fact. Statements overheard out of context, offhand remarks, quips and witticisms, and gossip take on the aura of hard evidence when captured by the misplaced literalist.

Behavioral scientists, when studying business, are especially prone to such misplaced literalism. To those not coming from the context of the plant or office, common language and phrases used there take on heightened significance; the same people may treat other, highly relevant information cavalierly.

One useful species of such misplaced literalism is found in the work of Melville Dalton, whose book *Men Who Manage* was derived mainly from overheard comments and casual conversations conducted in the vicinity of a plant. Talks with truck drivers, taxi drivers, bartenders, and workers from the plant provided him with an amazing network of information about the informal organization of the plant.[6] Since much of it was in the rumor category, its authenticity is founded wholly in his subjective ability to weave it into a coherent pattern. It also provides some excellent examples of misplaced literalism. Persons with experience in a plant know that the language there is ordinarily exaggerated for effect. The boss whose door is often closed is reported authoritatively by the help to be sleeping in there. It is an article of macho faith among plant help to believe that male managers with good-looking female secretaries are sleeping with them. Purchasing agents are always tipping the till and taking kickbacks from suppliers. Anybody who walks through the plant without saying hello to anybody is a sourpuss who probably spies on the help and betrays a best friend whenever possible.

Another source of misplaced literalism is found in the reports of behavioral scientists who supplement questionnaire results with "quotable quotes," purported to represent a real-life example of what the survey results really mean. Doctor Bright has an especially keen ear, akin to John O'Hara's ability for dialogue, and his often sophisticated research studies are made more readable by such quotes as "Hell, Doc, who'd want to work with *him*?" The danger in such quotes is that they will color the entire result of the research, for they are a source of misplaced literalism for decision makers. These people read the quotable quote—ignoring the research— and take sweeping action based upon it.

Much of human relations in the world of work consists of lighthearted badinage. Sales representatives may exaggerate how much time they have actually spent on their lunch hour, or how many martinis they have consumed. The common parlance for identification of expense accounts is "the swindle sheet," even among those who treat every item on it with the meticulous detail of a certified public accountant. Office messengers who go in and out of executive offices carrying messages and performing other menial chores sometimes exaggerate the moods, statements, and attitudes of the denizens of those inner circles.

The grapevine is a seething mass of inaccurate data, as well as a hard core of factual information. A story that starts out in one dimension becomes enlarged, shrunken, stretched, and filled with important embellishments. The grapevine also becomes a source of much misplaced literalism. The words of the higher ranks are especially subject to such misplaced literalism. A male vice-president refers to a shapely female clerk as "my dear," and a dozen listeners have already established as

---

[6]M. Dalton, "Conflicts Between Staff and Line Managerial Officers," *American Sociological Review,* 15, no. 3, 1950.

a fact a series of trysts and assignations, and possibly a divorce. The women in hearing distance hear blatant sexism.

Such misplaced literalism has innumerable value in establishing as a fact that some proposed change will not work, thus reinforcing the activity trap. The humorous card found in stationery stores, "Look alive, you can be replaced by a button," becomes the seed of some mass anxiety in the work force when it is reported that a new computer has been ordered or a transfer machine has been received for installation in the manufacturing plant.

**6. The use of irrelevant precision**  Irrelevant precision is a final form of fact evasion that helps mightily when the need comes to perpetuate the activity trap. An old shop story describes a journeyman machinist who was teaching an apprentice to read a micrometer, an instrument for measuring the thickness of flat objects. First, he wound the mandrel down to a fine line and held the micrometer up for the youngster to see. "That is one thousandth of an inch," he declared solemnly. The boy was clearly impressed. "Gosh, Hans, that's really small. By the way, how many of those are there in an inch?" The journeyman shrugged and said, "I don't know, there must be millions of 'em."

The number of people in business, government, churches, homes, and clubs who solemnly count, measure, gauge, and weigh things about whose meaning they haven't the slightest inkling is beyond calculation. The emphasis upon *doing things right* rather than *doing the right things* requires an increasing precision in day-to-day work. The accountant who spends hundreds of hours finding a fifteen-cent error in a financial report is caught in the activity trap, with all attention focused upon misplaced precision. Editors and teachers of writing who become obsessed with punctuation and grammar at the expense of thought, style, or the effectiveness of communication are thus ensnared in misplaced precision. This, of course, does not mean that good editors, who are concerned with communication, are always sloppy grammarians, for good grammar can assist in communication.

Government auditors are prone to seek out any conceivable deviation from customary practice, which then elicits a loud public announcement of "variances from prescribed practices." Turned into a headline or a TV news story, the variance, which might have been a mistake in addition or a wrongly numbered page, is enlarged into major corruption and a possible scandal for the millions of readers and listeners.

Such precision becomes a form of reality evasion and a strong inducement to risk aversion when the slightest error in precise details becomes the basis for rejecting the entire new idea. In one Western state an economist was engaged to prepare a complete strategy for the development of the state's travel and tourism industry. His report was professional, informed, and imaginative. However, a minor state official, threatened by the change, noted that in one place in the lengthy report the economist had misstated a date. Seizing upon this minuscule and wholly unimportant error in fact, he built this into a major case against adoption of the proposed strategy. Endless days of dispute delayed the initiation of the new program while the official pounded away at "inaccuracies."

Lawyers, whose trade is admittedly that of advocacy of a single position rather than divulging the complete truth, know the advantages of misplaced and irrelevant precision. Dealt a weak case to defend, the skilled barrister draws the jury away from the damning truth by misplaced precision. A damaging witness can be discredited if he or she can be caught in an error of fact, however minuscule. Credibility as a witness is thus attacked, and the damage done in the finding of a small imprecision might, in the hands of a skilled advocate, be extended to taint the large body of testimony.[7]

The activity trap breeds anti-planners, advocates of the status quo. When decisions are being made to adopt the innovative and creative idea, the executive may be placed in the position of judging among alternative advocates. In such a court, the defender of the status quo finds that misplacing precision will help his or her cause greatly if the executive decision maker is able to be persuaded by misplaced precision.

All of this avoidance of fact is perfectly sensible for the person who is struggling hard to avoid being turned into a misfit by change, by planning, by innovation. The power of the human mind in resisting change cannot be underestimated.

## THE FACT-FOUNDED DECISION

Management consultant Marvin Brower, writing of his many years of counseling America's top executives, places making "fact based decisions" among the most prized of skills.[8] This is made especially hard when the facts are not being reported, and even more difficult when they are not even considered fully. The powers of people in the middle and lower ranks of an organization to disguise facts from themselves, and thus from others, grows out of their desire to retain the status quo. Of what value then is such a detailed display of the ways in which facts get lost?

By recognizing and enumerating the sand bars in finding facts, we make the navigation among them easier, and possibly enable the change-seeking reader to avoid some of them. Recognition might also, we hasten to note, assist the confirmed occupant of an activity trap to employ these obstacles to ensure that no change takes place. For those whose commitment is to the old activity trap, the list of obstructions offers a systematic guide to immunizing themselves and their surroundings against what Professor Alvin Toffler has called *future shock,* a malady that afflicts people when the rate of change is simply too fast for their minds and metabolism to bear.[9]

For managers who hope to introduce change while hanging on to the already satisfactory, and to retain control while introducing innovation, an ability to get facts and use them is vital. From these specific instances cited emerge some positive rules for making fact-based decisions in human affairs:

1. The best facts are affirmative, not negative.
2. The burden of proof ordinarily rests upon the advocate.

[7] F. L. Wellman, *The Art of Cross Examination* (New York: Macmillan, 1948).
[8] M. Brower, *The Will to Manage* (New York: McGraw-Hill, 1964).
[9] A. Toffler, "Future Shock," *Horizon,* 1965.

3. Establishing a fact requires the tying in of a direct relationship between hard evidence and the proposition to be proved.
4. Evidence of fact should be relevant, and relevance is established first by the evidence itself, or, in its absence, by fragments from which it can be constructed, and finally by indicators or links of indicators.
5. Facts are more apt to be probabilities than proofs, and such probabilities can be stated in weather forecast language as percentages of likelihood.
6. A fact is no better than the evidence presented in its establishment.
7. A fact is only true in the context within which it was born.
8. The emotional condition of people directly alters, amends, and distorts their perceptions of evidence.
9. The weight of evidence can ordinarily be expected to produce facts that point at a decision to do nothing.

Those organizations that have generated a capacity to be innovative and creative in the ways they do things have learned these nine practical guides, perhaps intuitively. For most organizations, where activity traps prevail, the arts of circumventing them have been equally well learned.

# four

# The professionals
# as failure exploiters

Daniel Moynihan, as senator from New York, was strongly engaged in a verbal battle protecting his constituency from a government tariff policy that would have created a higher level of unemployment among garment workers. The policy in question would have made it easier for foreign manufacturers to compete with New York firms, throwing several hundred workers in that industry onto the unemployment lines. In the course of the ensuing debate, his antagonists conceded the effect he described but proposed that "the government would provide for the victims of the unemployment which would follow." Moynihan, with characteristic insight and wit, observed that Moynihan's law would undoubtedly be applied. In effect, this law, he said, is that government aid to the unemployed laborer would consist of hiring two $8-an-hour counselors for every $4-an-hour worker laid off, "and of course the victims would be unqualified to hold the position of counselor for they would lack credentials for such high level work."

The results of the debate are of course not the point; it is rather how we have come to rely increasingly upon *failure* to provide opportunity to a rising tide of professionals. If unemployment did not exist, a substantial number of professional aids, counselors, social workers, analysts, economists, clerks, administrators, and high-level civil servants would themselves be unemployed. This idea demonstrates just one instance of how we have created a plethora of failure professionals: people who have made a profession and a well-paying career out of the failures of our society, our inability to fulfill our goals, and our apparent propensity to labor in vain in so many areas of our society.

The respectability of failure as a profession was demonstrated in 1977 when the Massachusetts Institute of Technology (MIT) School of Engineering, School of Management, and Department of Urban Studies jointly offered a new course called "The Failure of Human Systems" in recognition of the theme that failure has become such a dominant issue of our times.[1] The course was originated by Pro-

[1] *New York Times*, Nov. 14, 1978.

40

fessor Frank P. Davidson, appropriately, perhaps, a lawyer by training and an expert in "macroengineering." He reported to the *New York Times,* "I was struck by the fact that so many of the institutions of society are really set up to deal with failure." The case Professor Davidson makes can be corroborated by such institutions as the courts, prisons, bankruptcy and tort law, the welfare system, the insurance industry, medicine, social work, juvenile officers, truant officers, remedial education, the military, quality-control departments, customer relations departments, and product liability suits, to mention just a few.

By definition, failure has traditionally been assumed to mean unsuccess, and has had an invidious tone. Othello's "lame and impotent conclusion" was the substance of tragedy and agony. The words *fiasco, fizzle,* and *washout* from popular language are all words indicating disgust and disappointment. Yet, in modern times, we have empirically constructed a whole new definition of failure to make it synonymous with professional opportunity. Failure is one of the fastest growing industries and occupations. One of the first tasks for the MIT seminar was to rewrite the definition of failure. The traditional definition makes it a positive thing rather than setting up failure as a polar opposite of success and then defining one in terms of the other. This new definition calls failure an inability of a mechanism or a human being to fulfill the function for which it was designed. One student in the MIT course chose to create two definitions: *failure-bad,* which is laden with guilt and inadequacy, and *failure-learn,* which is what happens when a scientist fails but the experiment leads toward a better theory. The trial-and-error system of experimentation, which Edison is reported to have employed in finding materials to perform satisfactorily in an electric light, is an example of failure-learn.

## FAILURE-GOOD: THE PROCESS OF CREATIVE DESTRUCTION

The destruction of the obsolete through the failure of the less suitable, it should be noted, is part of our tradition. In science and in the economic system of capitalism the mental method consists of asking certain questions, and asking them in a certain way to produce the new and better. Schumpeter called this "creative destruction," and this attitude was such that less useful ideas were supplanted by better ones, and in that sense produced the failure and destruction of the old in order to make way for the new and improved.[2] The high failure rate of business in good times and bad, where a modicum of competition is permitted and encouraged, is well known as a risk of business. It is exactly this risk of failure that produces a climate where science and engineering can also function well. The manufacturer who must choose between two alternative machines will choose the better where costs are the same and the less competent or less perceptive will fail. Few will lament this destruction, for the greater good emerges for the larger number when the best machines and methods can squeeze out and bury the lesser good. Even the losers and failures

[2] J. Schumpeter, *Capitalism, Socialism, and Democracy* (New York: Harper & Bros., 1947).

recognize the merits of the system in which they have done their best but are outdone—or have failed.

The creative-destruction hypothesis resembles many of the systems of nature. The natural processes of evolution imply that change will occur and in the process some species will survive and others will not. In this way, the species that do not make it through the evolutionary process can be said to have failed. Jean Baptiste de Lamarck described the processes of change in evolution as consisting of four elements: (1) a striving for perfection, (2) an ability to adapt, (3) the frequent occurrence of spontaneous generating of the new, and (4) the inheritance of acquired traits. While Lamarck's fourth principle has not been proved, most evolutionary theory emerges from Darwin, whose theory of the survival of the fittest—and the corresponding destruction or extinction of the less fit—highlighted the adaptive process as a cardinal principle of evolutionary change.

Biological processes, as we are prone to learn from TV shows of animals in their wild milieu, are seldom mild. Wolves prey upon the lame and old moose, and keep the deer herd in line with the available forage. The deer, even when not threatened by predators, may fail from too much prosperity and excessive breeding. This overly rapid growth of population will pressure the food supply to the point where some members of the herd will starve. As stern-voiced announcers are prone to remind us, this is all part of a natural process and reflects that most familiar of conditions, "the delicate balance of nature." This kind of assurance makes the younger members of the watching audience feel less pained at the apparent ignominous failure of the lesser species as it is quite violently devoured by the one successful species. In fact, this whole process is part of nature's plan and is therefore failure-good; however, it may cause the more tenderhearted to flinch in empathy.

## HOW PROFESSIONALS USE FAILURE TO EXPLOIT

During the more frenetic days of New York City's race with bankruptcy in 1977, a startling example of a new kind of failure was uncovered, one in which the professionals used the failures of our society to exploit the situation to their own advantage. Because of the pressures to reduce expenses, the office of the controller was obligated to cut back on certain expenses previously incurred. Among them was the program to provide child care for women who were heads of families. By ordinary or perhaps traditional standards, women who were the heads of families— many of whom had been abandoned by husbands, others of whom had never been married—were the object of a social welfare program. The program's main effort was a system of some 350 child care centers where such women could leave their children to be properly cared for while they worked. The logic of the program was civilized and sensible. The women, whose lives were made desperate by their lack of a husband or other familial status, were able to work, and jobs were often available. The only thing stopping them from moving off the dole and onto a payroll was the presence of small children. The child care center would provide them with a vehicle for working, and the assurance that their responsibilities for their infant children would be well handled.

Under the financial pressures of the time, the city concluded that it must close some 50 such centers and move the children in those centers to one of the other 300 remaining centers. It was discovered upon investigation that when the 50 centers were closed, there would be a saving of $100 million or more in salary costs but the effect would be a mere 125 children who would be obliged to transfer to the remaining child care centers. A quick calculation revealed then that fewer than three children per center would be transferred, and that in the process hundreds of social workers staffing these centers would be discharged. In other words, there were some twenty baby sitters for every three children in these centers. The average salary for each of these employees of the baby-sitting centers was reported at some $21,000 a year. This case, for which full coverage was provided in the *New York Times,* produced little chagrin among the professionals affected. Rather, they rushed their story to the press and TV in defensive and aggressive behavior. "The children are being sacrificed for money," was the gist of their indignant pleas.

Doubtless the original purposes of the centers was worthy. The possibility that women on welfare could be brought into the mainstream of society through easing a barrier to their working was sensible from a social viewpoint. Yet that worthy purpose was exploited by the professional failure exploiters. Nobody questioned the credentials of the staffs involved. They all held appropriate degrees, and all pursued their tasks with professional aplomb and zeal. It was not asserted that the professionals in every case were not hard working. They wrote extensive reports, attended meetings, typed their letters and documents and filed them, enrolled in courses to upgrade themselves professionally, and worked at methods improvements. The only visible defect was that most of what they did was wholly useless, being executed, however, with professional efficiency and skill.

The role of the professional social workers and administrators in the child care centers of New York was not nearly as exploitative, however, as that of the centers' landlords. It was to become a basis for criminal prosecution when it was learned that the housing for these useless programs was even more extortionate, to the point of lawlessness. Long-term contracts for floor space for the programs were uncovered, as was some illegal conflict of interest in securing them. Several of the principals were convicted. All of which reinforced those who were opposed to any form of social assistance to the welfare mothers, and in the end eliminated many socially useful and even necessary programs.

The realization that humans are venal and apt to pursue their own interests should hardly be a shocker to most people. It is, however, less likely that we realize how deeply the professionals of the world have become involved in creating the harmful and hurtful situations they subsequently will be prepared to alleviate through their professional ministrations. In such a professional ethic, the most "creative" of the professionals is *the person who can devise new job-creation programs for other members of the profession.* This sequence goes somewhat as follows:

1. The first glimmerings of an excess of professionals in the field produces some job pressures on the marketplace.
2. The prices and wages and job opportunities for new entrants go down, and the promotional opportunities for the experienced professional are blunted. Long stretches of stagnation and apathy appear imminent.
3. The educational establishment appears to be threatened with cutbacks in faculty, research grants, and professional mobility.

At this stage, the necessity for finding new "opportunities for service" produces the discovery of needs previously undiscovered or overlooked. Articles are written, speeches are made, the professional association lobby begins to work, popular audiences are made aware of this problem. Needs studies are followed by feasibility studies, proposals are written, and legislation drafted. Lobbyists shift their attention to demonstration grants, which become akin to the proverbial camel's nose in the tent. Once it is ensconced in somebody's budget, its removal therefrom becomes a matter of shifting the burden of proof to the cost cutter. "After all, there are many professionals and workers who will be without jobs if this program is eliminated." Thus goes the argument of the failure professionals.[3]

When the Office of Economic Opportunity—a regiment in the war on poverty—was created, it proposed to overcome the failure of society to provide employment opportunities and skill development for poor people. The result was a new bureaucratic organization made up of people who were far better educated than the victims and whose role was to perform professional services that would end poverty. The idea that some organizations have as their objective to put themselves out of business was implicit in the program. But that self-abnegating purpose is one of the first casualties in the war on failure. Thus, when at a later date a suspicious and truculent Congress concluded that the war was producing no victories and chose to abandon financial support of its efforts, the response was a plaintive appeal to the legislators that to cut off funds now would mean a loss of jobs for a number of professionals. At this point, the actual nature of the war was revealed in its true colors; it was not really a war on poverty, but a job-creation program for professional poverty fighters. The conclusion that the war was having no discernible effect upon the enemy was ignored by the failure professionals.

## THE HEALTH CARE INDUSTRY AS A CAPTIVE OF ITS PROFESSIONALS

Such modern versions of poor-box robbing appear even more blatantly in health care delivery and hospital management. If there were no sick people, then there would apparently be no need for hospitals. Since people are mortal and can become

---

[3]For one example, *see* "The Mental Health Lobby: Provider vs. Consumers," E. F. Torrey, *Psychology Today,* September 1978.

ill, however, hospitals are indeed necessary for repairing and maintaining the sick, and the basic need for health care is evident. A solid core of professionals in the health care enterprise could quite readily be conceded to be members of a category of failure professionals of the growth and improvement variety. The declining death rates for certain germ-borne diseases such as tuberculosis, diptheria, and the like are evidence of the ability of our race to overcome past failures and accordingly to help us all to grow and to live longer and better.

But such is not universally the case in health care, nor are all health care professionals so engaged.[4] By 1978, President Jimmy Carter had introduced bills into the Congress requiring that costs of hospitalization be contained, for such costs had reached unconscionably high levels. These costs were mainly salaries, especially those routed to professionals, whose fees and income were rising at rates in excess of thirteen percent a year. Not only were the incomes of doctors and nurses rising, but the numbers of persons required to staff the health care industry rose far faster than the demand for their services. Hospital administrators built lavish buildings for which no patient demand could imaginably be foreseen. A giant 800-bed hospital in Brooklyn was erected at a cost of some $200 million and never opened its doors. In Louisiana, a new Naval medical center of equal grandeur suffered a similar disuse: it never opened. More widespread were the overbuilding programs of local hospitals, which were typically found to be twenty percent equipped with excess rooms, for which no patients could be discovered. In a typical medical center in a small city it was common to discover that hospitalization costs for the genuinely ill person probably included at least $10 per day to pay off bond issues or loans on these unoccupied rooms.

The medical staff of one Eastern hospital having 300 beds was made aware of the fact that 100 of those beds were chronically unoccupied, and as one staff physician described it, "at staff meetings we often discussed ways in which that occupancy rate—we called it our 'census'—could be improved through longer stays, more in-patient admissions, and encouragement of elective procedures which in tighter times would have been handled in the physician's office, or in outpatient departments." Such pressures upon the staff were not visibly resisted by even the most professional medical staffs, and certainly not by the business managers of the establishment. Nor was the likelihood of its being policed too effectively by insurers, for they in turn were raising the rates for premiums paid by workers and employers for health care. One estimate by an automobile company executive is that that company's labor costs included an average cost of $2.65 per hour per worker to pay the premiums for health insurance. This hourly rate was five times the total hourly rate paid such workers twenty years before, and was of necessity passed along as a hidden tax to every buyer of an automobile that year.

Despite the widespread publicity given these facts, the lobbyists of the health care professions were successfully able to defeat legislative measures which would have contained cost increases to some six percent a year, which was closer to the average rate of inflation in the economy that year. Only in a few states, Massachu-

[4] M. Gross, *The Doctors* (New York: Dell Pub. Co., Inc., 1976).

setts, notably, was a liberal state legislature sufficiently taken with the undesired effects of these costs upon the working person to enact laws making all hospital budgets in the state subject to prior review by a state board before they were approved.

The pressures for cost increases in medical care continue through today from the failure professionals, whose aims are not only to cure the ill, for which of course they must quite properly be credited, but also to create pressures to continue wasteful and useless costs to workers and the public to support a nonproductive surplus. Seen narrowly from the viewpoint of the professionals themselves, their quite legitimate function of healing the sick also serves as a justification for adding luxurious and wasteful overrides to the real costs in order that the failure professionals' establishment might continue its highly satisfactory status.

The consequence of this rise of failure professionalism was an immense windfall to the professionals—the doctors, hospital administrators, and insurers. Between 1959 and 1969, the benchmark years for the rising tide of medical costs, hospital care rose 217 percent and payments for physicians' services rose 130 percent, reaching a total of $12 billion. Expenditures for medicines and appliances reached $8 billion, up 88 percent over ten years prior. This was in an era when inflation was a benign 3 percent annually. Every index of medical care rose at double that rate and often much more. The costs of a hospital room, the total cost of a stay in a hospital, and the operating costs of community hospitals all rose in a breathtaking fashion. The number of persons enrolled in health insurance programs rose, with proportionate increases in income of the insured at a compounded rate of 18 percent per year during this period.

By 1970, about 80 percent of the residents of the nation were covered by health insurance, which provided financial underwriting for the health of most people. It also provided a signal to the health care establishment to ignore costs and benefits and proceed to spend other people's money for the enrichment of the professionals in health care. In January 1971, President Richard Nixon directed the attention of the nation to a massive crisis in health care and warned that there would be a total breakdown within the decade unless changes were forthcoming. Private insurers providing health care were supplemented by government programs, Medicare, and Medicaid, which provided opportunities for the new failure professionals to enrich themselves beyond their wildest dreams. Going beyond the many excellent services which were demonstrably being provided the genuinely sick, the failure professionals were revealed to have added on "fringe benefits": needless surgery, billing for undone procedures, and charging the government for phantom patients and undone work. The massive flow of funds provided also the wherewithal to lobby against any legislative attempts to monitor, control, and curb the failure professionals in health care. By 1979, there were strong efforts but few tangible successes in stemming the rising cost of health care and its extraneous appendages of failure professionals.

Medical schools are well known to have some elements of the same beneficial add-ons, which serve more to preserve the well-being of pointless professional staffs, in addition to the acknowledged invaluable function of medical research and high-technology medical practice, and the education of new professionals. My own study of the student-teacher ratios in university hospitals, which are teaching hospitals, reveals that the average teacher-student ratio is about 10 to 1. That is, there are on an average ten professors of medicine for every medical student. Even if we concede that medical education is expensive, and that the ratio of teachers to students should be much higher in medical school than in law school, for example, that 10 to 1 ratio borders upon the extortionate. The ratio of law students to law professors runs closer to 40 to 1, in the opposite direction. That is, there are apt to be forty students in a large auditorium listening to the lectures of one professor at any single time in law school, with the main reliance for learning placed upon the student, who must read cases and master texts upon his or her own initiative in the library study carrel, or in study groups of other students. Although admittedly nobody would relish the prospect of being treated by a self-taught physician or surgeon, a significant margin remains of failure professionals whose major function is taking care of the job security of other professionals, with a resultant cheating of the patient and the taxpayer, to say nothing of the rest of the university, which struggles along with the leftover resources after the medical school has absorbed the giant portion. Confronted with one prominent and prestigious medical school with a ratio of fifteen professors for every student, one wag in a school of business at the same university was noted to have quipped that he intended to establish a "rent a student" business for medical professors, whose opportunity to ever meet a student before commencement was really quite slim.

## THE LEGAL PROFESSIONS AS FAILURE PROFESSIONS

Law schools, however efficient they may be when described in terms of the student-teacher ratio, have hardly come off looking better when it comes to engaging in failure-professional production. The result of expanding law schools and the increasing graduation of law degree holders has produced a well-publicized surplus of lawyers whose major anxiety appears to be in finding things to litigate. Despite their admitted efficiency in operations, the schools' long-range planning ability leaves something more to be desired. The production of lawyers because of the proliferation of law schools during the seventies was hardly deterred by studies showing that there was already a surplus of lawyers, many of them unemployed, and even more of them employed outside the practice of law in business, government, and nonprofit organizations.

The legal profession is widely recognized as an example, perhaps even a model, of failure exploitation.[5] Despite the widespread criticism of it for its exploitative character, the profession has to date shown no evidence of a willingness to reform itself. Exposés in *Time*, denunciation by Supreme Court justices, and occasional muckraking books about superlawyers and million-dollar lawyers leave them unscathed, and probably unmoved. For there is no reason they should eschew a strat-

[5] J. Goulden, *The Super Lawyers* (New York: Putnam's, 1972).

egy that is succeeding in making the legal profession central to the life of the society.

A character in one of Kurt Vonnegut's novels describes a lawyer as a person who has an unerring eye for money and how it flows. This ability to see money flowing is turned into profit by lawyers when they interpose themselves into the stream between two parties, holding before them the prospect that all the money in the transaction may be in jeopardy for some obscure legal reasons that only a professional lawyer can see. Thus, if there is any such transaction as buying or selling a home, building, business, or piece of land; dying and leaving an estate, or giving a substantial gift to a beneficiary; obtaining a divorce and dividing the property; or creating a trust with our assets—for any of these we call a lawyer to protect the bulk of the property and our rights from being diverted or diluted. For this service, the lawyer takes a piece of the action, thus becoming a switching station, so that money going from A to B will not go directly but will go from A to the lawyer and hence to B with a certain portion of it removed.

Admittedly, the need for protection against loss is a valuable service, and most people are willing to pay the price—really quite modest in most cases of property transactions—for the peace of mind that comes with having a legal opinion of the transaction's soundness. But the torrential, Niagara-like production of young lawyers from newly minted law schools has created more lawyers than there are such transactions needing scrutiny and security. Hence, the rise of that segment of the legal profession that must devise new and more ingenious ways of becoming professional exploiters.

Once the volume of transactions between buyers and sellers and ordinary day-to-day business is fully satisfied, it becomes necessary to *create failures,* or at least to discover new ones that might produce the possible flow of money from one person to another. This generates the failure exploiters in the profession. One variation of this is to produce complexities in what might otherwise have been a simple transaction. A more notable example of this variation is the divorce proceedings between wealthy and notable persons who have fallen out of marital bliss. Obtaining more than equitable or even decent proportions of joint property for one or the other of the marital disputants creates a financially lucrative practice. This, of course, entails setting aside any such archaic values as reconciling the parties, or providing justice to either side, especially one's opposing mate.

The divorce itself is routine. It is the property settlement between the now separated parties that comprises the area of exploitation. The more the aggrieved party can take of the whole sum owned by them jointly, the larger the fee accruing to the lawyer. Such eminently successful lawyers dealing almost exclusively with the divorces of the well-to-do are known in New York as the "bombers." About ten in number, they live at a six-figure income by aggressively attacking the whole sum and channeling most of it to their own clients to the dismay if not impoverishment of the other. The strategy is not justice or equity, but attacking and winning. In the process, the professional exploiters create new demands for their service by an expanding level of divorce. As one of them told me, however, "We can hardly be charged with responsibility for the fact that one of three marriages will end in divorce in the first ten years, and if we are vigorous in our advocacy that is the function of lawyers." It is true that the cause of divorce is not lawyers. Still, the existence of such a failure of the marital establishment has been heightened by possibilities of great gain and exploitation, for the victorious partner and the lawyer have sound economic reasons to applaud the entire process. Even the losing lawyer in divorce settlement cases has small reason to lament the outcome. Only the losing partner has reason to mourn the system.

The old saw about "ambulance-chasing lawyers" is nothing current, but the growth of the insurance industry has created a new form of liability and tort law that has produced what Joseph Goulden calls the "Million Dollar Lawyers." These are the liability lawyers who take on clients of low station for a contingency fee where the target of the suit or complaint is an insurance company or other corporate giant with resources which run into mind-boggling figures.[6] Such suits seeking redress for wrongs or injuries done which would make the damaged person whole and provide full payment for lost money, lost time, and even grief and suffering are admittedly justifiable and even necessary. Yet, the professional failure exploiter goes well beyond such simple justice and produces settlements which make millionaires of their clients, and ultimately of themselves. The surplus of lawyers and the limited number of torts that could support the legal establishment requires ever-increasing levels of imagination and ingenuity to devise new means of exploitation.

*Product liability suits,* in which the aggrieved party has been injured through negligence on the part of a manufacturer, have been enlarged to a new industry that provides income and employment for thousands. Even if we allow for the many legitimate complaints that flow from a mass-production society where imperfections must be found, there are a growing number of individuals stretching the application of product liability suits, the major beneficiaries being the lawyers. From a relatively simple base, the growth of product liability suits has erupted into a torrent that promises to stem the growth of many industries and add billions of dollars in operating costs—and ultimately product costs—to American manufacturers. This is more than a simple extension of the suits of the past. A whole new family of complaints is being developed.

## THE NEW ENVIRONMENTAL PROFESSIONALS AS FAILURE EXPLOITERS

One such manifestation of product liability has been the tying together of cancer fears with product liability. A leader in this campaign in the late seventies was the National Resources Defense Council, or NRDC, a nonprofit organization "dedicated to protecting America's endangered natural resources and to protecting and improving the quality of the human environment." In a two-color brochure mailed broadside to millions of Americans, NRDC asked its direct-mail clientele, "How safe are you and your family in an environment where the food you eat, the soda

[6] J. Goulden, *The Million Dollar Lawyers* (New York: Putnam's, 1978).

you drink, the air you breathe, the materials you use every day are hazards to your health, perhaps to your life?" The purpose of the brochure was to announce a new fight against cancer, which could, they proposed, be attributed to water pollution, children's art materials, industrial plants, nuclear facilities, city smog, and unsafe packaging.[7] Boasting forty thousand members with a full-time staff of twenty-four lawyers and scientists, NRDC operated in Washington, New York City, and Palo Alto, California, to create a fear of cancer from the ordinary things of life around us. The program includes legal action, scientific research, and citizen education, as well as vigorous lobbying to incorporate into law and administrative regulation legal systems to create a whole new industry: the appeal to a fear of failure of our cells to remain normal in the world in which we live. The appeal to the year 2000 asks, "Will some form of cancer still strike one person in three?"

In the first eight years of its operation, NRDC reported that it was able to achieve some tangible effects upon the thinking of citizens through such actions as forming a network of lawyers to monitor legislation to protect fragile coastal environments, forestalling the plutonium breeder, ending the killing of Alaskan wolves, and requiring that corporations disclose environmental policies. The unifying link in many of its suits, and a stated strategy for the future, was to be centered around the cancer-preventing character of many of the environmental protection projects it would undertake in the future.

This relatively small organization proved that professionals can indeed take real risks and threats and turn them into a new industry, exploiting the feature of failure. In fastening upon cancer, they chose the ultimate fear of failure, that of our bodies to adapt. The willing response of the Department of Health, Education and Welfare, and the adoption of a similar pattern of fear induction by the Occupational Safety and Health Administration to cancer-inducing elements, are evidence of the success of their approach.

The hard fact that cancer is a major cause of death is indisputable. It is certainly understandable that people do not want to be afflicted by it, that in fact they seem to be in absolute terror of it. It is the symbol of death, the hidden and terrifying grim reaper. Whether it is especially useful to exploit that fear, to say nothing of ethical, through fund-raising brochures is perhaps more a matter of taste than anything else. As biologist Lewis Thomas puts it, we all will die anyway, and the rapid rise of cancer is not really a change in the cancer-causing forces in life as much as a reduction of the other causes that used to take us away. When we cured diptheria, pneumonia, and other insect- and germ-borne diseases, we merely assured ourselves that we would more likely survive for other causes of mortality, which would be degenerative. This means that as we get old we degenerate in our organs, our circulatory system, and our hearts.[8]

We might also consider it a bit unimaginable to list 2000 influences in the world around us that cause cancer with any sane expectation that either OSHA, NRDC, or HEW will really isolate all of the causes and subdue them. The very num-

---

[7] "NRDC and the Fight against Cancer," (brochure), New York, 1978.
[8] L. Thomas, *The Lives of a Cell* (New York: Bantam, 1974).

ber 2000, which is the length of the current list being promulgated by OSHA as cancer-causing agents, invites generalization. Unfortunately, the generalization that has 2000 individual causes, with possible combinations and permutations, leads to a rather fruitless conclusion, the not especially novel revelation that everything in our life leads to death. The professional failure exploiters, in suggesting that lawyers and special "movement" people can reverse that trend, pending only the mailing in of your personal check (tax-deductible) today, are appealing more to paranoia than to reason. The exploitation of other people's misfortunes is indeed something to be lamented. Even more lamentable, however, is the deliberate cultivation of new forms of paranoia created to produce employment opportunities and income for special professional failure exploiters.

## SOCIAL WORKERS: THE NEW LANDED AUTOCRACY

Among the more nobly motivated and ignobly enmeshed in profiting from failure are the social work professions. Clearly, if there were no poor, no ill-educated, no delinquents, no criminals, no handicapped, no ex-convicts, there would be no need for social workers, at least of the present repertoire of skills and behaviors. But, you might rightly protest, surely nobody charges social workers with *causing* poverty, or of willfully perpetuating it. Why, look at how hard they work to stamp it out and ameliorate its effects. They even search out its causes and attack them, in denouncing corporate greed, middle-class indifference, suburban isolation, and flight from one's fellow human beings. Still, the mechanisms are firmly implanted in social work to create the problem social workers hope to convince us they are laboring to alleviate.

Take the problem of definitions. The poor are defined as those below a certain level of income for a family of two or three or four. This figure rises annually as inflation and real income together rise in the economy. The architects and the principal beneficiaries of this definition of poverty are the poverty workers, not the poor. By defining poverty at some figure, say $7000 a year for a family of two, they take a host of people who might otherwise never be considered poor and cast them into that category. A retired couple living on social security plus a pension received by the retired breadwinner may own their own home, a car that is aging but, being well tended, runs perfectly fine, and a houseful of furniture that is well maintained and pleasing if not modern. It might even be that they have some other assets or, perhaps if they are aged enough, have engaged in estate planning and disposed of their assets to avoid estate taxation. If, as well, their consumption habits are less self-indulgent that yours or mine, they in fact live well within their income at a level most satisfactory and pleasing. Yet, they are poverty-stricken according to the social workers' definition if their income falls below a certain level.

Now it would be plain nonsense to suggest that everyone who is poor has a fine house and car and is living well. There are many people who go to bed hungry, wear old clothes for years, and are cruelly pinched by rising energy costs, food costs, and medical bills. But that group is not as large as the total number of people who are encompassed under the rubric *poverty.* Only the professional social workers have a vested interest in selling us a definition that includes both groups.

The means by which this process occurs in the hands of the social worker and related poverty professionals is that of "blaming the victim," to employ the term coined by William Ryan.[9] We concentrate, he says, upon the black child—and all of his or her alleged defects—who, coming from a culturally deprived home, is to be blamed for his or her own miseducation. This is a shorthand phrase in which the victims are blamed for their own miseducation, for they contain within themselves the explanation for their inability to learn. Internalized cultural deprivation includes a family that does not subscribe to *Reader's Digest* or buy the *Encyclopedia Britannica,* that speaks only lower-class dialect, which adds up to social deprivation and explains why children squirm in their chairs, are inattentive, and play hookey from school.

This averts the necessity of looking radically at the low budgets, decrepit buildings, outmoded and battered texts, crowded classes, insensitive teachers, and blustering, frightened principals. This generic process of blaming the victim, says Ryan, is widely applied to almost every American social problem. The lack of decent health care is explained by the assumption that the victim lacks sufficient motivation and health information. Slum housing is caused by the culturally deprived background of the victims, who are Southern migrants not yet acculturated to life in the city. All of these influences add up to a cultural problem, which of course is understood by the social worker, who nevertheless cannot attack its causes, being so busily engaged in devising explanations based on the culture of poverty and in ministering to its victims. The creators of the practice of blaming the victim are producers of a false scientism of poverty professionalism, which alleviates the need to attack the causes and, accordingly, perpetuates the problem. They also perpetuate the demand for greater numbers of professionals, who as their numbers increase comprise professional growth and career development opportunity for those properly trained in the theory of the professional. This affords their means of living at a distance from the victims.

In many respects Ryan's thesis has similarities to a theory of poverty proposed two centuries ago by economist David Ricardo, who proposed an "iron law of wages." Wages, he said, are doomed to rest ultimately at, or slightly above or below, the subsistence level. Natural law produces in the lower social ranks among people who are paid above the subsistence level the damning effect of producing more children to enter the labor force. This added supply of child labor will quickly drive wages below the subsistence level until starvation and squalor put a natural stop to this reproduction. The shortage thus arrived at by misery will soon produce a labor shortage, which will drive wages once more above the subsistence level, at which point the iron law takes over. The higher wages will produce moderate wealth, which will enable people to reproduce again. Thus, God must take the rap for creating natural laws that make poverty a technical cycle, much like the hog-corn cycle noted by agricultural economists in our time.

---

[9]W. Ryan, *Blaming the Victim* (New York: Random House, Vintage Books, 1972).

Direct doles and subsidies take on the connotation of the error of "throwing money at problems," which is noted as useless if not downright hurtful to the victim in the long run. As in the Malthus theory of population, aiding the poor is less preferred to hiring more middle-class poverty workers to minister without end to the victims of cultural changes and to continually analyze their problems. Like members of the landed aristocracy of 1775, modern victim blamers reject such obvious solutions to the problem as either honest acceptance that they do not intend to help the victim or, on the other hand, a radical solution, since radical social change would endanger their own position. Nobody has a greater stake in poverty than the poverty professional.

The solution is a brilliant compromise. Neither radical reform nor simple acceptance will do. The ideal compromise is to turn upon victims as the cause, to make them volitional victims, to whom social workers will minister with genuine compassion and low in their postvictimized state. If the victims are fated to be poor or sick, or to be drug addicts, pushers, or street hustlers by their own inadequacies, cultural heritage, or genetic defect, then there is no alternative but to minister to them with social welfare programs.[10]

Many of the failure professionals—lawyers, doctors, counselors, and consultants—live such compassionate lives ministering to victims whose fates are sealed by the definitions and practices of the profession. The parallels to the unintended evils that flowed out of the poor laws for the English peasant have been noted by Professor Steven Marcus of Columbia University. The intent was to prevent the hard-working peasant from being exploited by the indigent but lazy poor. The effects were more widespread, and the laws reacted against the very group they purported to protect. Ira Glasser, executive director of the New York Civil Liberties Union, takes the viewpoint that much of the work of the "caring professions, doctors, judges of family and juvenile courts, social workers, custodians of the aged, the poor, the mentally ill, and other dependent weak persons, has the end effect of robbing them of their civil rights in the guise of helping them and ministering to their afflictions." Such caring tends to become coercive, and while it is not to be suggested that dependent people should be deprived of care and assistance, the care should not be coercive, for in becoming so it coerces all of us. Glasser suggests that the caring ministrations of the failure professions have turned into an adversarial relationship between power and liberty. The professionals, in their caring behavior, have found an area for the exercise of coercive power, and have deprived a large segment of the population of their power over their own lives.

## THE PROFESSIONS UNDER SIEGE
## AND THE BILL OF RIGHTS

It is exactly this latter point which suggests the route by which the reversal of the failure professionals and their dominance of our society will in all likelihood occur.

[10]W. Gaylin, I. Glasser, S. Marcus, and D. Rothman, *Doing Good: The Limits of Benevolence* (New York: Pantheon, 1978).

The protection of civil liberties and individual rights has a strong tradition in America. When colonial rules abridged individual freedom, a revolution and a constitution were deemed necessary to remedy the oppressive effects. When in the latter half of the nineteenth century business trusts became too powerful, antitrust and other restrictive legislation was enacted to restrain their accumulation of private power, greater in many instances than the power of the democratic state and certainly more than the power of any single individual in confrontation with it. During the 1980's, it is predictable that such a set of protections will emerge for the protection of the rights of individuals against the failure professionals, which is perhaps a way of saying that the professions themselves must become the subject of legal safeguards of the rights of individuals. After beginning in the sixties, and reaching a high-water mark in the late seventies, the feeling in many quarters that the professions are too powerful and need to be restrained is widespread.

Columbia University's Jacques Barzun, writing in *Harper's* in 1978, described the professionals as being "under siege," with the need of the public being weighed against the private practice of the professions.[11] President Carter that year twice called down two of the leading professions. Chief Justice Burger twice criticized the legal profession. Senator Kennedy, in hearings on medical cost containment, declared passionately to the leaders of the medical profession that "you will surely bankrupt the country" if their private practices were not restrained by legal means. Lawyers, rather than becoming defenders of the rights of people, are thought to be neglectful and distorting. Scientists, after Alamogordo and Hiroshima, were seen as amoral, and either treasonous or warmongering, or else they were under attack for being tools of the utility corporations, and for constructing nuclear plants that would destroy life in our community. Accountants were barraged with charges of and lawsuits for self-dealing, and of concocting rigged books and being masters of misrepresentation. Admittedly, much of this is part of a more general malaise about the affluent and the successful of the world, represented by the well-heeled professional; in many instances emotional binges lead to an attack on the more visible objects of that malaise.

Perhaps, Barzun suggests, this new control of the professions will come from within. Internal reform is not an ordinary condition of institutions without pressures from without, however. Perhaps, Barzun suggests, the route will be realized through the demotion of the profession to ordinary trades. As the professions advertise and competition sets in, a breakdown of standard practices will ensue.

Creating a czar of professional conduct will not work, however, without the development of ethical norms and internal policing of the professions themselves. The hope for a moral uprising in the professions will, of course, not occur unless leaders within them—moral leaders rather than technical—gather the critical mass needed to strike the conscience of the main body and create a code calling for a more heroic behavior by the professions. Among the glimmering possibilities are those that have led to an infusion of more teaching of morals into the basic education of professionals in the universities. Business schools now have courses and

[11] J. Barzun, "The Profession Under Siege," *Harper's*, October 1978.

chairs in professional ethics in the face of scandals of bribery and malfeasance at the highest levels of corporate life. This is more than hiring industrial chaplains; it takes the employment of trained philosophers and theologians to teach courses in business policy and organization behavior, as has happened at the University of Connecticut, Stamford Campus. At least two of my colleagues at the University of Massachusetts School of Business are holders of degrees from theological schools, teaching management decision making and personnel management. Medical schools and law schools in a few isolated locales have made similar appointments, although most are still more like resident prophets preaching do-good courses as appendages to the important technical courses in torts, contracts, or human biology. Codes such as the Hippocratic oath, or the more trendy bioethics codes, or government regulations governing research into DNA, are fruitless if they are not embedded in the technical behavior of the professions all of the time. For the professionals, ethics cannot be an additional course or a supplemental kind of behavior, but must be a way of practicing one's profession.

The control of ethics lies not in governing behavior with rules of right and wrong, for this governs only the activity of the professions. Rather, the siege against the professionals, which is only now mounting to serious proportions, lies in the control of their purposes. The rightness or wrongness, the meanness or nobility of the professions, lies in changes in their objectives rather than in their technical achievements. The skills of medicine, law, or administration are neutral. To achieve this means more likely that the professions must manage themselves by objectives, and the choice of those objectives along right rather than wrong lines can only occur when the professions seriously attend to the processes for defining their own objectives regularly, systematically, and in a mandatory way. It is the activity trap that has caused the professions to veer from making any choice whatsoever except pursuit of activity for its own sake. When they turn their attention to objectives, the journey to internal self-reform will have begun.

Beyond czars as suggested by Barzun, or self-policing, proposed by many professionals themselves, more is needed.

## ANTIDOTES TO PROFESSIONAL IRRESPONSIBILITY

Despite the widespread misuse of professional capacities we now seem to find out about, there are some antidotes which could make a substantial step toward the uplift of professional contribution. The major loss entailed by professional irresponsibility lies in the waste of talent it produces. This means low-yield use of our best brainpower, to say nothing of the frustration and apathy that settle upon the professionals themselves when they do not know what is expected of them, don't know how well they are doing, and feel unfulfilled.

*The antidote to professional irresponsibility lies mainly in the management of professionals, often by other professionals, but just as often by nonprofessional managers.*

Antidotes thus begin with management practices that are rooted in the following guidelines; for most professionals work in organizations, not as individuals.

1. Emphasize the goals of the profession and choose noble and uplifting ones rather than pedantic and maintenance goals. Every manager and profession should spend time regularly, systematically, and unremittingly in finding such purposes to which professionals can be committed.

2. Divert resources to those things that promise to make the highest contribution to those objectives.

3. Build support systems of paraprofessionals, facilities, typing pools, libraries, and other aids to free professionals to focus their work on contributing to the achievement of noble and necessary social and technical goals. Withhold the same resources from those who use the position and politics of professionalism to stem such efforts.

4. Free the professionals from bureaucratic straightjackets and controls to allow them the luxury of freedom to find and pursue a clear path to the goals which society needs from them. Professionals cannot be treated as hired brain boxes and expected to produce noble results.

5. Upgrade their professional capabilities constantly through advanced professional education and training so that they rise continuously up the scale of competence.

6. Involve professionals, and not just their managers and administrators, in the discussions through which goals are chosen. People who participate in decisions that affect them will support and execute those decisions with greater zeal and intelligence than those who receive decisions from persons less aware of the perplexities and obstacles of professional conduct.

7. Reward and encourage those who demonstrate that professionalism is rooted in conceptualization and creativity rather than those who demonstrate their conformity and compliance with obscure and pedantic routine goals.

8. The rewards for successful attainment of socially necessary and uplifting goals should be proportionate to their worth. Many professionals today find that they are paid less than truck drivers, carpenters, plumbers, electricians, and others whose work is valuable but more procedural.

The breakdown of the professions, as Barzun proposes, is already far along. More and more are *employees* rather than independent, self-employed professionals. In such a role, the problem is good management, not revelations or new oaths.

five

# The malpractice society

During the sixties and seventies, a nerve-wracking development overtook the medical profession. Patients sharply increased the number and size of lawsuits filed against their doctors charging malpractice. The sheer volume of them was breathtaking, and the percentage of them that were handed down favoring the patient and making huge awards sent malpractice insurance rates through the rooftops. This produced a great leap upward in the insurance premiums physicians and surgeons had to pay to obtain such insurance, a cost they added to their charges for medical services to patients. This, in turn, angered even more patients, who became increasingly critical and rebellious against the "greedy doctors." The result was further malpractice suits, and so on. A few sober observers were alarmed and predicted that if the trend continued, the entire system of health care delivery to individual patients would collapse under the great malpractice binge.

More was at stake, however, than the mere income of physicians, or the vulnerability of their insurance companies. The basic relationship between physician and patient was brought into question. Was the physician in fact the true healer we had by faith led ourselves to believe? Numerous new studies of medical practice effectiveness were conducted and produced evidence that not all was perfect. A study showed that each year some twenty percent of all surgery was unnecessary. In view of the percentage of cases where people died in surgery, the chances are that there were probably thousands of deaths that could thus be attributed to needless surgery. Government administrative rulings, made pungent by the huge infusions of federal funds into medicine, sternly called for reforms including peer review boards and numerous other kinds of control systems that would ostensibly overcome the newly revealed fallible character of the medical profession and restore it closer to the image of perfection we held in our minds as the ideal.[1]

---

[1] J. Horn, "Making the Malpractice System Work Better," *Psychology Today,* September 1978.

# THE MALPRACTICE OF EVERYTHING
# PROFESSIONALS DO

While doctors were understandably distraught, there were other kinds of malpractice charges being leveled against different professionals. In education, there were numerous studies leading to extravagant charges that the professionals in education were guilty of malpractice. In some instances, parents and even former students were filing gigantic lawsuits against their former teachers, charging them with malpractice; to wit, they did not teach the kids under their charge to read and write. The legal profession, while less vulnerable to suits by the fact of its obvious ability to defend itself better than most professions against lawsuits, was nonetheless assailed by many important groups and members of its own guild for being guilty of malpractice. A justice of the Supreme Court told the American Bar Association that most trial lawyers were incompetent. Others, in a more sensational vein, wrote exposés of the shady practices of lawyers—how they exploited clients, were incompetent, and were generally of low quality in the practice of their profession.

Ralph Nader, a lawyer by training himself, was an important reformer who provided substantial leadership in creating the new malpractice mentality of our society. Starting with a book that exposed malpractice in automobile engineering by the large automobile companies, he expanded steadily to expose almost universal malpractice in all of the professions he studied. Tire makers, drug and pharmaceutical manufacturers, professional baseball teams, and government administrators were all guilty of imperfection and therefore malpractice. As a result of the movement he spearheaded, the National Traffic and Motor Vehicle Safety Act brought the design of motor vehicles under federal regulation. Within a year, Congress had passed the Wholesale Meat Act, the Natural Gas Pipeline Safety Act, the Radiation Control for Health and Safety Act, and the Wholesome Poultry Act, all advocated by Nader. Nader then turned his perfectionist eye upon the Federal Trade Commission, opposed the election of W. A. Boyle in his candidacy for the presidency of the United Mine Workers of America, and launched investigations into malpractice by officials of the Interstate Commerce Commission and the Food and Drug Administration. In 1970, the Occupational Safety and Health Act advocated by Nader passed the Congress. Meanwhile, Nader had taken on Union Carbide Corporation as a polluter. He then turned his attention to investigating the malpractice of the Congress itself. By 1970, numerous public interest research and raiding groups were abroad in the land, and the age of malpractice was upon us.

In 1975, an even more radical conclusion about professionalism in our society appeared, when Ivan Illich wrote *Medical Nemesis,* going beyond the suggestion that there was mere occasional malpractice in medicine. He proposed that "the medical establishment has become a major threat to health."[2] Because we have been made dependent upon professional health care, we have learned to neglect our own responsibility for our own health, he proposed. This dependence upon health care affects all social relations, and we have arrived at a "medicalized society." The doc-

---

[2] I. Illich, *Medical Nemesis* (London: Caldar and Boyars, 1976); *see also Deschooling America* (London: Caldar and Boyars, 1972).

tors, Illich propounded, expropriate the power of the individual to heal himself or herself and to shape his or her environment. Thus, he states, modern medicine itself is an epidemic, and we have built up an illusion of doctors' effectiveness which is, in fact, dangerous. We are accordingly more apt to suffer from *iatrogenic* diseases (doctor-caused illnesses) than from real ones. The healthiest world we could live in, Illich proposed, would be one in which people live in decent houses, eat healthful food, and are surrounded by an environment that supports rather than suppresses life. The role of medical doctors is occasional intervention, rather than dominance of health, which should be returned to the individual, whose main interest it should become.

Similarly, Illich had dealt with education in a book appropriately named *Deschooling America.* His thesis was the same. The educational professionals were going beyond malpractice at the ineptness level; they were trying to prescribe a social order. In fact, they were producing more ignorance than knowledge. Illich asserted that people should assume more responsibility for their own education and that of their children. Teachers and schools should serve the purpose of helping people attain the education they wanted. The idea that the educational system should become arbiters of ends rather than means was a whole new dimension of professional malpractice theory.

These two books, plus many more in similar vein, were not without practical effect. People during the seventies indeed did begin to seize more control over the maintenance of their own health and over their schools. Preventive medicine, and a general boom in personal physical fitness programs, swept the nation and the more affluent nations of the world. Jogging, swimming, biking, and tennis gained increasing numbers of new participants annually. Corporations' fitness programs quadrupled in number during the seventies to provide opportunities for people at work to take some control over their own health. A greater amount of nontraditional education emerged.

In its extreme, the malpractice mentality of the times went beyond the mere concern with professionals' mistakes. It proposed that professionalism itself was a fallible concept and that we should not really trust any of our professionals.[3] While this latter extreme was not universally held, those who adhered to it made enough noise that they were heard and made their influence felt.

## HUMANISTIC MANAGEMENT MEANS LIVING WITH IMPERFECTION

In an age when malpractice charges fly about freely, the fear of failing hangs over the head of every corporate executive, every research scientist, and every professional, and ultimately over every company or agency that produces or sells technically based products. The pharmaceutical company producing a drug for mass use will inevitably find that anything less than perfection in controlling nature will

---

[3] B. Barber, "Control and Responsibility in the Powerful Professions," *Political Science Quarterly*, 93, no. 4, Winter 1978.

mean that some people will become ill or even die from ingesting the drug. Thousands more will, of course, be saved from pain and death. The vaccinations against some diseases, such as poliomyelitis, produced cases where children actually incurred the disease and died from it when they would not have done so if they had not been innoculated. In the past, we accepted this small hurt—this failure—for the larger good. In more recent times, however, we have renounced such cold rationality and insisted that perfection be the goal. This quest for perfection has not taken the form of a demand that God or nature be kinder to humanity, but rather a demand that human beings be perfect in their cooperation with natural law or otherwise abandon all attempts at such cooperation and at discovery and development.

*The attempt to turn every technical problem into an artificial, humanistic problem has the ultimate effect of stopping all technical progress. It has turned the knowledge of failure into a preoccupation with the fear of failure.*

The seriousness of this unwillingness to live with technical errors pales when we turn our attention to problems that are more patently humanistic. We seek perfection in management, health care, government, and in social institutions, and thus insist upon malpractice mentalities in all aspects of life. On the one hand, if a physician using the best available knowledge of cooperation with nature makes a mistake, God will act consistently and unremittingly to punish the victim. It is not God who is sued for malpractice, however, but the physician. The next time around, the physician will be less willing to take the high-risk step that might produce a total recovery or preserve life, but will become cautious and even unwilling to make a decent effort.

The perfectionist mentality, which is unwilling or incapable of abiding comfortably with conditional outcomes and probabilities, is a special and more difficult kind of anti-planning mentality. If there is a chance of failure, or an element of risk, then that risk should be seen and known in advance—and if it is great enough, we should not undergo it. Rather, we should retain the status quo, or, even better, return to an imagined era of the past when everything (as seen from our present perspective) was stable, predictable, and faultless. Thus, *Split Wood, Not Atoms* adorns the bumper stickers of many cars in college towns across the land.

Much of our inability to cope with trouble is rooted in our confusion between what is natural and what is humanistic. Natural things result from acts of God. *Humanistic* means artificial. Water flows downward and seeks its own level. This, of course, is God's law, not that of the Army Corps of Engineers. Gravity causes a brick to drop on somebody's head, raising a large bump, but we blame the bricklayer, not the law of gravity. A hurricane starts in the Caribbean and tears up beaches and property on the Florida and Carolina coasts. Nobody calls for an investigation to discover what can be done to prevent God from doing such rotten things to us; but there may be a call to investigate the weather bureau for not preparing us for such disasters. We seem to have adjusted to nature quite well, and we recognize that the best thing for us to do is to learn what its forces are and to try to alter, predict, and use them to our advantage by a wonderfully ingenious kind of cooperation. The human heart can go into fibrillation and kill its owner, but medical science has uncovered the impulses that cause this and can block them by medication. We can make a drug that works because we have learned that beta impulses can be blocked by certain chemicals, and we cooperate wonderfully with nature to provide the patient with exactly the right material to carry out the function. It would be a foolish scientist who gave the wrong medication and then complained that God was perverse for not covering up the mistake. Nature, in this sense, is very unforgiving of our errors. A foot caught in a door is bruised. A capacitor that burns out will cause a whole computer to stop. Cursing God at such times is not considered very rational; therefore, we curse our own failures to skillfully cooperate with these inflexible rules.

Because of our skill in cooperating with nature, we like the occasions when we have developed a new cooperative scheme and it has worked well. Thus our liking for technology, new machines, electronics, nuclear energy, and creative chemistry. Upon reflection, we realize that we have not mastered nature but discovered it and cooperated with it in ways that produce felicitous results for ourselves.

In the sixties and seventies, a minority of extremists in society went too far in their support of a quite proper and necessary environmental movement. While much of the extremism was designed to produce a generation of radicalized students, the extremists' methods were to attack the failures in technology. This produced movements to stop oil drilling off the coasts of the nation, to ban nuclear power generation, and to limit the use of pesticides. Holding God blameless, the extremists fastened their attention upon the technicians who had the temerity to seek such pioneering cooperation with Him. Better, they said, to halt such attempts and live with the levels we knew in the past. Anything less than perfection is malpractice, which should be forbidden.[4]

## REALITY-BASED HUMAN RELATIONS: THE RISING TIDE OF EXPECTATIONS

A few years ago, I was touring a stamping plant for a large automobile company. Standing on the balcony overlooking the plant floor with the personnel director, we watched a worker insert large sheets of steel into the bed of a press and spray it with a drawing oil, at which point he stepped back and pressed a foot pedal. A giant crash followed, and a complete auto body shell was ejected on the other side of the press. The worker was clothed in a rubber suit and masked helmet. The roar, the splashing oil, the spray in the air all made it a most unpleasant job, I thought.

"Doesn't it make the company sad to see a person do that kind of work under those conditions?" I asked.

"Oh, they *like* it," the personnel manager replied.

That made me even sadder. The correction of the conditions would require elimination of the job along with the undesirable conditions.

---

[4] The *New York Times* of Dec. 14, 1978, on p. 1 reported a dispute between Transportation Secretary Brock Adams and the federal Environmental Protection Agency of New York, which opposed construction of the Westway.

Possibly, the evils of the job were willingly borne by the workers. There was plenty of competition among workers there to get that job. It paid extremely well; and the person doing it had some status within the shop, was able to afford such things as a camper and a home of his own, and was able to finance the education of his children. I have learned recently that that particular plant has since that time been reengineered to eliminate much of the work and, incidentally, the job of the person I observed. Now automated, it is quiet, pleasant, and free of human effort.

The engineering of that change undoubtedly was done in part as part of a cost-reduction program, designed to meet foreign competition and perhaps to upgrade the output of the press. It also could have been a product of a rising level of expectation people have about their work. Such rising tides of expectation among workers come in with every wave of new, young workers who have acquired them at home, in school, and from the social system. The "quality of work life" movement (QWL) is a symptom of that rising tide. QWL has been created not from the top down by management. Indeed, the personnel policies of the past were designed to accommodate and adjust the worker to the job, however bad it might be. Today it is far more likely that the worker and the professional will bring their separate sets of expectations onto the job, and that these expectations will be higher and more ennobling than those of the past. At least they will be different. Higher expectations eliminates many jobs, and the workers who held them.

To criticize management for not having anticipated these values is somewhat like criticizing it for failing to anticipate a natural disaster. Management behavior in the situation was not misdirected or inept, but perfectly sensible and proper in the light of its own experience and knowledge. Yet, the combination of unforeseen and mainly unforeseeable changes in worker expectations makes many managers of today misfits in the positions they hold.

## THE REASONS FOR THE MALPRACTICE MENTALITY

In the summer of 1978, when thousands of young people gathered at Seabrook, New Hampshire, to prevent the further construction of a nuclear power plant by the Public Service Company of New Hampshire, they received world attention. The ostensible purpose of the protest gathering was public health and safety. Nukes, it was proposed, were dangerous, and that was the reason for the demonstration—in effect, it was an attempt to save lives, at some time in the future. Yet, if that were the reason, the demonstration surely could have been focused upon more current and productive life-saving concerns. It might have focused upon automotive accidents, accidents in the home, or even being pushed out a penthouse window by a jealous spouse, all more hazardous than nuclear energy. The sober conclusion one could reach from studying the protest is that it had other objectives—not those often attributed to it by certain newspapers and political leaders in New Hampshire: a Communist plot. Rather, it was a protest of a small group of people who had found a means of expressing their dissent in a bureaucratic world where they felt powerless, a widely shared emotion.

The world of bureaucracy is aimed at producing efficiency. In order to do this, in a complex and highly populous world, there must be organization. The division of labor produces specialization, efficiency, and procedures and makes human beings instruments of the system, as well as beneficiaries.

It is this reaction to depersonalization—anger, alienation, and antipathy to the stated goals of the bureaucratic society—that has turned a small group of young people into rebels. While open rebellion, such as becoming a revolutionary, has some hazardous features, which rational radicals are quick to recognize, there are more sensible means of stopping things from becoming more bureaucratic and less responsive: Attack the unintended side effects of bureaucratic systems by using the system against itself. The customer who attempts to get an adjustment on a utility bill, or to persuade the book club to cancel his or her membership, becomes angry and alienated. The bureaucratic society has a systematic way of saying to individuals, "You are nobody." This is, of course, occurring in a world in which more and more people are living by the credo *I am somebody.* The ordinary person, often folded, spindled, and mutilated in the past two decades, watches the few who have taken some special measures to ensure that minority voices will be heard, and endorses those measures silently without joining in.

The sequence by which this malpractice mentality and the age of malpractice that ensued coincided closely with the growth of bureaucracies in government and corporate life, as well as institutions. Aided by the development of high-speed giant computers, the reduction of individual differences and concerns was astounding during the sixties and seventies.

When the bureaucratic form of organization was new, it produced some heartening improvements in standards of living. The actual efficiency and life of products and services grew. At the same time, paradoxically, the complaints against the quality and against the malpractice of managers and professionals in charge grew even faster.

As a boy, I lived in a small New England town which was serviced by New England Bell Telephone Company through what was known as a *party line.* Not ideological, but technical, this was a telephone system in which a single line was strung along a country road and ten or more telephone sets in ten or more homes were all strung off that single line. The distinction was in the number of rings the operator made to announce an incoming phone call. "Two longs and three shorts" was our home phone. Immediately upon picking up the phone we could hear the clicking of a half dozen other phones along the line being picked up to eavesdrop. Far from being depersonalized, technological, and bureaucratic, the system was highly personal and intimate. Consider the technical shortcomings of that system.

- There was no privacy, and wiretapping by nosy neighbors and operators was epidemic. No attorney general's order was needed.

- Technically, the service was horrible. Fidelity of tone and reliability of service were tenuous. A single squirrel on the line could knock out a dozen phones with a single bite and often did so, until the customers went out armed with a .22 caliber rifle or traps and halted this kind of interruption.

- Any technical service from the company was slow in coming, was often wrongly executed, and frequently needed redoing within a few days.

Yet, the clients seldom filed protests with a government agency, or even with the telephone company itself. The tribulations of the system were endured with casual good humor and small-town witticisms. The human frailty of the switchboard operator, who would leave her board unattended to gossip or even to go out for coffee, was well known and accepted.

Today, the quality, cost-effectiveness, and privacy of telephone service are unmatched. Direct distance dialing, a transistorized system, microwave communication, and satellite communication are accepted with indifference. What is less well accepted is the tiny irritations, such as a taped message when one makes an error in dialing or an overcharge of a few cents in billing. (There are few corresponding complaints about underbillings.)

Why in heaven's name are we so exercised about the minor glitches in the superbly sophisticated and flexible system we enjoy today when we were so blasé and indifferent to the primitive system of the twenties?

*The system today is depersonalized and impersonal. The customer and the employee are perpetually being told, "You are nobody." The system of old was defective but personal. We fight to restore that personalization.*

The steel-belted radial tire, which, we protest so loudly, does not perform for its whole guaranteed life of 40,000 miles in a few cases, is vastly superior to the miraculous "balloon tire" of the twenties. Yet we seldom protested the technical deficiencies of those earlier models. The reasons are not in the tires, but in our rising expectations, in our malpractice mentalities, and in the highly bureaucratic ways in which we are treated when we visit the dealer to protest a minor defect, or even a major mistake.

Angry clients and customers are at near epidemic proportions today. The courts are jammed with product liability suits brought by angry customers. The corporate response has been traditional: When faced with a problem, set up a systematic, often bureaucratic, piece of organization to deal with it. Typically, the company confronted with angry customers creates a new customer relations department with a WATS line through which customers can telephone long distance at no charge to air their grievances, large and small. One study by some marketing students of such telephone services was that twenty percent of such calls were greeted by a taped message, informing the customers in effect that "we care about you as an individual."

Frustrated and baffled by an apparent powerlessness in the face of a system that makes us conform, we raise our expectations even higher. Unable to get at the heart of the problem, we poke at the available targets, the localized underbelly, the most vulnerable spot. We attack the product itself as defective, even when by objective standards it is vastly better than it was before and is nearer ideal than we might expect.

People at work have similar responses to their sense of powerlessness in their work life. Procedures, policies, and systems require that things not be overly personalized. Women expecting equality of opportunity are baffled by a system which was designed for and operates mainly for males. Blacks and other minorities are frustrated by their apparent inability to unlock the doors to opportunity in a system that slowly evolved to fit whites. In their frustration, they find in the age of malpractice the small exposed edge that they can assail with considerable success. Since perfection is impossible, they must accordingly never run out of opportunities to be felt and heard if they are to continue their assault on the bureaucratic society.

Managers and administrators, legislators and elected officials work very hard at solving problems in traditional ways, while the attacks continue upon the small malpractices that are always present. In this sense, the managers are misfits and out of touch with reality. Perceiving reality means seeing things as they are and knowing both what expectations exist and how to respond to those expectations.

In human relations, Douglas McGregor suggested that today's managers are not in touch with reality in their own organizations. They make decisions as if they were, but they see reality through a set of rose-colored glasses that makes the real seem distorted and the distorted and bizarre appear real. The part of reality that managers miss most readily is the nature of the human beings who work under them, including their expectations. Also misunderstood are their value systems, motivations, and desire to work. Starting out with a nonflattering and inaccurate picture of the human character, the manager often presumes the employees to be averse to work, needful of orders and discipline, and in need of extensive controls so that the worst characteristics are not permitted to unleash themselves and thereby cause the organization to deteriorate and fall into chaos. Such a picture of reality, McGregor suggests, is false, for people can enjoy work that is productive and creative. They have wide powers of creativity which they desire to unleash, and they will do that exactly if they work in a supportive and reality-based managerial climate.[5]

Similar positions on the unreal focus of managers have been taken by other behavioral scientists, who propose that there are tools of research available that can be used to uncover employees' underlying attitudes and opinions and to verify where reality really lies. Arthur Kuriloff, who has both behavioral research and top-management experience, takes a similar position with respect to reality. Top managers, he states, have not got reality in hand; they have misconceptions.

The arguments the behavioral scientists make are impossible to refute, just as they are equally impossible to prove. You do not need to be a behavioral scientist, for example, to know that one man—as president—is indeed unable to know and become personally aware of the character, nature, desires, and opinions of 500,000 people, the approximate number working for General Motors. Nor could one know 100,000. It is a superhuman feat, attained only by some politicians, to be able to know and recognize even a few thousand people. The only way managers thus can know the realities in their own organizations—who are their people, what are their capabilities, what are their wishes and aspirations for the time being and the long term—is through statistics supplemented by personal impressions. Mainly, the chief

[5] D. McGregor, *The Human Side of Enterprise* (New York: McGraw-Hill, 1961).

can know these things from the reports of lesser managers, who in turn have gleaned them from lesser managers, and so on. General Motors has some eleven levels of management between worker and chairman of the board. Might reality be lost or slightly damaged in the journey from one end to the other? It would be amazing if it were not.

Isn't this then a powerful argument against *bigness* itself? Isn't such a removal from reality a telling argument for the vigorous enforcement of the antitrust laws, the divesting of major units by some large corporations, and the breaking up of others? Not necessarily. Such a case was made at the time of the great electrical conspiracy of 1959, when executives of major corporations went to jail for conspiring to fix prices with other large manufacturers. Ralph Cordiner, at that time president of one of the firms whose officers had been jailed, stated that he had no idea that such wrong behavior was going on. Immediately the response came from many, including the antitrust divisions of the Justice Department: If the top man cannot see improprieties only two levels from him, what other might possibly be occurring ten levels down that he must certainly know less about. Does this, the argument went, not suggest that bigness itself is the root cause of misbehavior? Only if reality can be found can the malpractice mentality be dealt with effectively.

Finding reality in a large organization requires that it be organized in such a way that various levels of reality are permitted to exist at various levels. The reality of the shop floor must be under the knowing eye of a responsible supervisor in charge of that area, and if this is so, then it need not be under the immediate surveillance of the peak leadership. The president deals with the realities of his or her own affairs. The generals in Washington cannot command the tactics of every platoon in the field. To attempt it produces the unreality McGregor describes.

> *Thus the realities of decentralization are the realities of several levels. Centralization almost inevitably breeds the world of unreality. The Washington bureaucrats who fancy that they can plan the nation's needs have lost touch with reality, and this work produces unrelated side effects. Only in reversing the mad race toward centralization in administration can the reality of human relationships and the management of human beings be located.*

This flight from reality in human relations has produced a mad world of increased controls over humans from distant authority, coupled with a sharp rebellion against those controls on the part of minority groups, women, and the young. In centralized organizations, people diminish, and reality becomes clouded. The absurd becomes commonplace. The world of Joseph Heller's *Catch 22* becomes so customary that there is little quibbling about the unreality of its details, for they can be found in organizations everywhere. The gang at the water cooler, the students sitting around the student union, the secretaries in the car pool, and the lesser-level managers become more and more cynical and alienated by the outcomes growing from centralized administration. Management information systems—complete with on-line, real-time, alphanumeric-boob-tube installations in every manager's office—and the growth of accounting and control departments to monstrous sizes are designed to facilitate top-management control over minor decisions. Procedures and inspections are designed to catch improprieties at every level. Personnel records and appraisals, designed to bar entry to management ranks to those who will not respond well to control, and the other familiar apparatus of centralized management scramble frantically to catch up with a reality that has been lost and cannot be recovered except through changes in organizations that free human energy and creativity and permit people to pursue their own image.

## MYTH AND REALITY IN HUMAN ORGANIZATIONS

In the vain attempt to maintain control of reality by complete knowledge of everything, many managers have opted in the direction of centralization, armed not only with a picture of an organization chart, but also with a belief that reality can be found in managing people. This *Theory C* is based on a myth that all authority and responsibility rest at the top of an organization. There are, therefore, as this myth goes, order givers and order takers. Those who are the order givers may delegate work to order takers, who, by division of labor, execute the orders and report back their results. If they have not been directed or permitted to act, they should not do so. If they are struck by some idea not within the purview of their orders, they are to go back to the authorities and seek permission. If, by chance, a subordinate's enthusiasm for an idea is sufficiently compelling and he or she should execute something independently, that subordinate will be required to describe "by what authority" such action was taken. In order to maintain control over this relationship, elaborate policies, procedures and regulations are required, and an organization plan is a design to control compliance. As Kenneth Boulding describes it, "The reports flow up, and the vetoes down."[6] Within an organization operated on such mythical grounds, people shrink. The absurdities of ordinary large organizations multiply, while the people at the top are out of touch with reality and accordingly cannot know of these absurdities.

In decentralization, the emphasis for realistic initiative shifts to the lower levels. *Theory D* suggests that the authority of lower levels to take independent action in the attainment of agreed-upon goals is unlimited, *except* that the final results must be satisfactory in terms of the objectives promised and the means must fit within the customary modes of human morality and not interfere with others' rights to take action. In Theory D, *policy* becomes the value constraint of the organization, aimed at preventing harm to the organization and its people, rather than, as in Theory C, *control* of every detail from the top.

*Decentralization then becomes increasingly crucial in achieving the reality-based organization that can live successfully with the malpractice mentality.*

[6]K. Boulding, *The Skills of the Economist* (Cleveland: World Books, 1961).

# EXISTENTIAL LEADERS AND
# THEIR FOLLOWERS

Reality-based leaders are *existential*. For them existence precedes essence; ego survival is the immediate issue. Pressures to oust leaders are widespread.

Astride these swirling pressures is today's leader. Hoping to move ahead or move backward, watched by workers and customers who pursue perfection in an imperfect world, there stands quivering and uncertain the modern leader in government, in business, in the institutions of society, praying "to whom it may concern" that he or she be allowed to continue existence in office and to keep the organization afloat.

Take the case of the Southern California Edison Company, a remarkably progressive and well-intentioned public utility led by people of good will and ability. Massive problems face the company management in providing power and light to millions of their fellow citizens. The company's power-generating plants rest nervously atop the San Andreas fault, which from time to time grumbles slightly, thus causing a major brownout. Its attempts at finding ecologically less noticeable power plants on the Kaiparowits plateau in Utah have upset the serenity of the region and aroused resistance among the Navajos living near there and among ecological advocates who would preserve the solitude and pure air of that isolated region. The government presses the company to do more to provide jobs for blacks, Mexican-Americans, and women under the equal employment opportunity laws. At the same time, the company requires a competitive level of profit in order to make future security offerings attractive to investors to raise sufficient capital for new facilities to continue the level of power required for a rising population in its area. Its executives are existential humans, for whom the problems of *being* are paramount.

Existence is the problem for millions of working men and women, even in a society where they are more affluent than any other workers in history. Since they are threatened by automation, unemployment, foreign competition, and rising inflation, which cuts cruelly into every increase unions obtain for them, since traditional seniority rules are threatened by equal opportunity hiring rules, since their children are less and less intelligible and less a source of joy, and since their work is sometimes sterile and unsatisfying, their very existence seems to be more of a problem that it used to be. The middle-aged male finds an affinity with Archie Bunker, the TV darling of the seventies, who articulated his frustration and defiance against the cultural, familial, and social forces that harrassed him everywhere. For many, only the voices of Spiro Agnew and George Wallace spoke of defiance and hope during the early seventies, thus providing a model for political hopefuls for the remainder of the decade. Even these ideals were to prove mortal or fallible.

For existential persons, whether workers or managers, the reversion to antiquities is a hobby of idle loafers and well-off youth. The futurist world is an incomprehensible collection of pipe dreams engendered by what their hero, Govenor Wallace, dubbed the "pointy headed pseudo intellectuals." Five major elements make up the realities of these existential people:

- *Luck* is the uncontrollable force that exerts an inordinate amount of control over their destiny. The rise of lotteries in dozens of states is far more than a source of revenue for beleaguered state treasuries; it is a wild dream of some golden salvation that may actually happen to a shipping clerk upon whom the kind face of luck shines. For the business owner, luck is what prevents rain the week of a clearance sale, when success is badly needed to turn overstocked inventories into cash. For the general manager, luck is what caused the credit crunch that wiped out the firm's debt financing and sent the company reeling into insolvency. Luck is the damnable occurrence that causes a president to select out of ten candidates for sales vice-president the one who will shortly go sour and prove a lush or a pleasure seeker at the expense of the entire sales program of the firm. Luck is thus generally *bad luck*. When things go well, it is justly deserved recompense for years of striving.

• *Conflict* is the second ever-present ingredient for the existential person. There is ever the competitor, the adversary, the snooping bureaucrat, the grabber who would take it all away if opportunity beckoned. There is the person at the next machine or in the next office who attempts to capture someone's job by making him or her look bad. At the very moment when things are going best, some calamity seems to appear in the form of competitors who snatch away customers, develop a new product that obsoletes one's own, or capture a market. Conflict and hostility are the aspect of reality that is in fact the most appealing to the modern manager. The bitter losses of today will be made up for by the sweetness of victory tomorrow. Conflict leading to defeat heightens the relish with which we can look forward to victory, which will be greater because we have come up from the floor to win it.

Yet, conflict is an indisputable fact, even when people collaborate and sometimes conspire to circumvent it. The extent of this fear that produces conflict, the raw nature of it, produces the hostility with which many business leaders view any attempts by lawmakers or the Department of Justice to enliven competition, widen it, or police its more destructive aspects under antitrust law. Business's best energies are aroused by its presence, but also some of our basest motives grow out of conflict.

• *Guilt* is another reality for the modern manager and worker. The task that could have been done but wasn't, the need to make personal decisions over people that destroy their careers, the need to inflict psychological shocks to people who are basically good people—these all engender guilt. Meeting organizational goals requires that guilt be *suppressed*. Developing a toughness to ask people to do the dirty jobs is a duty of the executive, lest one bleed too heavily for every subordinate's cuts and wounds and end up doing what David Moore has described as "usurping all of the dirty jobs while his subordinates stand around marvelling at the chief's ability to take it on the chin."[7] As Levinson put it, everyone has felt twinges of guilt or conscience for violating the rules and values by which he or she lives.

The president of Lockheed, referring to his company's downfall for bribing the Japanese, described this dilemma. As he sat in the outer office of the prime minister of Japan, he was confronted with the choice between paying a substantial bribe, which he found distasteful and repugnant, or sending back word to California that the order had been lost and thousands of workers were to be discharged. The

---

[7]Speech before the Bureau of Industrial Relations, University of Michigan, 1962.

need to cut corners to make competitors stay in line—this creates the emotions of guilt that must be kept in hand in the existential person. The failure of the company itself almost always raises in the executive the question, *If I had done so and so, could this have been averted*?

External pressures and organizational conformity are major influences in keeping guilt as a source of low-level tension, requiring people not to grow into their own aspirations on their ego ideals. One of the more common kinds of executive guilt customarily follows an outburst of rage at subordinates for failures. The outburst is not planned and is not controlled, and often it is followed by apologies for the blast, accompanied by chagrin and guilt at the occurrence.

• *Situationality* is a fourth ingredient of the existential manager. Hostility and resentment rise against consultants, news reporters, government regulators, professors, and eggheads who criticize business because it doesn't adhere slavishly to some theoretical norm. "If these people would get out and see what the situation really is like, they might talk differently," says one company president. Business is not organized to be anti-intellectual, and certainly not to be in opposition to education. More common is the scorn for the theorist who would run things from a book or according to some situationally unreal principle. If there are unending searches for general theories of management among management professors, they certainly haven't extended to company presidents and their subordinate officers. *I'm just a person trying to do a job* is a more apt self-description for executives. Expediency and practicality in the face of the unexpected and a confidence in their ability to see and solve new problems as they reveal themselves are part of this situationality. The skill of executives, who are scornful of ideology as useless, is the skill of the here and now, with some reluctant attention paid to those things in the future that already have evidenced themselves as potential problems.

• *Failure and death* are the final and perhaps the major remaining elements affecting the life style of the modern corporate leader. Death is not a common topic of discussion, for it is morbid and thus foreign to the executive way of thinking. Yet, the reality of finite careers, the executive replacement chart, the executive physical, and the fear of crippling heart attack, ulcers, or other disabling physical disabilities are always close to the surface. Finding younger people to move into managerial succession ranks, planning organization charts to allow for the ordinary mortality of executives, and keen attention to the physical facilities and prerequisites of office are designed to protect the executive from ordinary inconveniences that might make life more uncomfortable and perhaps foreshortened.

The forms of failure that confront managers are many. They may, for example, get passed over for a promotion they expect. This happens to most, for despite Mark Twain's advice to young men that "it is better to start at the top of the organization for there are fewer people at that level and therefore less competition," such a strategy is often not feasible, because the present incumbents haven't the decency to step aside, and among the breed called by Vance Packard the "pyramid climbers" there comes a realization that the top is very small and the ascent slippery. Most managers who don't get to the top accustom themselves to lower levels. The most painful failure is that which follows a long string of successes, perhaps even an uninterrupted series. This creates the condition Eugene Jennings identifies as the "executive crisis," which is personal, interpersonal, and organizational and can be most severe.[8]

Perhaps the most severe pain in failure comes to the executive who has risen over competitive peers to the top without serious interruption, attains the heights, then discovers that the company that he or she now commands is heading into serious business troubles. This is not uncommon, for the average length of life of a business in this country is *seven years*. Collecting a representative sample of company presidents in one room, one could address them as follows: "Look to your left; now look to your right. One of you will be out of business in two and a half years. Furthermore, two of you will be gone in five years, and in seven years, all three of you will have gone broke." Statistically, this would be a perfectly true statement. The reason, report Dun & Bradstreet and others, lies more in bad management than in any other cause. Ninety-two percent of business failures are due to failures of people to manage their affairs, the remainder to acts of God, natural disasters, and unavoidable risks.

*Statistically, at least, one of the more important realities of management is that it fails because of managerial inability.*

This embarassing and psychologically damaging reality has important effects on the introduction of change.

## THE REALITY OF HUMAN FAILURE

The business press is a constant source of news of top managers who try to break out of convention and fail in the process. Stepping into situations where caution or doing more of the same might be the politic thing to do, such managers become the expendables in moving things ahead. Jimmy Ling, the conglomerate builder, was forced from the management of LTV, the multibillion-dollar conglomerate he built from a garage-based electrical business, when his sources of cash dried up at a crucial moment. When William E. Roberts was hired from Bell & Howell to take over a not so healthy Ampex Corporation, he brought with him, a prescription for rapid growth. He set growth goals of 15 percent a year, principally by moving into the home entertainment market. Roberts resigned in 1972 after losses of $40 million were announced for Ampex's most current fiscal year. Analysts had a field day. "A case of growth for growth's sake," growled one broker. "Ampex home entertainment business just hasn't had 'strong acts,'" said a competitor. "Bad choice of technologies," explained another broker. "Too much debt financing," states another writer. Like the scribes watching the gladiators, all found it easier to sit in the stands than to jump into the pit and take on the lions. Yet, the supply of new gladiators, some of whom will become entrees for the lions, continues to be fairly plentiful.

At Arcata Corporation, which in five years grew to a $160 million diversified company from a $12 million redwood lumber operation, the two young men who

---

[8] E. E. Jennings, *The Executive in Crisis* (New York: McGraw-Hill, paper, 1972).

had built the business up were replaced in 1972 after a single profit-barren year. The analysts were less unkind in this instance, but the directors, nonetheless, dumped them, thus proving to thousands of people who never took great risks or broke out of the activity patterns of the past that innovation was after all too risky.

At Boise Cascade, a similar pattern of anguished cries from analysts, stockbrokers, and other fifty-yard-line ticket holders arose over $85.1 million in losses in 1971. After starting as the Boise and Payette Lumber Company, the firm had acquired a new look and a new vitality when Robert V. Hansberger became chief executive, changed its name, and started on an innovative course of growth and diversification. On the steepest part of its ascent it could do no wrong. Then there came a serious cash crunch and a recession when sales fell and financing on major projects became unconscionably high, and the drums began to beat. The 1971 profit blood bath was only one blow to be suffered; lawsuits in California and Maryland aided in the fall of the company's stock on the exchange from 80 in 1969 to a lowly 17 in 1972. The company was now deep in debt and held worrisome investments in Latin America; its corporate image took quite a beating, and so did its image of infallibility, which had come, probably quite unsolicited, to its top executives such as Mr. Hansberger.

In even more stable and longer-established firms, executives get caught, and the business press and the general public see the executive and his or her key associates in an unfavorable glare of publicity. It often seems that the corporate executive is invisible, compared to politicians and actors. This is true until one of them fails, or gets into serious trouble in business matters. Then he or she is quoted, photographed, and discussed by an endless number of analysts. It is rather unlikely, for instance, that Michael Daroff, sixty-nine-year-old chairman of Botany Industries, Inc., was a household name until his company's financial troubles forced it to close down its retail divisions, including such noted names as Weber & Heilbroner and Broadstreet's, following losses of $23.5 million in 1972. Competitors had explanations, including advice of what they should have done or not done five years earlier. They should have moved more quickly into knits, they should never have started retailing, they should have trained skilled workers. The sideline coaches burgeon with explanations.

In other instances, the failure is noted but not personally identified with anybody, as occurred when RCA dropped out of the computer business, selling all to Univac, or when a similar thing happened when GE sold its computer business to Honeywell. Within each individual firm it was a fairly sizable eruption, although it did not endanger the entire firm. Yet, it is predictable that for the individual managers involved, there were some fairly important personal readjustments and some bruised egos.

This bruising of egos for failure is an important ingredient in maintaining the status quo and preventing future risk taking. When things go well for the person who flies in the face of convention or takes risks that others do not take, there remains a huge body of the middle-management corporate body politic in business who draw their breath expectantly and await what they presume will be another fiasco. There is no natural cheering section for most business innovators. They, of course, generate their own cadre of admirers who have a stake in the success; and some other, similarly inclined innovators who have themselves taken strong risks in their own lines have empathy. For the most part, the employees, middle managers, staff people, engineers, personnel managers, and a rash of various analysts are standing on the sidelines ready to *explain* whatever occurs, but never really ego-involved and fully committed. It is this sideline group that finds sustenance in the activity trap. When all of the adventuring and innovating is done, they will all end up returning to *doing what has always been done.*

During the upward movement or the dramatic sweep into new fields or in new dimensions, there are enough people to accompany the innovators. The lawyers who take immense fees for providing counsel, the accountants who charge amazing sums to prepare the detailed estimates of glowing outcomes ahead, the brokers who take 15 percent on underwritings total, the consultants who calmly bill the firm at $1000 per day for technical assessment, and the reporters who do nothing but see all and write it down are part of the retinue that rides on the back of the leader who makes things happen.

When the leader flops, the retinue is no longer there. Perhaps a banker who rashly took a position in the game must now pick up the pieces and find a new champion to run things in order to get the bank's money back.

The myth that managers who fail are not really hurting is not true. After all, some suggest, they undoubtedly have been drawing high salaries, and have set aside enough so that they are reasonably well off, even if they are dropped from the organization. They hurt.

Interviews with numerous persons shortly after a losing battle in the field of business have shown that, although reactions vary from bravado to anger, they never refuse to admit that their pride is injured, and that they would like to come back. Accordingly, when the Penn Central went bankrupt, one of the senior men under the chief executive was Alfred Perlman. While some observers state "that had Perlman been in charge at Penn Central, the bankruptcy might not have occurred," there is no doubt that his pride in having a career destroyed near its end had been hurt. Thus, at age sixty-nine, in 1970, he took on the task of overhauling the nearly bankrupt Western Pacific Railroad. In his first year the railroad added $10 million in sales and turned a $14 million loss into a $3.9 million profit. When Perlman took over, the railroad was on the ICC list of railroads headed for bankruptcy. Within the year it was debt-free, in a strong cash position. What, beyond ego, should impel a man at sixty-nine to take on another sick organization? Perlman's record prior to moving to the New York Central, which subsequently merged with the Pennsylvania, was in turning around the insolvent Denver & Rio Grande during the 1950's.

*The visible failure of risk takers and innovators, coupled with the often anonymous and invisible nature of the successes, is an important reinforcer of the status quo in business. It produces risk aversion.*

Numerous visible failures over the past two decades have produced what many observers note as a public loss of faith in business ability to handle its own affairs. When the Penn Central went bankrupt, it caught many of the nation's largest banks unaware. Thousands of investors were decimated by the collapse of Wall Street, where the value of shares fell one third. Lockheed, ITT, the consumer movement, and the concern over pollution of the environment by manufacturing and utility firms operated for a profit have made the executive a ready target. The end result could be a further diminishing of the innovative drive that is necessary to make progress on some of the crucial social problems that can best be solved by business.

# six

# The idea killers:
## the creation of false obstacles by false argument

There are a few people in this world who have a grand idea and make it come true through skill, imagination, and leadership. Unfortunately, they are outnumbered and outgunned in today's world of activity traps, failure exploiters, anti-planners, and malpractice mentalities. There are, lamentably, far more people who create obstacles. Sometimes the obstacles they create are real, and in other cases the obstacles are imaginary. Some people create obstacles for others, and still other people create obstacles for themselves, then stand there in front of them helplessly deploring the fact that they cannot get anywhere. The result of these four varieties of obstacle makers presents the person who would make things happen with some special challenges.

Making things happen, of course, requires some ability to deal with obstacles. The same kinds of obstacles that stop one person will be overcome by another. Thus, it cannot be the obstacle that stops the initiators and creators, but more likely their ability or lack of it in coping. In this chapter, we will examine those kinds of false obstacles that have become very prevalent and highly developed, by false argument. There is little to be said in favor of beating your head against a wall, which will prove painfully real. But there is considerable benefit in knowing how to distinguish between a real wall and a false construction of a critic's imagination. Timing is also of the essence, for what is a real barrier at one moment may not be one later on. Creating diamonds was a maniac's dream at one time, but now General Electric does it commercially.

*A false obstacle is the creation of false argument in the mind of another or oneself by advocacy or argument that proves the error or fallacy of what is really a perfectly sound and practicable idea.*

## THE NEGATIVE ARTS OF ADVOCACY

The art of producing obstacles that are not there often employs the skill of advocacy, which is the basis of an important profession, that of the lawyer. Advocacy also is the province of the debater, the collective bargainer, the sales representative, the advertising manager, the politician, and just ordinary people when they engage in friendly argument. It is most especially the role of the manager. Some advocacy then is positive, while some advocacy is negative. It is the latter we look at here. It has two major dimensions. First we create by highlighting, by persuasion and argument, the vivid reality of things that do not exist, or persuade that the astronomically improbable is really quite possible. These are the arts of argument. When negative advocacy and persuasion work well, the obstacle will be agreed upon between advocate and antagonist.

A second and more substantive category of creating an obstacle where it does not exist is to define a difficult or impossible objective and demand that we achieve it. This is a valid function of the manager. The company president who pictures a great organization, employing hundreds or thousands of people, housed in a modern building, paying taxes, producing products consumed by millions of satisfied customers, is, at first, a visionary. Such a leader sees something that does not exist but which might. This president's efforts from then on are focused upon producing that vision. Such a function of leadership is the most important ingredient of leaders whose attainments are greatest. When de Gaulle returned as the head of France in the fifties, his visions included restoring France to its former rank as a world leader. The solution of the Algerian crisis, the divestment of the colonies, which were to be unified into a cooperative union of French-speaking nations, and the emergence of France as an atomic power were specifics of a larger dream and a master objective, which, in large part, he was able to attain in his seven-year term.

## HOW FALSE ARGUMENT PRODUCES OBSTACLES

The literature of argument and substantive fallacy is an important part of the literature of formal logic. Usually couched in Latin terms, such as *ad hominem* and *ad verecundiam* and the like, it has a formidable character that frightens off the casual observer.[1] In the world where managers direct organizations and people work, such argument is used regularly to get things done, and just as often to help create obstacles to changes or goals that might be unsettling. We use substantive argument and fall into substantive fallacies in order to perpetuate the activity trap. Persons working closely with creative people have found that there are some stock methods of killing innovation. The former president of Bambergers, the giant department store, once prepared a list of "killer phrases" that his experience had taught him people use to prove that a new idea will not work or should not even be attempted.[2] It included such expressions as:

- We tried that before.

---

[1] Several basic books on logic are useful here. I. Copi, *Logic* (New York: Macmillan, 1968) is one of the best. Also suggested is W. W. Fearnside et al., *Fallacy: The Counterfeit of Argument* (Englewood Cliffs, N.J.: Prentice-Hall, A Spectrum Book, 1959.)

[2] Speech at Rutgers University, 1955.

- The boss wouldn't approve that.
- It is against our policy.
- Somebody else tried it and it failed.
- It would cost too much.

Such commonplace expressions are far too simplistic for the critic who would really block change and reinforce the activity trap. There are in logic many more kinds of fallacious thinking that can be used to create obstacles.

Five such fallacies in substantive argument are described in this chapter, together with some allusions to the many other variations available and useful in creating obstacles and killing new ideas. The central idea of each fallacy is to disguise or conceal reality and produce a barrier either for others or, even worse, for ourselves. Let us examine each of these five obstacle creators.

**1. False appeals to authority** Since organizations have a tendency to slip into the habit of being dominated by one leader, such an authority figure has a formidable influence in preventing change at lower levels. The argument that "the boss probably won't like it" can be verified by bits and pieces as evidence from the boss's own words. In one large department store in the Midwest, it was forbidden for years to buy and display wicker furniture for sale in any home furnishings department because it was reputed that the big boss, a strong-willed man, hated wicker furniture. The rumor was false, but nobody was about to challenge it and risk his disfavor. Thus, no matter how profitable the line or attractive the deal, no buyer would break the taboo surrounding this item. Curious about such a strange disliking, the author, not being in the sphere of the old man's wrath, asked him if it was true that he hated wicker furniture. I explained the myth that prevailed.

"Why no, I love wicker furniture. I *did* see a couple of chairs in our store for sale one time which I thought were horrible and I explained why to the manager of the department, and they disappeared. Maybe that's where the story originated."

Despite the reassurances that subsequently followed—the clarification of the myth—the store still does not do very much in wicker furniture. Occasionally, some new young buyer who has not heard the full details on the likes and dislikes of the boss brings in an item, but in time catches on. As in Greek mythology, the pressures of the gods take up a sizable body of the literature, and a god apparently has to land pretty hard on the mortals to expunge the tale and substitute another.

There are numerous other fallacious appeals to authority that hit the opposition over the head with a big club to produce the appropriate change of mind. For example:

- It is fashionable these days in management to hand the other side a moderate karate chop by using better *numbers*. They may be simple statistical tables or complex models, meaningful or otherwise. A touch of complexity in the math is often all that is needed to add authority to the conclusions which accompany the argument, whether they are humbug or not.[3]

---

[3] A. L. Boone, "Wouldn't It be Nice If—" *Management Accounting,* February 1977.

• The reverence for the printed statement is another source of false authority. If the verification has been printed in a book, it has somehow thus acquired a character of infallibility, as if the process of being printed has touched it with divine endorsement.

• More likely to be found in the academic world than in business, but increasing rapidly even there as staff departments proliferate, is the use of quotations and footnotes in written communication. This heightens the impression that the author of the accompanying poppycock has in vast detail researched all of the available, and some not so available, data and produced indisputable truth. Often such abominations are sufficiently veiled that it is impossible to track them down. One either cites sources that require weeks to find, or copies from somebody else's footnotes without checking the originals themselves, and omits enough information in the notes that they cannot be found even if one tries. This conceals a fraudulent conclusion behind a note that does not say anything in support.

• There is muscle in professional status, and this is used to squelch the lesser ranks, especially younger people. In many organizations it is a cultural creation to teach humility to the young, by enhancing the infallability of the opinions of the old. That is, the older you are, the more logic you have mastered and hold available for instant application. This is not merely using experience, which has numerous underrated values. It is the idea that thinking itself, and even moral decisions, are better made by the old than the young. This idea tells these lesser lights that they are indeed lesser, and that *for that reason* they are in error. In other words, if you get caught in something stupid by a young person, don't refute the logic of argument or facts, but rely upon the argument that one must be wrong because one is young.[4]

• Appeal to the weight of dollars is another common fallacy in argument with authority. *We have invested twenty million in this and we know that the following is true* has much persuasion, especially in a world where dollars are an important measuring stick, a storehouse of value, and a criterion of success and achievement. Thus, my *wasting* twenty million gives me more right to decide the merits of an argument than someone else who has prudently spent one million. A variant of this is the salary of the person who is arguing. There is something fascinating about sitting in the presence of a millionaire.[5] Such opinions seem to have some kind of weight about them not found in the words, however wise, of the bartender or gardener. Even a $50,000-a-year executive has some clout in his or her own opinion because of what happens on payday when expatiating in the presence of lesser-paid persons.

• In a reverse kind of appeal to authority, there is the invoked *authority of the masses.* The labor relations negotiator, when losing an argument, may find it helpful to suggest tactfully that unless his or her opinions hold sway there may be horrible

---

[4] B. Greco, "Recruiting and Retaining High Achievers," *Journal of College Placement*, 27, no. 2, Winter 1977. Proposes some right ways of dealing with the young.
[5] *See* F. Lundberg, *The Rich and the Super Rich* (Secaucus, N.J.: Lyle Stuart, 1968); more current is K. Lamott, *The Money Makers* (Boston: Little, Brown, 1969).

consequences through the unleashing of mob power by the horny-handed children of toil, whose continued containment prevails only through the labor relations manager's skill and daring. *Can't exactly predict what the boys will say to this* has swung many a timorous company president into agreeing to a foolish stance. The ability of the black leadership to use this authority to change the minds of reluctant leaderships in many cities was described by Tom Wolfe as "mau-mauing the establishment."[6] This is a reference to the Mau Mau, terrorist groups of East Africa, whose willingness to engage in terrorism of the fiercest sorts against whites was a well-known bit of history. By alluding to such possibilities, the militant leadership was able to make its logic more persuasive to those who would otherwise have found it expedient to delay longer the granting of improvements to the blacks.

• The *ominous joke* is another kind of appeal to authority to win arguments that are basically weak. When the going gets rough, the person with the power to tell the rest of the people *You're fired* and make it stick can win arguments not by crass threats but by veiled allusions. The son of the founder who is now president can ask *Whose name is on the outside of the building?* and make his point. A smiling *Think of your mortgage, fellows* is a convivial bit of humor that has an undertone of ominous reality. It changes conclusions in the debate which follows.

• The "king's ear" approach to winning arguments is still another persuader of some weight. The disputant in a closely fought argument will have an immense advantage if he or she can claim to have the ear of the president, the boss, the king. This adds weight to the argument because of the height from which it apparently has fallen. Coming from a high place can assist a lightweight considerably, for lightness of weight is abetted by the height, which gives foot-pounds to an order when it lands on an opponent.

• Another kind of authority that is employed in argument is that of the weight of the paper generated in its defense. This is a favorite in government agencies, where often ten pounds of paper is generated for every gram of logic. In the age of the Xerox and other copying machines, such argumentative material is generated at ever-increasing rates, much of it pure puffery.

• A variant of the Xerox-copy argument is the computer printout, which hit people with an undeniable thud when it landed. It is often garbage of the sheerest sort, and is an attempt to win the day in persuasion when the weakness of the basic case would be apparent if not covered with tons of mumbo jumbo.

It would be possible to proceed thus illustrating many more appeals to authority and showing how they can be employed to create reality where it does not exist, or to win arguments, generally. Such arguments were once referred to as *ad baculum* argument, which is "with a stick." Lamentably, we have seen a rise of arguments carried on with sticks of various dimensions and should hope for a stemming of the trend.

**2. How to win an argument by attacking the arguer** The major idea in arguing

[6] T. Wolfe, *Radical Chic and Mau-mauing the Flak Catchers* (New York: Farrar, Strauss & Giroux, 1970).

to the person and not the topic is that it serves to shift attention from the argument's flaws or merits to the arguer's. Given a case in which someone is proposing a radical innovation that might be most inconvenient to you, if no major defect can be discovered in the logic, attack the person. A lawyer's joke, all too often employed, is *Hopeless case, attack the prosecutor*. The practice is not unknown in other fields.

For many years, the management training technique known as *sensitivity training* was practically immune to criticism, for anyone who criticized it was automatically demonstrating insensitivity and therefore was probably sick.[7] At one time, in a debate on the merits of the method, I predicted that I would be attacked as sick for being dubious of many of its medicine-man aspects. Such attacks followed; but even worse, the fact that I predicted the attacks, it was noted soberly, proved that I was even sicker than first thought. Today the evident nonsense aspects have become more clearly seen in the method.

In other ways, this form of argument to the person resembles the reactions of union officers when confronted with an organization drive by their own office employees at the union headquarters. These employees wished to form an office worker's union made up solely of office workers at the labor union headquarters. They were immediately attacked by the union's hierarchy, and some were fired for being *antiunion*. This charge, for a union organizer, for example, could be the ultimate personal attack. The employees responded in turn by charging the supreme chief of the union himself with being antiunion.

• Attacks upon the *motives* of the opponent are a customary form of circumstantial attack upon an adversary. Rather than pointing to such obvious facts as are evident to all, this line suggests or alludes to possible concealed and base motivations. Such arguments can take the tone of veiled kindness: "*I understand and sympathize with Joe, who badly needs a new idea after the series of failures he has had . . .*" is a bone thrown to a dog, upon which he might choke if not wary.

• Where the other person has been known to have developed personal associations that might indicate some character flaw or reflect upon loyalty or question his or her judgment, such argumentation is likely to appear when the going gets tough: *Your friends down at the club probably like this better than those of us who are just plugging away doing a job. . . .*

• The profession of psychology, which has made great contributions to industrial human relations, has also produced its share of snake-oil artists who have used the awesome power of an attack by a psychologist to achieve some rather mundane aims. For example, they have been known to overly extend a retainer contract for consulting in such fashion. They have, in more extreme cases, used arguments *ad hominem* to set aside the major person in the organization who has been opposed to their retention: *Considering Joe's own problems, it's understandable.*

---

[7] G. S. Odiorne, *Training by Objectives* (New York: Macmillan, 1972).

The major advantage in *ad hominen* arguments that attack another person is that they require no long personal acquaintance with the victim. Everyone's life is sufficiently filled with details to serve as target for an attack when one is engaged in arguments. The only way in which they can be averted is never to argue.

There is one commonly agreed-upon conclusion from arguments founded upon attacking the arguer: *Everybody loses.*

**3. Arguing to the crowd** Quite apart from the ominous practice of threatening mob action if one loses the argument is that of using the masses as a source of verification.

In an executive development program at the University of Michigan a few years ago, an eminent behavioral scientist was explaining some of his findings to a group of executives. They listened attentively and with complete understanding. Finally one of them stated, "Professor, I have no doubt that your data will fit exactly the populations you have sampled. I do, however, believe that your conclusion would not be true in my company in my region of the country, with my people." The professor lost his temper.

"My population," he shouted, "is the world, and includes the United States, and that includes every little burg like yours! Whether you like it or don't like it, my data is true in your plant." Perhaps it was courtesy of the group, or perhaps chagrin, but the argument ceased.

The argument to the crowd does not require that the crowd actually be on hand, as in a Hitlerian rally. It may be a massive group of people located in some major classification, such as a political classification.

In 1971, a flurry of campaigning occurred to determine the location for the takeoff and reentry base for the new manned space shuttle proposed by the National Aeronautics and Space Administration. Four sites were under consideration: Florida, California, Utah, and New Mexico. A Utah delegation prepared data of impressive credibility. Technically, economically, ecologically, and geographically Utah was superior. When the delegates took their tale to Washington, however, the argument *ad populum* immediately wiped them out. "How many electoral votes does Utah have?" was the only question asked. California and Florida, having several times as many, ended up dividing the project, to the utter surprise of nobody, except possibly Utah's two hapless advocates.

In other instances, the appeal is to the poor folks, the less affluent masses such as those concentrated in the ghetto areas of the big cities. Arguments which appeal to them have weight over those with sound logical and factual content. The rise of the populist movement in the early seventies was such an appeal. Sometimes referred to as the "aw, shucks" argument, it generally follows this kind of line: "Shucks, I guess I can't come up with answers to all those stay-tistical arguments, but the Good Old Folks back where I come from, they sorta like to say that . . ."; and of course if you are not attuned to what those folks are saying, the chances are pretty high that you are overly attached to some specious position. The rise of the Office of Economic Opportunity and similar agencies has bred a whole new middle-class advocate and expert on what the poor folks are thinking and saying, which is invoked against opposing arguments involving policy in these areas.

These are also variants of the "boys out in the field" argument. When something new is suggested, the sales manager who finds it threatening can readily throw the weight of the sales representatives' opinions into the breach: *I can tell you chief, that the people out in the field won't like this* one bit. The implication is that they won't sell as much and all the company's revenue is going to dry up. The customers also constitute a population that can be invoked to veto some new scheme that is afoot. One of the sales manager's most common experiences is to have the sales force go out and return with a collection of arguments why a new product will not sell, why it can't be sold the way the force was instructed to sell it, or why the price is wrong. The sales representative who actually contacts the customer has the weight of contact with the unseen body of people to use in discussions with the sales manager.

**4. Arguments to time gone or times coming** As we have noted earlier, there is a strong appeal for escaping from the present and its reality by appealing to time gone by or times to come. This is a form of argument that has considerable appeal.

• *Arguments to tradition* are not without tactical merit, for traditions have some tangible effects in providing roots for an organization, giving it continuity, and creating an important sense of belonging. A long tradition of service in a firm can improve the quality of the service provided today. The fallacy of traditional argument is that much of it is pure fantasy invented to produce a desired effect in argument. The amount of "old Western tradition" that is discovered each year to prove something or other is amazing. Similarly, residents from Nebraska, Oklahoma, and New Mexico who move to Vermont may be expected to invent an astronomical number of old Vermont traditions within a year of arrival. Statements that were uttered long ago likewise take on a patina of verity that newly discovered ones may not have. The persistence of illegitimate ancient arguments helps carry on errors from the past. Homilies, old sayings, and the irrelevant quotations from somebody long dead, usually out of context, make great hay for arguing against something new.

• *The stability argument* is a powerful influence in keeping things as they are and always have been. It is very obvious that a good manager does not want to run an *unstable* business, which is one that may simply flutter right out of existence at any moment. Such instability is evidence that the ordinary affairs of the business are not under control. It accounts for most management and business failures. The owner does not have adequate records, does not keep books to provide information where money is going or customers coming from, and is surprised when it finally all turns up its toes.

Yet there are businesses that are so much under control that the control system dominates the firm, the people who work for it, and even the managers who run it and finally dominates any impulse, however slight, to change things for the better.[8] In certain kinds of business—such as public utilities, medical supply and pharmaceutical manufacturers, and financial institutions—stability is of utmost importance for the survival of the firm. For the drug manufacturer, quality control over products that have life-or-death effects is imperative. For the utility, an interruption of consumer service, as happened in the great blackout of 1965, is unthinkable, and stringent controls are called for to prevent human error as far as possible. In such businesses, the excellent controls become overdone, and the virtues carried to excess become a vise, which latches onto everyone and everything in a tight grip, preventing change from occurring, or making its progress dependent upon a very few people at the top.

The arguments in such firms are representative of what stability-worshipping organizations everywhere say:

- *Remember the power failure of 19–.*
- *Remember Cutter Laboratories.*
- *Remember the XYZ company case where they had to call back all of their product.*

Yesterday's experience can be a valuable teacher, and cautionary tales are worth listening to, but when they dominate the present they become fallacious sources of reality.

Quotations from the chairman of the board, now deceased, often keep the company firmly entrenched in a disastrous course, or a wrong product line.

The major fallacy in antiquarian argument is that it denies that knowledge is cumulative, and that each generation stands on the shoulders of all prior generations and therefore has less and less to learn from antiquity.

- *The argument to novelty* is the reverse of the antiquity argument, and focuses upon the novelty of an idea. The management training and supervisory development field is practically dominated by such an argument. Each year must produce some new entertaining gimmick, as though the learning of last year were journalistic in character. Once I was conferring with a planning committee about possible instructors for its courses for managers. I proposed an eminent behavioral scientist, author of twelve books, an original and creative man. "Oh no, we *had* him," they responded. Often the search for new ideas is for newness alone, and anything that already exists is suspect.

This argument to novelty reveals itself in an appeal to staffing all positions with young managers who are bright, attractive, slim, tie-less, with flowered shirts and sideburns. The denim suited source seems to have become for some the source of the best knowledge, and arguments have been known to be shunted aside because of their originator: "Oh, he's a shorthair." For those who would win arguments, in such a culture, it is sensible to be accompanied by a retinue of the young

[8] R. Beckhard and R. T. Harris, *Organizational Transitions: Managing Complex Change* (Reading, Mass.: Addison-Wesley, 1977). Proposes a middle ground called "transition management."

ones when making a case. They are part of what Walter Guzzari labeled the "Young Managers" with the reasonably accurate prediction that we would be seeing more of them in the future. The term *new breed* has been attached to many different kinds of people who are being espoused for more important responsibilities, including, it should be noted, "the new breed in personnel," which was the basis of a college text in personnel administration published in 1971 by this writer.[9]

The arguments to times gone or times coming often use the same kind of materials. Arguments aimed at future events are often *arguments to risk*. These are a variety of the argument *ad novitatem* and serve to create some wonderful barriers to change. From the viewpoint of the person who would not like to see anything change, it is a natural, for it does not require any hard or empirical evidence that anything has happened or actually will happen. The risks are the possibilities of loss, danger, pain, embarrassment, or damage. An imaginative opponent can see the risks in a new line even without understanding the proposed change. The key phrase in using future events to prevent change is *But suppose that...* It might include such expressions as these:

- *But suppose the consumer taste changes?*
- *But suppose the money market tightens up?*
- *But suppose we can't sell the issue?*
- *But suppose the union doesn't like it?*

In their place such questions are valuable, and even indispensable. They help us see the risks that lie ahead and permit us to take steps to avert them.

The innovation-minded person has a different set from the stability-minded one. For one thing, being innovation-minded starts one off with the presumption that as one presses ahead into new things, the unforeseen problem will occur, but *can be solved*. The stability-centered person arrays all of the influences at hand right now and weighs the pros and cons of each. If the pros of the present are less than the cons of the present we are tipped in favor of moving, but often do not until we can see that all of the possible obstacles have been thought of and dealt with prior to entering the venture.

Arguments to maintain the status quo and reject the novel and the original will often base their conclusions upon a failure to see how future problems can be solved. Without a ready solution they advise caution or warn against adoption of the idea. The innovative person will move into new areas without full knowledge of the problems or how they might be solved. There he or she often fails. Were we to listen to caution, and then proceed, the chances of succeeding might be greater. If we were totally dominated by such caution we would never have started.

Arguments attaching special virtue to the newest things, the newest ideas, the newest product are fallacious and widespread in management. The use of the computer, aside from its numerous invaluable applications, owes much of its acceptance to its newness. The toy value of new hardware often accounts for its acceptance.

[9]Odiorne, *Personnel Administration by Objectives* (Homewood, Ill.: Richard D. Irwin, 1971).

Executives who have no earthly reason for wanting to get somewhere in a matter of minutes commit their company to a new Lear jet or a Gulfstream company plane, which often runs the cost of a cross-country trip as high as triple the cost of first-class commercial flights, purely for the toy value and novelty.

What is true of the fallacy of novelty is equally true in the novelty of ideas, which is demanded in part by the business press and the journals, which require a steady diet of novelty to catch the attention of the executive reader. Such novelty tends to run in cycles, with the new panacea of this year fading away only to return in ten years in some other form. The birth and death of ideas of this type has produced a kind of conversation-piece approach to management. Some of the novel buzzwords frequently have acronyms, such as OD, LRP, MBO, SOP, and PERT. The very appeal of their novelty is a limitation, for people of experience are apt to use this fashion show aspect of new ideas to outstay every new idea that comes along and never make any changes. "I've seen them come and I've seen them go. This one [the latest novelty] too shall pass away."

*Being immune to gimmicks is a dangerous position, for one day something utterly indispensable may come along, disguised as a gimmick.*

**5. A rogues' gallery of managerial fallacies** Constructing a truly exhaustive rogues' gallery of managerial fallacies would be a sizable task. Not only are managers very busy doing things, which means they err, but also the roster of possible fallacies is considerably larger than a single book can cover. There are numerous schools of logic: the syllogistic logic of Aristotle, the mathematical logic of Russell and Whitehead, the canonical logic of ancient China, and dozens more. All concern themselves in large part with finding fallacies so that we can proceed through life happily without them. The probabilities of doing so are minimal, but in knowing where they are we can do better and find reality with more confidence, and perhaps move ahead. Not all fallacies are commonly used in business, because of the prevailing culture there.

Some of the fallacies that are ordinarily considered bad form and therefore are ordinarily avoided are these:

• *Arguments that appeal to pity:* It is ordinarily bad form and considered maudlin and embarrassing to make a case for something in business by displaying abject and servile misery. *Pity me* is not a useful appeal. *Don't build the new hospital, I use that lot to walk my dog.* This may be somebody's purpose in following a line of logic, but the beggar and the suppliant who seek things simply because they don't have them are in bad form. Servility, when it reveals itself, shows up as flattery rather than pure begging.

• *Arguments that appeal to snobbery* must be carefully concealed. The idea that pervades some college fraternity rushes—that joining this or that fraternity will open doors to executive suites through which the brothers rush and meet vice-presidents, who upon being given the appropriate clasp and byword will discriminate in favor of the brother—is not in tune with realities. Snob appeals as obstacles, however, have a real existence: *We can't abandon that business, because it would make a couple of old Yalies look stupid.* Snob appeal can get one an intro-duction that might otherwise be missed. It might make one visible—something valuable—but raw appeals of "we Dekes must take care of each other" are ordi-narily an embarrassment when tried.

• *Arguments ad nauseam* are an almost certain route to becoming a shelf sitter in management. While great verbal skills are invaluable, the person who simply talks too much, and never uses one word when seventy-five can be employed, gets an almost certain routing to the sidelines. Yet many a good idea has been talked to death, and the filibuster in Congress is a revered tradition. It blocks majority will for some time and occasionally carries the day. High-level executives who engage in filibuster probably will not be fired, and most certainly will not be told they are too garrulous, but the habit will cost them dearly. This should not, of course, be construed as a case against full exposition of position. Arguments *ad nauseam* will probably have numerous irrelevancies, and sweeping digressions and will work over the same ground several times at least. Unless you own the business, such arguments are to be guarded against.

• *Arguments against change appealing to the emotions* are of course employed, but must be employed with restraint, especially when the opponent is inside the company. Against competitors or external antagonists, such as people in govern-ment agencies who have issued contradictory directives that affect your company adversely, it is acceptable to use terms usually associated with hatred to refer to their brains, their ancestry, or their anatomy. The most important distinction in using strong emotional argument inside the firm is that managers must compete without expressing hostility, and must maintain an air of calm judiciousness in their statements about one another. Since long-term associations must continue after the event of today, managers must be careful about using emotion on their peers. Emo-tional invective is much more acceptable and common in dealing with subordinates, but of late the constraints upon showing violent emotions are increasing. The appeals to fear (*ad metum*) nowadays are ordinarily more subtle or psychological in character and center around producing anxiety rather than terror. Even man-agement by anxiety has faded in popularity and, in any event, is more widely recog-nized when seen and is increasingly frowned upon as a mode of argument.

Those arguments which appeal to the emotions and aim at generation of en-thusiasm, happiness, pleasure, and, under carefully constrained conditions, greed are perfectly satisfactory forms of persuasion. Even though they may be fallacious, their special character is such that they may, in fact, not prove fallacious, for they become self-fulfilling promises. The sales manager who is desperately trying to lather up a sagging sales force may exhort them with appeals to their great spirit, their competitive skills, and their ability to work hard when, in fact, he or she has sparse evidence that such qualities exist. By fallaciously describing the nonexistent, one hopes to produce that which does not now evidence itself, and occasionally one does so. This harmless and sometimes helpful kind of sophistry and illogical appeal to emotions is perfectly acceptable in the hands of a skilled practitioner.

• *Appeals to gradualism and moderation,* on the other hand, are the most respected and accepted kinds of argument to defer change, and for this reason are most often the role of the successful obstacle maker. When differing opinions emerge, it is the mediator who emerges as the leader. Strong, perhaps even violent, advocates of one position or another cast mighty blows at each other, drawing advocates to one side or the other, and it would seem that if the struggle contined, it could destroy the organization. At such times, it is the gradualist—the person who produces the successful appeal *ad modum,* the person who brings proportion to both sides and converts a win-lose game into a unity movement with both sides apparently winning—who is most respected and followed.

The fallacy of arguments *ad modum* is that they are universally necessary. In the student riots of the sixties many universities deliberately sought out labor relations experts to assume their presidency because, it was reasoned, they would be best equipped to resolve the serious discords that were tearing the campus to pieces. The assumption worked well as long as the fighting continued. Once it was resolved, some of the presidents continued to stand about with their hands in their pockets waiting for another riot to erupt. Since none occurred and it was not their function to initiate one, many such organizations have gone into sideways skids, if not absolute decline.

• *Appeals to perfection* have temporary advantages to the person making them, but in business, being too good to be true or looking uniformly perfect is almost certain to arouse anxiety and opposition. The perfectionist is the person who masters every detail, which is excellent. He or she also corrects errors in other people's perceptions and facts, which is bound to infuriate them over time unless done with superhuman tact. Perfectionism corrects small errors, and makes right the irrelevant wrongs. Such matters as grammatical errors, mistakes in syntax and punctuation in others' memos, or even personal idiosyncracies are probably better left alone unless they are incidentally damaging someone in some serious way, or holding up the attainment of organization goals. The fallacies of appeals to perfection include the following:

1. Assuming that any kind of defect is some evidence of overall inadequacy, and that even a minor defect must be cured or the entire structure of the organization is somehow doomed.
2. Assuming that the form in which things are done is a reflection of the substance, and that they are being done sloppily, when there are grammatical or typing errors, the content is also defective. If people are permitted to park out of their stalls in the parking lots, the perfectionist mind goes, then they are probably doing shoddy work and possibly stealing from petty cash as well.
3. Assuming that any deviation from standards, procedures, or rules is an automatic signal of the depravity and dissolute morals of the offender.
4. Assuming that things that are orderly are correct and logical and things that are rumpled and sloppy are not.

Perhaps this final fallacy would be a word of caution in correcting the fallacies in your own life. Do not attempt to be a resident fallacist on small matters.

Catching a few major ones now and then will have made the time invested in this book worthwhile. Nothing can be more irritating than experts in formal logic, replete with Latin phrases, who, when confronted with a losing position, leap into the fray, not with more evidence to make their own case or ruin yours, but to twist the whole argument into one of which side possesses the greatest logic. For example:

> *Mr. A:* I think we should refer the whole issue to the policy committee.

> *Mr. B:* Naw, let's just talk it over with a couple of the key members and if they seem to think it's OK, go ahead.

> *Mr. A:* Aha, you have committed a logical fallacy, of argument ad vere-cundiam!

Such behavior has done more harm to the study of logic than all of the book burners in history. In extreme cases, it can get you a smack in the mouth.

## ANTIDOTES TO FALSE ARGUMENT AND FALSE OBSTACLES

Many of the false arguments used to oppose change and creativity aren't really founded in logic. People often start with a preconception and build a case to fulfill their emotionally based ideas. *Don't bother me with facts, my mind is made up:* so goes their reasoning. Thus the antidotes to the false argument based upon false obstacles don't begin usually with more and better facts, but with the skills of persuasion. Persuasion is based upon three major elements:

1. *Overcoming false logic with superior logic.* While false logic usually isn't the most likely root of the false argument, overcoming it is the first step in turning around an opponent. It may be that upon occasion the opposition to change is truly founded upon logic, and in such cases it must be met with logic. Better facts, superior definitions of goals, more lucid definitions of the problem, the choice of several optional courses, and finally a choice of the best solution from among them are all logical and rational ways of thinking about a situation. When one is confronted with an opponent who presents the false obstacle and engages in false argument, it is a necessary step to refute the arguments. Even though you may suspect a more deeply rooted psychological or personal motive for the opposition, don't neglect the logical step left untaken, such as debating and overcoming defects in the other's logic. Otherwise the false logic lies uncontested, and in such silence you assent to its truth.

2. *Seeking out and changing the attitude of the others.* It is far more important to recognize when the strategy calls for attitude change and when it should be considered the heart of persuasion. Having tried logic and facts to no avail ("dealing with such unreasonable people is impossible"), turn then to persuasion at an attitudinal level:

- Get at the roots of your opponents' attitude: What is causing it?
- State their case back to them in their own words and indicate that you understand their view even when you know it to be wrongheaded.
- Adopt and express positive statements, and speak the language of success.
- State your own understanding of the merits of your case in their own terms.
- Be positive in your affirmation of the improvements sought. Adopt the manner of the believer, the uplifter, the persuader. Try to strike the imagination of your opponents to see the features and benefits of the proposed advance and improvement.
- Remember that enthusiasm is contagious and your own enthusiasm will affect the attitude of the skeptic. Remember also that pessimism and negativism can be contagious and that in dealing with cynics, skeptics, and opposers you are prone to such contagion yourself.
- Concentrate on *what* is wrong, not the errors or shortcomings of the *other person or group*. Don't slip into their own ways of argument *ad hominem*.
- Speak to the imagination of your opponents once logic has failed to move them. Imagination, it has been noted, has a capacity to stir people's souls and to cause them to rise up beyond themselves.

3. *Changing the others' behavior.* If the use of both logic and attitude change doesn't seem wholly effective in refuting argument of false obstacles, try to stir your opponents into *some kind of action* in the right direction. One of the great phrases of persuasion is *Why not try it once?* Then assist them to get under way. While attitude sometimes controls behavior, it is equally true that getting people into behavior may change their attitudes. Often attitudes are held because of a poverty of imagination about what things would really be like if the proposed change were tried out. Try these steps:

- Ask for a single test or experimental run of the new idea.
- Choose an area where success is highly probable.
- Make the first trials easy ones.
- Start small and build from there.
- Let your opponents participate in shaping the first effort and ask for their suggestions for further improvements after the first test. Then incorporate their suggestions.
- Remember that false argument is mainly based upon an emotional condition, not real logic, so use support, encouragement, persuasion, and action as the new behavior slowly emerges.

# seven

# How to destroy
# a sound plan
# by false analogies

When a manager stands in front of nine employees and tells them to "get in there and hit the ball," it doesn't necessarily have to be the manager of an actual baseball team. It might be a way of speaking analogously. It might be the manager of the local McDonald's Restaurant exhorting the employees to get the French fries out on time, or it might be a jovial librarian instructing the assistants at the checkout desks to cut the number of errors in recording. Each is speaking metaphorically, or by analogy. Analogy is a form of communication in which we utter some words which are taken from one context and transferred to another, wholly new context. Thus, the McDonald's manager alludes metaphorically to baseball, but is not suggesting that the hamburgers be rounder (more ball-shaped) today than before. It is not intended that the employees actually hit anybody or anything physically, except perhaps the cash register keys or other ordinary things they contact. It is not proposed that something new be done, such as throwing an actual ball into the parking lot, or batting balls into the fried-potato preparation area. In fact the boss would be dismayed if you took things too literally, for the analogy is merely a figure of speech. Analogies are useful in bringing clarity and imagery to our communication.

Unfortunately, analogy used as a substitute for thinking, either at a superficial and trivial level or at a more complex, strategic level, can serve to disguise reality, not just from the outside observer but sometimes from the thinker as well.

## USING FALSE ANALOGIES TO JUSTIFY
## THE ACTIVITY TRAP

Using examples that are *like* something else (called *analogical inference* by the logicians) has an important and perhaps irreplaceable place in the process of thinking. Take something simple, such as saying that a plot of land is gull-shaped. "It has two wing-shaped halves, dipping down in the middle with the brook as a backbone." This kind of explanation quickly clarifies, makes simple, and relates an unknown thing to a listener wholly unfamiliar with it by relating its complex characteristics to something very familiar. Thus, the manager of the nine-person restaurant crew was perhaps struck by the similarities between this employee group and a baseball team; in each case they were nine in number, played different positions, had a common purpose, wore uniforms, performed for a public that they served, and were generally youthful. What our manager hoped to convey was that the employees should emulate the hustling behavior and the keen concentration on the immediate task at hand, should display cooperative behavior between cooks, cashiers, order clerks and operators, and should produce high-volume sales that day.

Analogy suggests that *if two things agree in one or more respects they can or should agree in another,* or perhaps all respects.[1] This process is familiar in all forms of creative invention. Galileo was struck with the theory of a pendulum when watching the motion of a lamp swinging on a chain in the Pisa cathedral. Physics achieved one of its greatest breakthroughs when light was seen as analogous to a wave in the water. In the modern practice of *synectics,* the first analytical step is to make the strange *familiar.* This is part of an analytical stage in which the realities of the problem at hand are plumbed and its ramifications and fundamentals laid out and looked at. It is here that analogy is absolutely essential to the creative process. It is useful not only in mechanical or physical reasoning, but in social and managerial reasoning as well. As William J. J. Gordon has pointed out, however, "If only this analytical step is taken, no novel solution is possible."[2] The human mind is essentially conservative, and is threatened by the new and novel. A sensible defense is to form the new thing into a familiar and acceptable pattern. The next stage in synectics requires more discipline: to "make the familiar strange." This requires that the observer and problem solver distort in some way the existing reality and see new things that don't presently exist.

*Managerial reasoning by analogy, when it stops at making the strange familiar, inhibits change and reinforces the present activities and rejects the innovative.*

## HOW MANAGERS THINK IN ANALOGIES

There are five ways in which managers think in analogies, even when they don't realize that they are doing it. For the person of action, the reflective thinking process is a luxury requiring time, which he or she does not have to the same degree as professors and perhaps a few longhaired researchers. Yet thinking *is* being done, and managers *are* managing by analogy. Many are like the pundit who reported, "I have been speaking prose all of my life and never knew it until now." These ways of employing analogy include the following:

1. *Sending for the facts and getting back a sample.* One of the most common kinds of managerial actions is a no-nonsense approach that rejects analogy but then ends up with a concealed analogy. The boss sends somebody out to conduct an investigation. "Go dig into this thing, and get right to the bottom. I want *all* the

[1] I. J. Copi, *Introduction to Logic* (New York: Macmillan, 1968).
[2] W. J. J. Gordon, *Synectics* (London: Collier Macmillan, Collier Books, 1961).

facts." Because the event is gone and the remains are all that is left to examine, what comes back is a kind of partial evidence. A good investigator will try to shape the available facts into numbers, for hard facts are most often considered better if they are numerical. What the boss gets back is a numerical analogue of the reality. The facts might, for example, resemble a skewed distribution curve, or something that shows numerically what the situation is. The boss orders the closing down of three plants, or the merging of five sales offices into one, or finds that there really is not any problem. That most business investigations, however complete, produce more than a sampling of reality, ordinarily stated in numerical form, is only a myth, however widespread.

2. *Using personal experience as an analogy.* There are numerous advantages in going out and taking a personal look at things. If a new job is to be started, or a new sales territory opened, it is good practice to go see the scene, and perhaps even make a few sales calls and get the "feel" of the territory or the problem. At the University of Utah, all administrators, including president, deans, provost, and department chairmen, teach a class each semester. The stated purpose here is laudable, for it gives the administrators a personal sample of what teachers face, what students are like, and what realities exist in the world of education. For many years in the automobile business, the first job a trainee had before joining the industrial relations staff was as a factory supervisor.

This "learning in your muscles" and not abstractly is *personal analogy.* It is most valid when current, and the experience of many years ago may not be valid; the manager who relies upon it once in a while should get out and see what is going on by doing the job for a day or so. One large airline regularly assigns its executives to return for a day to some operating job at the ticket counter, in baggage handling, on the reservations desk, or the like to foster this personal analogy capability.

3. *Direct analogy,* a kind of direct comparison, is another form of analogy. Alexander Graham Bell is reported to have proceeded upon the analogy to the human ear in inventing the telephone, when he noted that a delicate membrane in the ear could move massive bones and hypothesized, therefore, that a delicate artificial membrane might move a piece of steel.

Thus, if the Chicago plant has been outstripping the New York plant in production of cartons, we might send a scout to Chicago from New York and copy the plant's method or some of its salient features. If the Chicago plant has installed an automatic feeder on one of its presses, then the New York plant will install an automatic feeder. Here direct analogy might be applied further: "Let's go over all of our high-speed machines and see how many of them could be fitted with some kind of an automatic feeder." The results show that none of these can; but a stripper, which is at the other end of the line, can be so fitted, thus making a saving. A more sophisticated type of direct analogy is to fit something to a new application similar in principle to its old one.

A department head at a university was troubled with professors who were very late turning in final course grades for the last class of the year. Some even delayed well into the summer, and both students and administration were inconvenienced. Exhortations did not seem to do much good. The department chairman was talking to a sales manager and mentioned the problem. "Hell, do what I do," was the reply. "I don't release salesmen's paychecks until their sales reports are completed and turned in. I never have any late reports now, and I used to have dozens." By direct analogy, the department head found the solution. Professors did not get paid until their grades were turned in.

Such direct analogy is widely known and used, and sought after by managers. Much of the purpose of managers in attending management seminars, they report, is to "pick up a new idea or two." One new idea they can use makes the entire conference worthwhile, they report.[3] What they are really seeking is some direct analogies, and this search for direct analogies is the major selling feature of such seminars and of most management magazines. Some managers clip ideas that seem to be appealing and to have possible values for future direct analogies.

4. *Representational or symbolic analogy* is a somewhat more complex form of analogy, in which a problem of the real world is fitted into some kind of entirely different likeness. Sports analogies and analogies from family life, from community living, from politics, or from childhood experiences are used as explanatory models. The advertising agencies are satirically pictured as doing most of their thinking in such terms. *Run it up the flagpole and see if anybody salutes it* is an expression used for proposing that a market test of a tentative idea be tried on a small but representative sample before a full commitment is made to it. We suggest behavioral policies in such symbolic terms as *good neighbor policy, running interference,* or *par for the course,* or refer to a bad loser as a *momma's boy* or *crybaby,* or suggest an *end-around play* in collective bargaining. Sales rallies become *roundups,* in which case the meeting room is the *corral,* the hotel dining room becomes the *chuck wagon,* and all of the salespeople are *pardners* rather than colleagues. One large grocery company launched a symbolic ship for a *sales cruise,* and the sales manager became the *admiral,* complete with uniform and sword.

All of these, of course, are symbols. A new trend has been the use of symbolic analogies in the form of diagrams, numbers, and mathematical models. The operations researcher proposes that the essential features of a situation can be extracted and described in terms of a mathematical model. Such models as the break-even chart, the supply-and-demand curve, the decision tree, the decision matrix, and even the profit and loss and balance sheets are forms of symbolic analogy.[4] They are not the reality but *symbolic representation* of reality. Their rationality and proven usefulness are undisputed, to the extent that a case might well be made that the top managers in most firms are symbol manipulators.

A common management analogy that is mainly symbolic is to find a prior explanation and fit a new situation to the known theory. The behavioral sciences often provide the theory into which facts of human behavior are fitted. "He is be-

[3] *American Management Associations* (New York: *Annual Catalog,* 1972).
[4] H. Breimen et al., *Quantitative Analysis for Business Decisions* (Homewood, Ill.: Richard D. Irwin, 1965).

having like a Theory X manager," or "He is abdicating" (a behavior, in fact, limited exclusively to kings and princes). This has value if the theory describes the behavior explicitly and differs from the situation in no important details.

*Symbolic analogies are not merely neutral in their relationship to the change process. In operation they have a strong tendency to reinforce the present and the past.*

Because managers by habit, training, and the circumstance of time pressures and practical constraints are careless in handling analogy, a nice one-two punch knocks out innovative ideas (that's an analogy from prizefighting). Blow number one: They look at ways of taking the new idea and making it seem familiar. They do so by using analogies that are largely symbolic in nature, the symbols being tied to the past. Blow number two: They never get around to making the familiar seem strange, or looking for the small differences required for innovation; and any possible new ideas get lost in the first analogies.

Accordingly, for many experienced managers, there is never anything new under the sun, for everything first presented as new immediately reminds them of something else. "We used to do that stuff back in the old one-room school when I was a kid," declared one vice-president when first confronted with programmed instruction. "Reminds me of the old JIT programs we taught millions of foremen during World War II," proposed another. The new is now familiar.

The use of the wisdom of the village savant in managerial thinking draws heavily upon symbolic analogies. Such a beginning as *Kinda reminds me of a feller who used to . . .* starts a process of making the strange familiar, which is of immense value as a first step if it continues to make the familiar strange and hence leads to innovation. Unfortunately, this process is most often not taken, and the old activities hold sway. Change is managed into *no change.*

5. *Imaginary analogy* is a special kind of analogy that likens the new phenomenon to something fantasized and imagined. The childhood game of imagining shapes seen in clouds illustrates the process. To say a large white cloud "looks like a very fat owl with a crooked beak" would be an example of relating something to an imaginary yet familiar model.

In social circumstances, such as a business or a hospital, the imaginary analogy may compare or contrast new ideas with some kind of *wish fulfillment* model. Suppose an employee proposes to the boss that the parking system for employees needs improvement, but the boss has an imaginary analogy of excellence in administration in which everything and everyone is perfectly quiet and nobody complains—ever. No change will occur as a result of the employee's suggestion. The military hierarchy is riddled with such images of perfectly obedient subordinates, and the junior officer who makes suggestions to the colonel to change the way things are managed is in conflict with the brass's imaginary image of what the troops should be like and is put in his or her place.

Parables are imaginary and creative stories that are used to produce or create analogies. The parable was the method used by Christ to teach the abstractions of Christianity in terms of specific behaviors. His examples were couched in terms of the life of the people He taught: of sheep, vineyards, fathers and sons, and the elements around them. Aesop's fables made social, cultural, and political lessons by fantasy analogies. Swift's fantasy of the travels of Gulliver, and Lewis Carroll's *Alice's Adventures in Wonderland,* made contemporary events take on a new reality by analogy. Satire, paradox, and caricature are forms of imaginary or fantasy analogy.

> *Yet, this marvelous tool, this key to creativity and change in the hands of people who would clutch the present like a prize, becomes a vehicle for binding them to their present activity, and if they are in charge of others, of binding their subordinates also. Thus, the analogy serves to prove that the only reality lies in the commonplace.*

## HOW FALSE ANALOGY
## CONCEALS REALITY

President Dwight D. Eisenhower in his earliest years lived the life of the small-town boy. The clapboard house, the picket fence, the procession of horse-drawn buggies broken only by an occasional horseless carriage on a dusty Main Street, and the close contact with dirt, grass, fields, fishing poles, and limpid ponds were reality. For many of the older generation this is still reality. Their source of analogies then lies in treating the new as it relates to the old and familiar. As Gordon has put it, "The commonplace of the past was organic and concrete, the commonplace of the present is synthetic and abstract."

For leaders who have accommodated themselves to the new reality, change is welcome, natural, and sought after. For the elderly owner of the bank, the insurance company, the factory, or the store in hundreds of places like Muncie, Salt Lake City, Waco, and Montpelier, it is the preservation of the past through identification of everything new with it that prevails. Such older leaders think in metaphors, analogies, and similes, and employ the *metaphoric* mind to conceal the synthetic and abstract realities around them.

The criterion for selecting fact is whether and how well it fits into a conception of reality. If that conception has the purpose of suiting the metaphoric pictures that are available, it paves the way for seven reality-begging fallacies:

1. *The fallacy of the false metaphor.* Such common thinking emerges when people attempt desperately or intuitively to relate today's ambiguities to the familiar, common-sense realities of the past. Complex social and technical problems become ninth innings in baseball games, the fourth down on the goal line, the house on fire, the needle in the haystack, or a row of dominoes about to be tipped. Horses rush back into burning barns, and failures of managers are equated with the village loafer or the wayward child. Each of these terms has embedded in it an insidious fallacy that serves to distort our understanding of the object or circumstance it purports to describe. It *labels* problems, and the process reduces our understanding of their nature, to say nothing of distorting our knowledge of the basic source from which the analogy is drawn. Leaders who ask their followers' opinions "water down" their

leadership, like a bootlegger watering down a cheap rotgut. For some New Yorkers, everything west of Hoboken is "the cornfields." Common sense is what everyone has, except the sole offender who is about to become a "scapegoat."

No business or administrative organization could carry on the day-to-day communication needed to keep things going without using such metaphors and similes in speech. Perhaps the next generation of managers will communicate wholly by calculus if some of our business schools have their way. Meanwhile, we smuggle absurdities into managerial practices by overdependence upon this insidious fallacy.

2. *The fallacy of overexactness in analogy* occurs when a partial resemblance between two situations is expanded to make the similarities between them perfect. A is similar to B in one or two respects and accordingly can be assumed identical in every respect. In this fallacy, it is the actual dissimilarities that are discarded, which is useful and practical if the differences are small and reality isn't discarded in the process. Analogies by their definition can never be perfect, and the partial nature of the resemblance must always be borne in mind, or the traps of living in an unreal world and making unrealistic judgments may follow.

Company A expanded rapidly, and was caught by a credit crunch that made its debt financing structure disastrous and led to bankruptcy. Company B's management, in a period of plentiful debt financing and available money, reasons by analogy that debt financing is a certain precursor to bankruptcy and pays a high price for equity financing, thereby avoiding the poisons of debt financing, which, it is reasoned by analogy, leads to bankruptcy.

Learning from experience should include the discrepancies in analogies as well as the congruities if one is to avoid the fallacy of habitually seeing perfection in analogy. If a company pursues a course and is also making money hand over fist, then it must be a perfect guide to others, goes such fallacious analogy. The trap of seeing one situation or entity as "just like" another should send up a warning signal for the listener.

3. *The structurally false analogy* occurs when we shift an analogy from one situation in which it applies to another in which it doesn't and we leave out some important information necessary to understanding. A common one was illustrated in the early 1970's when General Motors built a highly automated assembly plant in Lordstown, Ohio. Subsequently, there were strikes at the plant. The conclusion arrived at by many journalists is that automation will lead to strikes. What is missing is the true reason the union struck, which was related to the rate of introduction of automation, some supervisory practices in the new plant, and several other variables, which were subsequently corrected.

Studies in the behavioral sciences have often produced such false analogies when converted into management prescriptions and into advice by management teachers and trainers. A plant was a poor producer under a manager who was autocratic. A new manager who came in to replace him was more permissive. Production rose. Therefore, the reasoning goes, managers should be permissive if they wish to attain high production. The false analogy lies in the differences in conditions under which the new manager operated. Not wanting to take on the tough job, he stipulated certain conditions that had to be met by higher management before he would agree to go in. For one thing, he needed several million dollars for new equipment, which he received. The new equipment had been requested by the old manager but had been denied him. The new manager went into a plant different in efficiency, and found less reason to get tough.

The structural fallacy overlooks inconsistencies between the two circumstances and distorts reality, producing fallacious decisions.

4. *The fallacy of lost relevance* helps managers miss reality in some instances. In comparing the qualities of A and B, the quality in A must be relevant to the quality in B which is being explained. Take the case of the sales executive who interviewed a candidate for a responsible post. The applicant spoke with impeccable grammar, and was rejected for that reason. "Homosexuals talk pretty, and so does he," he explained.

"I see, you feel that people who speak with proper grammar tend to be homosexuals?"

"Oh, let's say a little too *fancy,* and why take a chance?"

In other applications of the false analogy, selection of personnel seems to suffer from such fallacies especially. Here are some of the more common ones that have been observed:

• Since eighty percent of the present chief executives of the 8000 largest companies in the United States are college graduates, we had better not pick a non-college person for a new managerial position.

Thus, the company selects an educated dolt over a competent candidate who did not have a college education twenty years before.

• A large automobile dealer reported that "pipe smokers don't make good automobile salesmen." The reason? "I'm not sure *why.* All I know is that I have eighty salesmen, all are cigarette smokers, and I have the biggest dealership in the county, thereby proving that cigarette smokers make better salesmen than pipe smokers. Maybe it is because pipe smokers are too reflective or something."

Further investigation showed that for fifteen years he had been applying his selection policy, rejecting all pipe smokers and hiring cigarette smokers. If one smoker switched after employment, he was tipped off about the rule; and if he didn't straighten himself out, he was quietly let go.

The fallacy is so widespread in selection methods that it becomes almost fruitless to oppose it. Several leading corporations select people on the basis of high grades in college as a determinant of their promotability. Why? Because some years ago it was noticed that the top management of the firm all had high grades in college. But since the criterion had been applied faithfully during the intervening years, it could not be overwhelmingly apparent that quality A (high grades) was related to quality B (executive success). Since no person with "gentlemen's grades" of C had been promoted, the proof over time became even more persuasive, a form of self-fulfilling prophecy.

5. *The fallacy of the smuggled-in comparison.* Take the case of the firm that had

begun to expand through geographically dispersed units. One executive opposed the expansion with the often repeated statement, "When your limbs begin to swell it is a sign that the body is sick." This starts out with one analogy:

*a.* The company is analogous to an organism, a body with limbs.
*b.* In a body, when limbs swell, it is a sign of sickness.
*c.* This company's branches are swelling, and therefore it must be getting sick.

What was overlooked was a couple of concealed analogies:

- Growing and swelling are analogous.
- A sign of disease in a human body is the same as a sign of disease for a corporation.

The analogies between *organisms* and *organizations* have been put to fruitful use in understanding organizational behavior. The world and language of the physiologist is adopted without much modification to explain organizational behavior. Organizational communication is explained in terms of "synaptic transmission," and the messenger service, phone connections, and intracompany mail are part of the corporation's "central nervous system." The various-sized units of the organization are compared to cells, limbs, organs, and the like. While all of this has produced some reduction of the complex world of the corporation to recognizable dimensions, it must be employed with discretion to be careful to avoid the smuggling in of false analogies.

One of the effects of the smuggled-in analogy can be seen in the application of the systems approach itself, especially in financial controls and accounting. The corporation is seen by the financial executive as an electrical control system, with "feedback" an important part of the new business executive's vocabulary. The analogy may lead to overconfidence in the similarities, with the result that the very real individual differences of people will be overlooked.

Some other common analogies which have been productive, but which are prone to the error of the smuggled-in analogy, which produces false analogies, might include:

- The analogy between a factory and a single machine.
- The analogy between a sales force and an athletic team, or an orchestra.
- The analogy between a retail organization and a tree, showing many branch and even some "twig" stores.

One of the more probable results of such false analogies is that any change or improvement in the behavior of people or groups within it that is inconsistent with the analogy will be rejected, thus making this form of analogy a strong influence for keeping the status quo. For the preservation of organizational health, stability, homeostasis, self-healing, and mending of tissue are necessary but not sufficient conditions. *They also militate strongly against change.*

6. *The fallacy of using an analogy as proof.* This is an operational mistake in reasoning, in which resemblances are stated or accepted as proof of something else. Its

greatest danger lies in its plausible and persuasive nature. When the argument gets down to the struggle over fine issues, it is often the homely analogy that wins the day. The epigram, the earthy analogy, the wisecrack, or the witticism, especially if it can destroy the other side, has overcome many an argument that was sounder in concept and more probable of success in execution.

In a large automobile company, a fierce debate was under way about the merits of a four-cylinder versus a six-cylinder engine for a forthcoming model. After arguments and evidence were presented on each side, the day was carried by a grizzled old roughneck on the side of the six-cylinder car who declared scornfully that "a four-cylinder car is like a four-inch penis. It may be OK around town, but it won't be any good on the road." The ensuing laughter and the widely quoted wit were taken as proof of the case for the six-cylinder car.

In another instance, a policy issue in personnel procedures was being debated by the industrial relations staff. A new control procedure for preventing people from sneaking out early was outlined and vigorously espoused by one man. Another man, who was opposed, won the day with an analogy that seemed to be proof of the wrongness of the policy: "I was a prisoner of war in Germany during World War II, and that is exactly how the SS troopers used to control the prisoners," he stated. The opposition quickly collapsed.

Many a policy has been installed or removed because it was proven in the first instance by an analogy that had only the most precarious relationship with the case at hand. The dramatic example, the quip, the epigram, and the citation of an unfavorable experience out of the past that is painfully remembered by those present can have such a fallacious effect.

Unfortunately, this form of analogy is most effective in those instances where changes in existing systems, technologies, or procedures are involved, and it is a forceful tool of the conservator of the *status quo.*

7. *The fallacy of futurism by analogy* is prevalent in the installation of computers and in the adoption of many new theories of management. The fact that the number of computers has doubled in the past ten years serves a kind of analogical thinking that is used to persuade doubters of the practical value of buying a computer. Such argument is often found in the prospectus of high-technology businesses for potential investors. Each new invention in technology is equated with the development of the telephone or the railroad, the dawn of space age, and the growth of atomic energy. Isaac Asimov, the marvelously talented popularizer of complex science for the nonscientist, for example, has equated the development of the hologram with the creation of the human eye. While undoubtedly the field of holography has grown and results from a scientific breakthrough, as with other breakthroughs before it, some of the conclusions about it are tenuous where they rest upon analogy rather than hard research and scientific evidence.

Such futurism is even more unstable and conjectural, however learned, in the field of the social and behavioral sciences. When the theories of Professor A or Professor B are equated with those of Freud or Marx, this is analogical reasoning into the future and becomes part of a sales pitch rather than a prediction of any reliable nature. There are some methods of improving the accuracy of predicting the future by extrapolating from past trends and present evidence, as is probably possible with holography. Prediction is less tenable when its basis is to find some similarities between the nascent stage of a rather feeble idea and the nascent stage of some momentous idea out of the past and to equate the two as if their similarities were evidence of equal possibilities for useful application. Economists have developed an irritating but reliable system for taking care of prediction, which might be commended to other futurists: they hedge everything with the "if-then" reservation known as *ceteris paribus,* or *all else being equal.*

False futurist analogies can be dangerous, for they lead people into wrong and sometimes harmful paths from which it is costly to retreat. The best use of analogies in prediction is to suggest the possibilities and hypotheses that the analogy suggests, with perhaps some estimates of their probability appended to each.[5]

> *In government, the full effect of such overselling by analogy has produced a bureaucratic world of civil servants who have developed a healthy suspicion of every new administrative program that is sold as "the greatest new breakthrough since the end of the spoils system," or under some similar promotion.*

## NO ARGUMENT BY ANALOGY
## IS EVER VALID

Despite the inability to ever construct a perfect analogy, there are ways in which analogies can be handled that will keep their conclusions in line with their premises with a modicum of logic.[6] Because analogy is a powerful tool of resisting change, and vital to the arguments against change that crop up when innovative ideas are proposed, we can apply some tests to analogies to help find their most useful application.

1. *Keep the number of examples high.* Buying one bad loaf of bread in a store isn't as good evidence that the store sells defective goods as buying several bad loaves, plus some rancid butter. When a new secretary is late on the first day, it is wise to wait for further latenesses before firing him or her. The boss who walks around the plant and sees two workers talking instead of working does not have evidence of widespread soldiering on the job. If ten trips through the plant in a week show 100 instances, the case is stronger—you might say 100 times as strong.

2. *Examine carefully the ways in which the cases resemble one another.* If the boss on a plant tour sees a supervisor or other manager sitting at a desk reading a reference report, it is somewhat different from seeing an employee seated beside a machine reading a comic book. Both are reading, yet one is working for the benefit of the company and earning a salary, while the other is cheating the employer.

3. *Judgment about the strength of the conclusion is needed.* If a company sets up a branch plant and it fails to perform, it is a weak conclusion to assume that all

---

[5] R. L. Heilbroner, *The Economic Transformation of America* (New York: Harcourt Brace Jovanovich, 1977). A scholarly example of how futures are extrapolated in economic areas.

[6] P. Kurtz, *Decision and the Condition of Man* (New York: Dell Pub. Co., Inc., 1965).

branch plants will be weak. The strength of the conclusion lies in the nature of the connection. Is it the distance between home office and branch that loosens the ties of control? Or does the manager in the branch not behave the way other branch managers do, or the way a good branch manager should?

4. *Look for the dissimilarities as well as the similarities.* Analogies seem to be born out of finding similarities between some known situation and something new and unknown and then suggesting that the new is like the old in some respects, and therefore in most or all respects. For the most effective use of analogy, the differences should be clearly spelled out as well as the similarities. The failure to explore the differences will strengthen a false argument and lead to some false conclusions.

5. *Make an overall judgment of the relevance of the analogy.* This finding of *relevance* is the most important criterion in judging the validity of analogies. One good relevant analogy is worth a dozen irrelevant ones. The key to relevance is to find some strong causal relationship. Similarity alone is not always evidence of cause and effect. Analogies are attempts at proving some kind of cause and effect relationship, and where such causality is not found, the argument by analogy is irrelevant. The company that hires three black employees and subsequently has to fire all three for bad performance might by false analogy presume that all blacks will prove unsatisfactory employees. Yet the company may not have applied good selection methods to check qualifications as it ordinarily does with white employees. What is relevant in this case is whether qualified people are hired and then properly trained and motivated.

Unfortunately, analogy seems to be most useful in areas of decision where resistance to change is sought.

# eight

# Distorting facts to kill planned progress:
## a guide to false generalization

Getting an accurate picture of the facts that consitute reality, difficult as it may seem, is not enough. Somebody has to decide what the facts mean, if creative change is to occur. Following that, presumably, some course of action can emerge. A simple, hypothetical case study will illustrate.

Let's assume that several morons are sitting in a room and the room is on fire. Being morons, they have some difficulty finding *meaning* for what are obvious facts, such as the smell of smoke, the crackling of burning wood, and the visible orange flames. The thermometer on the wall has blown its top. All of these evidences are at hand, for their olfactory, aural, and visual senses are perfectly OK. It is just their power of generalization that is deficient. They are accordingly confused, frightened, and baffled by the facts.

Unless somebody explains the meaning of the facts, or generalizes the facts for them, they might be in trouble. For example, someone in the group, or somebody outside the group, such as their counselor, could explain the meaning along the lines, "This place is on fire; let's get out of here!" The first part of the statement is the generalization, the addition of meaning to what apparently did not have meaning before it was proposed. The second is an action plan.

*Adding meaning to facts* and then taking action is an essential managerial function. The manager either must do it personally or must assure that it is being done well somewhere else. Old-fashioned concepts of management elevated this role of action taking into the most important role of managing. More modern approaches suggest that this skill of energizing action should not be centralized but should be widespread in the organization. It is the essence of delegating decision making to lower levels.

Adding meaning, or generalizing, produces several different classes of generalizations:

1. There are those that classify, sort, and label facts into plausible classes and clusters. These may use either statistical description or a taxonomy of classes.

2. There are generalizations that show *statistical regularity,* such as saying that "ITT has produced an increasing rate of return on investment each quarter for the past 43 quarters."

3. There are *trends,* which can be expressed either statistically or verbally, as, for example: "During the sixties, the labor movement grew slowly in numbers of members, and declined in its militancy in bargaining."

4. *Limited trends* can be generalized: "Population in Southern California, while growing, did not grow as rapidly during the late sixties as in the prior decade."

5. Overall laws or global statements can be made: "Society is doomed."

6. Conditional generalizations can be defined, as in: "If the lab testing is finished and is favorable by the end of the year, we should be able to project a cash flow by the beginning of the following year."

7. A generalization can consist of an evaluative assessment: "The failure to reach our production goals last month is due to the failure of suppliers to meet their commitments."

8. A generalization can consist of slotting or dovetailing a fact or event into an existing explanational theory: "The reason our people quit so often is that our management practices are autocratic and resemble Theory X."

9. Policies and procedures are themselves generalizations. They are precut decisions, awaiting any data to come forth to be interpreted: "The company will refund tuition for courses taken by employees after work hours at accredited colleges, up to $75 per course."

Such statements deal not with the collection of facts, but with their *management*. They also open the door to a host of new pitfalls in managerial decision making, and in the choice of directions in which the firm will go. They are therefore crucial in breaking the activity trap, but can also be instrumental in reinforcing its clutches. The activity trap just uses data to prove that nothing need change. The innovative manager carries a burden of proof that certain facts indicate the necessity for change.

Each of the nine classes of generalization stated above lends itself to a number of errors in management. Let's look at each category, and some of the common errors.

## 1. ERRORS IN CLASSIFICATION OF DATA

One of the first steps in managing numerical information is to classify it.[1] When it comes in its raw, untouched form it is technically called an *array*. In ordinary language it is a mess. If you were handed the batting averages of 214 regular players in the American and National Leagues for 1972 in unclassified form, you couldn't do much with it. As a first step in managing the information, you would immediately start classifying it. For example, you might rearrange it from the highest to the lowest. Or you might do the same by leagues. You might classify names and

---

[1] F. C. Mills, *Statistical Methods* (New York: Holt, Rinehart & Winston, 1924).

averages alphabetically, which would make it easy to find out how well Hank Aaron did after his transfer to the Brewers. Or you might break it down into classes you create especially for your own purposes. If you were the personnel manager of a single team, you might want to break averages down by clubs to see how your team did compared with others, for purposes of salary negotiations. You might even set up classes by dividing the averages into groups of point ranges, such as .110 to .120 and establish classes for every ten-point spread.

One major fallacy in classification is that the classifier might create classes in such a way as to prove a desired point. One way of doing this is to make the classes unequal or *disproportionate*. For example, you could set up classes like this:

- .090 to .095
- .096 to .200
- .201 to .205
- .206 to .210
- .211 to .215
- .216 to .600

Even to the naked eye this looks suspect. At one end you have some fine discriminations. Then, between .215 and .600, you have a leap that catches everyone over .215 in both leagues. Furthermore, the .214 hitter is only one point off from the .499 hitter. This would obviously have Curt Flood as player representative in the commissioner's office filing a grievance if you were an owner and these figures were to be used for anything important, such as raises.

Further fallacies in classification are committed when comparisons between classes of different populations are required. Suppose I have six doctoral candidates in a seminar and I rank them in performance from 1 to 6, each one being in a separate class. The last student in rank gets flunked. This may overlook the fact that all six came out of the top two percent of their master's class and even the lowest is better than the best in another group of six at Siwash University down the road.

A classification system occurs regularly in corporate salary administration. Errors in classification here can lead to internal dissent, public scandal, and stockholders' suits if the employees happen to be officers of the firm.[2] One large oil company, for example, uses a forced ranking system for its senior scientists, on a project-by-project team basis. Each project leader is forced to fit the team members into a six-class dispersion. This rewards mediocrity, for the best scientist in the worst group gets the same classification as the best in the best group. It is not a coincidence that this laboratory enjoys the dubious distinction of having a disaffected staff of professionals and one of the few engineering and scientific labor unions in the country.

[2] S. K. R. Murthy, *Corporate Strategy and Top Executive Compensation* (Boston: Harvard Graduate School of Business, 1977).

Classification errors get worse when numbers are not involved but rather words and lengthy descriptions, called *taxonomies,* are used, as in biology. It is useful and necessary, and certainly it clears things up, to classify the main phyla (groups) of the animal kingdom into Protozoa, Porifera, Coelenterata, and so forth. In economics, management, and the social sciences, the groups get hazier, and are made doubly vague by the tendency of every independent-thinking social scientist to establish some new classification system.[3]

Leaders can be classified as autocratic, democratic, or laissez faire, suggest Schmidt and Tannenbaum. McGregor proposes that managers fall into two classes, described generally by Theory X and Theory Y.[4] Colin Wilson classifies people into insiders and outsiders. Nicholas Murray Butler proposed three classes into which people might fall: those who make things happen, those who watch what goes on, and those who haven't the slightest idea what's happening.

The main fallacy in such verbal classification is that once it is established, every bit of data must thereafter fit into the available classes, or a new classification must be created. Thus the data are sometimes distorted, and this distortion may serve to conceal an embarrassing condition, or to prevent change, and it offers one of the best ways to establish a punishing classification system. Imagine, for example, that you could smell some kind of change in the wind and understood that all plants making less than ten percent return on investment (ROI) would be closed. Your plant happens to be in a low ROI category because you have a new plant not yet fully in operation. On the other hand, you know that if they would rate the plants and classify them on another scale, either rates of improvement or outcomes on an employee attitude survey, you would fare better, because you stand in the top classification in these two respects. The obvious move is to ask the dealer to switch decks. After all, who wants to be transferred as a failure?

By the way, this chapter is organized along a classification line, a taxonomy of errors found in handling facts, numerical and otherwise. Where did this classification come from? Did the author join the ranks of those whom he describes above? Not exactly. I found that a historian named Patrick Gardiner had already set up such a classification system for generalizations in history and that with some modifications it might fit this book.

# 2. FALLACIES IN STATISTICAL REGULARITY

Once the data are clustered, arrayed, and strapped into classes ready for analysis, it is sensible to seek statistical regularities in them. The classes themselves most often emerge looking like a bell-shaped, or Gaussian, curve if the data are normal or follow the natural patterns of data arrayed purely by chance. Statistical description shows how the data look when fitted into curves, into pie-shaped charts with

[3] R. P. Runyan, *Winning With Statistics* (Reading, Mass.: Addison-Wesley, 1977).
[4] W. E. Natemeyer, *Classics in Organization Behavior* (Oak Park, Ill.: Moore Pub. Co., 1978).

slices drawn, into bar graphs resembling thermometers, and into other shapes. Its main purpose is to make the abstract and confused facts seem concrete and visible. This is called "regularizing" the data. This laudable purpose sometimes produces fallacies in the fitting of the data to the system. This fallacy resembles the man looking for his key late at night by a streetlamp: He explains to an onlooker that he has lost it someplace else, but "it's lighter here."

The major error is often in not fitting the presentation to the form in which it resembles life. This is especially easy to fall into in the case of sampling.[5] A sample is found by rowing out over a huge lake full of data and dipping down a little bucket and withdrawing one bucketful; you generalize about the whole lake. This is called *inference*, which is of such importance in generalizing that we will take a whole chapter (Chapter 9) looking at the errors of inference and how they trap people. For the time being, it is sufficient to note that sampling methods can change the apparent statistical regularity. For example, it is necessary that, in the example of the lake just described, the sample not be taken near the mouth of an especially polluted inflow stream, or exclusively from the shallows near another location where the water caught in the bucket will not be representative of the lake as a whole. The confusion between regularity within the sample and overall regularity of data is a common pitfall.

One large Western state, concerned with tourism, decided to get information from tourists on how long they stayed in the state and how much money they spent while they were there. Since it was impractical to interview every tourist, the state settled upon sampling. A rubber hose across the entry and exit road actually counted the number of cars, then detailed information was taken by interview from a smaller number and generalized from that sample. All perfectly normal and customary. The number 5000 as a sample size was chosen from a population of over one million visitors yearly. The method of sampling chosen to get the two sets of answers was to present the sample group a brief diary which they would maintain while within the state. It was requested that the diaries be turned in at a visitor center upon departure. Only 25 percent of them were. These 25 percent were subject to rigorous analysis, including a chi-square test to show any significant variance between the two variables, cost and length of stay, from those responding.

On the basis of these facts, the state spent some large sums of money in tourism development—in the millions of dollars. Yet there was some unease, because every year or two some dramatic, startling change in tourism seemed to take place, such as a drop in the average length of stay from five days to one day in a single year with no apparent explanation. "What are we doing wrong?" it was asked.

The first error lay not in the small sample size, which, if it were perfectly representative of the whole population, would be satisfactory for generalization. There were some other matters, however. To obtain diaries, the sampled persons

[5] L. W. Hein, *The Quantitative Approach to Managerial Decisions* (Englewood Cliffs, N. J.: Prentice-Hall, 1967).

had to visit a tourist center. They had to be willing to accept them. They had to keep them accurately during their stay in the state while they were supposedly having a vacation and enjoying themselves. Finally, they had to turn the diaries in or mail them back upon departure. Only 25 percent did so. Even though it was possible to work all of the tools of statistics upon the information received, the limitations in the method of obtaining the sample cast enough doubt upon its being truly representative that a great deal of humility in stating the outcome should have been displayed.

Unsound sampling and how to correct it have been adequately discussed by statisticians, but the products of it in statistical presentation are endless in management. *Wrong design in sampling cannot be patched up in presentation,* even though it is tried and often goes uncaught. When people rely upon the data for policy or decisions, the decisions will be wrong.

The skilled user of numbers also knows that in studying data, it is sensible to retain that small margin of skepticism that permits the dramatic exception to occur. In admitting students to large universities, the sole reliance on test scores often rejects before admission a potentially top-flight man or woman who would have been recognized by the professors doing the screening if they had been sufficiently willing to go beyond the regularities of their data *for a reason.* Perhaps the reason is that the applicant has attended a very tough school, has taken very tough subjects, or perhaps has experienced some intervening experience such as military service that makes the statistical record an irregular rather than a regular one. The fact that the student pleads vigorously for admission might also be a relevant fact, the point being that regularly a judgmental exception appears.

## 3. FALLACIES IN GENERALIZING FROM TRENDS

One morning in the Cleveland Airport Motel, I overheard a boss extending a trend into a generalization to his assembled subordinates: "Gentlemen," the voice boomed, "this division is on a collision course with disaster." Having ruined numerous appetites, the manager then went on to present a downward-sloping sales curve. His idea was noble. If you can foretell the coming of disaster, it might possibly be averted by taking actions other than the ones you might have followed otherwise. Odiorne's Law certainly expresses a similar idea: "Things that do not change will remain the same." Yet there are limitations and fallacies here that make generalizations of this sort of trend dangerous and subject to the manipulations of persons who would prefer to affect the outcome in a fixed direction.

One method of producing a fallacy from trends is to extend the trend line to some absurd length and presume that no other changes will occur, and then to treat this imaginary trend as an imminent reality. Ecologists, laudably desiring to clean up the air and water, have fastened upon population growth as the root cause of pollution and initiated a program of zero population growth (ZPG). To make their point, they extrapolate the population growth of the world from the year 1900 to the year 2050 and show that there will be some astronomically high level. From this they paint an imaginary word picture of what life will be like if the average human being has three square feet of earth to occupy. Their subsequent brief refers frequently to this horrible condition as if it were real and the need for ZPG were now. Other studies have shown that if the rate of population of black and white middle-class populations were to stabilize at the present rate but the rate of poverty-level persons were to continue the trends of the past, 45 percent of the population of the United States would be unemployed black ghetto dwellers by the year 2008. The author must confess to using this statistical trend in a book in 1968 aimed at business leaders to advocate the employment of more blacks.[6]

The fallacy here is to extend the trend with the presumption that nothing else will change. The absurdity of such blanket assumptions is illustrated in a paragraph by Mark Twain, in which he points out that the Mississippi between Cairo, Illinois, and New Orleans had been 1215 miles long 176 years earlier. It was only 1180 miles after the cutoff of 1722 due to flooding. It was 1040 miles after the American bend cutoff, and at the time of his writing was only 973 miles long. Extending this trend *backward,* Twain concluded that in the Old Ozoic Silurian period, millions of years ago, the Mississippi stuck out over the Gulf of Mexico like a fishing rod. In another 742 years, the entire lower Mississippi River would be only a mile and three quarters long and Cairo and New Orleans would be able to have a single mayor and city council.[7] As Twain put it, "One gets such wholesale returns of conjecture for such a trifling investment of facts."

Another common fallacy in interpreting trends is false interpolation, which is taking two separate points *A* and *C,* with nothing known about the intervening space between them, and confidently describing the character of *B.* Financial projections contained in prospectuses, and business descriptions prepared for potential investors, are riddled with such interpolations. A small firm in California presented financial projections in *pro forma* fashion for would-be investors, showing that a leap from "losses of $100 thousand per month in the most recent period to earnings of $200 thousand in two years . . . demonstrates that the firm will break even in one year." The accountant, presumably with this fact and a generous fee in mind, had prepared accounting projections accordingly. No variation between months was projected, but rather a straight line of steady movement in between, despite the lamentable fact that the new product upon which this bonanza was to be based was not yet fully invented and some substantial scientific barriers had yet to be overcome. If your son grew from four feet tall at age fourteen to six feet tall at age twenty-one, he would average 3.4 inches over the seven intervening years, yet nobody would propose that in any single year he actually grew that amount. A man might drown in water that averaged only two feet deep.

Fallacies in *statistical probability* are likewise commonplace in generalizing from trends. Given a bowl of beads about which everything is known, it is possible to predict the probabilities that a sample from that bowl will be of a certain com-

[6]G. S. Odiorne, *Green Power* (New York: Pitman Publishing Corporation, 1968).
[7]M. Twain, *Life on the Mississippi,* from *The Portable Mark Twain* (New York: Viking, 1946).

position. This suggests, however, that in the real world there is really a bowl, and not two or three or a hundred or more. Perhaps there is no bowl at all, but a series of wild shots.[8] A second kind of error found in probability management is the assumption that if a distribution is known, then the a priori knowledge for the general tendency can be used to predict a single specific outcome with absolute certainty.

Recently, as I was driving with a man in Salt Lake City, the center of Mormonism, we were cut off by a careless driver. My friend, a non-Mormon, immediately fell into fallacy. "Crazy Mormon drivers," he said through gritted teeth. As we overtook the offending car, we noted that it was driven by a Catholic priest, apparent from his reversed collar and black coat. "Goodness," I noted, "the Mormons are now wearing their collars like Catholics."

## 4. FALLACIES OF LIMITED TRENDS

During a management development program conducted by a large university, all the men attending were representatives of a single company, and all were middle managers from the home office. During the course the director of physical education of the university, at the company's request, organized an after-hours physical fitness program for the interested manager-students. As part of the program, he had each man who enrolled step on the scales at the gym daily, and unbeknownst to them, he recorded their weights. Subsequently, he produced a research report that stated that "American executives are obese," each averaging thirty pounds overweight compared with standard tables. It was seized upon by the business press and was editorialized upon by several.

The fallacy here was the limited trend. The standards for ideal weights were for 18- to 24-year-old undergraduates. The men were from one company, and from office occupations in that company. Only those engaging in activities at the gym were weighed. Two of the most obese refused to take part but headed for a bar. Those hiking or playing tennis or golf were omitted from the study. The subjects were middle managers, not top executives. Fewer than half the men were weighed. Yet the generalization was read by the majority of readers as applying to all American executives.

Journalistic research often has such characteristic fallacies. The reporter receives an assignment to investigate something or other. With limited time, he or she seeks out the *available* data rather than the important. The data gathering is ordinarily conducted through interviews, which limit the size and representative character of the sample. When surveys are made they may show some unintentional bias due to limited scope. Numerous such limited studies have been done to show the characteristics of successful executives. A sample of 300 top managers shows a rising trend of accountants in top management. Another of 550 reveals that engineers are rising in the ranks faster than persons with other kinds of educational back-

[8] E. Ferrell, *Proceedings of the Conference on Statistical Quality Control,* Rutgers University, New Brunswick, N.J., 1953.

ground. One of the effects of such management of information undoubtedly contributes to the lack of credibility of the press. One publisher, working for the government, was told by a student, "You are a journalist, and you now are on government duty. That is a double reason for not believing you."

The limited trend is also characterized in many cases by the fallacy of the dramatic exception, treated as though it were a minor trend in itself. In some cases, the lonely fact might even be generalized into a major trend. A training director during the 1950's appeared before a training directors' convention and explained in great detail the mechanics of a course designed to teach all of the managers in his organization how to read faster and better. When the time came for audience questions, somebody asked, "How did you determine that they all needed speed reading training?" Flustered, the training man blurted, "Why, I need it, and so do they." A vice-president of a large airline was served his martini in a highball glass on a flight from Chicago to New York while flying as a passenger on his own line. As a result, over 600 stewardesses went back to school for a full day for a review of beverage service procedures.

The most common of the dramatic exceptions with which every company seems to be afflicted is the phenomenon of the letter to the president. A lady in Denver wrote to the president of a consumer product firm complaining that her high-altitude cake mix had failed; as a result, ten thousand hours of investigation, reams of correspondence, and thousands of dollars of expenditures were wasted on what was an isolated instance. The president of a large oil company received a long-distance personal phone call from an irate customer complaining that one of the company's trucks had broken a fence and her prize cow had escaped. Letters and phone calls cascaded down the chain of command, and a team of staff experts flew a thousand miles to check out every detail. It appeared that there was some doubt that it had actually been their company's truck; it may have been that of a competing firm. It wasn't really her cow. The fence had been repaired, and the errant beast, an accomplished escape artist, recovered, but for a year afterward the security of cows was an important agenda item in that oil company.

## 5. FALLACIES OF GLOBAL STATEMENTS

Fallacies of global statements occur when someone generalizes from several factual statements, sometimes incorrectly, and then runs down the logical ladder to deduce a specific answer but produces something entirely new, which is then forced to fit the generalization—but shouldn't be. This can be illustrated with an example.

A famous study of insurance agents in Newark, New Jersey, produced two facts. Several departments were studied. Top management was asked to classify the departments according to their productivity, which it did. The workers in all departments were asked if their boss supervised them closely or loosely while they were working, and the departments were ranked according to the tightness or looseness of supervision reported. There was a close statistical correlation between those departments that were low-producing and those where tight supervision was practiced. There was also a correlation between loose supervision and high productivity. The generalization produced was: Loose supervision *causes* high productivity.[9] This conclusion has been taught as gospel to more than a generation of managers, supervisors, and business school students. Presumably, they then try to apply this global generalization to specific situations. Some dramatic personal failures have resulted from following the generalization in specific circumstances where it did not fit. What went wrong?

Inside the company, people were furious when they learned exactly how their departments had been rated low on productivity. "Standards of productivity were not that clear," they declared. For another, the generalizers did not ask the tight supervisors *why* they were so tightly controlling their people. If they had, they might have learned that the reason they were being so tightly supervised was *because the place was in trouble.* The loose-style supervisors would have reported, "When things are going well, why bother pushing people? If they do well, they get left alone."

When students and other observers began to ask the question that naturally comes to mind, *Did the loose supervision cause the high productivity, or did the high productivity cause the loose supervision?* an amendment to the data was appended. When one of the high-producing supervisors was reassigned to one of the low-producing units, its performance improved. This, of course, opens a host of new problems. What was there about this person's behavior that turned around the low-producing organization? Did the manager in fact use loose supervision to do so? Or was there some concealed classification of behavior involved? Did the same superiors rate productivity in both places? The experiment was discontinued prior to obtaining all of the answers the experimenters wanted.

Later, other experimenters, using the same kind of analysis, did similar studies with somewhat different conclusions. In other words, they took the generalization back down to specifics once more and attempted to duplicate the original data to see if the generalization proved out. But in the process, they studied added variables: the personality of the subordinate for one, and whether the supervisor showed enthusiasm for goals and employed loose supervision for another. Amid a certain amount of academic wing flapping, the latter experiments were hailed by some critics as a disproof of the original generalization. They were, of course, nothing of the sort, because the originals, themselves subject to question, had only to do with tightness and looseness of supervision, not the added contaminating (or purifying) action of different personalities or of showing enthusiasm for goals. Perhaps the existence of clear goals was the discriminative variable in every instance.

*Fallacious global statements* are generalizations that are, upon close scrutiny, considerably less general than they appear to be, as they are ordinarily based upon some widespread exclusions. The study of business by the behavioral sciences is replete with such overweening generalizations. A hundred engineers are interviewed and the whole style of managing eighty million American workers is now subject to a new global statement.

One of the results of such global statements is that the originator is prone to

[9] R. Likert, *New Patterns of Management* (New York: McGraw-Hill, 1961).

engage in what has been labeled *statistical pleading*. This is a method of handling data so that favorable data are treated one way and unfavorable in another, thus proving the truth of the global statement.

Take the personnel researcher who wants to test the hypothesis that "an autocratic manager's employees suffer from more stress than those of democratic managers." The researcher prepares a questionnaire, and the answers come back looking as follows:

### Employees Level of Anxieties

|  | *very anxious* | *somewhat anxious* | *no anxiety* |
|---|---|---|---|
| Autocratic managers | 10 | 80 | 10 |
| Democratic managers | 10 | 80 | 10 |

This does not fulfill the expectation at all, so the researcher then proceeds with a so-called analysis of the data. The first step is to examine the ten anxious employees of the democratic manager. The researcher now concludes that it was anxiety at the research, and not at their manager, that impelled them to reply thus, and then moves them to the "no anxiety" column. The researcher turns to the autocratic manager's employees next and discovers that half of the "somewhat anxious" managers have actually applied for transfers. This is interpreted as evidence of great anxiety. Accordingly, the analyst then moves all forty into the "very anxious" column. The results now look like this:

|  | *very anxious* | *somewhat anxious* | *no anxiety* |
|---|---|---|---|
| Autocratic managers | 50 | 40 | 10 |
| Democratic managers | 0 | 80 | 20 |

With a little more such analysis, we can perfect the case, or if no more is possible without outright falsification, we can explain what we have.

Global statements upon which the originator gets hooked sometimes produce *statistical nonsense*. Having arrived at the global statement by goodness-knows-what methods, the originator then produces bits and pieces to demonstrate the case. This occurs often in muckraking articles or testimony. General Motors, the world's largest manufacturing corporation, and one of the most profitable, finds itself especially vulnerable to having its tail twisted and its nose tweaked. In some cases, as with Ralph Nader, it has found its arm being twisted. But the statistical nonsense is not hard evidence of anything important on a large scale. It consists of making too much of some isolated or irrelevant statistical facts: *The measure of the effectiveness of General Motors is shown in the fact that 3125 of its employees were seen in local bars around Grand Boulevard on Friday night.* Usually, statistical nonsense is data taken out of context or related to nothing. In some cases, it is statistical description without any intrinsic interest or value, and with no comparative data. *The interpupillary distance between the eyeballs of company presidents was . . .* is statistical nonsense, to which sophisticated mathematical analysis would add nothing. Many tables included in management reports and the vast majority of computer printouts thrown in to bulk them out and add a touch of respectability and class to a weak report are statistical nonsense. The danger is that the careless or unobserving reader might accept them as verification of a global statement without examination.

## 6. CONDITIONAL GENERALIZATIONS

Conditional generalizations are those that state the conclusions from the facts in the form *If A, then B*. This is a form of generalization that protects two parties. First it protects the prophet or originator from being caught with his or her predictions or generalizations. One always has a safety valve. The economist's *ceteris paribus*, which means "all other things being equal," is about as conditional as you can get and places the economist well out of range of responsibility for the accuracy of his or her own predictions. While this may seem a cowardly evasion, stating this condition in truth protects the unwary from placing undue importance upon the strict construction of the generalization.

A narrower kind of conditional generalization is one in which the most likely outcomes are predicted when three (or some finite number of) conditions are met.

The most modern conditional generalization is that of the new Bayesian statistics, which states all of the possible outcomes in terms of their probability, such as "20 percent chance of rain."[10] This makes it possible to construct "decision trees," or networks of conditional probabilities, which cover most of the major possibilities in a situation. The fallacy of the decision tree is that it takes dozens of *judgments* and clusters them into a systematic pattern.[11] If the judgments are deficient or the judge lacks the information needed to make the judgment, the tree will be bad. Even worse, the decision tree becomes a kind of crossword puzzle to be filled in. The final probability statements at the ends of the branches require that some judgments be made on each branch and each twig, even if the person making them hasn't the foggiest idea of what should be included. To the extent that it forces one to go find out and get the facts, that is good. To the extent that is forces one to pick a number from the air—any number—it is bad.

## 7. THE EXPLANATION GENERALIZATION

The generalization that explains an event is the kind of generalization an expert witness produces in a court of law. The expert does not claim to have seen the murder and has no particular brief for either side. It is just that he or she happens to have a whole batch of impressive credentials that demonstrate his or her ability to search back into the recesses of the mind and pull out some generalization *that*

[10] P. G. Moore and H. Thomas, *The Anatomy of Decisions* (New York: Penguin, 1976).
[11] Moore and Thomas, *Anatomy of Decisions.*

*will fit the case.* An example is the psychiatrist who concludes from the evidence presented about the defendant's behavior that the defendant was insane at the time of the crime.

In management, this kind of generalization is ordinarily rooted in many years of experience. In theory, the old sage has been around for many years, busily observing everything, storing it all into classification systems in the mind, and learning constantly from experience and is now prepared to issue valuable judgments about specific situations that occur and to baffle those without the same richness of experience. In some cases, it works exactly that way, and all of us might hope that as we grow old we will learn in such a pattern.

The fallacies here grow out of the unreliability of lessons so learned; experience, or even extensive research, may teach us contradictory things. Thirty years' "experience" may be one year repeated thirty times. Whether our information has been obtained by meticulous research or from the school of hard knocks, it teaches varying lessons. Furthermore, it sometimes has taught us things we don't realize we have learned.

Tevye in *Fiddler on the Roof* was such an old sage. He had lived a hard life as a peasant farmer in Russia, raising a family amid poverty and constant threat of exile by a government that was anti-Semitic. His experience taught the value of the *double reverse,* or hedged judgment, which experience teaches many people: On the one hand maybe this is the whole truth, but then on the other hand maybe exactly the opposite is the whole truth. The major fallacy in the explanatory generalization is thus excessive reliance upon the kind of experience that produces hesitancy. Such generalizations are not generalizations at all, but a series of rounds aimed at the target, which achieve what artillery soldiers refer to as "bracketing" the target, but never hitting it.

Irrelevance of experience and the data thus obtained often creates a fallacy of the explanatory generalization. Secretary of Defense McNamara was reported to have been in discussion with an admiral who proposed acquisition of a giant piece of hardware in the billion-dollar price range. When the admiral cited his own combat experience and that of all of his senior colleagues in the naval officer corps as corroboration, the secretary is reported to have retorted, "How many nuclear wars have you fought, admiral?"

The point here is that a generalization arrived at by research or observation some time ago may not be supported by research done or observation made at this time. The fallacy grows out of a tendency to draw present-day generalizations from obsolete experiences or data. It is perfectly true that many fundamental things do not change. It is equally true that many of the things that were once true are no longer true. To judge the values of a generalization requires a judgment about the residual life of the underlying facts upon which it is based.[12]

---

[12] C. J. Hitch and R. N. McKean, *The Economics of Defense in a Nuclear Age* (Cambridge, Mass.: Harvard University Press, 1963).

## 8. THE EVALUATIVE ASSESSMENT

One of the crucial kinds of generalizations, which is close the heart of the activity trap, is the evaluative judgment about the success or failure of people, programs, organizations, or policies. Here the judge or judges weigh the evidence of what has been done or achieved and pronounce it good or something less than good. The major fallacies found in such judgments are numerous. A few of the more important ones follow.

1. *The criteria for judgment* are not clear. When this is the case, then the judgment is subjective, intuitive, and personal, and ordinarily does not meet the test of fairness. Often it is part of a domination technique, for the judge cannot lose and the judged cannot win unless the judge so chooses.

2. *The criteria are not explicit.* This means that it should be sufficiently clear that both the judge and the judged, as well as neutral observers, can agree by what criteria the judgment or assessment is made. Many of the modern "assessment centers" for choosing new managers have faltered because there was a pure assessment with no standards. Where they have been successful, the criteria for success or failure have been explicit.[13] The measurability of standards of assessment is a thorny issue, with many adhering to an overly quantitative approach. A mixture of numerical and nonnumerical seems to be a requirement of sound standard setting. One guide to the establishment of criteria for *utility measurement* is shown in my Exhibit I, "How to Measure the Unmeasurable."[14]

3. Another fallacy exists when the results are assessed, *but are not within the control* or influence of the individual or group being assessed. Assessment should not require that mortals be asked to control the vagaries of nature, but only that they be diligent in averting the risks of mismanagement. For example, if a salesman sold so much product per month last year and no radical upheavals in conditions have occurred in his territory, it is not unreasonable to have expected him to produce a corresponding amount this year. On the other hand, if a new competitor has entered the field, a major flood has wiped out most of the customers, and the government has declared that the company's product causes leprosy, it is not an impartial assessment to judge the salesman a failure for falling below last year's level.

4. A fourth fallacy in assessment exists when the individual or group being judged *does not know it is being judged,* or thinks it is being judged by one standard when in fact it is being judged by another, invisible set of criteria. In such situations the judged have no way of knowing how well they are doing while they are acting, which makes either success or failure an accident.

The increase of standardless judgments and evaluations after the fact is common in political affairs where the purpose is to embarrass and discredit one's

---

[13]C. Jaffee and F. D. Frank, *Interviews Conducted at Assessment Centers* (Dubuque, Iowa: Kendall/Hunt, 1976).

[14]*See* Exhibit 1 from G. S. Odiorne, *Management Decisions by Objectives* (Englewood Cliffs, N.J.: Prentice-Hall, 1969).

opponent. In the heat of the campaign, such assessment is fair, if not mandatory, behavior. It becomes more serious, however, when organizations such as state auditors, or the General Accounting Office of the United States, hiding behind a cloak of objectivity and impartial assessment, rush into headlines with sweeping charges based upon judgments for which the criteria are deliberately not made known until after the scandal is released.

For the victims, the outcome is similar to finding out that a duel has been under way for some time only after their opponent's sword has been thrust through their body and the hilt is projecting from the chest. If they had known it was a duel, then they might have unleashed their own weapon and engaged in a fair game of parry and thrust. Whoever won or lost, the rule of fairness would at least have been complied with, for whatever comfort that is.

## 9. POLICIES AND PROCEDURES

The final form of generalization which might be identified is that of the policy, which is a general guide to action, and the procedure, which is specific statements of means of compliance. Policies add rationality and predictability to a business and contribute to its stability, which is highly preferable to instability. It is not a good thing, however, when stability becomes subtly turned into rigidity and inflexibility. When this happens, the organization cannot solve many of its major problems, for it is muscle-bound in its own policies. John Gardner once wrote that as the last act of a dying civilization, someone will be writing a procedure. Policy statements as generalizations might be classified into two major divisions according to their relationship to promoting innovation, or inhibiting it. As in Chapter 5, let us call the two Type C (for *centralized*) and Type D (for *decentralized*).

- Type C organizations have policies that centralize all authority and responsibility at the top except for that which is specifically assigned to lower levels.
- Type D organizations have policies that assume that the authority of lower levels to take action in the achievement of agreed-upon goals is unlimited, except by policy.

Is there a significant difference between the two? An immense difference, I would suggest. The Type C organization is one in which innovation must start at the top. "If there are any good ideas around here, I will have them," states the chief in the Type C organization. Suppose somebody at a lower level in a Type C organization gets an idea: What should he or she do about it? Obviously, that employee must first obtain permission to act; independent action without prior approval can bring forth considerable difficulties.

In the Type D organization, the individual lower down in the organization who has a good idea consistent with his or her objectives simply goes ahead and does it. Does this add up to anarchy? No, it resembles General Motors more than a commune. Alfred P. Sloan spelled out the explicit relationships between higher and lower levels under a decentralized organization, and the role of policy in that relationship.[15]

Fallacies in policy and procedure often center around the choice of Theory C as a means of organizing and of setting policy. These fallacies in policy include some of the following major ones:

1. The fallacy of *lost objectives*. The executive who wrote the original policy is gone, the reason for its creation is forgotten, and it continues without modification. "There's no reason for it, it is just policy." The cure is to revise policy often enough to be responsive to major changes in corporate strategy and goals.

2. The fallacy of the *traditional policy*. "The Navy has been in business for nearly 200 years and that's the way it has always been done." This is then assumed to be firm evidence that it should continue to be done that same way.

3. *The no-recourse fallacy*. When a policy has been stated but it becomes necessary to violate it in order to achieve an objective, there should be means of ensuring that such highly necessary action will not cause the boom to be lowered on the person who deviates in good cause.

4. *The absurd procedures fallacy*. Since procedures are specific ways of implementing policy ("Send the salmon-colored copy to data processing"), it is possible for two procedures to be mutually exclusive and produce absurdities that drain human confidence in the organization.

5. *The informal policy fallacy*. Many organizations assert that "we do things informally here," which ordinarily means, "We never use the right principle voluntarily, but we wait until a blowup has occurred and then create a scene and produce a taboo for the organization thereafter." The solution to the fallacy is obvious: Write down your policies and disseminate them before you enforce them.

6. *The nonresponsiveness fallacy*. Policies, being for the guidance of people as well as directing the use of money, materials, and machines, must be responsive to the needs of the organization. They cannot simply respond to the requirements of the money markets, the technical processes, or the customers, although they must obviously also do these. In recent times, it has also become apparent that policy needs to be responsive to public opinion and governmental opinion as well. The major ill effect of Ralph Nader upon General Motors did not ensue from the company's ill-advised investigation of his character, or even the defensiveness of its testimonies in reply, but the lack of responsiveness of its policies to a new and heretofore unseen influence. Today the company's policy is more responsive to such influences as consumerism and equal employment laws and the like.

## SUMMARY: HOW TO MAKE A FAIR GENERALIZATION

The list of improprieties that can be slipped into in managing factual data is obviously larger than the few noted here. There are some conclusions about making generalizations which are worth highlighting, however.

[15] A. Sloan, *My Years with General Motors* (New York: Doubleday, 1964).

1. The kinds of bloopers in interpretation we see in statistics, such as are abundant in accounting or marketing reports, are not limited to statistical reports, but are a kind of lapse in human logic generally. Therefore, some time spent looking at the statistical fallacies will help you recognize them when they appear in non-statistical thinking.

2. In order to qualify as a *general law,* a generalization must be true in all cases where a certain cluster of conditions is met.

3. An *explanation model* should meet the test that the only complete explanation is one in which the conclusion must follow *necessarily* from the premises. An explanation is not what *can* be, but what *has* to be.

These are very tough conditions to meet, but they constitute proof, and for the most part managers will seldom meet the full tests of proof and finding a universal law. Thus, working under uncertainty a fair portion of the time seems to be the condition of managing organizations.

Living constantly in an environment of uncertainty means that the action-centered manager, who would attack problems and solve them, who would set impossible goals and achieve them, will be surrounded and probably outnumbered by activity traps full of people who seek certainty and predictability before they will change. When people who prefer certainties are accosted by people who apparently are indifferent to security and have high confidence in the future of things, they (the security seekers) both use and misuse the tools of logic to prove that the innovative is not attainable because it is uncertain. The person who climbs a mountain "because it's there" is expressing exactly the reason that most people will go *around* it. The infusion of scientifically educated persons into managerial ranks brings the rationalizing skills of the engineer, the accountant, the mathematician, the statistician, and the metallurgist. Thus, management is staffed with security seekers who abhor the entrepreneurial and innovative behavior which crops up at lower levels. The power to engage in orderly scientific experimentation ensures that no rash moves will be made, that the best of all possible worlds, that of the rational mind, will prevail. Both theoreticians of management and plumbers, to paraphrase John Gardner, should be competent, for if they are not their creations will not hold water.[16]

Breaking the activity trap is thus not a totally rational process. "Men strive to become what they are capable of," says Harry Levinson.[17] This is beyond rationality, for how can one demonstrate with proof that some image one holds or dream one pursues is provable? The pursuit of an ego ideal, while explainable in psychological terms, is no great shakes as an explanation model, for it does not really meet the test that the conclusion must necessarily follow the premises. What makes up the ego ideal for one person may be woefully inadequate for another.

For better or worse, one of the fascinations of the activity trap is that when people are left alone and like themselves in their activity, no amount of logical

---

[16] J. Gardner, *No Easy Victories* (New York: Harper & Row, Pub., 1968).
[17] H. Levinson, *The Exceptional Executive* (New York: Mentor Books, NAL, 1971).

persuasion will break them out of it but may help them preserve the status quo. Maurice Barrès once said of a particular man that, since he was "a shrewd man, he only wants what he can get." This leaves the tools of logic for those of us in the activity trap, and assures us of a satisfactory role with which we can live. For the rest, the appeal is expressed by Robert Kennedy when he said, "Some men look at what is and ask 'why?' Others look at what could be and ask 'why not?'"

# Nine ways
# of using false inferences
# to prevent change

There are certain articles of faith that some intelligent people take pride in. For example:

- They don't believe in ghosts.
- They can't be convinced that extrasensory perception really works, even if a professor develops statistical proof that it does sometimes.
- They don't believe that witches and devils inhabit the earth. On the other hand, they consider it a mark of high rationality and sophistication to rely upon logical *inference.*
- Inference takes signs and turns them into complete scenarios.
- Inference is completely rational, whereas belief in ghosts is superstitious and founded upon emotion.
- People who make decisions based upon superstitions are backward, primitive, and barbaric. People who make decisions based upon inference are intelligent, educated, sophisticated, and civilized.

  *The sad truth is that fallacies of inference cause people to act as if they were reading horoscopes or tea leaves or listening to spirit voices. At the same time, such fallacies can surround witchcraft with an aura of scientific method.*

## HOW MANAGERS ARE TAKEN IN BY
## THEIR OWN INFERENCES

People who are tough often take pride in that fact. To them it is not a defect like a wart or calluses to be hard-nosed. But being a hardnose usually means leaping to conclusions from inferences more quickly than others do, and taking corrective action. The hardnoses pride themselves upon their realism. They presume that they are in touch with reality. Yet they depend upon fallacious inferences to tell them where reality is.

Valid inference is an immensely versatile and useful tool. Fallacious inference is a menace.

Reality is so complex it's hard to find. Close to the heart of finding reality is the process called inference. What does inference do? It *draws out meaning* from information. The common error in speech of confusing *infer* with *imply* is an error of perspective. An implication presents the facts. The inference "hears" them. Inference may hear statements in such a way that the reader or listener can easily draw a conclusion from things beyond what is actually said. Thus, if the janitor were to suggest to a visitor, "The president is sober again today," the listener might infer that the chief was, in fact, a regular lush, but that today at least he was on the wagon. Note what is *said* and what is an inference on the part of the listener. In fact, the president might be a confirmed teetotaler, in which case the janitor would have stated a false implication, and the listener would have made a false inference.

This handling back and forth of ideas, words, and conclusions is sometimes where reality gets dropped, amended, or enlarged. A person reaches out to pick up one thing and finds he or she has grasped something entirely different. The reality in a statistical chart or table is only in part in the numbers appearing in it. Its reality lies also in what people draw out of the numbers. Thus, the statistician has some responsibility in data preparation, for "figures don't lie, but liars figure." Presenting raw figures or data that can be easily misinterpreted or perhaps are *most likely* to be misinterpreted is the preparer's responsibility to avoid. Yet, as in the marketplace, the law of *caveat emptor* applies: let the buyer beware.

Some of the common fallacious inferences in statistics were discussed in Chapter 6. The discussion of bloopers and pitfalls in this chapter deals with the more ordinary transactions between people: how inference causes people to see or hear something that is not there, or perhaps to miss something that is, when information is received in verbal form (and most information is received in words).

In popular speech, the term *inference* is widely used in some pejorative sense. Most people do not think of or use *inference* in the sense of *I draw a lot of favorable inferences.* Rather, they think of putting together an unfavorable, critical, or scandalous story from patches of evidence, or threads. Even a single smidgen of evidence can be used to imply vast expanses of sin, venality, and corruption.[1]

Take a case reported in the press during the election campaign of 1972. Representative Les Aspin of Wisconsin, it seems, obtained a General Accounting Office report on a sample of fourteen hospitals in five states that showed that nearly $500,000 had been illegally charged to Medicare out of a total $20 million paid in Medicare claims. "Federal Funds have been used to pay for private duty nurses, TV sets, and telephone service for medicare patients—all illegal under federal law."[2] The possible inference here is that the entire $500,000 was paid for these classes of expense. Congressman Aspin then enlarged the possibilities rather generously. "If the Department of Health, Education and Welfare and Blue Cross administer the whole medicare program as indicated by the sample GAO report, then the

---

[1] For a veritable encyclopedia of deceptions, see A. Herzog, *The B.S. Factor: The Theory and Technique of Faking It in America* (New York: Simon & Schuster, 1973).

[2] The basic source is the *Congressional Record* of October 1972; this material was also reported in *The New York Times*.

Federal government has been gypped out of approximately $380 million," he concluded. Now the TV's, private nurses, and telephones were by inference at a third of a billion dollars! Congressman Aspin goes on then to discuss the $380 million (not the $500,000) and draws an outsized inference from this huge sum and concludes that the reason for the overcharges is "pervasive mismanagement, administrative procedures, and incomplete audits by HEW and private insurance companies."

Of course, in politically active years, which are customarily holidays from logic, the press is filled with such examples; and the point here is, of course, not to judge the accuracy or inaccuracy of the charges by the politician but to illustrate how one ten-cent drop of information can become a tank car of inference worth millions. The best part of the whole thing from the implicator's viewpoint is that it isn't really necessary to state that any facts are available about the whole thing, but only to note soberly that the available facts have been highlighted and a conclusion extrapolated from them.

The violence done to the truth in such instances is severe, but not that done in this case by the GAO, or even by Congressman Aspin, whose expansion of $500,000 to $380 million is a mere 760 to 1 growth. This merely initiates the process. The follow-up consequences are where reality is hopelessly lost. The interest groups begin to line up behind the Aspin case, citing it as proof that Medicare itself is riddled with joyous corruption and self-dealing highbinders who are robbing the taxpayers, and so on. It is a sobering thought to realize that some of our nation's legislation may be a product of such reasoning.

The key issue of fact is more mundane, in all likelihood. We should concentrate upon the $500,000 and the illegality of that expense. It comprises 0.13 percent of the whole amount. Does this fall within the special emergency provisions for extraordinary therapeutic and health care services permitted? Or did the hospitals, Blue Cross, and HEW all in turn err in their interpretation of the procedures? What is *their* explanation? Is it indeed an illegality in the sense of violating a statute, and criminal in character, or is it a somewhat lesser level of peccadillo, such as unacceptable variance from a procedure which the GAO discovered after the facts were gathered and which it then applied to the data, a not unknown practice in that arm of Congress? Or, is there indeed some heinous conspiracy to rob taxpayers on the part of an agency carried away by sentimental foolishness on behalf of the old folks? Reality in the case, having now been permanently put into abeyance, can never be evoked in the case, in all likelihood.

## HOW INFERENCES CAN
## BURY REALITY

Tomes have been written on extracting meaning from received information.[3] The subject includes topics such as semantics and communication. We should be able to

---

[3] P. F. Strauson, *Introduction to Logical Theory* (London: Methuen, 1952); *see also* W. Dray, *Laws and Explanations in History* (London: Oxford University Press, 1957); and R. Braithwaite, *Scientific Explanation* (Cambridge: Cambridge University Press, 1953).

find nine major fallacies of inference that cause managers to see things that are not true and miss things that are:

1. They catch only a fraction of the information, and that portion is not the vital part.
2. They do not have the same kind of vocabulary used in the message.
3. The words have two or more meanings and they choose the wrong definition and go from there.
4. The wrong medium of transmission is used.
5. The meanings are distorted by faulty emphasis.
6. The listener's emotional condition screens things selectively.
7. The meanings of terms change as they change hands.
8. The information is being sent over one channel or medium while receivers have their ear glued to another, or the medium used is defective.
9. The listener is cataloging meaningless information into a personal system of classification.

In business, as in government administration, the false inference is growing in volume and seriousness, as we add staff specialties. Each functional expert has his or her own jargon, and in some instances insists upon adding tortured and special meanings to ordinary words. The search for clarity of communication is a search for clearer meanings and ways of transmitting them. While the emphasis has been upon the communicator to produce everything in crystal-clear form, there is a further responsibility among listeners to interpret it honestly.

What does honest inference require? First, that *context* be considered. Second, that *textual analysis* be accurate. Third, sound inference calls for fair *application* of the first two to the real world. This fairness doctrine fits both statistical and nonstatistical information.

What is the difference between the kind of inference that statisticians talk about and the kind that produces the reality losses described here? In logic, there is perhaps none. In statistical inference, you dip a small pail into a large lake, then study the contents of the pail in great detail. From your findings about what is contained in the pail, you *infer* certain things about the whole lake. This is pure inference, and with the constraints noted it should provide accurate data about the larger body. If the sample is representative, if the choice of times and places to dip the bucket is meticulously managed and there are no secret or unseen strata or sub-pools within the lake, you are safe to generalize from that sample.

This is far less true in the instance of oral, written, and semantical problems of inference. Here no lake has been defined. The small bucket may consist of a single drop, or it may consist of a fire hose turned on you full blast. The data come in ordinary, day-to-day business intercourse and arrive in all kinds of forms. How do people who handle that information miss reality? How, for example, can a manager sit on top of a large organization and not be in touch with reality?

**1. Most managers miss more information than they get.** Because the top manager is one person and the activity of the company is diverse, varied, and geographically spread out and is carried on by many people, the top manager simply cannot see it all. This means that he or she is somehow being *protected against* information that will never reach the top. But even when information reaches there, the decision maker won't get it all, just selective bits of it.

For one thing, there is a mechanical problem of simply not being able to listen fast enough and with enough skill. Studies of listening skills have shown that one month after receiving it, the average person retains only a quarter of what is received aurally. People's listening skills are not developed as well as some of their other communication skills. People sit through lectures or conferences, nod attentively and walk out with less than a quarter of the information to which they have been exposed.[4] Listeners fail to hear because they are prone to distraction, they fail to listen for ideas, they avoid listening to things that are foreign to them, they dismiss topics as uninteresting, they concentrate upon the speaker's style of delivery or appearance rather than the message, they are diverted into daydreams and faking attention, and they engage in other bad listening habits that produce a major loss of received information.

The distinct impression that a boss is not listening to a subordinate much of the time is reported by many subordinates. "She doodles, does filing, and takes interruptions such as the phone, and I get the impression that she is not hearing the most significant stuff."

The boss who has the answers in hand has a selective screening apparatus already erected when somebody comes into the office with new information. "He doesn't hear half of it"—the research shows this is just about accurate. This leaves the boss with fragmented and partial information upon which to draw conclusions, make decisions, and solve problems.

On many occasions, subordinates are engaged in a post-mortem on some terrible error which was made. The boss, now contrite, asks, "Why didn't somebody tell me about this situation earlier?" and the response frequently is, "We tried, but I guess you weren't listening, boss."

Although reality is there, it remains invisible and unused—no dumping of the contents of even a small pail out on the table and scrutinizing it in minute detail to find meaning, just a crazy quilt of bits and pieces, for the receiver won't have it any other way.

2. **The ambiguity trap likewise assists in concealing reality.** Professor Ed Wrapp of the University of Chicago, a long-time corporate director and adviser to top management, proposes that things are not as neat and tidy as some management theoreticians would have us propose at the top of large organizations. Managers at the top, he proposes, are not models of efficiency and smoothly operating machines, but rather live in a world where ambiguity is rife. They are more apt to think in wheel-and-deal terms than in the neat, orderly patterns of efficiency.[5]

Ambiguity can consist of using a word that has two or more meanings without specifying which one is intended. It also can refer to a climate created by actions that are intended to be clear but are not because of conflicting interests

---

[4] R. G. Nichols and L. A. Stevens, *Are You Listening?* (New York: McGraw-Hill, 1957).

[5] E. Wrapp, "Manage by Objectives—or Wheel and Deal?" *Steel*, 160, May 1967.

pressing for diametrically opposed outcomes. In administrative relationships, where neatness and clarity of purpose is rare rather than common, people with a high tolerance for ambiguity thrive.

At one time a professor was employed as an executive for a large corporation. It was customary in this organization for everyone from president on down to be on a first-name basis. Yet one morning the chairman of the board met him in the hall and said calmly, "Good morning, Doctor." He immediately rushed back to his office to mull this new development! It was well known that the ex-professor had a Ph.D., but he had made no special point of it. For one thing, he might be called to help if somebody were run over in the parking lot, and he could be made ill by the sight of blood. Yet, even with such a model of rationality as this man, this remark in a context not ordinarily found was unsettling and created an air of ambiguity, from which a host of interesting inferences could be taken.

*Inconsistent behavior* can produce inferential ambiguity and generate numerous specific false inferences. The boss who is smiling one day and growling the next produces inferences that have such a wide range of interpretation as to make reality unknowable. For a boss, inconsistent behavior in a subordinate makes that person's reliability of doubtful quality, and when an otherwise good person makes a drastic breach of faith, we are impelled to ask, "Which one is the real Mary?" Years of steady performance often are undone by a single error in judgment, for those observing the person infer that this is a concealed defect, well hidden up to now, which reveals an underlying weakness. Most people like unchanging information from which to draw their inferences.

Much of what we purport to know about principles of human behavior is really inference. A person stalks out of a meeting and we infer that he or she is angry at the proceedings. That person in fact, *may* be enraged, but we don't know that. It might be some other cause. The whole fabric of personality is inference, for there is no explicit physiological organ called "the personality." When a man or woman behaves in a certain fashion regularly, we, by inference, some organizing central core in his or her mind or spirit to explain these behaviors and call it personality.[6] Much of the literature of behavioral sciences is really a highly refined study of inferences about behavior. Not that this is bad, or useless, for it helps explain, predict, and control the behavior of others and of ourselves. Nevertheless, the ambiguous action can produce false inferences about that behavior. We have come to rely so strongly on this inference that when we observe excessive variability and ambiguity of behavior we are apt to consider calling it erratic, which is often a synonym for mentally deranged.

3. **False inferences can grow from semantic differences.** The meanings of words differ. This is less true of words that have a hard referent, such as *automobile* or *tree;* but it is especially true of words whose only definition is in terms of other words, words such as *truth, values, liberty, democracy,* and *love.*[7] Even the hard

---

[6] B. F. Skinner, *Science and Human Behavior* (New York: Macmillan, 1953).

[7] C. K. Ogden and I. A. Richards, *The Meaning of Meaning* (New York: Harcourt Brace Jovanovich, Inc., 1936); *see also* S. Chase, *The Tyranny of Words* (New York: Harcourt Brace Jovanovich, Inc., 1938).

words often have different meanings to different audiences. *Grass, pot,* and *hash* could have different meanings for an urban dweller than they might have for a middle-aged rancher in Montana.

Semantic differences might be the cause when forms of communication do not produce an exchange of meaning. This failure, of course, may result because the sender has not clarified mentally what he or she wants to send. It may fail because this idea is not couched in a language the receiver can unscramble and decode after receiving it. Perhaps the medium it is sent through is inadequate or too weak or does not use the same bandwidth as the receiver's. It may be that the receiver's equipment is not tuned in.

All of these troublesome possibilities might account for the communication failure.[8] Ordinarily, that part of the failure that involves the code into which the message is formed is in the domain of semantics. Some of the most common managerial fallacies in semantics are these:

- *Speaking in technical jargon to nontechnical people.* The accountant, the engineer, the chemist, and the data processing expert all have special vocabularies. In their own quarters, the language becomes familiar and commonplace. When they use it outside their quarters, they can sow confusion.

- *Using special in-house language.* There are numerous private communication systems, often nontechnical in nature, that are ordinary and clear to their users but are Greek to outsiders. Young people use them to exclude others. Double talk and the language used by the violence-prone teenagers in Anthony Burgess's *Clockwork Orange,* and the numerous other special insider languages, are nontechnical but obscure. They create a distinct impression of exclusion of those not abreast of their meaning and produce barriers that lead to misunderstanding and a loss of touch with reality. They also immunize the insiders from new ideas that impinge upon the group from outside, unless somehow they can be translated readily into the insider language.

- *Forcing ordinary words into affected and stylized precision.* Perhaps the worst offenders here are personnel departments. Since there is little real technical language of personnel administration, with the possible exception of behavioral science jargon, they turn ordinary words into a forced technical vocabulary. Such words as *assessment, objectives, goals, results,* and *discrimination,* which are common words, are assigned explicit meanings that are pounded home with great emphasis in personnel procedures. In one firm where, for example, a "goal" is a one-year target; a five-year target becomes an "objective." Since these are synonyms in ordinary language, there is a created need to explain the difference and correct errors. The result is a loss of communication between personnel managers and others, for whom such distinctions are trivial. The others may infer that the rest of personnel administration is of comparable moment.

[8] D. Kirkpatrick, *No–Nonsense Communication* (Brookfield, Wis.: K & M Publishers, 1978).

The sad part about such artificially produced communication failures is that the listener hears something that was never intended. If someone cannot understand what is said because the meaning is distorted (or because the communicated form is totally devoid of meaning), he or she infers wrong information. The receiver also infers something about the sender, such as *He is contemptuous of me.*

Few things tear up relationships, or produce hostile behavior, more readily than inferred insults, even though no implied insult may have been uttered or intended. The semantic gap between classes of people, between occupations, between generations, between races and the sexes is likely to produce in the receiver the impression of an insult even though one was never issued. This insult is *reality* for the false inference maker, as real as the clubs and stones and guns that may naturally follow.

**4. When the wrong medium of transmission is used, reality gets lost.** Wrong inferences, and misrepresentations of reality, may be a product of the medium used in transmitting the message. The most important failures occur when things that should be spoken are sent in writing instead, or at least are written without being said first.

a. *The overlooked importance of face-to-face dialogue before memos.* The value of personal, face-to-face discussion to produce an exchange of meaning has been emphasized widely and demonstrated repeatedly in theory and violated widely in practice. The ability to see and hear the other person and to be seen permits communication to be enlarged to include *all behavior* and not merely written behavior. While there have been some studies done of "body language" and of the various meanings of facial expressions, it is mostly a personalized art. The "silent language" requires personal contact.[9] Often the very act of writing memos out of the blue, without prior discussion and face-to-face meetings, creates great inferences of insult, personal slights, and an authoritarian image on the part of the writer, even where it is not intended.

Three major kinds of communication call for face-to-face communication, all in the category of *transactions.* A transaction is what you engage in when you are going to bargain with someone, resolve a disagreement, or change his or her behavior. Such relationships will call for face-to-face contact, where the full powers of behavior can be put into play. Such transactions will be the site where the realities of the world exchange hands. Eric Berne, a specialist in transactional analysis, compared such communication to "games people play." He classified these games into symbolic games, which call for "stroking" behavior from the other player ("I am wagging my tail, pat me"); pastimes ("How did the Colts make out?"); and, more seriously, life games, which, if won or lost, can have drastic effects such as placing the loser in the poorhouse or the morgue. It is likely that certain kinds of symbolic games can be played impersonally, as through sympathy cards, birthday gifts, and get well cards. Pastimes might possibly be carried on by written

---

[9] K. Back, *Communication: The Art of Being Understood* (New York: Hastings House, 1963).

communication; many people play chess by mail. But life games require that the transactions be face to face.[10]

Forcing communications into the medium of personal communication will improve the quality of understanding and avert the false inference by which reality is lost. A safe guide when confronted with delicate and important communication is *Go talk to the person!*

b. *The inept use of written memos.* Written confirmation in memos is as important to the transfer of reality in communication as is the original transaction. It rounds out and makes the transaction whole. In labor relations, the two-part process is spelled out in the Labor-Management Relations Act of 1947. The parties shall meet at mutually convenient times and places and bargain in good faith, and later, the agreements arrived at shall be reduced to writing and signed by both parties, and shall be enforceable as a contract. This fundamental rule of good administrative practice is an assurance that the communication, which was so vividly real and shining when the discussion ended, will remain tangible during the life of the agreement, the peace pact, or the assignment. Reality then becomes something tangible to which both can agree.

Bad writing, bad syntax, or even wrong punctuation can mar the intent of the original agreements. The written content should be a faithful representation of the agreement made, the constraints included, the conditions under which it was made—a sort of minutes of the meeting, with provision for the recipient to correct errors in fact.

**5. The distorted-emphasis fallacy** Still another fallacy in inference is that which *distorts meaning by changing emphasis.* The American newspaper industry is presently confronted with a serious problem of credibility growing out of this tendency. Attacks by leading politicians upon the credibility of the press have centered mainly upon this distortion of emphasis, which produces inferences that change meanings of words and statements, while the press and media have vigorously denied the charge. The press infers in turn that the politicians may intend to use their powers of office to suppress freedom of the press (itself an interesting case of inference).

Many editors and publishers privately concede that the inferentially biased story is a difficult one to manage. In part, it is a product of the publishing industry's problems, which often make circulation dependent upon an unending diet of sensation, stories of conflict, and novelty in the news, where factual news of such a nature may be sparse. The problem is exacerbated by the low wage scales paid to reporters, which mean that younger people ordinarily staff most of the news-gathering positions, bringing some of their values to reporting.

Hardly any prominent person can escape the experience of having publicly uttered something, only to see a single bit of it blown greatly beyond the intended proportion, thus producing an inference in print which is then disseminated to the readers as a flat statement. The baiting question, the innocent question

---

[10] E. Berne, *Games People Play* (New York: Grove Press, 1964); *see also* T. A. Harris, *I'm OK—You're OK* (New York: Harper & Row, Pub., 1967).

designed to induce the prominent person to state something that can become the basis for a journalistic headline, is a reality-distorting fact of life for most important people. Persons who have gone through the white glare of publicity, which involves public notoriety, almost unanimously report that they "didn't recognize themselves."

The deep resentment such people have of the distorting influence of emphasis upon the reality of their intentions is apparent. Presidents of the United States inevitably end up being hostile to one or more elements of the media. General de Gaulle, during his hectic struggle to end the Algerian crisis, commented on the apparent inability of those who speak and write for a living to report the situation accurately. Company presidents who have been through the experience of meeting the press and stating facts as they know them, only to have a single item boldly distorted into the lead paragraph with inferences not intended, have learned to shun the news conference.

Mistaken emphasis also comes from the *omissions* accompanying communication, and mistaken inferences take on the reality of spoken error. One president was talking to his executives about the objectives of the company for the next five years with respect to mergers and reductions of present lines. A question from the audience asked him if he intended to distribute his remarks in writing. He replied that he did not intend to. The silence in the room that followed this off hand comment, and the discussion in the halls afterwards indicated a great loss of credibility in his comments because of his refusal to publish them. What was inferred was that he was not firm in his resolve.

*Phraseology* in communication can create inferences, intentionally or otherwise. When used consciously, complex phraseology produces subtlety in communication. When used through carelessness, it may distort reality, and people will see something that is not really there. Such phrases as these could be subjected to several inferences:

- *Honest John, the treasurer. . .*
- *If this campaign fails, gentlemen! . . .*

There are many such styles in which understatement, sarcasm, affected uncertainty, the ominous pause, the gentle spoof, the biting satire, the paradoxical statement are used to produce inferences where direct statements are not made.

Reality can be distorted by emphasis employed in a way that converts it into *innuendo*, which is the responsibility of the sender. In other cases, the emphasis is placed there by the reader. The executive who cheerfully told his competitor "I hope your mother bites you" was only a hairsbreadth from calling him an S.O.B. On the other hand, even the most skilled writer will find it hard to prevent a biased reader from supplying innuendo if the reader so wills it. Even the flat monotone voice can speak volumes of innuendo, as David Brinkley has demonstrated in his descriptions of behavior of congressmen. His flat, factual, accurate descriptions of behavior and verbatim quotations often have the effect of producing an image of an utter scoundrel, an incompetent, or worse.

All this demonstrates the importance of the emotional condition of the hearer. Many of the fallacies described here result when the listener is guided by his or her emotional condition.

**6. Fallacies of emotional distortion** These cannot be managed by the sender, except in controlling the frequency and intensity of messages sent. Emotionally aroused receivers are in no condition to interpret things in any way except in the light of their emotional condition. Their central nervous system acts as a filter through which reality is received. Threatened people receive messages as hostile attacks, while frightened people seek defensive materials to erect barricades, or weapons to destroy their harassers. Simple admonitions such as *Now cool off, Harry* will not clear the air, and further emotional responses will serve only to heighten the emotionally charged condition of the receiver.

People are different when emotionally charged up from the way they are when cool. Their adrenal glands issue a stimulant into the bloodstream. Their muscles are stronger and more tensed for action. The liver emits sugar, which must be consumed, and the lungs and heart respond with greater activity to burn off this fuel. The increased flow of circulation stems off certain segments of the brain, the face is flushed, and the temperature rises several degrees. Saliva ceases to flow and the mouth is dry; the enzymes that digest food stop flowing; the vision is impaired; and the entire process accelerates if there is evidence of rage or hostility on the part of the other person.

In such a condition, the only possible way of restoring people to normal and achieving reality in the relationship is to allow them to settle down. The non-directive methods suggested by psychologist Carl Rogers seem to be the most fruitful approach.[11] It requires that the other person avoid strong affirmative or negative action, but instead *listen* actively to what the charged-up correspondent is saying. Simple acceptance, rephrasing of words, indication of understanding of the other's position, waiting for insights of a rational nature to appear, and then rephrasing these rational comments until the real nature of the problem can be identified constitute an overly brief description of the Rogerian method.

To illustrate, a man is enraged at what seems to be an insult to his honor.

"You scoundrel. You have called me a thief, and I shall get revenge!"

"Hmm, I see that you are angry. You feel that I have attacked your honesty." No satire, no emotion, no counterrage—simply restatement of the feeling expressed. Although not an easy form of transaction to carry off, the sympathetic explosion is well known to demolition experts and applies as well in human communication.

The avoidance of acceleration of the emotional state is the first step in the creation of reality-based communication, and the reduction in fallacies of inference. Even emotional conditions generated in the heat of battle can be frankly stated if they are stated in factual terms.

"I am angry too, and would like to suggest that we agree to talk further of this." While it may seem to take a superhuman effort, the professionals in international diplomacy and in labor-management negotiations have demonstrated that

---

[11] C. Rogers, *Client Centered Therapy* (Boston: Houghton Mifflin, paper, 1965).

it is a human skill that can be acquired and developed. The consequences of its not being more widespread could be that our world will be reduced to rubble.

7. **False inference from jumping definitions** Changeable definitions are a certain method of destroying reality and meaning in communication. A management-development manager made a presentation to the general managers of the major divisions of the firm, selling them on the virtues of a results-oriented appraisal system for the managers in the company. It covered all aspects of a manager's performance. Their acceptance was necessary for the successful application of the new system, and he explained it as fully as possible in the time allotted at the meeting. The general acceptance level was high, except for one general manager who directed one of the largest divisions.

"Aren't you just talking about budgets?" the manager asked. "Hell, we have had budgets in our division for years, and therefore I don't see anything new."

"Goals should be stated in measurable terms wherever possible," was the reply, "but should include other programs as well."

"That's right," the reply came back, "you are just talking about budget numbers. If I am making my numbers I am already using your idea, which is pretty old hat in my opinion." In some instances, facts can be given false definitions.

Suppose, in a study designed to discover the amount of stress executives confront in their jobs, the researcher designated several classes of stress the executives could report. The highest order was the choice "considerable stress." Following this was "some stress," "little stress," and "no stress whatsoever." The results came out something like this:

| | |
|---|---|
| Considerable stress | 10 percent |
| Some stress | 41 percent |
| Little stress | 42 percent |
| No stress | 7 percent |

In the verbal report the results might come out, "A majority of managers in American corporations in a recent study suffer from more than a little stress in their work." The equivocation here comes in the evolving definition of stress as argument emerges. The sample group is defined to include all executives. The responses on a paper-and-pencil test become defined as "suffering." Reality is the potential victim.

This jumping of definitions is easily accomplished when it moves from one hand to another. Much information suffers in transmission. I report to A that I have just sneezed and she reports to B that I have a cold, which becomes a *serious* cold when C receives the bad news. Within six such transactions, I have recently passed on, or am about to do so, from viral pneumonia. Information does not always enlarge, but sometimes diminishes. I return from a world trip and am ready to describe it mile by mile to all listeners. The first victim is unwitting enough to ask about it. "Tell me about your trip around the world." He gets the full story. The next one hears that I "had been away awhile." From then on, if that trip is mentioned at all, it is probably along the line, "Haven't seen you for awhile. Been out of town?" The reasons for the degrading of information, including the charge of definitions during the transfer, are that:

1. People receive and use information according to how useful it is to their purposes, not to fit some abstract principle of accuracy of transmission.

2. Information will be altered in meaning upon transfer when the favorable consequences outweigh the unfavorable consequences for changing it. If the consequences for fidelity of transmission were highly favorable, the accuracy of the information would improve.

Take the case of a passenger who is flying into O'Hare Airport in Chicago. He is arriving on airline A, which uses terminal 1. He is scheduled to make a connecting flight to depart from another airline in terminal 2. The incoming plane is late, and he is concerned whether his baggage will be transferred to the outgoing flight. He has some important papers in his baggage that must be on hand upon arrival at his new destination. He approaches a passenger service representative from airline A who is standing at the exit ramp in terminal 1.

"Sir, will my bag be transferred to airline B in terminal 2 in time for a 2:30 P.M. departure?" Without hesitation, the representative lays a hand on his arm and says, "Absolutely sir, without a doubt."

Later it proves that this charming touch is not to come true. The bags cannot possibly be transferred in that time, and the passenger is seriously inconvenienced, more so than if the information were accurate, for he might have made some allowances or taken remedial action if he had known the truth.

Why does the young man respond with erroneous information?

This can be explained by a grid that displays the various consequences to the person. Across the top we show the major kinds of actions available, in this case, lie or tell the truth. Down the left side we see the kinds of consequences or payoffs for each of these kinds of actions. Then we complete the details in each square. If the unfavorable consequence for accurate information transmission outweigh the favorable consequences, there is one strike against an accurate transfer. What could befall this employee if he did the right thing (told the truth, that the passenger was too late, the time was too little, and the bag would not make it)? The passenger might immediately chastise him, call to see his boss, perhaps abuse the airline and its employees. To lie produces a smiling passenger, a cheerful thank you, and a rapid end to a sticky problem.

On the other hand, if all kinds of favorable consequences for transmitting the information are visible, and no unfavorable ones, the possibility exists that there will be some other kind of communication failure. Perhaps the young man does not really know. Perhaps he thinks the bag should make it. Perhaps he is correct but somebody else fails to meet the schedule. Within such limits, however, the production of better inferences from information, and more accuracy of communication of reality, will occur when their are fewer unfavorable consequences and perhaps more favorable ones.[12]

[12]G. Rummler and K. Brethower, "How Training Changes Behavior," *Training and Development Journal,* July 1979.

**8. False inferences occur from defective channels** When Paul Revere planned his famous midnight ride, he had arranged as a signal, as every schoolchild was later to learn, "One if by land, and two if by sea/And I on the opposite shore will be." This medium of communication, lanterns in a church tower, apparently was sufficient to send Paul on his now famous ride through every Middlesex village and town. One teacher reported that a question from a worried little girl asked, "What would have happened if the man in the church hadn't had a match?"

This young lady identified a weakness in that particular communication system. The inferences an impatient Paul could have made if the anonymous lamp holder had been unable to light the lantern are endless. Paul might have cursed the blockhead for being delayed in a bar. He might have assumed that the British had called off the maneuver or had captured the man. He might have assumed that his signalman had been bought off.

Inferences that require high-fidelity transmission will inevitably suffer when the medium used is inadequate. In some cases it is because the sender is transmitting information over one channel and the receiver has an ear glued to another. This becomes especially vexing when technicians of various sorts communicate. Even in closely related special areas, such as accounting and finance, there are differences in theories and procedures that cause gaps. *Sources of funds* can have two different meanings, one to the treasurer and one to the chief accountant. For engineers, the most significant data may be quantitative data, and they are especially attuned to anything which is "hard" or shown in figures. Engineering reports are thus reliable, others are not. For the public relations expert, the numbers are a mere starting point for the more sophisticated readings of attitudes, perceptions, trends in feelings, and the like, and engineering reports are meaningless.

*The most effective channel is that which reaches into the understanding of the receiver, rather than meets the needs or convenience of the sender.*

This means that translation into the vocabulary of the audience is a preliminary and necessary step in the avoidance of false inference. Even more, it is necessary to make an estimate of the mental set of the receiver, for that attitude will be the receiving channel to which the ear of the listener is attuned. Kenneth Boulding suggests that much of this receiving attitude is formed by the images we carry about.[13] We are concentrated upon one thing and selectively tune out everything else. He notes that when one is working attentively at something, the numerous ordinary noises, such as cars passing by, a lawn mower on the next block, or birds singing, are as unheard as if they did not exist. The fact that information is bombarding us makes such a mechanism necessary in order to preserve the concentration necessary to get things done at all. The mechanism screens out some stimuli and "screens in" others that we consider related to the set that grips us at the time. The receiving channel, then, is influenced by the mental set we have adopted at the time of the incoming information.

[13] K. Boulding, *The Image: Knowledge in Life and Society* (Ann Arbor, Mich.: University of Michigan Press, 1961).

**9. The fallacy of bizarre classification** One of the common fallacies in business that produces false inferences is the number of strange classification systems for information that exist. These are similar to the experience of the family traveling with small children in a cross-country automobile trip. Bombarded with new sensations, the children may develop new classifications of receiving them to pass the time. "Well, we just left Ohio. What did you think of it?" might produce a reply such as "Thirty-eight gas stations" from the information receiver in the back seat. For the child, the time was spent counting gas stations, and accordingly, Ohio becomes a number of gas stations (or red barns, foreign cars, or brown cows).

Numbers have such a quality for many people. I once knew a timekeeper in a factory whose knowledge of people was mainly by their employee number. He was able to keep everyone's identification clear, being able to connect face with number, but was totally unable or unwilling to connect faces with names. When a dispute occurred among several female employees, he subsequently described exactly what happened in his own terms:

"I saw it all. Employee number 1931 was walking out of the lounge and jostled 1156. They started arguing when 1678 joined in and took sides with 1931. That apparently made 1482, who is 1156's sister-in-law, mad because she took a swing at 1678 and fetched her quite a whack on the head with her purse."

Such a bizarre classification system often shows up as a *black-and-white* classification system. The employment manager in a small plant located in a small town once explained to the author his system of selection of employees. "I can smell a potential union organizer in disguise the minute he walks in. I have a sense for telling whether a man will or won't join a union when I first see him, and if he is one of them, I send him packing." Apparently, his black-and-white classification worked, for despite whatever shortcomings he may have had as a personnel manager, his bosses were apparently pleased that the plant had never had the faintest murmurings of union organization attempts.

Eddie Rickenbacker, the war hero and racing driver who later became president of Eastern Airlines, reported similar abilities to classify people according to their trustworthiness. If they looked him straight in the eye they could be believed. During World War II, when he was on a technical mission to Russia, he unearthed the amazing fact that the Russians could be trusted, and attempted to transmit this information to President Franklin D. Roosevelt. To his disgust, Roosevelt simply did not give credence to his opinion, and as a result, Eddie reported, we had to go through the entire cold war, which was probably unnecessary.[14]

One of the more bizarre classifications, which has attracted some of the best managers and behavioral scientists, has been a polarized classification of managers according to whether they hold Theory X or Theory Y. First presented by Professor Douglas McGregor of the Massachusetts Institute of Technology at an alumni conference in the fifties, the classification struck a responsive chord in managers everywhere.[15] Theory X is a set of beliefs that suggest that the average person dis-

[14] E. Rickenbacker, *Rickenbacker: A Life* (New York: Dell Pub. Co., Inc., 1969).
[15] D. McGregor, *The Human Side of Enterprise* (New York: McGraw-Hill, 1961).

likes work and avoids it whenever possible, and thus must be directed, coerced, intimidated, or controlled to produce anything useful. Theory Y, on the other hand, assumes that people find work as natural and pleasant as rest or play and, given some goals and a reason for getting there, will be productive and creative without the whippings and scourgings of a boss.

In its vagueness and imprecision, this classification system is marvelous for finding the good guys and the bad guys. Everything good managers do falls into Theory Y, and everything bad managers do falls into Theory X. If a company fails, it is because the managers in it must have held Theory X. If a company grows and makes good profits and its people are productive, socially aware, and responsible, then by definition it must be a Theory Y company. If a manager proves to be extremely tough but the organization does well, the tough boss nonetheless "must have been tough in a Theory Y fashion." Despite the fact that the boss was kindly, rational, and considerate, if the company failed, it is probably because "he or she was *secretly* an X person" who used the facade of kindliness and manners to conceal a basic desire to manipulate people. As an exercise in discussion of the effects of management styles upon employee behavior, this polarizing is extremely useful in displaying the issues. As an exercise in logic, it is lamentably bad.

Numerous other examples could be presented showing how executives polarize things. The danger here is that polarized words are vague and practically invite wrong inferences. They display some of reality while concealing most of it. Words such as *hot* and *cold*, *black* and *white*, *autocratic* and *democratic* have meaning in various degrees. Turning long lines into two points does damage to reality. Forced choices that turn several shades of gray into black and white become meaningless nonsense.

## HOW TO AVOID SEEING THINGS
## THAT AREN'T THERE

From this chamber of horrors, perhaps it might be useful to pick out a few positive steps to avoid these errors of human inference. The steps are already with us in information theory, but haven't always been as well applied in social communication as in physical communication, such as in telephony.

1. *Be sure to clarify the idea before sending it.* When an intent or idea is unclear, it will be sent unclear and received in error. The less the idea is clarified, the more confidence we may have that the listener or receiver will get it wrong.

2. *Encode the message in a form easy to decode.* The vocabulary of the listener or receiver is an important part of the message. If the information is classified in any way, be sure the listener knows how to use the classification system. If a word is being used in some special way not found in the ordinary vocabulary, explain it. If you are adding a new word to the listener's vocabulary, define it. If you are communicating something about a class of things or people, either name them explicitly or define the limits of the class so that wrong people aren't included and right people omitted. If you are defining an event that requires a time frame for correct understanding, frame it between what preceded and what followed. Illustrative

examples of definitions will clarify them, especially if they are apt to be foreign to the receiver. (Talk to a plumber about pipes, not fluid dynamics.) Defining how the object is constructed, naming another object it resembles, and saying what its parts consist of or how it works are all part of the encoding process.

3. *Use media that will reach the sender.* Knowing what channels the sender is attuned to, and which ones he or she has no access to, is part of the attenion-getting process. The transmission medium should have enough pulse strength that the message can get through. This must include a consideration of noise and interference in the system. If you are competing against union officers, the competition, critical government reports, these are ingredients of the medium that must be allowed for.

4. *Estimate the receiver's decoding equipment.* Playing tunes uncoded with exquisite fidelity does not do much if the receiver's equipment is rudimentary, old, and scratchy. The receiver's vocabulary, self-image, attitude toward the sender, and emotional state, as well as the consequences of faithful transmission, constitute *filters* built into the decoding equipment. A clear picture of the decoding capability of the receiver is part of the projection of reality. Our intelligence, prior training, formal education, cultural background, and value systems are the shapers of our decoding equipment.

5. *Obtain feedback.* One of the surest ways of clarifying reality in communication is to obtain steady information from the receiver about what information is being received, what understanding he or she has of that information, what is not being received, and what misunderstanding is obtained. The illusion that communication is an *act* rather than a *process* is an overriding error that distorts meaning and reality. The ridiculous sense of pride that persons in authority sometimes take in being able to assume that they can get through without continuous communication is the producer of numerous misunderstandings. *I am going to tell you all of this just once. . .* is a preface to false inferences.

> *From these illustrations, then, it could be inferred that false inferences go well beyond the statisticians' and logicians' realm, for most false inferences are rooted in social and psychological barriers to reality.*

# ten

# The ideology
# of anti-planning

In the world of politics a common ideological division is made between liberals and conservatives. Liberals, at least in the stereotype, adhere to a strong belief in planning, whereas conservatives do not. In the black-and-white world of political left and political right—which of course consists of various shades of grey in real life—things are very clear. Yet, there is little doubt that liberals are more often advocates of government legislation that imposes plans on societies and even on branches of government. Such central planning impels further planning at lower levels. The only viable response a corporation has when it lives in a world of a politically planned economy is to privately plan more itself.[1]

Once one has moved to the corporation level, however, much of the planning is *defensive planning,* done under compulsion and, even when skillful, done with the utmost reluctance. Even in the most successful corporations, this attention to defensive planning occupies an inordinate amount of time and money. General Motors was reported to have budgeted some $1 billion a year for research in the late seventies, sixty percent of which was devoted to meeting new governmental standards for air emissions, energy consumption, and automotive safety. Research aimed at reducing the weight of the car and at designing restraining devices for passengers and drivers and fuel economy devices was a kind of responsive planning, all done defensively after the company gave due attention to governmental interference with the free enterprise system.

A similar response pattern is shown by all levels of industry and society in general. Central planning requires defensive planning at lower levels. This is all a source of vast irritation and a cause of the anti-planning response on the part of conservatives in society.

[1] A. B. Carroll, *Managing Corporate Social Responsibility* (Boston: Little, Brown, 1977); *see also* "An American Approach to Planning," *Challenge,* 19, no. 6, January 1977.

# THE CONSERVATIVE AS ANTI-PLANNER

The profile of a conservative is not really all that clear, but it is reasonably safe to state that most conservatives are out of sympathy with a government that does too much societal planning. The conservative might be a philosophical type that adheres loftily to the beliefs of Edmund Burke or of a more current political type of the Eisenhower-Goldwater-Nixon-Reagan school. You can probably count on such a person to take a dim view of global governmental planning schemes that produce heavy intervention of government into the lives of the people. Even more important, the conservative opposes government planners' impinging on the decision-making processes of management. Not all conservatives are alike, of course. It therefore requires some definition of terminology and beliefs to identify the various sorts of conservative who are anti-planners upon ideological grounds.[2]

Clinton Rossiter suggests that there are four distinct definitions of conservative, which are also convenient for purposes of identifying levels of anti-planning.[3] The four forms of conservatism Rossiter proposes are *temperamental conservatism, possessive conservatism, practical conservatism,* and *philosophical conservatism.* Since conservatives of the four types all would apparently view planning—and anti-planning—somewhat differently, their viewpoints make a fine takeoff point for seeing the anti-planner in still a clearer perspective.

**The temperamental conservative.** The man who wears a belt and suspenders is a temperamental conservative. He has anticipated awful, embarrassing consequences of a predictable although improbable and even implausible event should there be a failure of a single source of support for his trousers, and he has covered himself against at least one failure that could change for the worse his manner of life, work, and enjoyment and his reputation. The temperamental conservative is quite likely to engage in habitual behavior, and changes are less likely to be quantum leaps or erratic changes. Rather, the conservative person of this breed lives within an activity trap, which is altered only by the slow formation and even slower change of habits. These habits, which bring great pleasure in repeated use, are often a product of past cultural influences to which the person has worked out a satisfactory adjustment. The possibility that a change in that culture might be of sufficient magnitude that it would require some change in habits to adapt anew is hardly something this conservative greets with tumultuous enthusiasm. Some kinds of change require both physical accommodation and, more important, mental effort in untested areas. Such exploration is often frightening in prospect and is therefore to be opposed.

To the temperamental conservative, planning ordinarily does not project a perfect extension of the present; otherwise why bother to plan? Thus, it appears to

---

[2] The most popular at this writing is W. E. Simon, *A Time for Truth,* (New York: Berkley Publishing Corp., 1978).

[3] C. Rossiter, *Conservatism in America: The Thankless Persuasion,* 2nd ed., (New York: Random House, Vintage Books, 1962). Much of this philosophy is also exemplified in B. Goldwater, *The Conscience of a Conservative* (New York: Hillman Books, 1960).

be a technique for upsetting the present arrangement, which is largely suitable. Government planning almost always hold forth unsettling changes for the temperamental conservative. People who now know their place in life will no longer be situated in that comfortable role, but will be demanding new opportunities and new entitlements under new laws. This could turn strengths of the conservative's position into weaknesses and expose him or her to mortifying consequences, including deprivation of property, income, or security. All of this tends to place planning into the category of threat and alienation from a highly satisfactory present.

**The conservatism of the property owner.** It is a common article of faith that the solution to a young man's student radicalism is employment for a good salary and the acquisition of such material things as a house complete with mortgage, a steady paycheck, a car, and perhaps some appliances. Once the advocate of overthrowing the system has been equipped with a garageful of recreational vehicles and equipment, a boat on a lake, and a house beside it where the kids can enjoy themselves during the summer, he views with considerably less jubilation and fervor the idea that radical dream planners of such lofty visions might intervene and diminish the volume and quality of those possessions. Equal employment laws that have a long-range goal of providing special compensatory advantages to minorities and women for their past deprivation could mean that a black, a Chicano, or a woman might get that next raise or promotion which has traditionally been exclusively his entitlement.

Recently, a liberal and outspoken woman advocate of women's rights confessed privately to me that the fervor of her convictions had been diminished somewhat when her four sons, one by one, graduated from college. They discovered that in the field for which they were trained, employers were strongly favoring female candidates, whatever their qualifications, in order to comply with laws against sex discrimination.

This same principle elevated to a larger scale is the basis of the conservatism and the resistance to planning of the factory owner or large stockholder. The government planner often produces schemes that will cost money, thus raising taxes and diminishing wealth.[4] In many ways this produces less accumulation, either through higher costs and hence lower profit, or through cutting off sources of income and revenue, which likewise dries up profit. Lower dividends and a decline in the value of assets bring out anguish, anxiety, frustration, and angry reaction to the plans and their effects. Professional managers who see their rank and accordingly their salaries, bonuses, and perquisites threatened may not find it sensible to merely state their possessive position in such bald terms but rather to couch it in the language of a conservative philosophy (see under "The Global Conservative").

Having substantial possessions that would appear more than ample to most

[4] J. E. Anderson, ed., *Economic Regulatory Policies* (Lexington, Mass.: Lexington Books, 1976); *see also* C. Schultze, *The Public Use of Private Investment* (Washington, D.C.: Brookings Institution, 1977).

people seldom deters the possessive conservative from fervently promoting the firm's property interest. Mobil, in 1978, assumed a more reasonable but nonetheless self-interested plea in its series of advertisements on the editorial pages of the *New York Times* in a series called "The Standstill Economy," which made a sophisticated and complex attack upon inflation through wasteful government spending, which it noted is a result of "chronic expansion of government." Such inflationary behavior on the part of government it termed "the big lie," which diverts funds that might otherwise be invested to increase productivity and create jobs. Incidentally, one might note that such chronic expansion of government also diminishes the growth of assets and earnings of firms such as Mobil, although this was not stated explicitly in the ads. The target of the ads is not only the possible new inflationary government programs, but also those past programs that have already produced inflation. Inflation, then, is clearly seen as a consequence of program plans that add to the cost of government. Planning usually means new programs, which cost more money, a cost shared by all, including the wage earner and small property owner, as well as the corporate owner.[5]

This suggests that possessive conservatism is not to be found solely in the board rooms of corporate giants, for it is apparent that the large labor unions whose members have improved their economic position in the past by higher wages and salaries are equally possessive. The construction worker wearing a hard hat is well known to be opposed to most changes in any form or from any direction that would upset a self-centered state of mind to protect the present level of income and prosperity against erosion from without. The corporation, like the welfare chiseler or the food stamp recipient, shares the possessiveness motive, as do the small group of doctors who become rich on Medicare payments, or even the retired persons whose pension is threatened by inflation or by a decline in the market values of securities in their pension fund. Even at the lowest levels of society, this possessiveness and the desire to protect the smallest advantage over others in a relative sense is readily observed. It makes people possessive conservatives, uneasy about plans that might change things.

Possessions are the basis for status. When planning affects the amount of property one owns or controls, one can quickly imagine the possibilities of decline in standing in the community, in self-worth, and, ultimately, in one's comfort and well-being. Moving to a smaller house, owning a single car rather than two, and being obliged to restrict one's social and cultural activities are thoughts that bring forth the possessiveness that opposes planning of the sort that changes the distribution of property and the ways in which it is acquired, held, and consumed.[6]

**The conservatism of social arrangement**   Resembling closely the adherents to what Rossiter refers to as "practical conservatism" are those adherents to traditional morals, manners, and social structures. Opponents of the widespread use of abortion

[5] H. B. B. Cleveland and W. H. B. Brittain, *The Great Inflation* (Washington, D.C.: National Planning Association, 1976).
[6] E. Z. Friedenberg, *The Disposal of Liberty and Other Industrial Wastes* (New York: Doubleday, 1976).

view with considerable concern changes in the ways in which women function in society. When women can with apparent ease "do their laying about without concern for raising the offspring which might result," it encourages more such immoral shenanigans. Thus states one group. It upsets society, for it provides a relatively easy way of dealing with the crop that comes with sowing what the conservative deems wild oats. People who adhere to such immorality, they suppose, will not be limited to merely this class of immoral action, for all kinds of wrongful behavior can be winked at if this particular evil is permitted to be commonplace.

People, the practical conservative holds, should stick to the tried and true social mores and values, and not suggest loosening those standards, or the entire fabric of the social structure that has afforded conservatives (sound people) many benefits will be threatened.[7] The legal profession fights advertising by other lawyers, not only because it will divert legal fees from the present established lawyers, but because it weakens the fabric of professionalism that has been the basis for building that establishment. The existing community of successful physicians must carefully police any variations from its canons of conduct, lest the structure of the profession topple like a house of cards, incidentally leaving new people atop the restructured professional pile. The feeling of satisfaction and identity that comes with status in society and its subsections is deeply rooted in a kind of tribalism that rejects the stranger as a bearer of change, and possibly as a disruption of what are perfectly comfortable and satisfactory arrangements.

The man who enters the suburban train at an intermediate station and seeks a seat may ask others to move their briefcases and coats to make room for him. He feels entitled to enjoy full-fare rights from his ticket, but is confronted with disgruntlement. The other commuters silently and perhaps with covert glances of discomfort and distaste comply only grudgingly with a disruption of what they feel is their right to the arrangements worked out since the last stop. Once seated, the newcomer will accordingly join the group in glaring sullenly at the boarder at the next station who demands, however quietly, to share the remaining space. An arrangement, once in place and accommodated to, speaks out silently against anyone whose plan calls for some disruption of the status quo.

Even the process of adjustment appears to follow a standard ritual. Once it is learned that the same commuter will board the train every day at the same station and seek out the same seat, a normalization occurs, and curt greetings might even occur, indicating that his entry is now to be treated as an ordinary and even expected event. If the intruder were to commute daily for some time and not show up some morning, this would be a cause of minor concern. "What happened to Jones this morning?" might be asked around.

Older communities such as New England towns are replete with such practical conservators of social arrangements. When the Pyramid Corporation, a shopping mall builder and developer, attempted to construct a mall of seventy stores in a

---

[7] N. W. Chamberlain, *Remaking American Values: Challenge to a Business Society* (New York: Basic Books, 1977). Notes the conservative tendency and proposes that business must lead the change movement.

small town outside Burlington, Vermont, in 1978, the merchants of downtown Burlington successfully resisted with formidable energy and anger this unwanted example of the free enterprise system in action. It would, they pointed out, destroy the existing arrangements of the central business district, and however beneficial it might have been to shoppers in the long run, it was soundly defeated. In Ithaca, New York, the mayor mounted a war against the Pyramid Mall outside his city, going to the extent of visiting the new mall personally after it was built and accosting citizens of Ithaca he recognized, asking them why they were being disloyal to the merchants of the central business district. The attitude that systems and social structures that have been working satisfactorily should be left undisturbed is common in all societies. It is basically hostile to reform, change, and planning that would produce such restructuring of current arrangements.

Not only are social structures the object of this conservatism, but so is the natural environment. Environmental laws essentially conservative in character would preserve the right of even the smallest animal or plant to retain its standing in the world unhampered by the plans of people. A minor flap ensued in New York City in the winter of 1978 when Transportation Secretary Brock Adams engaged in a verbal tiff with the federal Environmental Protection Agency, which had successfully blocked the construction of Westway, a highway designed and planned to rejuvenate the West Side of Manhattan Island. In letters to two senior officials of the Environmental Protection Agency, Adams protested the very successful attempt of Eckardt C. Beck, regional administrator, to block construction of the new superhighway because it would add more automotive pollution to New York's air, as well as disturbing the migration and breeding habits of certain fish in the nearby Hudson River. The Tennessee Valley Authority was likewise halted in constructing the new Tellico dam in the Tennessee Valley because it had been discovered by environmentalists that the project would upset the habitat and perhaps threaten the existence of the snail darter, a tiny species of obscure fish. The snail darter, previously unheard of by almost everybody, became famous for having halted multi-million-dollar construction plans that would have provided electrical energy to the region. In the Hudson Valley, and in southern Utah, power plants were opposed by environmental groups for wholly different reasons: they would disturb the aesthetic configuration and skyline of the area. Thus, pure conservatism dictates that really nothing must be changed, however noble the objective or however pressing the necessity of the plan to a majority of the citizenry of the region. The preservation of Arctic tundra and of streams and the survival of an unheard-of species of toad living within the city limits of Houston all took their places as reasons for opposition to plans and planners, and to that most detestable of creatures, the *developer*, who would not only make plans but also execute them in the face of the practical conservatism of nature.

**The global conservative: The philosophical and radical anti-planner** None of the three brands of conservative described so far are new in history, nor are they unfamiliar in human experience. They are simply behaving in a very human fashion and are prevalent in all societies and times. They are as present in communist as in fascist states, and in democracies as well. The fourth category of conservative, the philosophical-radical conservative, is a cumulation and summary of all of these melded into a system of thought and belief that transcends all of them. Conservatives of this type live in a passionate state of mind that stresses the principles and underlying theories of conservatism rather than their effects. While the behavior that follows is often like that of the practical conservative, there is more to its makeup. Such conservatives may, in fact, have evolved or acquired from education and upbringing such deeply rooted beliefs that they will pursue them *even when their own self-interest might be adversely affected.*

It is easy to understand people who pursue their own selfish interests and are to be faulted only for displaying the normal human condition of greed, which is as widespread now as it has been in the past. It is less likely to be noted that philosophical-radical conservatives are true believers and accordingly will expend money, time, and their own well-being to pursue the conservative ideal.[8] Other brands of conservative often are not conscious of their own conservatism; they are only so labeled in the eyes of beholders. But radical conservatives engage in speculative thought and are consciously radical in their conservatism. They study history and economics and political science to find the essence of what should be preserved. They spend energy and money to preserve and restore traditional things in society, religion, and education.

During the bicentennial year 1976, such radical and traditional conservatives were very likely to be engaged in fund raising to restore old colonial inns and to re-form old colonial military units. They often purchased expensive uniforms resembling those of the Continental army, and probably marched up and down village commons to fife and drum corps resembling those of 1776. In the Western states, the pioneer lore inspires philosophical conservatives to grow beards and raise expensive horses and to parade about reenacting the traditions of the golden past. These displays are, of course, not the essence of philosophical conservatism, for it is argument, historical study, and the statement of principles that are the essence of radical conservatism. For some, such as Robert Welch, the founder of the John Birch Society, the toll in criticism, scorn, and alienation from most of society, as well as the tangible cost of supporting conservative causes, is apparently a small price to pay for relief from the aching belief that restoration of the traditional past is worth whatever price must be paid.

In its more severe forms, this philosophical conservatism emerges as a basis for radical behavior. The underground Minutemen of the fifties stored arms and trained cadres of guerrillas for a war against the tyranny of a socialist government in case one ever came. The Klan and the tiny nazi parties that have sprung up often consist of fanatic conservatives who pay a heavy price in social acceptance and economic well-being to turn their philosophy into action programs. Even the anti-nuclear movements, such as the Clamshell Alliance of Boston, which has engaged in civil disobedience at the site of the Seabrook nuclear reactor in New Hampshire,

---

[8] E. Hoffer, *The True Believer* (New York: Harper & Row, Pub., 1951); *see also* E. Hoffer, *First Things, Last Things* (New York: Harper & Row, Pub., 1967).

are a special brand of radical conservative. They would return us to more conventional energy sources for generating power for our homes and industries. While their bumper stickers proudly proclaim *Split Wood Not Atoms,* they seek a return to colonial means of finding energy.

The conservative probably fits the model of Douglas McGregor's Theory X manager in his or her attitude toward people at large. The average person, to the conservative, is probably corrupt, depraved, lazy, and untrustworthy. This means, of course, that ordinary people are incapable of making proper decisions about their own governance and need a more disciplined, somewhat aristocratic kind of person to provide the goals, methods, discipline and control to make up for that shortcoming. The common people acquired their wickedness and irrationality from heaven, and there really is not much one can do about it but to recognize it, for the explanations of the inner nature of humanity are too deep to plumb. These deficiencies, of course, can be helped by education and some strongly binding customs and traditions, if they are adhered to. Despite these lamentable faults, the individual is a physical and spiritual entity that must be treated as an end rather than a means. People tend to have varying amounts of this base nature, and it is the continuum of the ability to overcome it, from very high among the leaders and aristocrats to almost total absence among the masses, that is the basis of the rightness of aristocratic rule. Humankind, being imperfect and imperfectible, requires a government which is stable, constitutional, and assuring of a rule of the better types.

Property holds a high place in the conservative philosophy, for it is property and its holder that represent the highest order of society. Property makes it possible for fallible beings to be free, to have duties thrust upon them, and is essential to the existence of the family. Property also imposes discipline on people, and ultimately is the main conservative agent. While we all have a right to collect property through subduing our animal instincts, not everyone will demonstrate such self-mastery, but those who do should have the right to be in charge of things. Property, in the mind of the conservative, takes precedence over ideas, imagination, thought, and concepts; and professors and intellectuals are ordinarily to be viewed with considerable suspicion. Religion is somehow to be tied to property, and many conservatives, if they dared, would happily assert that "God has entrusted the rule of industry to a few Christian gentlemen of property."

Reverence for history, property, and God are somehow tied together into a philosophy in the mind of the conservative, which calls for moderation in all things. There are no free lunches, only the fruits of proper thought and action in subduing the flesh and the pursuit of pleasure. The heart of conservative philosophy is to defend the established order and pass it along modified only in the slightest possible way. Because most people in the scheme of things are sinful, weak, and imperfect, they must be reminded of their condition periodically and governed by those trustees of property and religion who have somehow mastered their own passions. The conservative realizes that most people will tend to see the conservative people in charge as mean-spirited, selfish, materialistic, callous, anti-intellectual, antidemocratic, and antihumanistic, but is willing to accept that as a penalty—or a proud badge—to be assumed as a function of leadership in society by the propertied excellent.

All of this produces an aristocracy for whom strident calls for reform and the schemes and plans of the masses are repugnant, and adds up to a revulsion against planning, which usually is an egalitarian and democratic activity designed to produce changes to benefit the masses.

## THE CONSERVATIVE CASE AGAINST PLANNED SOCIETIES

The core of anti-planning scripture for the conservative is probably contained in the writings of Friedrich A. von Hayek, whose *Road to Serfdom* outlined the case against social planning most clearly and explicitly.[9] The anti-planning conservative is not really against planning, but against explicit planning. Planning, in fact, should consist of those private, nongovernmental decisions and opinions of the trustees of property and sobriety, who have demonstrated their right to rule. Whatever the ruling class chooses to do comprises the only form of satisfactory planning, and is implicit in the choice of leadership. The conservative does not dispute the need to make intelligent decisions among alternatives, but is rather adamant as to who should make those decisions.

*Socialism* is the rubric with which all explicit planning by government is labeled by the conservative. If the planning is by a central government agency and directs the organization of our activities according to some conscious blueprint, it is obnoxious to the conservative.[10] For the conservative, the alternative to going down a road to serfdom is to stress the power of competition among freely competing private forces in society. Competition, suggested Hayek, does not simply mean leaving things as they are, but is a means of coordinating human effort. Not only is this freedom seen by Hayek as more effective than centralized or socialistic planning, but it produces another, more desired effect: it permits the individual differences among people to be the basis for the distribution of income and wealth.

This does not, Hayek suggests, mean the elimination of government, but rather calls for a specific kind of legal framework in which the free exercise of individual planning is protected from constraints and suppression by central planning over the market forces. It thus reduces tyranny over the lives and activities of people in the economy and society. The kind of planning Hayek is against mainly is that form of planning that restricts competition, if it does not eliminate it altogether. The mechanism of the price system, unhampered by conscious, central, socialist control, is the implicit plan for control of society by which the advantage of the largest number of people, both economically and socially, will be produced.[11] There is nothing in technology or politics that makes central planning

---

[9] F. von Hayek, *The Road to Serfdom* (Chicago: University of Chicago Press, 1944); *see also* L. von Mises, *Omnipotent Government* (New Haven, Conn.: Yale University Press, 1944).
[10] L. von Mises, *Planned Chaos* (New York: Foundation for Economic Education, Inc., 1947).
[11] M. Friedman, *Price Theory* (Chicago: Aldine, 1976).

necessary and inevitable. Rather, it is the complexity of the division of labor and the large organizations that exist under that division that make the price mechanism and the market mechanisms the only viable method of social control. The common feature of all collectivist planning systems lies in their desire to produce a deliberate organization of the labors of society to achieve a definite social goal.

Such centralized or socialist planning aims at the general good or common welfare, but, Hayek proposes, such planning is antithetical to the very goals the socialist aims at attaining. All-inclusive general goals will inevitably be initiated by saintly idealists who end up being tyrants, says Hayek, for such plans can never comprehend "the infinite variety of different needs of people which compete for available resources."

Such centralized planning works only where there are common goals held by all. Yet there will be delegation to small groups of agency administrators, whose individual wills will be imposed upon the majority. The effect will be the end of democracy and individual freedom, and the serfdom of the many to the few in bureaucratic positions of power.[12] Democracy is not an end in itself, but a means— a device for securing internal peace and individual freedom.

Centralized planning, then, even when democratic in its basis, will supplant the rule of law, which plays an important part in Hayek's scheme of things. The rule of law will define the rules by which competition will occur; it should not replace that competition by centralized direction of particular activities. The rules must be universal rather than particular, and the benefits will be to all rather than to those who have mastered the devices of democratic machinery to their own advantage. Economic control that produces centralized plans is readily subverted into dictatorship and totalitarianism when it supplants the messy if somewhat more efficient mechanism of the market of individual freedom and individual differences.

Thus, the *universal* role of town government in a small New England town would be to plow the streets in winter. Without such a function, the entire citizenry could not function. The *particularistic* role of protecting tenants against landlords, or vice versa, would, in Hayek's scheme of things, not be a legitimate function of government, but should be left to the rigors of the free-market system.

## THE CONSERVATIVE'S VISION OF SOCIETY

When one considers the conservative as a type, it must be the *philosophical conservative* who stands as the archetype and model. It is the vision of society of the philosophical conservative that determines the core content of conservative programs, and all modifications and variations must be from the philosophical extreme.

The planning that is permissible for the conservative rests in the planning which is done by God. Natural law is the implied basis for planning, and it is the normal, unfettered functioning of that natural law that replaces explicit planning.

---

[12] H. Simons, *A Positive Program for Laissez Faire* (Chicago: University of Chicago Press, 1934).

"The socialist government should keep its hands off God's laws!" In the conservative vision, people would operate according to their own self-interests, seeking their own welfare and that of their kin. An "invisible hand" thus lies behind a free economy, its mechanisms working naturally, without conscious regulation, for the good of all. When profits become excessive, new businesses will spring into being to share them, thus creating surpluses of supply, which will drive prices and profits down and so benefit consumers. Wages will rise when there are fewer people in the labor market seeking work, and thus more people will be impelled to enter the labor market, pressing wages down once more, and the cycle will repeat itself. Once wages have fallen below suitable levels, people will move out of their jobs and into more lucrative occupations, and the cycle will continue once more. Interest rates when high will draw more money from consumption into savings and investment until there is too much money available and interest is forced downward. With these three elements all fluctuating about a normal equilibrium level, all other influences of the conservative vision will likewise adapt themselves under this invisible hand.[13]

The only fly in the ointment for the conservative vision is the persistence of liberals in insisting that human interference should take place through the conscious plans of a socialistic government. For the pure conservative, such as Mises or Hayek, even child labor laws and pure food and drug laws are interferences with the vision and are counterproductive to the very goals they seek to attain. Government's role is to maintain the peace, issue currency, and perhaps protect competition from monopoly, and above all to protect the rights of property and the individual. The individual, however, is not to be protected, in the conservative vision, through specific or particular interventions on behalf of specific interest groups. Such groups, it is envisioned, will be better off if they are allowed to suffer the temporary inconvenience of unemployment or bankruptcy in the larger interest of all.

Planning, for the conservative, then, is simply the laissez faire, natural working out of multiple conflicting interests for the greater good of all. Explicit planning is tantamount to and perhaps even synonymous with that repugnant condition: socialism. If the real world of business and government seems most remote from the envisioned world of the conservative, such present reality is hardly important to the truth of the vision. All of the real world adds up to frictions and interferences that have to be reduced and perhaps abolished before the visionary world can hold sway.

The vision of the conservative is most likely, then, to exert its greatest influence and become policy when the impingement of government has gone to such extremes that specific interferences chafe and abrade against the lives and interests of too many citizens.[14] When the state of California in 1978 allowed property taxes to rise to levels that threatened the ownership of most homes, the people of the state overwhelmingly voted into law Proposition 13, which

---

[13] A. Smith, *An Inquiry into the Nature and Causes of the Wealth of Nations* (New York: Modern Library, 1937).

[14] J. Gunther, *Moralists and Managers: Public Interest Movements in America* (New York: Anchor Books, 1976).

reduced allowable levels of property tax to one percent of the value of the property. This created shock waves, not only in California, but in dozens of other states and in the federal government. A conservative wave of cost reduction in government and the elimination of many regulations and constraints upon industry and taxpayers became politically popular. President Carter budgeted substantial reductions in social programs aimed at assisting specific groups such as the old, the unemployed, and the ill in a wave which was popularly described as a "resurgence of conservatism." For the visionary conservative, however, such a movement was only the beginning. Not only were budgets to be reduced; but specific interferences in management decision making and regulations promoting the environment, safety, consumer protection, and affirmative action, all of which were past liberal successes, now seemed to be threatened or diminished by the vision of the conservative.

## THE SPECIAL CONSERVATISM OF
## THE PROFESSIONAL MANAGER

The meetings of the Business Round Table or other high-level corporate executive groups ordinarily are supposed to be a clustering of conservatives. Yet, in a world where business and government are often partners in managing the economy's affairs, the conservatism of the corporate giant takes a special shape. Rather than an ideological conservatism in action, the corporate planner relies most heavily upon a *conservatism of adaptiveness*. Lenin is reported to have said that if communism were to come and all businessmen were to be ordered hanged, there would be vigorous bidding on the part of business for the rope contract. Whether or not this grisly comment is true, it contains a germ of wisdom in understanding the conservatism of adaptiveness.

Professor Sidney Sufrin suggests that when devices are used to regulate or influence industry, the firm's decision-making processes will adapt to consider governmental constraints in a new light. The market is changed; the firm adjusts. If a minimum wage law is passed, that will be programmed into labor cost calculation and prices adjusted accordingly. The added cost will be borne by consumers. This conservatism of adaptiveness simply means that the firm now must engage in more sophisticated managerial planning practices: (1) It must scan the environment more regularly and systematically to discover what kinds of interferences might obstruct the invisible hand, and, even better, to forecast which ones are likely to occur. (2) It must adapt its practices to allow all of the mechanisms of the free market to suit the new guidelines imposed for social purposes. In such a system, government intervention has about the same effect as the cycle of rain and drought has on a farmer, or the sickness of a beast of burden on a peasant: it is simply a constraint having the same effect as a natural law that varies statistically or predictably within limits.

For the more progressive and skillful corporate management, such environmental scanning can take on the characteristics of a business advantage when the company is more imaginative than its competitors. Although it was denied by many automobile company executives, Ralph Nader has cited a variant of the

Leninist prediction: When automobiles were ordered recalled for quality defects under government laws, the automobile companies responded by vigorous sales efforts to sell added services to those owners who brought their cars back to the dealer for the legally required corrections. Statistics of automotive recalls for defects during 1977 revealed that of over 300 recalls, but ten percent of them were actually directed by the automotive safety agency in charge. The others were voluntary on the part of the automobile companies. Certainly much of this may have been in anticipation of mandatory recalls, but perhaps much of the voluntary nature of those recalls was due to the fact that both service sales and periodic service visits by owners are considerably higher for those cars that are recalled. One auto dealer said, "I really find that the recalls have had a good effect on my service department's sales volume. I even try to sell the people a new car once I get them back for a recall under the auto safety law. After all, the recall expense is paid for by the corporate warranty, but the service profit which I can make on top of it is for me."

The Occupational Safety and Health Act (OSHA) of the seventies produced some stringent and often irritating inspections of factories aimed at reducing occupational injuries. This would be a clear example of the kind of interference the philosophical conservative would label socialistic. It subverts the pure and untrammeled function of the free market. Yet the electrical supply and component industry quickly seized upon OSHA as a means of enlarging sales and profits in new safety devices, modified forms of old components, and systems newly engineered to comply with the law. The Environmental Protection Act produced a similar effect. When Kennecott Copper was obliged to engineer and install elaborate air scrubbers on chimneys at its smelters, manufacturers of air scrubbers seized on its misfortune as a business opportunity to be exploited. Water pollution laws produced business in pollution control, which grew in assets and sales by producing filters, sluice gates, and processing plants to clean polluted water. Tax laws produce not only government revenue but also tax lawyers. Company practices quickly modify the ordinary ways of adaptation to nature to maximize advantages to the firm. The firm then is invited by adaptive conservatism to guess the shape of the future when the government permits alternatives in policies such as depreciation policy, consumer protection laws, or employment regulations.[15]

In this sense, the firm that has learned to adapt successfully has acquired a stake in government regulation, and its ability and desire to adopt a conservative mode or vision lies more in the predictability of that regulation than in its existence, or even its absolute amount. When the government—socialist or democratic—intervenes into what is described as free enterprise, it does so with no special harm and damage to the corporate firm if it is consistent, holds to a steady course, and does not make its changes willfully and capriciously with respect to individual firms. In such instances of intervention, the government behaves under what Hayek himself would have to identify as the rule of law. When it is first imposed, the law govern-

[15]P. N. Bloom and L. W. Stern, "The Emergence of Anti Industrialism," *Business Horizons*, 19, no. 5, October 1976.

ing the entire market may be shocking and painful to some. Once in place, it becomes an environmental constraint to be noted and adapted to.

The case is somewhat less lucid and simple where the intervention of government takes place on behalf of particular groups. Affirmative action laws that intervene in favor of women or minorities will not fall evenly upon all employers; millions of tiny firms are usually exempt. Nor does antitrust law have any effect whatsoever upon the millions of small firms that have no significant impact upon the total supply or demand in a market, but only on the very largest. The heartily hoped-for ideal of adaptive conservatism is equality of treatment, but this is only meaningful where there is equality in fact. As the French aphorism goes, "The law in its majesty prohibits the rich and the poor alike from sleeping under bridges," illustrating how equal laws equally applied will rest unequally upon firms that are not equal. Yet even here, within each industry, adaptive conservatism means that the resistance to change is in actuality resistance to *new change,* and not a trend toward pristine philosophical conservatism.

**How adaptive planning preempts innovation** When a large corporation spends forty percent of its research funds on adaptive, or defensive, research and planning, it has shifted emphasis away from innovation and invention. The flow of patents for defensive research will increase while the number of those for genuine innovation will level off and perhaps decline.[16] Strategic planning and strategic management during the eighties will probably follow the patterns laid down by such leaders as General Electric during the seventies. There, in that electrical giant, "strategic business units" (SBU's) were created for every cluster within the corporation that comprised a "business." Such businesses as medical electronics and other product and market clusters were intensively analyzed. From such studies came some definite new strategies that changed the character and direction of the business. Yet, the most brilliant achievements of the SBU's were often in their mechanisms and systems for scanning the environment in which the business would operate. This environmental scanning came up most often with pictures of strengths, weaknesses, problems, threats, risks, and opportunities. The opportunity-management outcomes were far less likely to come out of such a scheme, however. More likely it would produce the triumph of strategic planning, a list of businesses that should be abandoned. Appliances, computers, and components all fell to the abandonment emphasis of strategic planning.

Admittedly, this preventive abandonment was made necessary by forthcoming changes, but it likewise fed on itself. New heroes of planning emerged whose insights into what should be abandoned then produced people whose expertise lay in creative methods of abandonment.[17] Once such skills of abandonment were developed, it became necessary to find a steady stream of projects and studies that required them. The inventive engineer and the creative scientist thus were accorded a formidable set of barriers through which an invention had to go before it could

---

[16]L. S. Robertson, "The Great Seat Belt Flop," *Journal of Communication,* 26, no. 1, Autumn 1976. Details the failure of government-enforced innovation.

[17]G. S. Odiorne, "Seventeen Ways to Abandon a Business," *Management Review,* 1978.

prove itself a viable commercial product; they were in a race for prestige with strategic planning, and most of the time the innovative idea lost.

## ANTIDOTES TO CONSERVATISM

When you find the barriers to change, progress, and planned progress in any of the four brands of ideological conservative just described, you can either confront the conservatives or cooperate with them to get them around to your way. The willingness to compromise with and to outwit opponents to change has been demonstrated most effectively in such cases. Here are the ways of dealing with each of the types:

1. Dealing with *temperamental conservatives* is hardly worth the effort of attempting persuasion, especially if they are along in years. Rather, it is best to work hard at lining up your votes to get your own side in agreement and confront the opposition. Nothing you can do will change the temperamental conservative viewpoint that no form of change is worthwhile, and the view that planning is probably applied socialism or communism of the most rampant sort. After a few sorties just to test the true mettle of the temperamental conservative, once you have determined that conservatism is deep-rooted, it is best to start surrounding, isolating, and overwhelming your opponents with a majority opinion. There are, it seems, some who will never accept change. Get the votes lined up and isolate them. They are a small minority.

2. Dealing the *property-ownership–based conservatives* is really quite easy if you put on your thinking cap. Show that the proposed change will probably benefit them in some tangible way. Point out opportunities to be exploited in the change, profits to be gained, and losses to be reduced.

3. Dealing with *conservatives of social standing* is best done by demonstrating that their social standing might be enhanced by the change and not reduced. If an ecology-based group is protesting a development project, hire some ecologists and use them as advisers. They then become part of the planning of the project and an important element in shaping its direction. This meets not only the needs of the environment, but also those of the ecologists. If people protest because they see an incipient threat to their present status, show how the new events can actually be employed to enhance their standing in their own eyes and others'.

4. *The global or philosophical anti-planner* is usually more highly educated and is perhaps engaged in work that requires powers of the mind. Such people are prone to talk incessantly and argue endlessly and are subject to compromise and logic rather than persuasion by power or money. It is disastrous to attempt to move such persons by offering them financial rewards, for they often hold their present views at the expense of their own pocketbooks. Here, the approach should be:

  a. Listen to their arguments and make sure they are really philosophical or radical conservatives.
  b. Engage your own philosophers or logicians to take them on in a verbal and mental argument.

c. Isolate both groups from the main decisions, by forming them into seminars off to the side on some mountain, where they will chatter on soberly and incessantly.

d. Make every effort to get their arguments turned toward more esoteric and arcane bases, which will immediately cause them to be lost to the population at large and from the decision-making process.

e. Encourage the philosophers to talk to one another rather than to the world at large, a preoccupation which they are readily prone to accept.

5. The *conservative professional manager* is perhaps the easiest of all of the ideologies to deal with, for such conservatives have rank and status to lose, and opportunities for gains in those areas. The antidote for such conservatism is in establishing high goals that call for growth, and withholding rewards for failure to produce growth, change, and systematic improvement. Give them a goal and ask for a plan for getting there. Give them a reason for moving and a reason for not standing still. Promote to high ranks only those who have a demonstrated commitment to planned change, and leave behind or demote those who have an affinity for maintaining the status quo. Build your reward systems to pay off handsomely for those who take risks and succeed. Such things as pay, bonuses, promotional criteria, performance appraisal forms, management development courses, coaching, and recognition all should be geared toward moving upward the innovator and the person who makes things happen. The rest should remain in the lower ranks.

# eleven

# How chronic childhood reinforces anti-planning

One of the more common reasons planning for orderly change is unpopular is that so many people have never left childhood or adolescence behind to become adults. Planning is a general characteristic of adult behavior. We deposit money in a bank with the expectation that it will be there when we come back to take it out. We plant a seed with the expectation that a flower or a cabbage will grow. We buy insurance policies to provide security for events that we do not really know will happen, but which, if they should, we will want to be prepared for. We expect and hope that the sun will come up in the east tomorrow, as it always has before.

Normal children do not have to worry about the future, for they are protected and buttressed against thinking about it. During their formative years, they engage mainly in receiving support from older people, and in play. Play is a common kind of childlike behavior in which the child experiments with adult skills, develops adult tools, finds adult purposes. Just as young kittens affect ferocious combat in their play, the young child uses play to develop skills. The games of war and soldiers played by the six-year-old were often noted by combat soldiers later in life as the arena in which their best skills in soldiering were devised and shaped. General Douglas MacArthur once noted that on the playing fields of West Point the skills and habits were developed that would protect the nation's safety in war on other fields at other times.

When Tom Sawyer was caught playing hookey by Aunt Polly, he was punished by being assigned the dreadful task of whitewashing a fence on Saturday morning. As Mark Twain wrote in his immortal novel of boyhood, Tom did not face the prospect with much relish. As one of his companions approached to jeer at his sad fate, a burst of cunning overtook the unfortunate Tom. "How often," he asked, "does a boy get to whitewash a fence?" He artfully applied a few deft strokes of the whitewash to the fence. His erstwhile tormentor was intrigued. Shortly he pleaded with Tom for a chance to try his hand at whitewashing. Tom quickly rejected this idea. After all, this was an important fence, and Aunt Polly was most particular about it. In a spasm of frustration his friend now offered to give Tom a

153

small, token gift for the privilege. Reluctantly Tom acceded to this bribe. Soon, other boys came along and were accorded the same treatment. By noon the entire fence was sparkling with three coats of whitewash, and Tom, seated in the shade, was proud owner of countless treasures, including a jackknife, a dead cat, and similar valuables. Twain noted that if he had not run out of whitewash, he would soon have cleaned out the entire stock of valuables owned by every boy in town. Naturally, Aunt Polly was pleased and amazed at Tom's new-found maturity and the job he had done on her fence.

This childhood episode, in which Tom applied the skills of negotiation and delegation of responsibility, undoubtedly was a forerunner of the many times in later life when Tom would demonstrate the leadership skill of delegation.

Playful behavior is where many of life's skills, as well as the tendencies of motivation in later life, are shaped. The use of toys that are manageable by the child creates images of a future that will be manageable. The representational play of cowboys and Indians, cops and robbers, good guys and bad guys is a kind of make-believe in which feelings are imprinted for life. Underlying the period of play is a knowledge that fear, conflict, and danger are being fended off by parents and do not really exist. The reversion to play carries with it a kind of *implicit planning,* which makes explicit planning both undesirable and unnecessary. One wag noted that the only difference between men and boys is the size and cost of their toys. The computer and data processing executive is an irrepressible toy buyer and toy user. The soldier and the police officer are enmeshed in a grown-up game of war or cops and robbers. Mothers sometimes play house when they grow up, only this time with real babies. Engineers build real bridges instead of Tinkertoys or Erector Sets. The father and child who battle in deadly seriousness over who will have access to the model trains, or the electronic computer games played on the TV set, live at the same level. Dad demonstrates both at home and at work that the play stage of development does not disappear as years advance.[1]

Much corporate and governmental planning is game playing because of the unwillingness of adults to drop their game-playing behavior and preconceptions. A ready repertoire of juvenile skills is in hand for most situations and will be employed, even where a more rational, orderly, innovative kind of planned behavior would be better suited to the situation. War, politics, industry, to some extent, all become such games.

## THE TOY MAKERS AS PLANNERS, OR THE TROUBLE WITH ENGINEERS

As the research study described in Chapter 3 indicates, we really are not all that troubled by change if the change is technical or mechanical. Social change, on the other hand, comes less easily. We like superhighways, electronic computers and cal-

---

[1] The seriousness of games is noted in J. von Neumann and O. Morgenstern, *Theory of Games and Economic Behavior* (Princeton, N.J.: Princeton University Press, 1944), and numerous other works that followed this germinal work.

culators, jet airplanes, and modern fertilizers. We especially like those changes that seem to produce quantum leaps in our physical life style. When the managers of a utility company like the one described in Chapter 1 start their course of development in nuclear power, they are almost unanimously applauded. Their satisfaction is great. They may have $400 million to spend on new toys, for which they receive much praise and reinforcement. Nuclear energy seems to hold forth a new kind of mastery and success.

Indeed, much if not most professional planning in this country and in Russia has been centered around toys. The building of a new dam is often nothing more than an enlargement of blocking up a stream in the street outside one's house after a large rainstorm when one is seven years old. Floating a matchstick or two down the stream, piling snow or mud to divert the stream, and packing it with debris to form a small lake becomes Grand Coulee, Aswan, or Tellico. Planning for public utilities has almost always been centered in the engineering department, with the financial people assisting by finding the funds to pay for the toys. Town and city planners have been designers of roads and streets or sewage plants for the most part, carrying on their childhood pleasures of making new ruts in the dirt with play cars and trucks.

Finding housing for poor people has all too often consisted of tearing down old houses and having unlimited money to build new ones in their place. The pleasures of destruction are dealt with in Chapter 12, but it is part and parcel of the toy maker and toy player's satisfaction. Urban development means building a sand house at the ocean's edge while being able to watch the seas wash older houses away. For the builder who can combine construction of the new with destruction of the old, work echoes the pleasures of childish play on a grander scale.

The puzzling part of it all for the engineer-planner comes when people interfere in ways totally outside the logic of the toy maker and toy user.[2] The blacks who were residents in the older housing grumble at the tearing down of their old neighborhood and the breaking up of the existing social structure. Environmental advocates protest the possible damage to their oceans or rivers or air from nuclear power or large dams. People who have not been consulted over the unintended side effects of the toy-centered games insist that the games are wrong and foolish because they were not consulted. Of course they were not consulted! They are not even engineers, so how could they have the experts' knowledge of toys? Such concepts are foreign and hostile to the technical changes the technical planners produce and therefore do not even exist in their plans.

Margaret Mead once accompanied a team of agricultural engineers to Greece to observe them in studying and producing a plan for improved agricultural production for that country. The engineers mapped out logical plans as if playing in a giant sandbox, diverting streams and collecting tiny peasant plots into manageable farming plots where modern agricultural machinery could be employed. Mead studied

[2]W. W. Miller, C. T. K. Ching, and G. N. Benesch, "Framework for Making Resource Use Decisions: An Application to Subdivision Development," *Long Range Planning,* 11, no. 1, February 1978. Shows the full range of influences needed in such decisions.

the social and cultural arrangements of family, religion, birth, death, and marriage. To impose the engineering scheme of things upon the nation would have required moving a cemetery or two, breaking up plots old men had set aside as dowry land for their unmarried daughters, eliminating a haunted swamp where ancestors hung out as spirits, and undoing the domain of a druid priest and his court. The highly efficient plan was of course never used. It would have required overcoming some Gods, graves, ghosts, magic brooks, and dowrys, which are not part of the toy-play behavior of engineers.

The point, of course, does not have anything to do with Greece, or agriculture. Rather, it suggests that planning for change that interferes with culture is childlike. Many a town or city has struggled along for years with an inefficient road system or traffic pattern because of traditions and superstitions that were firmly implanted.[3]

In one Central American nation, the Agency for International Development (AID) found that industrial growth was inhibited by poorly designed and archaic traffic flows in the main cities. The agency engineers reverted to their sandboxes with play toys and laid out the most efficient traffic flow plan possible. In its construction, they would have wiped out or rearranged several city squares, in each of which was standing a statue of a local hero, a founder, or a long-dead priest or folk hero. The traffic plan, of course, never left the drawing board in the ensuing cultural uproar. The engineers threw up their hands in despair at the ignorance of the people who were so emotionally attached to error in their opposition to the toy players and sandbox experts.

## OUR CHRONIC CHILDHOOD AS A
## BASIS FOR ANTI-PLANNING

Long after we have grown up and have experienced dozens or hundreds of new beginnings as adults, echoes of childhood continue to dominate us. Sober bourbons and mandarins, judges and potentates, moguls and managers revert to adolescence and beyond. A convention of lawyers, or of executives, will produce some behavior that is clearly regressive to an earlier time in life when play was the dominant concern. When this occurs, attention to such adult behavior as thinking, planning, making blueprints, and bringing about orderly change is not only set aside but is probably also stoutly resisted. It is the child in all of us that helps the anti-planning tendency remain strong.

## THE CYCLE OF OUR LIVES

Growing up is no cinch, especially when traditional kinds of adjustment to the process are changing. This is hardly news. The book of Ecclesiastes admonished people

---

[3] M. Mead, *Cultural Patterns and Technological Change* (New York: Mentor Books, 1955).

several thousand years ago of the changing stages of life. There is, the preacher intoned, "a time to be born, and a time to die." The gist of the message was that time produces changes and people must adapt to those stages of change. Saint Paul wrote to the Corinthians, "When I was a child, I spake as a child, . . . I thought as a child; but when I became a man, I put away childish things." Terrific advice, no doubt, but apparently not easy to do when technological invention is making old cultures shake, when a worldwide revolution in moral values makes the family less stable, and when women move out of the home into the marketplace. As a result, a rash of books dealing with the stages of growth have emerged in recent years. Having found an exposed nerve ending, such books as Gail Sheehy's *Passages* and Roger Gould's *Transformations* have raced to the top of best seller lists. Erik Erikson's term *identity crisis* has impelled people to see themselves on every page of such works. All of these books share the idea that the customary, normal discomfiture of moving from childhood to adolescence and then to adulthood and so on to old age is now worse. They all point out that external changes in values and in social influences have made such passages, transformations, and growth in ego strength tougher for more people.

As people become unable to make the adjustments to such shattering changes, the transformations to adulthood no longer take place neatly, and even professionally competent technicians remain childlike in the emotional conditions governing their life and outlook. Husbands and wives fail to bring adult behavior to the marriage state and behave like children, with a resultant escalation in divorce. By the end of the seventies, more people than ever were avoiding marriage and its required sacrifice. Plans often call for strength and lasting power in home life, work, or civic responsibility. In aging chronologically, people do not age as well in human strength, and mature people are not mature any more. In a world where more and more such eternally childlike people occupy adult positions in society, planning and the attendant change is one of the casualties. Not the only one, but for the purpose of this book an important one.

## THE FOUNTAIN OF YOUTH
## AND HOW IT IS DISCOVERED

When Freud theorized that our personalities consist of a conscious and an unconscious, it was the powerful existence of the unconscious basis of our behavior that struck a responsive chord in many. The content of the unconscious, which was used first in therapy for the mentally disturbed, became the basis of psychotherapy and psychoanalysis. Freud proposed that the unconscious was only to be probed by persons trained in helping people to see back into their own childhood and infancy, where much of the adult personality was shaped. People lay on their analyst's couches and spilled forth the childhood events and traumas that led them to problems in later life. Their defenses, or lack of them, against life's attacks real or imaginary could be reconstructed if this childhood and infantile influence could be brought to the surface and explained and mastered.

While much of the profession of psychiatry turned from the details of Freudian methods in mid-century, a Canadian physiologist discovered that there was indeed some basis for the idea that *childhood ego states* were retained in the brains of all humans.[4] By physical means, early childhood memories long forgotten could be triggered and elicited and reproduced with considerable faithfulness. This research suggested to psychoanalyst Eric Berne that there are three ego states that come into being as humans transact with one another: the child, the parent, and the adult.[5] The *child* state is an ever-present and available condition to which normal people revert simply because they have never lost it. Likewise, they retain a *parental* state, said Berne, in which they are able to reproduce the admonishments and actions of parents or similar authority figures from their past. As Erik Erikson put it,

*Every new beginning in later life and every new attachment and involvement reverberates in the childhood strata of our images and our affects where all kings and leaders are Fathers or big brothers and all countries and ideas, Mothers.*[6]

The child state, Berne suggested, is characterized in two ways. One way is a natural childishness, involving such things as love, life at an emotional level, dependence upon others for everything, and a need to be directed and judged constantly by older people such as mothers and fathers, teachers, and police. The other is the state of the adaptive child, who has learned that most of the nurturing mechanisms of society, including the family and the adult world in general, are geared to protecting, training, and taking care of its offspring. Growth into adulthood is based upon protection for many years by the layers of successive life stages, each giving the child a stipulated role to play, and all roles enacted in an organized setting. For the infant or the adolescent, this assigned role is to grow competent in some life skills, and to acquire confidence that many decisions for the future will be taken care of without any effort on the part of the child. The child trusts that mother and father will feed it and provide barriers against the world. The expectation that father will bring home the bacon, and that the child need accept no responsibility for hustling about for a meal or clothes or a bed, is socially normal.

Faith in the future is based on a past, and on a childhood lived without concern for the means of support or even a knowledge of danger and deprivation.

Erik Erikson, perhaps the paterfamilias of the modern school of development theory for humans, has illustrated the difficulties of growing from childhood to adulthood in a normal fashion as shown in the following chart:[7]

---

[4] W. Penfield, "Memory Mechanisms," *AMA Archives of Neurology and Psychiatry*, 67, 1952.

[5] E. Berne, *Games People Play* (New York: Grove Press, 1964).

[6] E. Erikson, *Life History and the Historical Moment* (New York: W. W. Norton & Co., Inc., 1975).

[7] Illustration is reproduced from *Insight and Responsibility* by Erik H. Erikson, by permission of W. W. Norton & Company, Inc. Copyright © 1964 by Erik H. Erikson.

| | | | |
|---|---|---|---|
| Stage C | Childlike Adult | Adolescent Adult | Adult Adult |
| Stage B | Childlike Adolescent | Adolescent Adolescent | Adult Adolescent |
| Stage A | Childlike Child | Adolescent Child | Adult Child |

The normal growth of a human to adulthood would proceed as follows:

- Stage A. *The childlike child* is the baby who cries when hungry, screams when deprived of anything, and acts in a similarly childlike fashion, which is perfectly normal in a child.
- Stage B. *The adolescent adolescent* behaves like an adolescent when he or she is adolescent. Attainment of genitalia, the physical changes of puberty, and all that goes with being an adolescent are normal.
- Stage C. *The adult adult* is the ultimate stage of development for the growing human organism. We grow up and behave in an adult fashion when we are in fact adult.

The problem in managing change in a planned fashion is in the number of variations possible on this normal pattern. There are six possible departures from these normal stages A, B, and C.

1. *The childlike adolescent* does not become a practicing adolescent in due course but retains childlike behavior, wetting the bed, engaging in tantrums, refusing to clean his or her room, and bullying everyone around, especially adults, and otherwise acting spoiled. This is the familiar "brat."

2. *The childlike adult* in its simplest form is the older person who engages in adult tantrums, throws things about, fouls his or her environment, and willfully destroys. In such a state excessive selfishness and egotism emerge. In a more acceptable and manageable form this is the naive and technically competent but irresponsible professional and can be a scientist, an engineer, a general, or an autocratic boss. This figure is an important anti-planner and change resister.

3. *The adolescent adult* is a more familiar and often admired figure. The male is apt to be playful, prankish, and sexually aggressive; and the female is likely to be girlish and to engage in surprising, charming, good-natured, and jubilantly happy overt behavior, which may be strategically designed to exploit. The beguiling smile of the tyrant, the use of coyness, and the frequent use of the sheep eyes that once

swept mother's disfavor into the dustbin are common practices here. The adolescent adult male often seeks to simulate the physical attributes of the teenaged male. The fifty-year-old who affects the manner of the superjock and who wears the clothes and hair style of high-schoolers is in this adolescent adult category.

These three forms of adjustment are clearly recognizable and are sufficiently familiar that they must be considered normal forms of maladjustment for most of us, albeit a source of some anxieties. There are indeed useful and even socially necessary times for such diverted forms of adjustment to growth. The charismatic leader is often successful because of his or her adolescent adulthood.

The next three variants I see upon Erikson's growth stages are more likely to be considered favorably than unfavorably by those surrounding the person.

4. *The adolescent child* is somewhat precocious. Advanced in learning skills, naturally enthusiastic rather than suppressed, more emotional at a deeper level than children ordinarily are, more advanced in competence or physique, or perhaps generally brooding and unchildlike, such a child can be a source of both pleasure and dismay.

5. *The adult child* is abnormally advanced and is loved by his or her parents. The child genius, the precocious and exceptional child, usually is discovered early because of some exceptional mental and learning capability. Ability to do advanced math, to engage in extraordinary mental gymnastics, and to show astonishing feats of memory are ordinarily the first recognizable symptoms. The child genius who finishes Harvard or Yale at age twelve or performs some similar, abnormally early accomplishment has been reasonably well studied, is admired more than understood, and is sufficiently rare in fact as to be a small possibility.

6. *The adult adolescent* is apt to be widely admired by parents, teachers, and other parental figures. This is the adolescent who has chosen a career at age thirteen, whose purposes are well in hand, and whose mien and demeanor remind one of little old men and women. Youths of this sort are sensible, informed, and reasonable adolescents, who, by definition, are rare.

## THE GADGET MAKERS: THE GROWTH OF THE SKILLED BARBARIANS

Most of the mechanisms for recognizing the prematurely adult human focus on some kind of technical precocity. An unusual ability to master mathematics is perhaps the most common trait. Few child geniuses, for example, are given that designation by adults for their performance in the social sciences. The idea of a six-year-old who developed a new theory of political economy, or a new economic model for preventing inflation, would on its face be absurd, and such a child's theory, if produced, would be ignored. The amount of verbal, social, and cultural background needed would require *time,* which is not yet available to the precocious young. Thus, recognized precocity can emerge only where phenomenal memory, exceptional ability to calculate, or astounding ways of manipulating memories become the coinage of the latent genius. The five-year-old who performs new feats of logic in calculus is apt to be quickly identified as advanced above his or her peers.

This *adult child* indeed often continues this precocity in the technical and quantitative area, but is less often likely to show a correspondingly balanced advancement in social and behavioral skills. Several studies following up on child geniuses of yesteryear found that they were quite likely to have ended up as fairly normal adults, few having attained exceptional social rank and attainment. More likely they became competent doctors, engineers, or teachers, and in that role were hardly the standouts they had been as exceptional children. A more common pattern was to follow the growth pattern from *adult child* to *adult adolescent* to a long run as a *childlike adult.* Having enjoyed prestige and acclaim as children for being different, as adults they cultivated their individual differences without veering from the technical or mathematical-scientific areas that had brought them favorable attention. As a result, in maturity they often became childlike in social and cultural skills, in the political arts, and in the cultivation of the common touch that gives a sense of what the mass of people of lesser talent think and feel.

The engineer at work and in society may become a skilled barbarian, a member of an elitist group that hits other people over the head with their own incapacities to do technical thinking.[8] Managers of engineering departments and scientific labs, and college deans are well acquainted with the troubles in managing organizations of such individuals. The Industrial Revolution was built on mechanization, and the postindustrial society is often dependent on the scientist, the knowledge worker, and the professor. The world in which such intellectuals live is peopled by those who are like themselves in intellect—most especially persons of quantitative intelligence. All others they deem lesser beings who need to have decisions made for them. The hierarchy of science is quite clearly demarcated into pure scientists, who are of the highest order, engineers, who are converters of pure technical knowledge into useful and beautiful objects, and that most detestable type: laymen. Laymen are those people who are concerned with love and hate, politics, social structures, and self-indulgence.

Change—and the planning for change—accordingly is pursued most strongly by the technical person in technical areas of invention, discovery, and development. Thus, early childhood continues its grip, and a persuasive case could be made that most planning for change emanates from the technical changes of a technical elite. Social planning, to this group, is unnecessary, for the other kinds of people are volitional victims.

## THE VOLITIONAL VICTIM, OR HOW "HELPING" ORGANIZATIONS BLAME THEIR VICTIMS

While the man who is a victim of crime seldom blames himself for his plight, the police force is less charitable. The study of victims shows that many of them are

[8] G. S. Odiorne, "The Trouble with Engineers," *Harper's,* April 1953.

repeaters, and police often rationalize crimes upon persons by blaming the victims. If the woman had only stayed out of that hazardous neighborhood at night she would never have been attacked. If the man had not been drunk, or pumped full of drugs, he would never have been robbed. Thus, people become volitional victims, and many of the misfortunes people suffer are volitional misfortunes. Social workers and teachers share this propensity to blame the victim, as William Ryan has pointed out in his book *Blaming the Victim.*[9] To Ryan, victims are held responsible for their own plight by those who design the system to *help the victims* but who do not incorporate measures in their planning to remedy the victims and release them.

The effect is to perpetuate the kind of behavior that creates victimized classes. The schoolteacher and the school administrator who blame the bad school system and the failure of pupils to learn in ghetto schools upon the home environment of the students operate a school that does the planning of the students' lives. School lunches, a stern system of control and welfare-mindedness, serve to perpetuate the childlike notions of the victims that indeed there is some kind of master plan in which their role of victim has been masterminded and provided for. The kid from the South Bronx who knows no father and whose mother is shiftless and perhaps immoral must be managed by an organization designed to care for the children of the shiftless and immoral. Such social workers, welfare teams, drug control units, and crime squads start with the assumption that there is no way such people can be taught to plan, or can be allowed to participate in plans that will emancipate them from their plight. The operating role of such helping units, thus, is to do remedial personal life planning for the victims, not to train them in how to plan escape routes, or to teach them how not to be victims.

The ideal victim, then, becomes one who is passive, dependent, and grateful for the remedial services and protection. In effect, the helping institutions and professionals seek to work their way upon the deserving poor and afflicted, and to withhold their help, controls, and plans from the undeserving poor and the ungrateful victimized clients. The mechanisms of welfare and corporate discipline work in much the same way to make the people in their control passive and dependent, which Chris Argyris equates with preventing them from ever attaining maturity. Starting with the assumption that adults in this clientele are really childlike adults or at best adolescent adults, the systems are exquisitely tooled to deal with childlike and adolescent clients. This, in turn, creates and reinforces in a hundred ways the tendency of people to retain their childlike behavior in order to cope. Planning is punished and accordingly disappears.

Blaming the victim extends beyond the poor and socially deprived, however. Corporations with executive development programs almost universally adhere to the principle that "all management development is self-development."[10] Those who respond poorly to such a theorem are, of course, volitional victims; they have failed to pay the price, lack the capacity, or otherwise are deficient in what the more suc-

[9] W. Ryan, *Blaming the Victim* (New York: Random House, Vintage Books, 1972; revised 1976).

[10] E. Schein, *Career Dynamics: Matching Individual and Organizational Needs* (Reading, Mass.: Addison-Wesley, 1978).

cessful have seized upon as opportunity. Mature managers, according to such a principle, are supposed to be able to work simultaneously at two levels, by learning:

1. How to develop enough ego strength to try to manipulate their social environment, at the same time the social environment is rewarding passive compliance and lower ego strength
2. How to engage in the kind of social planning for the organization that will produce compliance and conformity to organizational goals in its members

The result is that organizations all tend to report sadly that too many of their fifty-year-old middle managers are largely deadwood. They are volitional victims of their own inability to develop themselves at the same time they develop organizational leadership skills. People so labeled no longer seek out the meaningful experiences they have been persistently denied in the past. No longer able to find mentors who will help them through the maze that has been planned so expertly, they no longer become mentors for others. They become what Eric Hoffer calls misfits. They lose face, lose friendships, and are apt to be depressed, feeling trapped or feeling foolish for having trusted the organization's high promises. This is the definition of the "career crises" so beloved of those who blame the victims.

**God takes care of fools, drunkards, and little babies** The main recourse for most people, then, becomes one of throwing themselves at the mercy of fate. An old piece of folklore, variously attributed to the Irish, the French, and other sources, suggests that God indeed has a special kind of watchfulness over fools, drunkards, and babies. In their reckless behavior, which has little thought for the consequences of present actions, the three are a vulnerable and all-too-pervasive trio. The person who has learned to be the fool does not see that today's mindless actions produce tomorrow's consequences, disasters, and ruinous events. For the fool there seems to be a deliberate policy of ignoring this cause and effect. Often, the old folklore goes, the consequences will never come, and thus there must be some kind of providence. The solemn virtues of prudence, thrift, foresight, anticipation, and preparation for contingencies never enter the fool's mind. The hope that things will ultimately turn out OK overrules logic. Impulsive and even irrational behavior with no thought of consequence continues without interruption or second thought until it is indeed too late.

The point, of course, is not that societies' fools have greater faith in God than more intelligent people. Rather, they have a more pagan faith in the all right-ness of things in the world, which will carry them through without much planning. Nor is the point that only fools fail to plan, for ordinarily sensible and adult people may fail to plan because they habitually fall back upon momentary foolishness in facing an uncertain future.

This foolishness, which resembles the logical patterns of the inebriated person or the little child, is often applauded and tolerated with easy amusement by the majority. The victory of the country boy who in his innocence defeats the giant bureaucracy without an ounce of planning strikes enough sympathetic response in all of us that we act as if the protective-God theorem were true. If you get some money, spend it. If you can obtain credit, use it. If you live on the edge of an earthquake fault, ignore it. If continuation of your present disastrous course will naturally lead to endless trouble, ignore that too. Somehow, this faith goes, the best way to live is to assume that there is an implicit plan in nature and life that will spare us that final blow.[11] Often this takes the form of a fatalism, in which whatever will be will be and no planned course can affect it. John O'Hara's *Appointment in Samarra* tells of the man who learns that Death has come to town to pick him up. He immediately mounts his horse and races madly out of town toward the distant town of Samarra. Death watches in amusement as he checks his schedule book, for he notes that he has an appointment with the man in Samarra the following day.

The basis of anti-planning for many is thus a kind of fatalism that has been ingrained through the lengthy period of being protected as a child and has continued in adulthood. Mothers and fathers who are overprotective in time and intensity produce childlike adolescents and childlike adults who persist in this belief in a fatalistic idea of security against the future. If experience is any kind of teacher, it reinforces for many adults the lessons of childhood that planning has already been taken care of by hidden forces which protect us against harm, and that planning is nothing more than an exercise. Only the more worrisome and ridiculous people who don't know the real story would bother with such fruitless work and worry. If by chance the worst should occur, then people can expect relief, sympathy, and compassion from others for their ill fortune.

For some, this god is not an actual deity but is some organizational Jolly Green Giant who has great enough power to act as God's surrogate in caring for the nonplanners. When Ford workers were on strike in 1977, one union member reported to a news reporter that "I am Ford's man, and Ford should take care of his men." Substitute "Lord Ford" for "Ford" and you have a perfect description of feudalism. The fact that Mr. Ford was not at all disposed at the moment to assume God's role was a source of considerable disappointment. The worker in the paternalistic company, or the welfare recipient in the inner city, may have learned in a good school of experience that the organization will take care of its members. Thus, no planning by the individual is needed, for the government, the welfare agency, and the company have already done all of the planning necessary, and therefore growing up is not important or necessary.

Nor is such belief in the omnipotence of the organization limited to machine operators and clerks. Middle managers and professional workers have similar beliefs. As organization people, they rely upon their childlike intuitions, which tell them that IBM or the Bell System has made plans that incorporate timely personal relief making them whole if life should deal them a foul blow. Therefore, planning is irrelevant, for it has already taken place under a master plan of the elite top management.[12]

**The planned social climate which releases volitional victims** A hundred ways are open when we seek to turn such anti-planners into planners. Most of them have

---

[11] K. Horney, *The Neurotic Personality of Our Time* (New York: W. W. Norton & Co., Inc., 1938), describes such a state of mind as a kind of expectation that all will be right.
[12] W. H. White, *The Organization Man* (New York: Simon & Schuster, 1956).

nothing to do with the techniques of professional planning by staff experts. They require a managerial climate that aims at generating ego strength in the deadwood and in other volitional victims. Organizations that create excitement in their members are one element to be sought out and aimed for. The possibility of advancement, more creative challenges, more feeling among the employees that they can influence the decisions that affect them, more respect, more pride, and a sense of self-esteem are the ego-building elements that produce self-development. As Professor Paul Harmon describes it, people can have the feeling that they are living life "on an inclined plane upward." Through these basic elements are ego strength and social plans to encourage personal growth more likely to be attained.

The dilemma of eternal childhood among adults at work is that if we stand up and make real plans, we feel alive but threatened, and that frightens us. If we don't stand up and make plans for change, we feel deadened, demeaned, and stunted. *I could be more than I am if the people up there knew what I want to do, can do, or even what I am doing now.* Our social plans create an image of a giant who does not want us to grow and will cut us off at the knees or the neck if we try. All of our plans are rooted in science, weapons, computers, mathematical models, and technology produced by childlike adults.

## ANTIDOTES TO CHILDLIKE OPPOSITION TO PLANNED CHANGE

It is necessary to realize that all of us are prone to slip into one of the childlike stages of development at some stage in our lives, and most of us will revert to some more immature stage under social pressures. The major emphasis, then, cannot lie in expecting to produce adult adults all of the time. Yet there are some rules for managers, leaders, and administrators when they are confronted with this childlike opposition to change.

1. Childlike behavior is most likely to become adult behavior when there are good examples given to the children by adults who are visible to them. This means that leadership that produces adult behavior by good example is the best vehicle for creative adults.

2. Coaching and counseling of children by adults is not to be confused with admonishing and reprimanding. Nurturing actions are important skills of the top leader. The senior executive who lacks such coaching skills should not be in such a position, for that skill is an important part of the leadership function.

3. When confronted with childlike behavior, stick more firmly than ever to an adult mode of behavior yourself, despite efforts of the childlike to reduce you to their level. As Eric Berne suggests in his *Games People Play,* don't let them "hook you" into a childlike, or a parental (admonishing judgmental), behavior. Be orderly, rational, conscious, and human in your behavior, and if you stick with it people will come around.

4. Be reasonable, understanding, nondirective, and patient in dealing with childlike behavior. Restate others' childlike assertions without acceptance or censure, and prove that you understand. Then state the adult position.

# twelve

# The new luddites:
## how the desire to wreck things subverts planning and change

As the growth of government planning and the corporate planning that trails it expanded during the seventies, planning often fell more and more into a path toward destruction of something rather than into the creation of something new. This sequence or pattern emerged somewhat as follows:

1. Under the pressure of problems, threats, risks, and opportunities, the planners came forth with new, clever, innovative, and often noble plans. Government planned for a safe work environment, accident-free vehicles, and an economy that would provide full employment without inflation and the like.

2. Corporations and government administrators were required to initiate capital-budgeting programs that were defensive against the effects of the new rules of the road provided for in government plans. These capital budgets shifted traditional ways of doing things and brought forth more formal and explicit planning.

3. In the process of planning, the planners discovered that implanting new ideas, systems, and goals in their target areas often required that they remove and eliminate certain existing factories, organizations, and systems. In the process, the planners became taken with a very human delight in wrecking things, and the wreckage of the old became an end in itself for substantial portions of their time. As their skills of negation grew, their propensity to apply these skills grew apace.

This destructiveness in time turned many ambitious programs to remake the world through planning into a succession of campaigns to stop something or other. Nuclear power was once seen as a clean source of energy and started along that path with the Atomic Energy Act of 1954. Soon, the private utility companies had invested billions in constructing giant nuclear generating plans, which remade the face of utility financing and power generation at large. This, in turn, remade the entire face of the managerial planning of utility companies as well. Environmental protection laws concurrently produced whole clusters of private devotees on campus and in public interest groups who sought to ensure greater safety in the nuclear plants. These ultimately became so enmeshed in picket lines, mass demonstrations, getting arrested, and similar media events that the goal of greater energy combined with higher levels of public health was forgotten in the desire to stop nuclear power plants. College towns were peppered with bumper stickers which advised us to "Dismantle Nukes." Environmentalists, both inside government and out, became notable in proportion to their ability to noisily stop something or other, or to turn back the clock a decade or more.[1]

The production lines of automobile companies, appliance manufacturers, and tire makers ground to a halt; or their products were recalled for corrective repairs, ostensibly for safety reasons. While this safety motive had indeed underlain the original laws, it was apparent by the end of the seventies that stopping a product, a program, or a system in its tracks had become an end purpose for many of the people engaged in such endeavors. The instincts of the wrecker turned to new weapons, to old and new insecticides, to fluorocarbons, to over 2000 substances that were alleged to be carcinogenic, and to multinational corporations in general.

The mechanisms by which the original purposes had been converted into the motto *Stop Anything New* became sufficiently well developed that as new recruits entered the battles, they had to take sides as good guys and bad guys, leading to further polarization and lending an air of excitement and intensity that drew still more recruits. Numerous individual programs in time added up to an overall movement that formed a common bond for all of the progress stoppers. Think Small and Zero Population Growth, philosophies aimed not at a specific social ill but at generally stopping things, replaced the original, particular purposes with a more universal goal. The counterculture of the seventies attracted numerous supporters from the ranks of the college-educated, the radical right, and the radical left, and expanded its targets to include sugar-coated cereals, TV commercials, pornography, union monopolies, high taxation and government spending, gas-guzzling cars, corporate power, defense spending for new arms, arms sales, infant formulas sold in underdeveloped countries, strip mining, drug consumption, motorcyclists without helmets, marriage, divorce, abortion, anti-abortion, and corporate investment in South Africa. Each could at one time or another produce an organized group with picket signs, petitions, or lawsuits to wreck its target.[2]

The point here, of course, does not have to do with the merits of the case of any of these groups. It illustrates instead the emergence of a new Luddite class, or machine wreckers' movement, on a widespread scale in Western society, and even in China and Russia.

The original Luddites were workers in England in the early nineteenth century who saw technological improvements in factories as a means through which they would be thrown out of work. No theorists, the Luddites were directly and personally affected by labor-saving machinery. Quite understandably, they had little evidence other than the statements and assurances of the inventors that more jobs would be created from mechanization than would be destroyed.

[1] H. P. Metzner, *The Atomic Establishment* (New York: Simon & Schuster, 1972). A serious review of and attack on atomic development.
[2] C. McCarry, *Citizen Nader* (New York: Saturday Review Press, 1972).

The automation movement in industry in the 1940's and 1950's produced a small resurgence of Luddite thinking. The servomechanisms that produced automatic control, workers supposed, would produce vast unemployment. A think tank in California that called itself the Ad Hoc Committee on the Triple Revolution comprised of economists, labor leaders, and even a corporate executive or two, solemnly predicted that automation would soon wipe out millions of jobs and leave us with a depression greater than that of the 1930's.

The widespread attention paid to such ideas was in part fed by a press wanting to flesh out its Sunday supplements. But it also fed on a latent and close-to-the-surface willingness of many people to join any kind of movement that had as its underlying purpose the stopping of change, the end of planning for further change, and the reversal of some of the more flagrant changes existent at the time.

The presence of this pursuit of the pleasure of destruction is an often overlooked element which stops planning, and even engages many planners in its work.

## THE PLEASURES OF DESTRUCTION
## ARE WIDELY SHARED

Many years ago, I was for a brief time a member of a volunteer fire department. In addition to the sociability of hanging out at the firehouse, traditionally a male haven from more responsible pursuits, there were other compensations. The power to race around on a spectacular if somewhat ancient red truck, siren keening, and to drive down the left-hand side of the road and drive ordinary citizens' cars onto the sidewalks in terror was added to that of chopping up and hosing down other people's property with impunity. Even a defeat by a fire that got away from the firefighters had its concealed compensation for some of our members.

I became convinced that much of the pleasure of membership in this civic-spirited group was in its basic nature as a socially acceptable vent for latent arsonists and property wreckers. Of course, the cultural demands of the role required a horrified denial of such an attitude. Yet, I noted that everyone showed up for the fires and the burning and the chopping and the hosing down of people's possessions. But it was like pulling teeth to get anyone who could find the time to conduct *inspections* of people's property to prevent fire. Sudden imperative demands of family and job kept the members of the company away in droves when such tasks were announced. The point is not that firefighters are all arsonists, but rather that there could be made a persuasive case that people enjoy destruction and disasters that tear things down more than they enjoy planning and preventing such things.

Historians have puzzled for centuries at the apparent eternal propensity of the human race to engage in destruction of property and of other people. General George Patton is depicted as having said of war, "By God, I love it." Apparently this love of destruction has some kind of cultural if not psychological support that makes bombing, shooting, and firebombing a bizarre kind of pleasure for some. Ordinarily constrained by civilization, beneath our mask there often lies a beast straining to be free to tear things down in an hour that have been painstakingly built up by thought, planning, work, and creativity.[3]

The practice of surgery is a socially approved modification of this desire to cut and slice, all the more desirable because it produces approval and admiration rather than reproof and disgust.[4] With long study and exquisitely developed skills, the surgeon can wield a scalpel upon a human body and cut out the offending diseased part. The readiness of the surgeon to pop into the operating room at the slightest pretext is, of course, like arsonists in the fire department, hardly to be conceded by these technicians. Rather, it is a proposition to be vehemently denied. Yet, studies by the Department of Health, Education, and Welfare reveal that needless surgery during the seventies ran into the hundreds of thousands of cases, with some eleven thousand deaths attributed to such needless cutting and sawing. It was not the pain and agony growing out of this overzealous practice which produced a response, however, but its high cost. The Blue Cross–Blue Shield medical plans attempted to counter the growth of unnecessary surgery by offering to pay for second opinions when requested by patients as a means of dampening it.

Developers are widely recognized as wreckers of one thing to create something new. The lumberjack likewise finds a respectable and plausible career in chopping down giant trees that may have been growing thirty years. The bulldozer which tears up the natural landscape is driven by a skilled operator whose work is widely admired. Every construction project draws spectators who gaze in awe as the crane operator with a giant ball swinging on a steel line smashes old buildings into dusty wreckage to create room for a new glass and steel palace. When a giant chimney is to be felled, every TV news photographer for miles around stands breathless awaiting the detonation that will send the awesome edifice crumbling into a pile of rubble. At the moment of destruction, the event is recorded for the viewers in millions of homes, who can start their evening watching this glorious event, vicariously sharing the destruction on their TV screens.

News itself is far more likely to consist of coverage of wrecks, fires, violent collisions, and assaults that have left the victim bleeding and dazed, than of coverage of a competent worker building something. Wars, revolutions, riots, and possible mob action are always quick to attract reporters and photographers, who help to sell papers by making the details of destructive behavior in our society available to a viewing or reading public. When nature goes on a rampage, flooding cities, burying the ordinary affairs of life under four feet of snow, or dashing a giant airliner into a burning hulk, the event will be faithfully reported in preference to the mundane work of building something in the first place.

The entertainment industry in general senses this popular trend and obliges with weekly TV series that pander to this desire to see things wrecked. From kiddy

---

[3] The enormity of our commitment to war is clearly spelled out in A. Yarmolinsky, *The Military Establishment* (New York: Harper & Row, Pub., 1971, a Twentieth Century Fund study).

[4] M. Gross, *The Doctors* (New York: Dell Pub. Co., Inc., 1966).

shows in which cartoon cats are pounded into shreds by aggressive mice, to adult fare where automobiles crash in flaming balls of exploding gasoline tanks, this wreckage permeates the lives of TV viewers. Races of cars through city streets, tearing up property and plunging through walls, have become common fare. Violent death and mutilation and destruction of both heroes and villains in ever more spectacular fashion have made a folk hero of the *stunt artist,* a superwrecker who substitutes in the more dangerous scenes for the star, whose countenance and body are to be protected for the final love scenes.

Quite naturally there have followed movements proclaiming TV violence bad for children and for the peace and sobriety of society. In time, even these anti-violence movements have become more generalized attacks on privately sponsored television, to the point where public broadcasting has become more of a crusade against the profit system than an alternative  system of innovative programming. The commercial itself becomes the target, and thence the sponsors and their profits. Meanwhile, people vote with their feet by walking into supermarkets, fast-food chains, and automobile dealerships to buy the products advertised in the wrecker brand of entertainment. The question is no longer whether or not to be a wrecker, but which side to take in a polarized battle of wreckers. Wreck cars, or wreck private entertainment: that is the choice. By and large, the wreckers win either way.

## CORPORATE COMPETITION AS AN OUTLET FOR DESTRUCTIVE INSTINCTS

The birth of most corporate planning departments was in the development of modern marketing theory. Originating in a few large corporations, most notably General Electric, but widely adopted in other corporate giants, the "marketing concept" became pervasive during the sixties. This concept suggested that *selling* was only an incidental part of the total effort of the company to produce an expanded growth in sales and revenues from those sales. Intensive growth strategies for the firm meant finding new products to sell, finding the best applications of those products, finding new uses for old products, and selling more of the same product to the same number of buyers. This produced a kind of analytical science that might easily be described as the most sophisticated modern application of applied statistics and behavioral analysis to be found. Selling operations became subordinate to marketing strategies.

Finding, screening, and appraising new products is an important part of the profit-growth–planning process for the corporate planner. In these activities, the new form of market competition takes a new shape closer to that of the wrecker of tradition than that of the creation of the new. Donald A. Schon recognizes this when he declares that "the notion of innovation as an orderly, goal-directed, risk reducing process must appear as a myth." The actual process by which innovation occurs is a "conservative dynamism," says Schon.[5] The society of the corporation

---

[5] D. A. Schon, "The Fear of Innovation," *International Science and Technology,* 14, November 1966.

attempts to maintain a stable state, and innovation is an attempt to wreck that state, ostensibly for the production of a higher and better state. While this better state is highly desired, innovation is not to be taken lightly and left to run unopposed and unquestioned. Technological innovation disrupts the stable state of the corporate society and attacks the corporation's energetic efforts to stay as it is. In response to the assault of innovation, the corporate planning staff will reject the effort, get rid of the people identified with it, and place it in isolation from the rest of the corporation. If innovation continues at all, it does so under strong constraints, or it is made to fit within the framework of modification rather than radical change. It vacillates between verbal support on the one hand and massive system resistance on the other.

The major influences favoring product innovation, proposes Robert R. Rothberg, are ordinarily external to the corporation. Left to its own instincts not to change but to remain stable, the corporation faces the risk that some competitor will get there first. The introduction of a toothpaste with fluoride captured a market and left those firms which had avoided this change far behind. A new cake mix introduced by Procter & Gamble that made cakes with superior freshness and moistness caused its competitors to fall far behind in their share of the market. Changes in consumer buying patterns and dietary practices can leave the stability seeker high and dry. Changing levels of income change demand for products. These influences press the firm into innovation against its strongest instincts, which tell it to do nothing differently.

Innovation, then, takes on a quasi-scientific character. It is found in three major forms, suggests D. G. Marquis.[6] First, it may consist of complex systems changes which require many years and millions of dollars to bring about. Second, it may be a major breakthrough in technology, such as the electron tube, the transistor, the jet engine, or xerography. These innovations are both rare and unpredictable, and usually appear in the world of the university or the independent lab or are made by an individual inventor; researchers inside corporations are more apt to be concerned with short-term concerns such as cost reduction or product improvement.

The third kind of innovation is competitive innovation: that which is necessary to keep up with competitors' innovations. When Procter & Gamble captured the lion's share of the cake mix market, General Mills had to respond wholeheartedly or lose its important position in that market. This catch-up kind of innovation calls for a recognition of technical feasibility and market demand, and elicits some conceptualizing and problem-solving behavior inside a firm that might not ordinarily be permitted; the corporate planner is faced with the dilemma of having to please the stability-loving management while not falling behind in the competitive world outside.

One of the ideas that have sprung up to deal with such a tension-laden existence is that of a product *life cycle*. The product line of the firm consists, says Peter Drucker, of yesterday's breadwinner, today's breadwinner, and tomorrow's

[6] D. G. Marquis, "The Anatomy of Successful Innovations," *Innovation*, November 1962.

breadwinner. Each of these products has a life cycle that adheres to an inverted U-shaped curve. Marketing planning, then, consists of competing on a twofold basis, suggests Donald K. Clifford, Jr.:[7]

- It must reshape and control the life cycle of individual products.
- It must improve the overall mix of life cycles in the company's product line to keep corporate profits ever rising.

This means that life-cycle planning, an important part of marketing planning, requires that a company be in the product-wrecking business in a major way. It must on occasion obsolete its own products, as IBM did when it introduced its System/360 computers in 1964. Otherwise it may attempt to obsolete its competitor's products through a new kind of product, as Hewlett-Packard did with the sophisticated hand-held calculator. The development and management of the product life cycle calls, then, for the skill of learning how to abandon formerly successful and profitable businesses. Thus the skill of the dismantler and wrecker becomes an important skill of the planner.

The idea that such dismantling is always easy can be quickly dispelled. People become emotionally attached to the jobs, the customers, the procedures, the business arrangements, and the personal lives that have been built around the now declining product. Yet, the impulse to wreck is strong. It is not surprising, then, that the skill of abandonment and destruction of an existing business has risen in importance in the modern planning system. For many firms, the innovation stage requires endless amounts of bureaucratic approval and review, but the decision to abandon seems to become easier and easier.

## ANTIDOTES TO LUDDITE OPPOSITION

The perceptive reader has probably already noted that this chapter equates such people as youthful opponents of atomic energy with the Luddites, which is a kind of false analogy. In fact, the Luddites were no more than peasants, whereas modern Luddite-like opponents are highly educated. For another thing, today's Luddite-like opponents are usually young, the children of the middle class, and don't fear the loss of their jobs but have more vague apprehensions that impel them. The original Luddites were peasant factory workers who feared losing their manual jobs to machines. The modern machine stoppers and wreckers may in fact be engaging in a middle-class cop-out. Few blacks, children of the poor, or children of working-class parents engage in such demonstrations. Many of the wreckers have income from trusts or grants. Nonetheless, there are sufficient similarities that the Luddite label is useful, even if the analogy is less than perfect. Here are some ways we might deal with the modern Luddites:

1. *Wait them out.* Clark Kerr, long-time chancellor at Berkeley, is reported to

---

[7] D. K. Clifford, Jr., "Managing the Product Life Cycle," in *The Arts of Top Management: A McKinsey Anthology* (New York: McGraw-Hill, 1971).

have opined that "there is no student problem which can't be solved in four years." This represents exactly the most thorough and effective strategy, where it is possible. Many of the college students of 1965 to 1972, who made up most of the demonstrations against the "establishment," are now employed, have mortgages, are running for Congress, or have joined a government bureau regulating something or other. A few have become social isolates, but even these are quiet.

2. *Get them involved.* Make the demonstrators and wreckers part of the solution by asking for their assistance, seeking their advice, finding the root of their problem, and getting them to help solve it. Participation in solving the problem is a growth experience, and often the destructive behavior is a continuation of childlike behavior which needs nothing more than a dose of adult treatment. Remain adult in the face of all juvenile acts.

3. *Refute wrong facts with right ones.* Because the new demonstrators and wreckers tend to be college and university graduates, it is safe to assume that they are above the intelligence of the population at large. Thus, arguments they make that are rooted in wrong facts should be refuted with evidence stating the case more accurately.

4. *Use argumentation and debate.* Many of the demonstrators identify themselves as radical leftists. Such people are not affected in most cases by money or self-interest. They are, however, capable of being persuaded by logic and debate. Engaging in discussion ("rapping") has a beneficial effect for both sides. Louis Lundborg, chairman of the Bank of America, the world's largest bank, who engaged in such rapping with radical young people, concluded with tongue in cheek that "you can hear a lot by just listening."[8] More dialogue and discussion between people in charge of things and people who would ostensibly wreck things would materially advance the management of change.

5. *Avoid strong-arm put-downs.* People who oppose us sometimes get cast into the category of being "bad people" and in that classification deserve anything that happens to them, or so we conclude. Often this produces strong-arm, even violent, suppression of those who disagree. This of course materially strengthens their cause rather than weakening it, for it thrusts their opposition into the public media, and generates further support for the opponents. Media have a way of following violence, as has been noted. When radical groups start their programs and projects, they aim specifically at "media events," which will produce such widespread attention and increase support. The change maker thus must avoid like the plague those kinds of responses that produce counterresponses of more intensity, generate media events, and cement the hostility of the opponents.

[8] L. B. Lundborg, *Future Without Shock* (New York: W. W. Norton & Co., Inc., 1979).

# thirteen

# How our appetite for crises obliterates change

Most people who are competent at their jobs enjoy the crises and problems associated with their work more than they would care to admit. Many a job-pressed professional has ended the day happily at a nearby watering hole with the perfect excuse for a martini: "What a day, what a day! Give me a double, Joe." The pleasures of imbibing, however, are trivial when measured against the more permanent satisfactions of being totally engaged in solving an apparently endless array of problems. In time, such job pressures and intensive work schedules may produce such satisfactions that even the drinking habit becomes moderate and unnecessary. The stimulation from chronic crisis management, and the resultant sense of achievement, and the recognition from others for the extraordinary powers of mastery displayed are handy returns for the price paid in hours and energy. The ego satisfactions that come from the mastery motive required by constant crises are often present when one is working full tilt at pressure-intensive tasks.[1]

Planning, thinking, reflection, invention, and creativity, however, are likely to disappear under the pressures of such crises. Planning and creativity of a long-run character are not a vehicle for the instincts, but for the mind. Thus, the crisis and its cultivation become a potent anti-planning force in many of us, for crisis management engages only a peculiar quality of the mind.

## THE COMPETENCE MOTIVE AND WORKING UNDER PRESSURE

A card often found among those humor cards in airport newsstands goes, "When you are up to your ass in alligators it is sometimes difficult to remember that your

---

[1] Some basic sources here include E. E. Jennings, *The Executive In Crisis* (New York: McGraw-Hill, 1972); S. Freud, *The Problem of Anxiety* (New York: W. W. Norton & Co., Inc., 1936); *see also* K. E. Boulding, *Conflict and Defense* (New York: Harper & Row, Pub., Torchbooks, 1962).

objective was to drain the swamp." On its surface, the saying might seem a form of protest against the ungodly pressures of work, but the protest is blurred by an air of pride and pleasure at the commitment and competence implied. To fend off alligators while one is doing an important job such as draining a swamp suggests a high level of urgency, importance, and overriding priority in what one is doing. The vital significance of each move and every instant of time is apparent to everyone who sees it. A false move, a slip in technique, or a lapse in attention could produce terrible consequences.

Such pressure sets all other behaviors or more reflective and thoughtful actions aside. Under such pressures, the priorities have arranged themselves without question or doubt. People who work under such pressures probably achieve more in a shorter time than people might ordinarily be expected to accomplish. Revised schedules, new plans, changed priorities, and reflections about the propriety and wisdom of the long-range strategies of draining the swamp can be put out of mind, as events pile on events and add up to a satisfying sense of competence. Finding oneself able to deal effectively with the problems and crises of the moment over and over again turns into a sensation of mastery that feeds on itself. Once mastery is attained, it will be practiced with considerably increasing levels of pleasure and satisfaction.[2]

The development of competency is especially important early in one's career, for the young enter the work place without such competency and spend their early weeks, months, or even years in acquiring it. Competency, once in hand, becomes a personal asset, a source of security against being replaced, and a source of authority in one's life work. The company commander in the army who can maneuver things in the field under combat conditions, the plant manager who can get the goods out the back door on time within the budget, and the sales representative who can produce an ever-higher sales volume find most of their job satisfaction in their competence. Frederick Herzberg's research into motivation on the job places the highest levels of motivational effects within the job itself, and identifies competence in doing things as the engine of motivation.

This knowledge that one is adequate and perhaps even superior, once built up, often appears as technical competence, social competence, organizational competence, or interpersonal competence. Combined into a total job competence, it adds up to a feeling of mastery. Abraham Maslow describes "the peak experience" which comes to people who combine mastery and competence with the opportunity to apply it, with the result that people can tell themselves, "This was my finest hour." The times when people report having felt very good about their work were those when they had displayed superior abilities to make things happen where others might have failed or been overwhelmed.[3]

To suggest that this ability to get things done is a vehicle that supplants rational and strategic thinking is not to suggest that such work and behavior may not

[2] K. Herzberg, *Work and the Nature of Man* (Cleveland: World Book Co., 1966); *see also* H. Levinson, *The Exceptional Executive* (Cambridge: Harvard University Press, 1968).
[3] A. Maslow, *Motivation and Personality*, 2nd ed. (New York; Harper & Row, Pub., 1970).

in fact be creative. More likely it calls for short-term imagination and quick response, and channels combativeness and mental agility into an apparent connection between ends and means. Its gratifications are immediate. Such work opportunity and the attendant successes are not in fact fatiguing to the performer, but create more than enough energy to accomplish the work to be done. The variety of problems and crises that confront one and an ability to deal with that variety generate a high level of motivation. Such words as *zest, enthusiasm,* and *challenge* are apt descriptions of the attitude with which people having competence and mastery in crisis handling approach their tasks.

To ask such a person, then, to turn simultaneously or alternatively to a different mode of thought, to question the rightness of the goals and the usefulness of the whole thing, is only to be viewed as threatening to that competence and to the personal well-being of the worker. The idea that the crisis-based work is wrongly oriented, or even mistaken, in its purposes is frustrating and frightening. It threatens the competence so painfully achieved, and leads to possible frustration, apathy, and resignation. Small wonder, then, that strategic thinking, multiyear planning, sober questioning of long-run goals and purposes, and the introduction of major changes in the character and direction of the job itself are ignored or rejected by the professional engaged in it.

> *Crisis management, to the extent that it produces an obsession with the day-to-day, short-run aspects of the work, is a key ingredient in the antiplanning mentality of most of us.*

## THE CRISIS LEADER IS ONE WHO CAN CREATE CRISES AS WELL AS SOLVE THEM

The existence of occupations that live on crisis-based competence has been noted in Chapter 4. The *crisis* professions have much in common with the failure professions, but the source and direction of crisis management is somewhat different. The crisis manager must avoid innovative planning that might change the *status quo* in order that there be no diminution of a continuous stream of crises.

It is the unremitting character of crises—their steady supply in quantity and quality—that is the responsibility of leaders who would play the game and survive. Leaders in crime prevention must produce every new form of evidence that crime is on the rise, not only in amount, but also in the shocking new varieties that have emerged. J. Edgar Hoover could point to the ominous rise in the percentage of certain forms of crime and thus produce new staff positions, higher budget expenditures, and corresponding job security for the people who were ready to scramble into battle with criminals—organized and unorganized—in dramatic chases in new cars, using new weapons and new technology. More current methods of estimating crime statistics have suggested that much of this was little more than a perfectly understandable effort of a leader of a crisis-fighting organization to provide enough crimes for his organization to deal with. If bank holdups go down, then white-collar crimes must be suspected and then researched, until a whole new arm is required to deal with the crisis of this new form of crime. This is not to suggest that we do not have crime, but that leaders must continue to find crises to fight, rather than doing things of a more fundamental nature, such as discovering the root causes of crime and working and planning to alleviate those conditions.

Similarly, a host of people in Washington, some 17,000 of them at the present count, have positions managing the energy crisis under the rubric of the Department of Energy. If there were no OPEC nations holding meetings and creating timely crises, there is little likelihood that as a nation we would have created an agency known as the Department of Energy. Once it is created as a crisis-management organization, however, it behooves its leadership to appear in public periodically whenever a price increase by OPEC appears or some OPEC chief of state is toppled, to present charts to the TV news cameras revealing a looming crisis which the organization will worriedly but dutifully be obliged to tackle with competence, professional skill, and dedication. The point, of course, is not that the Department of Energy placed all that oil beneath the sands of the Middle East and then prompted the various sheiks and emirs to withhold it; it is, rather, that crisis-management strategy prevents its leaders from having any motivation to lean back and think deeply about ways to break up OPEC, or otherwise think up creative and innovative ways of changing the entire character of our energy supply system.

Inside the corporation, the executive must similarly provide grist for the staff mills. A staff department such as public affairs and public relations, then, resembles the old definition of a spouse: a person who sticks with you through all of the troubles you wouldn't have had if you hadn't been married in the first place. Crisis management, as an antidote to planning and innovation, has thus become a new form of gamesmanship for executives. As Michael Maccoby has described him, the executive who rises to the top in today's corporation is the *gamesman*. The games-man is a leader who has learned how to carefully select the issues that must be dealt with, and who engages in those social and personal behaviors that turn crisis management into a well-defined art.[4]

## EXECUTIVES UNDER SIEGE: STRATEGIES FOR SURVIVAL[5]

The emerging gamesman in executive ranks then is not the innovator and bold creative captain who sails his ship into new waters to exploit new opportunities. He is most likely to be the leader in applying craftsmanlike skills of *response* to events that appear to have been selected to be the crisis of the moment. These crises will project the executive into the public eye, and where the chief is unwilling or unable to respond professionally in a gamesmanlike fashion, he is apt to find himself replaced by one who has a more appropriate response. *Response management* does not make things happen, but rather watches what goes on and solves the problems

[4] M. Maccoby, *The Gamesman* (New York: Doubleday, 1977).
[5] Adapted from G. S. Odiorne, "Executives Under Siege: Strategies for Survival." Reprinted by permission of the publisher, from *Management Review,* April 1978, © 1978 by AMACOM, a division of American Management Associations. All rights reserved.

it discovers. The terms of the battle are of the enemies' making and the end goal is to maintain the status quo. Problem solving, suggests Peter Drucker, should not be the function of the corporate chief, but rather the creation and exploitation of innovation and new opportunity. Yet, the crisis mentality pervades and the skilled crisis leader is selected and succeeds according to his ability to scan the environment and adapt to it. Since he is chosen for that adaptive skill, it is a natural consequence that corporations will increasingly live in a world of crisis which creates a demand for crisis-competent leaders.

Heat rises, and the top executive gets warm indeed during a crisis. Whether it is a congressional inquiry into corporate political contributions or stockholders screaming about ecology, intense and unique stresses are borne by senior management.

During the turbulent sixties, a whole new set of stresses emerged. More recently, scandals have shaken the boardroom and the government agency, causing a decline in public regard for business and a lowering of organizational morale. There is open dissatisfaction with managerial decisions and continuing concern about policies toward the environment and occupational safety, the uses of the atom, the reliability of CPA reports, and a host of continuing problems.

As the laws and standards of conduct for corporations change, so do the standards of performance for those at or near the top. While the problems facing corporations are real and pressing, for the top executive there are others that are unique and more immediate. Many levels of the organization share the stresses of corporate life, but the engineer, line manager, and machine operator are not the persons likely to be hauled before a legislative committee or slapped with charges of bribing a foreign official. They are less apt to be kidnapped or picketed outside their homes, or shouted at by stockholders angered by corporate losses.

Little work has been done on these special traumas for those near the top. Aging and promotion to higher corporate levels produce their own stresses, of course, but there has been no real measure of how these myriad stresses affect the environment of the top manager.

In an effort to gain some insight into this side of managerial activity, sixty-one executives whose lives and jobs had been directly affected by traumatic events were interviewed. They were asked what strategies they took or might take to avoid a bad situation. Their confidentiality was assured, and they were remarkably willing to discuss their experiences and philosophies about such crises.

The attitudes revealed in the interviews fall into three rather predictable categories:

- Fight the adversary. In at least two cases I was treated to an approximate recitation from Hamlet about "whether 'tis nobler in the mind to suffer the slings and arrows of outrageous fortune, or to take [up] arms." In these cases and others, the besieged executives obviously relished a fight. This was particularly true where the chief executive founded the firm and perhaps saw it as his fiefdom. An attack on the founder was an attack on the company and vice versa. Also, an attack on either was often seen as an attack on America, free enterprise, and so on.

• Run away. Those who had little advance warning of crises often reacted with dismay, shock, chagrin, and consternation. Taken by surprise, these executives—who usually had records of unremitting success—frequently had heart attacks; others turned to alcohol. Many avoided their employees and would enter and leave their offices when they would be seen by the fewest people. Others did not return calls or answer letters, surrounded themselves with guards, or got unlisted home phones.

• Respond professionally. This category includes those executives who would step back from the predicament, analyze it, and then devise tough and adroit responses. Such professionals generally anticipated or at least considered the crises. Even so, one noted;

> Having a personal stake in the outcome can cloud your judgment. That's the best argument for using experts to review the situation. The old saying that the person who is his own lawyer has a fool for a client applies to more than court cases.

> Executives must make decisions that have an even greater impact on the lives of others than on their own. In such cases, getting all the facts and clearly examining the situation is how a rational person would proceed. But that's not always the case, and it's easy to be objective, even Olympian, about other people's problems. We all learn to suffer others' aches with considerable equanimity.

This executive emphasized that, when an executive is directly affected, outside advice becomes particularly important. "Oddly enough, that's the very circumstance where your vaunted objectivity is apt to desert you quickest," he said. "Getting the best possible advice from those who won't lose their objectivity is a pretty sound idea."

Another executive told how a friend had been chased around the boardroom by a small group of hostile board members:

> He was tempted to give the whole board an ultimatum and nearly forced a showdown. But he decided instead to discuss what to do with trusted and objective advisors, and they suggested options. Finally, he simply smiled his way through and let the opposition blow its game by going to excess. His first impulse would have led him astray.

Where a decision has high personal impact, the instinct is to emotional response. That can be just what the people on the other side are hoping for. Tensions can build to where it seems necessary to take action—any action—without gathering enough data for an objective decision.

The three general classifications above were the broad groupings of the interviews. Out of these, a system of possible personal responses to crisis emerged. The following responses were all drawn from actual cases.

1. *Freeze!* Only shortly before the media reported it, the head of a medium-size

firm learned that his sales department and his controller had bribed a foreign agent to get business. Immediately howls went up for explanations and for costly remedies, not to mention his scalp.

"I didn't know what to do, so I did nothing," he said. "I froze like a pheasant in danger. I didn't do it rationally; I just froze and couldn't move." This reaction apparently worked well in his case; he avoided aggravating critics and was able to respond quietly later.

2. *Become an ostrich.* One executive allowed us to interview his officers but not him. They reported that he stuck his head in the sand when he learned about his company's practice of dumping toxic wastes into a river. Publicly and privately, he would not agree to rationalize the problem. When his aides went to hearings and negotiated a costly settlement, he neither asked about it nor commented on the cost. For him it was as if nothing had happened.

3. *Lash back fast.* One corporate office took on the air of a war room when the SEC and a prosecuting attorney charged the officers with wrongful insider trading in the company's stock. News releases and press conferences were assembled with fantastic speed. The charges of wrongdoing were hotly denied, the motives of the agency chief were impugned, the capabilities of the agency's staff were scorned, the quality of its data was downgraded, and grand generalizations attacking the motives of the agency and the administration of which it was a part were issued. Sometimes this strategy works, but frequently it does not.

4. *Raise the issue to a higher general plane.* This response is highly risky. It can steel the offense and perhaps accelerate what could have been just a lost skirmish into a major battle. For example, an executive precipitated a Supreme Court suit over the right of OSHA inspectors to enter his plant without a search warrant. The cost of the suit far exceeded the possible losses from any safety actions and fines resulting from the inspection. Such actions usually are motivated by deep-seated ideologies, principles, or values that overshadow the case. The long-running court fight of Vivian Kellems, the Connecticut manufacturer who for years refused to pay income taxes, didn't save her any money. The IRS simply impounded her bank account and took what it claimed, plus interest. But her fight centered on some elevated issue of the proper relationship of business and government; the actual issue of taxes was subordinated.

Business leaders who have such strong ideological casts of mind are apt to favor this response. One executive, who was a member of the John Birch Society, responded to threats and crises this way, and some subordinates suggested that he cultivated crises that placed him in the center of controversy.

5. *Let your lawyer handle it.* This was a common solution to ordinary crises. For example, where one company and some of its officers were charged with failure to pay income taxes properly, there was no visible effect on the daily routine of the company or its executive offices. The lawyer was instructed to "fix up this damn mess *you* made," and he was empowered to commandeer any help needed. All hands received stern lectures. The implication was that "if the damn lawyers and tax people had done their jobs right, this never would have occurred." In at least one instance after the corporate counsel had done Herculean work at near-

genius level, the entire legal department was quietly eliminated and a private law firm retained.

On the basis of evidence collected in these interviews, it would not be sound career policy for a counsel or tax man to spend time crowing that "I told you so" when crises occur. The messenger who brings bad news should keep one foot in the stirrup; prior warnings are often forgotten when the crunch comes.

6. *Tough it out.* In situations where the originators of crises were a counterculture group or some ethnic or racial minority, the favored response seemed to be to wait for the problem to go away or to assign a low-level staffer to meet the unhappy group's representative. If doing nothing means that the problem will solve itself, there was a consensus that it is pointless to spend money or time on fixing it.

7. *Round up your gang.* While these crises often centered upon the chief executive, one response favored by skilled professional managers was to call in key executives and announce that "we" have a problem. "This means that if I fall, somebody is apt to fall with me, if not ahead of me," said one chief executive coolly. "I guess there are probably a couple of these guys who wouldn't mind seeing me slipped quietly over the side, because one of them might move up. I want to cool that idea very quickly. I make it clear that, like all problems, we are going to work on this together. I organize my defense so that they become spokesmen, advocates, and defenders along with me. I bind us together at the ankles, which helps in the battle."

One large food company was hit by charges from a Congressional committee's surprise witness, who presented on TV what he said was damning evidence about one of the company's products that is sold to children. The accuser asserted that the president of the firm knew and condoned the poor quality ("profits ahead of kids") and recommended that the company officer be hauled in to explain his malfeasance to the committee.

The company president immediately rallied his team, making it clear that the head nutritionist and director of research would be the first to go to Washington and that, if the president were called, he would immediately volunteer all of his team to attend and sit behind him in symbolic evidence of unity.

In another case, a committee for defending the company was appointed, and a well-known critic of the president was made chairman. The responsibility for clearing up the mess was placed squarely in his lap, and he worked hard and successfully to refute the charges against the president and the company.

8. *Make like a duck.* The late Bill Powers of the American Banker's Association had a tactic for crisis situation—"Make like a duck: Be calm and serene on the surface, but paddle like crazy underneath." When confronted with a devastating report from an examiner, he calmly agreed to read and study the report and then sought a delay. Then he worked like mad to limit its exposure, talked to key directors so there would be no surprises, and whaled backs to get everything corrected as quickly as possible. This would often permit him to report back, "We thank you for your report, and can now report that everything you found has been corrected."

9. *Contain the damage.* A chief executive who advocated this strategy was a for-

mer high-ranking naval officer who said he learned in combat that when you are hit, there is no use panicking or jumping overboard. "It's better to assess the damage, close off the most damaged compartments, and save the rest of the ship by sound emergency procedures," he said. "The objective is to save the entire vessel. It may even be necessary for the captain to accept some casualties in the containment of damage in order to save the entire crew. I guess the key to my strategy is to contain the damage." In short this means sizing up the damage, writing off what may have to be sacrificed, setting up a line of final resistance, and making a strong stand there.

10. *Act like Mayor Daley.* One executive of a large Chicago firm suffered through a traumatic experience inflicted by a hostile newspaper's investigative reporting.

> *I learned from our late mayor how to respond to personal attacks, especially when they seemed to have really caught us short. Mayor Daley, when confronted with a smoking gun case of misfeasance in his administration, would express shock and then fire a department head in a somewhat conspicuous way. The expendable subordinate usually understood the mayor's motives and normally accepted it as necessary to keep the party organization afloat. This managerial logic is very tough but clear—a manager must accept responsibility for his department, and, if something goes wrong, should be ready to depart.*

This kind of response usually involves a private consultation between the boss and departing manager, in which it is explained that there is nothing personal in the firing but that the action is necessary for the good of the organization. A generous termination settlement and strong assistance in outplacement usually are provided to help ease the transition.

11. *Attack the other's motives.* Perhaps more instinctive than logical, the defense of charging the attacker with the wrong motives must be used very well to work. "This is politically motivated" is seldom an effective response to a substantial charge; hard evidence is needed to impugn the attacker. Defamation laws must be considered, since a charge like "he is seeking revenge for being fired for incompetence" must be defensible in court.

12. *Countersue.* While using the courts to fight personal battles is illegal, a countersuit is a defense against a noisy and troublesome suit. One executive stated:

> *I resigned from a board because I suspected the president of cutting corners in stock selling, and I joined the board of another firm that indirectly competed with the first. The president of the first firm filed a noisy suit charging me with conflict of interest. After some thinking and consultation with a tough lawyer, I countersued for ten times his suit, describing his malfeasance. I sent the facts to the Justice Department, the attorney general, and several other regulatory agencies. The president withdrew his suit in a hurry.*

Such counterattacks should be waged only by those with clean hands. For example, after charges by Ralph Nader, General Motors had his morals and character investigated. This counterinvestigation outweighed the alleged wrongs in the public's eye and put Nader on the road to acclaim and power.

13. *Pick your best option.* Anger, panic, and stupor prevent most persons from listing available options, defining objectives, and weighing each option for contribution and cost.

Even if you use rational analysis in your normal dealings, when your adrenalin is flowing and the media is showing caricatures of you to millions of people you probably will have trouble. You may not recognize yourself and may detest what is happening, and this may be the time to call for some detached advice.

14. *Win on a higher level.* Dissidents charged in public and in the boardroom that one company founder was not competent to be CEO and chairman because of ill health (he had had one heart attack). The old man appeared to be defeated but made a last-gasp request that his removal be deferred for six months for personal reasons. It was granted.

With the pressure off, the CEO put himself under the care of a leading heart specialist. He lost weight, exercised, got a tan, and surfaced three months later with his doctor. "I'm back in the saddle," he announced to his board and the press. The physician chimed in that "In my opinion the best therapy for him would be to return to work at once." The rebels hastily retreated, leaving the CEO in charge for ten more years.

**The ideal response** The interviews suggested that an ounce of prevention will prevent a pound of panic. The ideal pattern of preparation for crisis appears to shape up like this:

1. *Manage by anticipation.* The "how I responded to crisis" interviews suggested that the best strategy is to be prepared—that is, consider in advance all plausible crises and have response tactics prepared for each. Specific options must be devised for the kinds of threats, risks, and opportunities that are out there. Most lawyers will be of maximum value in response (at your expense) rather than in prevention. A solidly grounded public relations director will think strategically before he thinks operationally, so you can expect more crises if your PR chief is more of a fire fighter than a preventer.

The president of one large corporation donated funds to his alma mater for a building and, with a go-ahead from his PR director, agreed to speak at its dedication. The situation soured, however, when a crowd of hostile students appeared at the ceremony, jeering and shouting insults about his company. The shocked executive did not handle the confrontation very well.

The PR man should not have allowed his president to be caught in such a situation. The president should have been warned of the possibility of a demonstration and been better prepared to handle it and even turn it to his advantage.

2. *Make better use of environmental audits.* Companies that operate in high-risk environments should be committed to surveying those risks regularly and assessing the possibilities of exposure. This requires constant staff attention to threats and consideration of ways of turning them into opportunities. The most professional executives reported that they really welcome some of the challenges and crises;

they saw opportunities where others might only have seen dangers or, at best, nuisances.

3. *Keep physically fit.* Maintenance of a steady state of physical health, mental outlook, and equanimity seemed to be a major part of the preparation of the professional managers. One executive said:

> *I find that if I am overtired, overworked, and overtaxed, I am apt to blow my cool at something rather small. I found that rage is something I fall back on when I haven't had enough rest—working too many hours, traveling too much, and not taking a vacation. I now plan a winter vacation in the sun for a couple of weeks every year, and I don't let anything stop it. I look forward to a fully occupied period with my grandchildren, some reading, and some long spells alone or with my wife.*

4. *Develop personal skills.* Executives who faced crises that required talking with reporters, personal appearances before investigative bodies, or sessions in court reported that they fully appreciated any previous training in public speaking, communication skills, and how to work in front of a TV camera. Past experience as an officer in a trade association, conducting seminars for professional groups, and speaking to educational groups proved to be excellent preparation for the kinds of appearances that placed the executive under duress.

"I found that my evening teaching in a college many years before was probably the best preparation for dealing with the press and media," said one president. "It taught me to deal with tough questions from relatively uninformed people who wouldn't mind catching me in an error."

5. *Plan things right all the time.* One president of a large insurance company quoted La Rochefoucald: "Perfect virtue is to do without witnesses everything that one is capable of doing in public view." Still another read a quote from Eldridge Cleaver: "Doing right is a hustle, too."

# fourteen

# How bureaucracy makes cowards out of heroes

In the course of a major antitrust suit against a corporate giant a few years back, a lot of intimate details about how that giant firm operates were laid bare. Among the more interesting facts uncovered was the system by which decisions are made at its upper levels. The following came out in the wash:

- It took as many as 2500 individual approvals or concurrences before a decision to introduce a new product was approved.
- Any one of thirty-five different staff departments had veto power over changes in major procedures.
- The failure rate of new products was in excess of eighty percent.
- A significant number of new ideas that were ultimately adopted started not inside the corporation but outside it, through the action of a competitor, a change in laws, or a market demand.

Yet this was a most successful corporation, so successful in fact that it dominated the market and was being charged with restraint of trade!

## THE INNOVATIVE IMPORTANCE OF SMALL FIRMS

The figures cited from the large corporation are rather different from those of the small- to medium-sized firm. For one thing, the large firm is more apt to see innovation as what D. G. Marquis calls "complex system change" than as a single breakthrough in technology or an invention. When IBM introduced the System/360 computer, it was more than a simple process of invention. The corporation at that time was a multi-billion-dollar firm and had plans to grow even bigger. Every decision to change a product line carried a multi-billion-dollar price tag. Dozens of factories, hundreds of service offices, and regional sales offices, and thousands of customers had to be changed. A major mistake could cost billions. Certainly, IBM's preeminent market position could have been the price of failure. Accordingly, it was necessary to act in a somewhat bureaucratic style in order to make change.

The small firm, on the other hand, has fewer customers to change, fewer employees to retain, fewer salespeople to update, and perhaps only one factory to convert. Even more important, it can get top-management decisions faster because there are fewer top managers. In many small firms, there is only one mind that needs changing: that of the owner.[1]

This means that the smaller firm can provide a vital ingredient in the market-place and, accordingly, in the economy. When a new idea strikes a small firm, it can move quickly to exploit the idea. It often has trouble finding financial backing to exploit the idea, it is true. But it also has fewer staff experts who can study fine details and prevent change if the top person wants to change. The small firm must press on through several stages, each of which it discovers as it presses toward exploitation:

1. It must develop a product that is technically sound and also fills some need. Usually it does not have expertise in hand to do a scientific market study, and it may push forward on the faith of the inventor alone. If the firm's instincts or luck are favorable, this hurdle will be passed successfully.

2. It must find a market big enough to justify the innovation. While the big firm can do size estimates of the market pretty accurately, the small firm often presses on with the blind assumption that "everyone will want to buy one." Here, too, the element of lucky guesses or sound intuitions can make or break the effort.

3. It must hone its ideas down through product development to get production bugs, tooling mistakes, and high costs out of the product or service. Often it has not the giant engineering staff with experience at this debugging process. If it fails to do it well, it will probably be noncompetitive in the long pull of operating a business against eager competitors.

4. It must build an organization, including a marketing organization, with all of the pitfalls inherent in doing so. The large firm has a ready-made marketing organization which is *adding to its product line,* or adding a new marketing effort based upon solid experience in marketing and service. The start-up of businesses based upon innovative ideas thus naturally suffers from a lack of resources and experience in planning. For the small, innovative firm, the biggest barriers to planning lie in lack of financial strength, lack of skilled personnel, and lack of experience.

While this is a painful process for most firms, and the majority of them fail, for the economy it is a healthy process. For those firms that luck out or have sufficient energy and skill in a few areas, innovative ideas become business and economic realities. Digital Equipment, Wang Electronics, Data General, and others in the computer business started small, headed by innovative and imaginative leaders who went through this maze and became successful where many failed. For

[1] J. H. Bunzel, *The American Small Business* (New York: Knopf, 1962).

the economy as a whole, this created new jobs, new products, and a new industry in minicomputers.

## THE CORPORATE BUREAUCRACY AND INNOVATIVE PROCESSES

Once the company has become large, it has the resources to exploit innovation and invention. At the same time, it has become a bureaucracy and is slowed down by its own internal constraints. This produces a paradox.

*Small firms don't have the resources or the experience to plan innovation. Large firms have the skill, but their decision processes are made cumbersome and Byzantine, and planning becomes a bureaucratic exercise.*

There are some ten ways in which bureaucratic management can slow down the process of innovation.

**1. The division of labor is finer in large organizations.** The whole idea of a bureaucracy, and its great strength, lies in the efficiencies of the division of labor.[2] From Adam Smith's *Wealth of Nations* onward, students of organization have pointed out this advantage of modern organization. The lone craft worker who makes the entire product from start to finish gets more pride out of the work but is woefully inadequate competing in an industrial society. Rather than a specialist in each village to make hoes, or kettles, or dishes, the industrial society creates entire villages—or even cities—of people making some small part of a hoe, a kettle, or a dish. Ten pin makers working on the whole pin will produce ten pins—one apiece. Ten pin makers in an assembly-line pin factory, with high-speed automatic equipment, will make millions in a single day.

This is all very fine for a stable business, where there are pins, cars, or bars of soap to be made, year in and year out, by the millions. But when the shape or style, or even the character, of the product is constantly changing, the bureaucratic division of labor serves to slow down change. The plant manager must grumble at new models that call for stopping production and retooling every so often. Long runs, standard quality, and lower costs are characteristic of production efficiency. The idea of change is not handily managed by the assembly line, the production schedule, or the mass marketing system. The division of labor builds up fine skills in tiny portions of the job, and when changes take place frequently, they disrupt, and they require people to learn anew what they should do. They also produce human misfits.

*The division of labor is not readily accepting of change, and when a planning department created to invent change comes on the scene, it must be considered an enemy of efficiency.*

[2] M. Weber, *The Theory of Social and Economic Organization,* trans. by A. M. Henderson and T. Parsons (New York: Free Press, 1947); *see also* E. Durkheim, *The Division of Labor* (New York: Free Press, 1933).

**2. Procedures are not conducive to change but to stability.** Very large organizations need procedures that describe how work shall be done. This attention to uniformity is necessary for standard costs, for uniformity of quality, and for ease of service to the customer. If a Caterpillar tractor breaks down in Colorado, it is far simpler to get it going again if the spare part can be ordered by number from Peoria, or from a regional warehouse. It is ordered by number and year and shipped according to a procedure, and the people follow standard practices in handling orders, preparing invoices, shipping the part, and billing the customer. The procedures for handling and restocking inventory mean that the right parts in the right quantity will be at the most valuable place at the best possible time, and that serves customer needs very well.[3]

Those changes that are modifications of procedures can, of course, be handled by a "change-procedure" order, which is itself a procedure. To the extent that change is itself a procedural matter, change is easy for the bureaucratic firm. If, on the other hand, the change is something that falls outside the procedure and calls for something innovative, individualistic, or particular, it is often bad news.

**3. In order to maintain stability, systems of control are needed.** For the large organization, the year begins with some assumptions that many of the things that happened last year will happen again this year at about the same level, and in much the same way. Sears sold $17 billion worth of goods in 1978 and started 1979 with the expectation that 1979 would be slightly above that level, with a few predictable changes, for the better, it was hoped. Contracts are let at the beginning of the year, employment relationships with workers and managers established, and capital investments made on the assumptions of stability—within definable limits. Control grows out of this predictability. If things vary from the predicted level, then certain responses are called for, all of which should have been foreseen and described in advance. The three-part cycle standards/operations/review-and-correct comprises the essence of managerial control.

Control does not change things; it assures stability and predictability.[4] Even the crises fall within certain upper and lower limits of variation. People who require changes that fall outside such standard variations are often treated to a certain amount of hostility, as would be deserved by an enemy. If planners confine themselves to *controlling,* then they are tolerated, even welcomed. If, on the other hand, they start making troublesome moves to change the character and direction of the business, they threaten stability and must be subdued. All forecasts should be made with three possible levels of output: the normal or expected, the maximum possible, and the least permissible levels. If actuality departs too sharply from these limits, a *crisis* has been created.

Some crises are understandable, especially those created by the actions of others outside the firm (for Sears, the actions of Kresge or J.C. Penney, for example). If customers' tastes change, this too can be accepted, since it is part of the luck of

---

[3] R. L. Cron, *Assuring Customer Satisfaction* (New York: Van Nostrand Reinhold, 1974).

[4] J. Juran, *Managerial Breakthrough* (New York: McGraw-Hill, 1961).

the game. If, however, the crises are deliberately created by *planning from within* the firm, even when it comes from the very top of the organization, it runs into resistance by the bureaucracy.

*Internal planning often creates an internal crisis and is apt to produce fervent opposition.*

**4. The fear of failure is widespread in bureaucracies.** The people who have learned to follow procedures and have been rewarded for conformity ("being a team player") fear changes that stem from nonconformity.[5] Old forest rangers faced with new theories of forest management from new, young, ecology-minded park managers are frightened by the threat to themselves from the obsolescence of patiently acquired experience and skills. The machine operator who has learned to cut cloth, or mix paint, skillfully is frightened silly and turned into an irrational being when the machine is automated or placed under computer control or when the procedures are completely changed. The arguments made against the change are all stated in rational and logical terms—or as appeals to experience; but the underlying cause for argument is the possibility that the new method or the new machine, or the new form of organization, will leave the worker obsolete, vulnerable, and exposed to being an organizational misfit. Past training, in the face of major changes, is now seen as useless and even foolish; self-esteem is lowered; and anger and dismay increase.

**5. Decision making in large organizations is shared by many persons.** In bureaucratic organizations nobody seems to be able to make a decision all alone. Too many people can point out some undesired side effect, some unforeseen cost, or some concealed trap in argument against the change. All of these many voices must be heard and their interests and opinions incorporated into the final decision. Such an array of voters, all of whom may have veto power but whose stake is mainly in the status quo, slows down the implementation of change. A new plan must fit the model "Victory has a hundred fathers and defeat is an orphan." Even people in highly placed positions will think twice before insisting that incessant talking cease and action begin. To shortcut the many judges sitting on the sidelines means that the responsibility for the mistake will be clearly identified with the overly assertive decision maker.

Rensis Likert, in his *New Patterns of Management,* clearly spells out the many advantages to the organization in this joint and group form of decision making.[6] People who participate in the decisions are more likely to support the final choice when it is made. The group is also an excellent morgue for foolish ideas. It also, we might note, is an effective method of killing some good ones. The end result is apt to be the death of some good ideas that might succeed along with the bad ones that do not make the grade. Much of the effect of group decision making among multiple decision makers is also to *slow down* the process, to reduce flexibility, and to

---

[5] D. Katz and R. L. Kahn, *The Social Psychology of Organizations* (New York: John Wiley, 1966).

[6] R. Likert, *New Patterns of Management* (New York: McGraw-Hill, 1961).

limit the firm's mobility in introducing change. The quality and acceptance of decisions is the aim of such multiple decisions. The unintended and unnoticed effect is to stop more than would be stopped by fewer decision makers.

**6. Individual responsibility disappears.** Many years ago I was on the staff of a giant corporation. Among the interesting assignments that befell me was an occasional call for my services as a writer of speeches for executives. In preparing me for this important chore, however, the vice-president in charge of personnel and public relations warned me soberly, "Please don't let any false *pride of authorship* get into your work." With these words this well-meaning and experienced man was telling me that the final speech was to be censored at least ten times before it would finally be allowed to be read aloud before some audience by an executive of the firm. All of the vitality, originality, and pizazz were consequently wiped out in the process. What came forth from the speaker's mouth was a well-pasteurized mass of verbal milk toast. Occasionally, I was able to slip something in that had some vigor, but most of the time if was bland stuff, and the note of appreciation that followed the speech was a hollow token that only depressed me more than if the speech had been honestly acknowledged as tripe.

This case illustrates the way in which so much of individual effort is homogenized in the bureaucratic organization. The people are fine folks, they are well mannered, and they want only the very best to come forth; and, to be honest, there are many reasons why the verbal peppers and spices that would have pleased the audience and the press had to be covered over with verbal gravy to kill the more piquant flavors the speech might contain. Yet, individual initiative, imagination, flair, style, and originality all too often are the first casualty in the battles the bureaucracy fights against its competitors and the environment. Automotive engineers with daring designs, utility managers with candor and openness in public statements, or personnel people with humane and caring ideas in dealing with people find that they must suppress their best shots. It would make the bureaucracy and its top people *vulnerable* to criticism, and the avoidance of criticism occupies much of the time and energy of the people engaged in bureaucratic work. The fact that the criticism is petty, or even invalid, might be conceded, but the existence of criticism as something to be avoided altogether has a dulling effect upon innovation.

Criticism is something that must be treated, dealt with, and perhaps responded to in a bureaucracy—not listened to. This will occupy the time and energy of a lot of people and thus is a painful nuisance. The safest way is to do things in such a fashion that criticism is avoided and short-circuited before it starts. The end result upon the organization's people is that they learn quickly to operate in a bland style that makes responsibility something to be *shared.* The pride of innovation, of invention, of authorship, then, is a personal affectation to be set aside and subdued in a self-abnegating way for the good of the organization. The natural consequence deriving from this *self-censorship* and self-suppression of form soon becomes the suppression of substance. If the original and daring thought must always be suppressed, then the natural, easy way is to avoid having it. After a while, it is not even missed, by either the organization or the individual.

After a year, I concluded that it would be wiser to get out before I had acquired such a mind set, and I returned to college teaching. For the first year at the University of Michigan, I reveled in my new freedom and engaged in making speeches and writing articles that in my exuberance, I must confess, all too often bordered on the inflammatory. Soon the faculty of that fine institution had shown me that it did not really care and had an easy tolerance for my fireworks displays, and I was able to retreat to a more responsible style. The security of knowing that I would not have to defend myself against censorship or criticism for thinking my own thoughts and speaking my own mind mended my trauma of the large bureaucracy, and I was able to become somewhat more sensible in my verbal behavior. This grew out of the freedom and toleration of the organization, and I began to assume a more responsible attitude toward writing and speaking.

What bureaucracies don't realize is that when people are always treated as responsible, they will do better things and will learn to accept individual responsibility for their own ideas. Censorship and suppression are powerful forces against originality and ultimately intellectual responsibility.

7. **Bureaucracy inevitably produces an organization of pipsqueaks.** The small firm that grows large with its founder still alive and in charge has been described as "the lengthened shadow of a man."[7] This has some suppressive effects upon change and innovation, it is true, especially when *the man* has a suppressive bent or autocratic style of leading. On the other hand, many such strong people like to surround themselves with equally strong people and thus to grow individuals who show imagination, individuality, and character.

The bureaucratic organization starts out at the same place and draws its recruits from the same human race and same labor market. But after it works its homogenizing effects, making decisions a matter of team effort and collaborative thought, it has separated individuals from making decisions and, accordingly, from personal responsibility for the good or bad effects of those decisions. The effect upon people over time is a distinct one; where there are few opportunities for decisions except the most routine, individual differences tend to disappear. This does not mean, of course, that decisions do not get made, but rather that they consist of bits and pieces from many people. You might even make a fairly good case that these decisions are *better-quality decisions* for the most part than would be made if a single heroic decider were to decide. Their *acceptance* as well as their originality is lower, for they represent compromise that leaves everyone slightly disgruntled.

Wiping out individual differences among people at work is not the purpose of group decision making in the bureaucracy. It is an improvement in quality of decisions and protection against error and failure that is sought. Individual differences mean that people have widely varying opinions and conclusions which they pursue. Some of them might be the voice of genius, but it is highly likely that some of them will be the voice of the crackpot and the fanatic as well. Cultivating indi-

---

[7] R. W. Emerson, *Collected Works of R. W. Emerson* (Cambridge Mass.: Harvard University Press, 1971).

vidual differences means allowing both to cultivate whatever kind of individual virtuosity they have. The pooled decision may, in fact, protect the organization better from its resident geniuses and nuts, but the resulting people can only be described as pipsqueaks.[8]

As a case study, modern university administration provides a ready example. For the administrator, such as a department chairman or a dean, there is almost no latitude to make many of the important judgments that are available to management in even the most restrictive and bureaucratic corporation. Personnel decisions for such matters as tenure, promotion, merit pay, and other rewards are all held tightly by a layered series of committees. The departmental personnel committee recommends personnel actions upon all of the departmental faculty in such matters. These go to the chairman, who may concur or dissent, but who will send the two resultant recommendations to a college-level personnel committee. After these deliberations, the well-layered question now rises upward to a dean, who studies the three prior levels and makes a fourth recommendation. The four cumulated recommendations levitate further to a vice-president or provost, who studies all the prior decisions and either concurs or demurs. This package now goes to the president of the university, who also studies the whole packet. This is now a paper accumulation of several pounds. If the aspirant for higher rank has passed through all of these filters, a recommendation then goes to the trustees, who approve or deny. It is true that usually the higher levels will overturn a lower one only where there is "compelling reason for doing so," but ordinarily any single level has more powers to reject and knock out than to recommend approval.

The result is that the aspirant to academic rank and status must be a *pleasing person* to multiple groups of people with declining levels of knowledge of individual qualities. The product is a dampening of many of the individual differences that would enhance the development of superior qualities of scholarly curiosity, intellect, invention, and innovation. In all fairness, the system works fairly well for the early-blooming genius who has produced a major, widely recognized breakthrough in thought or research. It likewise quickly screens out the small number of least productive teachers, researchers, or service persons in faculty ranks. It is the persons between those two ranks who are turned into pipsqueaks. A steady eight- or nine-year diet of watching numerous judges for cues and innuendoes as to what will *displease* them and the assiduous avoidance of such acts exacts its toll on the person.

Occasionally, a rare one comes along, like a young colleague of mine who patiently suffered through a ring of such assessments for seven years, until finally the trustees voted her tenure and full-professor rank. The next morning she burst into my office and, smiling from ear to ear, announced, "Okay, you bastard, that's it, no more Mr. Nice Guy! I can start being myself." Not everyone has the ego strength, the salable skills, or the financial lasting power to display such durability

---

[8] C. Argyris, *Personality and Organization* (New York: Harper & Row, Pub., 1957); *See also* C. Walker and R. H. Guest, *The Man on the Assembly Line* (Cambridge, Mass.: Harvard University Press, 1952).

in the face of bureaucratic decision making. Most will simply come closer to being a pipsqueak.

The procedure also explains why universities have such poor track records in producing good administrators. Robbed of individual decision-making powers in vital decisions, the department chairman, the dean, and even the provost are reduced in the ability to decide, and thus to grow, in the power to make wise, bold, or even competent decisions.

**8. Large organizations are best at large deals.** Once the annual revenues of a firm get over $100 million, it seems rather foolish to spend the time and energy of officers and other key decision makers in small transactions.[9] Unless the potential revenue added by an innovation will get into the multi-million-dollar range, it will probably be deferred, ignored, and brushed aside. To the ordinary citizen, for whom a $10,000-a-year raise in pay would be a bonanza, it may seem inconceivable. Yet, those who work around corporate offices know that this orientation to the big deal is a fact of life for most giant firms. One large food company, for example, will only enter a new competitive market if it promises substantially in excess of $100 million in revenues after the second year and if it can become a leading seller in that field in two years. Thus, some small, enterprising inventor of a spectacular new snack or a nutritious item could not expect this firm to show even a glimmer of interest in the idea. Only if it could have an impact at the $100 million level by supplanting an existing product would it be entertained.

This does not mean that such a firm does not enter start-up markets, but that it would be a rare case. Procter & Gamble, for example, entered the snack market that had previously been held by potato chips with a composite potato snack, which *did* start from zero and which leaped beyond $100 million in sales within two years. Mead Johnson started into the diet business with Metrecal, a diet supplement that assisted people in losing weight, and generated over $100 million in sales in two years with the new product. In such cases, the innovative idea may be a product differentiation—a special twist—or it may be a technical breakthrough that comes from long research in a well-financed lab.

For many other large firms, however, innovation is clearly a multi-million-dollar affair. A new kind of automobile is not a one-shot burst of genius. General Motors Research Lab has hundreds of engineers and scientists. The Chevrolet Division alone has over a thousand engineers working on future models, as do other divisions of General Motors. The Ford Motor Company engineering center is a large, campuslike atmosphere. During a single year, the organization of the engineering function will include several years of effort in a finely organized tier of assignments. One group will be designing the 1982 model, another the tooling of the 1981, while still another is doing advanced styling for the 1983 and beyond. All of this will actually be happening in the year 1980. The pipeline of research and development is such that it can hardly be said to be dependent upon the genius or individuality of a single person.

[9] A. A. Berle and G. C. Means, *The Modern Corporation and Private Property* (New York: Macmillan, 1932).

Similar patterns of development are apt to appear in petrochemical research, steel, and pharmaceuticals. Organized into functional departments such as chemistry, virology, microbiology, and the like, the lab does most of its work on a *project system*. Each person has a home department which represents his or her discipline, but one's productive work as a scientist, engineer, or technical expert will be done under the objectives of the project. This is shown in the illustration below.

This means that individual differences and performance possibilities must be demonstrated within an organizational framework that sharply limits the conditions under which excellence of performance can be displayed.[10] The large jet engine maker will have administrative home departments for engineers, service personnel, marketing, and manufacturing. From these groups will come the know-how to produce the new jet engines for the eighties that must fit certain constraints. The new jet must have sufficient thrust to carry wide-body planes with large payloads. It must also meet new noise-abatement standards, be fuel-efficient, and accordingly be lighter in weight than present forms.

Obviously it is a major decision to establish an innovative project. For one thing, funding for the project will probably come from some customer or client, such as the government or the military, or from a major marketing program within the firm. Before an idea can obtain the funding, it must be spelled out in advance in exquisite and costly detail to predict all the possible advantages and disadvantages. The project certainly calls for high levels of intelligence and is a great user of high talent. But the intelligence is also highly disciplined and organized, and the role of the isolated and brilliant inventor and innovator is almost nonexistent or is the rare exception. Star qualities are not sought, for they are more likely to lead to disputes and delays, which add to cost without necessarily adding to value. Thus, the general manager becomes as much an arbitrator as a leader.

The work of the project is highly subdivided into specialists. In electronics, these may have such exotic titles as *white noise* or *vibration and shock*. The

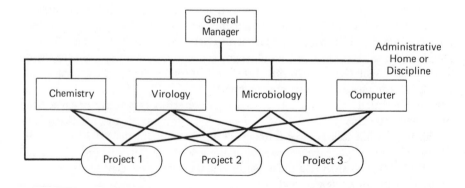

[10]H. I. Ansoff and J. Stewart, "Strategies for a Technology Based Business," *Harvard Business Review,* November-December 1967; *see also* A. Chandler, *Strategy and Structure* (Cambridge, Mass.: MIT Press, 1962).

project also produces a status system. The mathematician and the computer expert and the chemists and physicists rank high in the pecking order, while the technical writer, draftsperson, or machinist ranks somewhat lower. Ordinary workers, such as sweepers and typists, rank lowest of all.

The requirement of conformity to the procedures and policies of the firm, and most especially to doing a small segment very well, is more important than being a change agent, innovator, or imaginative planner. Only the few people clustered around the president or general manager have such power, and even here it is widely shared. The engineer must consult the marketing manager to be sure the product will sell before choosing a technical direction.

It is for this reason that small, start-up firms are most likely to produce the basic research and truly innovative ideas. (Yet they are more prone to make the mistakes of economic misjudgment, marketing mismanagement, and financial weaknesses that cause the great majority of them to fail.) It is thus that the bureaucratic and large organization serves to stop far more change than it produces.

**9. Large organizations operate best as assembly lines.** The genius of Henry Ford was less in the invention of the internal-combustion engine than in the creation of the assembly line for cars. The division of labor which assigns to each worker one small function on the line is perhaps a thousandfold more refined and sophisticated today than it was in 1910. Electronic control, automated transfer machines, numerically controlled machine tools, and automatic testing equipment have elevated the specialties to a higher level of importance. Such automated systems permit the programming of more variety into the line, but nonetheless it is still the programmed production line that dominates the idea of large-scale enterprise. Repetitive patterns, standard costs, and standard behaviors of people surrounding the process are still the heart of efficiency in the large-scale enterprise.

Because of the electronic and automated control, there are, it is true, many more jobs in the modern production plant that are creative and technical in character and permit more work of that technical nature than in the past. Still, the work of the production engineer, the quality-control specialist, and the electronic engineer is fragmentary and quite narrowly defined. A former student working for a large automobile company reports that his work as a "chief engineer" is to direct the design each year of windshield-wiper motors for one model of car. His work must fit into the design, the engineering, and the production constraints of the model, over which he has little decision-making power. Furthermore, it must fit the weight requirements, which are often defined by energy pressures, and must meet standards for safety set by automotive safety laws. His final product will be approved at several levels, almost as many as for the assistant professor seeking promotion to associate at a university. If his work proves to be sufficiently wrong, however, that the car has to be recalled after production and sale, it is quite unlikely that he will be held individually responsible for such a flaw, for approvals at all of those levels above and around him have immunized him from blame in the whole. Thus, his work is actually part of a giant system of rationalized and finely divided technical effort, and his individual creativity and innovative skills are sharply contained.

The Opportunities Board at Litton Industries, and the management review procedures at ITT, have clearly been productive of the goals the corporation desires. They combine the work of innovative and creative people with that of a powerful group of analysts, budget makers, program planners, and staff experts in accounting, traffic, law, personnel, public relations, and the like who scrutinize every proposal coming from the creative initiator. The big error is avoided, for no decisions are made on intuition alone. Confronted with the unknown, the creative person who follows his or her instincts will often rely on intuition and experience. The managerial organization, on the other hand, will immediately start screaming for facts, and if there is a tyranny of anything, it is a tyranny of the facts. It is thus a *mix of people* that bureaucratic organizations require to get innovation done at all. With nothing more to go on than sound review procedures, there would be no innovative, entrepreneurial types to make the proposals that would be available to be scrutinized. Without the domination of the reviewing managers, the innovative managers would fall into social, economic, and cultural pitfalls. They might also not be able to see the opportunities and avenues for exploitation.

Nonetheless, at the end of the corporate decision-making production line, which functions on constructive conflict, there are negative decision makers in more cases than approvers. Innovation and creativity are tightly disciplined, and when no outside influences are at work, such a new law, or intense action by a competitor, the tendency to turn down is often overpowering. The bureaucratic organization functions best at a "no surprises" level.

**10. Creativity is personal and bureaucracy is depersonalized.** The imbalance between creativity and stability produces a system that ends up depersonalized. Bureaucracies are efficient in production and selling, and in doing routine decision making.[11] All of this means that individual differences will be subsumed under the efficiency rubric, and people will be pressured to become amenable to enumeration. They have social security numbers, employee numbers, ZIP codes, area codes—and for good reason. If they can be identified by that characteristic they have in common with all others of their class—a number—they can be processed more economically. There is little room in a payroll for personal likes and dislikes, only the numbers. The customer, too, becomes treated with quantitative efficiency, and products, processes, and procedures are subject to quantification.

Five people on a pin assembly and production line will stop being John, Jane, Harry, Harriet, and Sal. They will become 1, 2, 3, 4, and 5. Their similarities are more likely to be respected than their differences. Their uniformity is the basic building block for the division of labor. While this is perfectly sensible from the viewpoint of cutting cost and improving yields, it has some unintended side effects. People who are first assigned numbers and, following that, become numbers, act as if that description were factual. They learn to subdue any flickerings of individuality, and in so doing subdue the instincts that would impel them to make changes,

---

[11] J. Jewkes, *The Sources of Invention* (New York: Macmillan, 1958); *see also* A. B. Stafford, "Is the Rate of Invention Declining?" *American Journal of Sociology,* 57, May 1952.

or even to suggest them. Finally, they find it comfortable to avoid even thinking about change, and then to suppress thinking about it when others propose it. This process usually does not fully suppress the natural desire of people to propose new ideas that would alter and modify the present ways for the better. It is in defensive methods improvement and new ways of doing the present things that innovation is most likely to occur.

The great barrier, however, comes in the immense fear and trembling created by a *new theory*. The new ideas to alter present methods are often apparent and visibly beneficial to eveyone and will accordingly be accepted. The entirely new idea, however, is one that can change the character and direction of the entire enterprise. It asks the question *Are we doing the right things?* rather than merely asking *Are we doing things right?* The latter question is often quite acceptable, and in some organizations even encouraged. The breakthrough level of thinking is far less likely to be greeted with great enthusiasm, and thus will not appear.

Modern medicine is said to have emerged when it was discovered that specific germs cause specific diseases. It supplanted a whole approach to human health care that was based upon some vague and vaporous theories of the causes of illness. While this "germ theory" is not to be denied as a basis of modern medicine, it covers up many of the most important public health problems of the last half of the twentieth century.[12] The era of miracle drugs, such as antibiotics, is a product of the theory of specific etiology—or specific causes for specific diseases. Yet, the problems which can be traced to multiple causes are not especially manageable by such an approach. The suspicion that cancer and heart disease are in need of a new theory rather than a specific cure has already made considerable headway in medical science. Yet, because it flies in the face of the established theories of doing things, it is not widely accepted and its proponents are treated to some rather disdainful kinds of rejection in many cases. The idea that human health may be substantially affected by the environment and substances within it is already beginning to find acceptance, many of its advocates apparently not even realizing that they are dealing with a wholly novel approach to the study and practice of human health care.

Much of this *resistance to new strategies,* new theories, and novel ideas about the fundamentals is rooted in the huge, well-entrenched organizations that are in place and at work under the older theory. As Bernard Dixon points out in *Beyond the Magic Bullet,* it is often the style of living and personal habits of people that may be more important in curing cancer and heart disease, the major killers, than any of the presently available forms of medical or surgical intervention.[13] For the Third World, better sanitation and nutrition are likely to do more good than shiploads of Western drugs, medical equipment, and doctors. Yet, it is the latter that are the tools and procedures of the medical and health care establishment and bureaucratic organizations.

---

[12] I. Illich, *Medical Nemesis* (London: Caldar and Boyars, 1975).
[13] B. Dixon, *Beyond the Magic Bullet* (New York: Harper & Row, Pub., 1978).

In innovative areas of science, it thus becomes nearly impossible to be successful in thinking big thoughts, undertaking imaginative enterprises, or using speculative intelligence. The bureaucratic organization of industry, government, and science stresses bread-and-butter payoff, short-term return, and cost-effectiveness in the near term. As a result, the young are trained to live within limits.

# fifteen

# How people can band together to resist change

One of the most fascinating novels in the English language is *Robinson Crusoe,* written by Daniel Defoe two and a half centuries ago. Defoe based this fictional account of a marooned sailor upon the diaries and written accounts of a Scottish sailor named Alexander Selkirk, who was marooned on the South Sea island of Mas á Terra from 1704 to 1709. For four years Selkirk lived in isolation before being rescued. He wrote his story for publication in 1713, to the fascination of the reading public, which included Defoe. The fascination we have for the story is the abnormality of the epic fight Selkirk (and Crusoe) made against being wholly isolated from all contact with other human beings. The fictional Crusoe, of course, exceeded the model of Selkirk, being marooned for twenty-eight years. In prisons today it is considered a cruel and inhumane practice to place an inmate in isolation for a month or more.

This *threat of isolation* is an important enforcer of conformity and compliance with group standards in modern bureaucratic organizations.[1] The military academy at West Point for many years exercised this kind of punishment by placing socially obnoxious persons in "Coventry," a condition in which a cadet who had somehow violated the standards of the corps was never spoken to again if he persisted in remaining at the academy. Such treatment is widely recognized as a special and most horrible kind of sanction for one group of people to lay upon another. Its very possibility comprises a potential kind of behavior modification technique by which discipline is maintained in organizations without resort to more physical and immediate kinds of punishment.

The power of a group within the bureaucracy to control behavior, however, is rooted more in the self-discipline that a *feeling* of isolation brings to bear upon

---

[1] The effects of isolation are well documented. *See* K. Davis, *Human Society* (New York: Macmillan, 1949); J. Bowlby, *Maternal Care and Mental Health*, World Health Organization Monographs, no. 2, 1952; *see also* H. F. Harlow and M. K. Harlow, "Social Deprivation in Monkeys," *Scientific American*, November 1962.

deviants; the isolation imposed by the group upon the member is actually a figurative condition of isolation. The group may isolate people consciously, either as punishment or for some other purpose. Or it may isolate people unknowingly, as occurs in large city populations where everyone goes about his or her own affairs. Without the slightest intention to punish anyone, each citizen maintains an aloofness and silence in contact with strangers. A person thus treated, however, may feel the pain of isolation just as greatly as if punishment had been willfully imposed. The loneliness of the city dweller, even if it is a social accident, inevitably produces anguish to the person without social connections. Such people are apt to engage in all kinds of strong reactions to overcome this isolation.[2] Mass killers usually are from the ranks of social isolates.

The potential of being consciously and deliberately set aside from the group is a powerful basis for conformity to the will of the group in an organization. The skill of the manager in the corporation, government agency, or other work group in manipulating the group's influence on members' behavior is freely labeled "leadership," for leadership means that groups of followers are being led in the direction of some goal.

Beyond its punishing sanction, the group also has certain other benefits for the employing firm.[3] Norman R. F. Maier has systematically listed the assets and liabilities of group decision making as it is practiced in modern bureaucratic organizations.[4] The advantage of group decisions, Maier proposes, includes the fact that the individual members' knowledge can be pooled into a whole which is greater than the sum of its parts. "There is more information in the group than in any of its members," suggests Maier. Another advantage of group decision making is its ability to produce a larger number of approaches to a problem than a single person, however facile, might generate. This opens new options for final choices. For still another advantage, group decision making allows every member to participate in the decision affecting him or her, which has the tangible effect of enhancing the acceptance of the finally chosen course of action. A lower-quality decision, Maier suggests, can be more effective than a high-quality decision if that higher-quality decision lacks acceptance by the group that must implement it. Finally, Maier states, decisions made by individuals must be communicated to others, and in the process of being relayed, clarity and fine details are often lost. On the other hand, where the group itself has shaped the decision, there is greater clarity and more insight

---

[2] Social isolation's effects are described by E. Raab and G. Selznick, *Major Social Problems* (New York: Harper & Row, Pub., 1959); *see also* W. S. Goode, "Family Disorganization," in E. Merton and R. A. Nisbet, eds., *Comtemporary Social Problems* (New York: Harcourt Brace Jovanovich, 1961).

[3] F. Roethlisberger and Dickson, *Management and the Worker* (Cambridge: Harvard University Press, 1939); *see also* E. Mayo, *Human Problems of an Industrial Civilization* (New York: Viking, 1931).

[4] N. R. F. Maier and J. J. Hayes, *Creative Management* (New York: John Wiley, 1962); *see also* N. R. F. Maier and L. R. Hoffman, "Using Trained Developmental Discussion Leaders to Improve Further the Quality of Group Decisions," *Journal of Applied Psychology*, 44, no. 4, 1960.

into the purposes of and alternatives to the final decision. Having been in at the birth, and in the preliminary development, the group can have a full knowledge of its goals, details, and factual information, all of which will be missed in ordinary superior-subordinate communication.

Offsetting these assets of group decision making, Maier has pointed to some limitations. Social pressures will impose the will of the majority upon a minority. Furthermore, once the consensus of a group has been arrived at, the tardy appearance of a superior solution is highly likely to be ignored. Groups can often be manipulated by a dominant leader who uses logic or persuasion or simply outlasts and wears down the others to produce a decision close to his or her own. Also in the group process, there is a danger of discussions in which the alternatives presented by various members stop being logical issues and become emotional goals around which people rally strongly. Winning the argument takes on a higher priority than making the best decision.

There are also other factors in group decision making which, depending upon the skill of the group leader, become alternatively assets or liabilities in attaining agreement on quality decisions. Disagreement and dissent can lead as easily to polarization and endless argument as they can to consensus and innovation. Group members may have hidden interests not especially relevant to the immediate decision at hand. These interests, however, will have an important bearing upon the outcome, for people will pursue those interests strongly without revealing the true basis of their position. While groups are generally more apt to accept risks willingly in decisions than individuals, the time required in making such decisions is longer. Thus, when quick decisions are needed, individual decision is superior.

*The conclusions from Maier's research point to the importance of the group leadership in determining the propensity of the group to accept change and creative new ideas.*

The tendency of leaders to be mastered by the group and accept a kind of egalitarianism is frequently due to a lack of leadership skill, something not easily acquired. Where leaders fade back into the group and assume only a convening and membership role under the impression that there is no such thing as creative leadership, an environment is produced which is more likely to resist change.

When *concurrence seeking* seems to be the major purpose of group decision making, the attention of the members turns to maintaining members' morale and membership status rather than improved decision making. This concurrence-seeking behavior has been identified by Irving L. Janis as "groupthink." This is the condition that exists when a cohesive "in" group seeks to retain its unity and overrides any dissident opinion or suggestion of alternatives. Having too many options to consider can generate lower mental efficiency, an absence of reality testing, and avoidance of moral judgments. Watergate, the Bay of Pigs, and similar shocking experiences have well documented the power of groupthink to overcome the hesitation and dissident thought of members that might save the entire group from subsequent disaster. Conformity tends to increase under groupthink almost in direct proportion to group cohesiveness. The possibility of antagonizing the group or its leader overpowers any such motives as morality or humaneness.[5]

## HOW TO RECOGNIZE GROUPTHINK

It is apparent that groupthink and consensus thinking are not universal. At the same time, it is apparent that they exist rather widely and where they reign will serve to resist change. As a means of planning, they can be either good or bad, according to the leadership of the group.

How can you recognize groupthink when it appears, and what are some antidotes to it? There are many evidences you can use to spot groupthink in your organization. Ten examples taken from the author's case studies in corporations follow.

**1. The ruling group gets along famously.** The management committee of a medium-sized western bank consisted of people who had worked together for more than twenty years. They had started with the bank when it was small, and as it grew, it had promoted strictly from within. The people on the committee were all officers, all had known each other for the entire twenty years, and a generally good level of personal friendship and support pervaded the bank. The president, who was sixty-seven years old, was almost like a father to the others, or at least an older brother who was viewed with considerable fondness. When it came time to decide something, consideration for the views and interests of others was also a paramount value. Nobody would disagree out loud if any other member of the group appeared to hold to a single view rather strongly, or it might ruffle somebody.

In 1978, the state banking commission sent a new auditor to the bank to audit the trust department, and the auditor issued a rather stern report about what he found. For one thing, the bylaws were short on defining the role of the department. Several potential areas of possible self-dealing were noted, including deposit of trust funds in the commercial bank itself. The people who authorized checks were also the people who could sign the same checks, which, the auditor sternly noted, was prohibited under the law. In all there were some thirty specific findings made that were critical of the stewardship of the department. In private conversations, many of the members of the management committee were interviewed about whether or not they had read previous audit reports, or were otherwise aware of the thirty points.

> 'Sure, I had known about many of these things, but I didn't want to raise a stink. After all, Bill has been the trust officer here for a good many years, and he was always assuring us that everything would be fine. It wasn't until we got a new auditor who was more of a stickler that we found we were wrong. Now it will take quite a bit of work to straighten up that department. But after all, we all knew Bill and nobody wanted to raise Cain over something

---

[5] I. L. Janis, *Victims of Group Think* (Boston: Houghton Mifflin, 1972); *see also* I. L. Janis, "Personality Correlates of Susceptibility to Persuasion," *Journal of Personality*, 22, 1954. Often this rejection affects new product proposals as well. *See* R. R. Rotherbert, "Playing It Safe in New Product Development," *Advanced Management Journal*, 4, Fall 1975.

*that was merely a potential problem that seemed very small at the time. I guess we should have spoken up a little more forcefully.' So stated the vice-president and lending officer.*

The antidote in this case was the outside auditor, who shook up the cohesive nature of the group by acting as a critic and attacker. This, of course, can be damaging to reputations and even to group performance in the future. It is better if the leaders require that the group practice self-criticism. The creation of stricter internal audit, or even personal criticism of one another, will often overcome the groupthink effects of the widely prized cohesiveness. This does not necessarily mean the end of cohesiveness, but a modification of it by which people learn to live with the pointed questions of others, and to respect others' motives in asking them.

2. **The group screens out warning signals.** Another characteristic of groupthink-dominated organizations is that they will pretend that danger cannot possibly reach into the closed circle which they have constructed. In one eastern manufacturing plant, the accident rate was double that of similar plants inside the firm and in the industry. The management team, however, ignored occasional letters and spoken complaints by the plant safety director, the union, and the corporate risk manager. "It really is a matter of careless employees who don't use their heads and take too many chances. It is really because this is a new plant and our people are younger and more rash in their way of working," said the manufacturing superintendent. Since a cohesive group was being addressed, this explanation was quickly agreed to, and no major effort was made to face facts and to study the causes and possible corrective actions needed. One day the inspector from OSHA came to the plant and filed a devastating report. It required not only major revisions, including some rewiring of a major section of the warehouse, but also the purchase of new equipment, which was very costly and wrecked the capital budget for the year at that plant. To top that off, the group was stunned when a very heavy fine was subsequently levied. They appealed, but the inspector was upheld and the fine came out of operating costs, which further ruined profits for the plant for that year.

The group responded by charging that the inspector was incompetent, that the judge who had heard the case was biased and antibusiness, and that the safety director should have caught it all. Ultimately, the plant manager was replaced. His replacement created a new safety advisory committee charged with conducting safety audits and reporting directly to the plant manager all weaknesses and potential dangers. This committee was established as a high-level critical body. It operated outside the central decision-making management committee and challenged that group with citations of threats and risks to the safety of employees in the plant it uncovered. The plant safety record improved sharply in the ensuing year.

3. **The group uses rationalization instead of action.** In a large firm in the Northwest, a common practice when unfavorable conditions were brought to the attention of the management group was to spend time and energy building elaborate excuses for the condition, rather than dealing with it as a problem to be solved.[6]

---

[6] L. Festinger, S. Schacter, and K. Back, *Social Pressures in Informal Groups* (New York: Harper & Row, Pub., 1950).

This practice reacted against the company in its affirmative action program, with the result that it was sued by women employees, who won a substantial sum of back pay in a consent decree. The rationalizations had consisted of such statements as, "Our women really prefer the jobs they have, such as typing and shorthand, and don't really want responsibility." Some other alibis that had become articles of faith to the management committee of the firm included the following:

- After all, no qualified women had applied.
- The population of this region is different.
- After all, we advertised and posted jobs before we selected the best person.
- The women are apt to have pregnancy leaves, which leave us shorthanded.
- People don't like to work for women managers; they are too picky.
- Women can't do some of the heavy, dirty jobs.
- Women only want to work at clean and dignified work.

All of this became evidence of discrimination when it was presented in court. The judge, speaking in open court, chastised the management for its violations of Title VII of the 1964 Civil Rights Act.

The antidote came with the appointment of a strong affirmative action officer, who taught people the law and made them aware of the threats in not complying. A women's caucus was formed to keep a watchdog role on affirmative action, and the personnel manager met with it regularly to hear complaints. These were filed in writing, and the copies to the management committee were often used to discuss new means of compliance.

**4. The group finds new meanings for morality.** In an electrical components firm, the manager of the sales department and the vice-president for marketing often met secretly with competitors to illegally fix prices and divide the market. This became a crisis when the FBI and other federal agencies uncovered the situation and filed criminal complaints against the officers for violation of antitrust laws. Several stiff fines and a few short jail sentences for officers were meted out by the court amid screaming headlines in the press. The crestfallen officers reported sadly that they had been seeking some higher goals. "We were trying to save the jobs of our employees, as well as protect the stockholders. If we hadn't conspired, we would have let down the many people who were depending upon us," one said. When the president of Lockheed was discovered to have been bribing an official in Japan, he reported some time later that his motive had been dominated by the desire to protect the jobs of thousands of Lockheed workers.

In still other cases, the morality isn't necessarily a higher one claimed for the group, but a lower one for its enemies. In one grocery wholesale firm, when competition got too heavy, the management committee tacitly approved a course of hiring some consultants who would provide "tougher competition" to the competing firm's truckers. This was a shorthand description for hiring goons to dump the competition's products into the street, throw gasoline into its produce, and engage in other, similar shenanigans. At no time did the board that had approved the letting of the "consultant" contract ever consider the morality of what it was undertaking as anything but the best. There was a certain amount of boyish laughter and glee when the reports began to come in that a competitor's tires were punctured or its windshields broken. "There was no real rough stuff, no physical injury to any persons, and certainly no killings or anything like that," explained the president. "It's just that we are playing a bit tougher hard-ball with a bunch of boys *who don't have an ounce of ethics*." The apparent rationale for this goon squad, then, was not that the damage and intimidation was moral, but that the competition was immoral.

Groupthink or its equivalent has to work out some kind of moral argument for the group.[7] Except for those very few groups that are collections of maniacs, every group needs a morality upon which it bases its actions. The terrorist group cannot function without a higher morality, which is usually the cause of some oppressed group. "We must engage in these acts in order to gain what is truly ours, and restore to us what we have had stolen from us." So goes the morality of anarchy, terrorism, conspiracy, or simply thievery. The process of groupthink in justification is somewhat similar for most cohesive groups, be it the missions board of a church or the gang of muggers in Central Park. Once this morality has been hammered out and put in place, all kinds of behavior can be justified under its sponsorship and justification.

**5. The group sees all opposition as one-dimensional.** In shaping their consensus through groupthink, boards and teams often find it convenient and even necessary to see the opposition as having but a single dimension.[8] That dimension may be simply "badness" throughout, or it may be a single obnoxious feature. All Germans were seen as huns, all Japanese as fanatics during World War II. In the area of labor relations, one large firm's management committee had cast the labor union into a mold of being "pinko" and anti-American. Every action, however simple, the union proposed was then treated as though it were a Communist threat to the free enterprise system. In private conversations, the members of the board referred to the president of the union and his officers as "the comrades" and always referred to the union itself as the "Commune." The union newspaper was never referred to by its actual name but was called the "Daily Worker," or alternatively "Redbook." Even the most amicable overture by the union, or its most reasonable concession, was promptly labeled as a "commie trick." Even when the officers of the union changed and its policies were revised, the management committee hung persistently to its one-dimensional stereotype. Naturally, all of its relationships with the union were transacted exactly in accordance with the stereotype, rather than with the reality of the situation.

Still another way in which people see the opposition as one-dimensional is illustrated by the image one firm's marketing policy committee held of its customers. Apparently the committee members felt that their customers were not the brightest people in the world, for they were always alluded to as the "rubes" or the "targets." They were seen as coming from somewhere like Dubuque or Fort Wayne, glued to the front of their TV tubes, clad in an undershirt, holding a beer, and

---

[7] G. C. Homans, *The Human Group* (New York: Harcourt Brace Jovanovich, Inc., 1950).
[8] E. Hoffer, *The True Believer* (New York: Harper & Row, Pub., 1951).

watching a quiz show or sitcom. All of the marketing policies of the company aimed squarely at this one-dimensional person. From time to time the young experts in consumer behavior on the staff would come in with scientific reports showing actual customer profiles and behavior patterns. They were noted with interest, and the researchers were thanked profusely. But when the time came to make decisions, the basic one-dimensional customer always prevailed.

Such one-dimensional outlooks produce marketing programs, personnel programs, or public relations programs which assume the stereotype to be true, and often such programs are self-fulfilling. The content of the concept becomes operational in the details of the implementation. If the customer is seen as a kind of idiot wedded to the boob tube, the tube will then beam messages which offer options to beguile only a TV-bemused idiot.

6. **The group sets standards and enforces them.** The ease with which groups make decisions on all issues is a function of their unanimity and closeness as people. If they seldom disagree on issues, the chances are very high that they have members who like one another, and that some members accordingly are not really agreeing but voluntarily suppressing.

The noted experiments at the Hawthorne works of Western Electric in the 1930's were the first widely publicized case in which the ability of groups to set norms for their own members was recorded in industry. The workers in this factory, in addition to doing their own work, also noted the output of others in the group, and when it was too low or too high, group pressures were applied to maintain standards. One form of pressure was "binging," a form of playfully striking the offending worker on the upper arm with a fist. Satire, sarcasm, and other forms of pressure included isolation from certain kinds of social gatherings, such as eating lunch or sharing rest breaks. In other social science experiments noted since the original Hawthorne experiments, observations of group standard setting have been recorded. Workers set standards of output per hour and per day for the entire group. People who insist upon exceeding that standard are apt to be subjected to social ostracism, threats, and in some instances physical retaliation.[9]

In organizations where the output is not tangible but consists of ideas, decisions, and choices, the standards nonetheless exist, and the enforcement is present. Often the cohesive and closely knit group will allow the presence of dissidents if they act according to an accepted code for dissident behavior. For one thing, they should have a plausible reason for their interest in their dissident position. In one large firm, the manufacturing manager was predictably opposed to all programs which would liberalize and ease the plight of labor in the plant. He felt that this was soft, weak, and probably socialistic. Furthermore, it would add to the costs of doing business and would make his job harder. The management committee was made up of people with a more humanistic bent and often outvoted the manufacturing manager. This was always done only after a predictable period of loud dissent, predictions of disastrous effects, and threats of bankruptcy. His role was seen as acceptable as long as it wasted itself inside the group and wasn't carried outside the group.

---

[9]F. Roethlisberger and Dickson, *Management.*

If the plant manager, for example, had gone over the head of the group to the chairman of the board or had gone to the union or the newspapers to fight his case on that different level, he would have been expelled, or at least severely punished by the group.

During the seventies it was common for newspapers to encourage and abet government employees who wished to "blow the whistle" on their boss, on the agency for which they worked, or on some other group of which they were a member. Controllers in the military often lost the battle for cost savings, only to carry the issue to the public at large by leaking their position to the public media. The media in turn, encouraged by the salubrious effects of such inside stories upon their circulation, rose to heights of higher moral fervor, appealing to the public's right to know. Whenever such a leak occurred, however, the group from which the leak emanated would predictably put the informant into a deepfreeze socially. The group standards were not changed in most cases, but the dissident was rejected.

**7. Conformity to the group produces self-discipline.** Not only does the reality of group pressure actually suppress deviation, but it also suppresses the individual's desire to engage in it. The control of the group is not that of the schoolmaster who catches mischief making in the student body and administers punishment. In such a form of discipline, the greatest sport for the members is to misbehave and get away with it. This differs sharply from groups where the members are closely knit and group thinking prevails. There, the members work conscientiously to discover what the group standard might be and then discipline and control themselves. They refrain from any action to weaken the group's position or differ from its will.

In one bank, the directors were presented with a report from a labor relations consultant who reported that his interviews with supervisors indicated that a proposed union organization drive among employees was highly likely to succeed. He made a strong recommendation to remove one supervisor, to raise pay, and to transfer several employees. Even though two members of the board were very experienced in labor relations from their own companies, they did not demur when the board seemed to be in unanimous agreement to follow the consultant's recommendations to the letter. The results were disastrous. The bank was found guilty of an unfair labor practice, the discharged officer sued and won a handsome settlement, and morale sagged badly in the bank. Said one of the directors, "I knew I should have spoken up, but it just wasn't the way things are done on that board. We always seem to move quickly and unanimously to decisions, and it would be sticky for me to take exception, so I kept quiet."

In the early stage of group decision making, a closing of the decision-making process occurs when the decision-making group is unified into a coherent body. Unity and unanimity become the same thing. From this grows a method of operating which *contains* possible dissent. It is agreed that all decisions will be made within the confines of the group, and no outside fliers or adventures will occur. The welfare of the group is used as the rationale for this containment: "We must all hang together or hang separately" is the idea that seems to prevail.[10]

[10]M. Argyle, *The Scientific Study of Social Behavior* (London: Methuen, 1957).

Once containment has been achieved, then suppression of dissidence and innovation results. The objective in the beginning generally is not the suppression of innovation or change. It is more likely to be identified as the achievement of a teamwork and unity of purpose. The major emphasis along the way becomes *affiliation* rather than *achievement*. The ideal condition is then the continued membership in the group, and the association which attends such membership and affiliation. The members of the board are spoken well of by other members, and recommended for other benefits outside the board, as long as they remain members in good standing. Conformity, then, is not the objective, but a means of retaining the unity of purpose so highly prized. At this stage, the membership will police itself, and no need will occur for punitive or disciplinary sanctions upon the deviating member.

**8. Silence implies assent in group decision making.** Most of the dissent from the course of action a board or group is taking usually takes the form of silence. The self-disciplined member might even hold some rebellious and contrary judgments about an issue in which the entire group appears unanimous. The silent members often harbor uneasy thoughts, different perceptions, or contradictory facts. In order to retain unanimity, however, such discomfort with the decision is customarily greeted with silence. The other members of the group, not hearing any tangible evidence of a disagreement, will presume that silence is to be taken as acceptance— even full acceptance.

In a medium-sized insurance company the insurance commissioner of the state had conducted an audit and found that all was well within the firm. One director, however, was aware of something that had been overlooked in the audit and suggested to the board that this condition should be pointed out to the commission. The response was surprising, for immediately several other members of the board spoke up and indicated their agreement with the idea. Ultimately, the board addressed a letter to the commissioner, which produced no major ill effects and increased the credibility of the firm with his office. Said one of the members, "I really wanted to do it from the beginning, but since nobody else brought it up I thought I would just let it go. After all, I didn't want to take up too much time and cause a lot of dispute, so I kept quiet."

Those who wish to generate some kind of change can use this process in the group to produce an apparent consensus. Prior to the meeting of the group, they simply talk to three or four other members and get their private concurrence with their suggestion. Thus, they can be almost certain to persuade the others. "If I go to the meeting with the knowledge that what I propose is already acceptable to three or four others, I know the remainder will go along," one director told me.

**9. The use of consensus in place of voting.** Unlike the legislative body, where partisan divisions may make a majority of one or two votes adequate to carry the day, coherent groups such as management committees and boards of directors are more apt to rule by consensus. Usually this means that the issue is stated in reasonably black and white terms. The number of options is limited, and the process of opening more options once the issue is before the group is not ordinarily acceptable in a consensual group. Consensus means that the membership is of one mind, or, at least, it is decided within sufficiently narrow bounds that a few fuzzy side conditions will not be considered important. The presence of fallacies of logic is not of great moment, as long as personal attacks, rancor, and strong argument are avoided.[11]

When the W. T. Grant Company chose to change its marketing posture from that of a five-and-ten-cent store to that of a general-merchandise product line, it faced the problem of attracting people into the new stores who had previously fixed its image as a five-and-ten-cent store in their minds. In order to overcome this mind set of customers, it was concluded that the company would issue its own credit cards, and issue them widely to the population at large. Even though some of the management were concerned that collecting on such credit would be a problem, there was no serious debate or consideration of other options. There was no weighing of cost-effectiveness of this method against other possibilities. Even though some directors had some reservations, they approved the move when it seemed to be strongly believed in by the management and other directors. The result led to endless debt and ultimately bankruptcy.

The consensual discussion often has an air of being a complete discussion, but usually deals with questions of whether the *entire plan* is good or bad, not the specific details. Few decision-making groups operating by consensus will do an adequate job of digging deeply into the facts, nor will groups extend the implications of the decision forward into the future to see the possible side effects. Most discussion is of the character of a summary statement: "In my opinion the evidence we have in hand seems to bear out the relative worth of the project, and I think we should probably go ahead with it." Or perhaps the statement to deny the project would sound somewhat as follows: "On the whole, I have some very serious concerns about this idea at this time, and think we should defer action until some time in the future." The process then becomes less a debate upon the merits and more of a tallying of summary positions and personal attractions to one another. If the prevailing opinion of those who speak up is in favor and the others remain silent, the leader or president may then issue a consensus statement. Once that consensus statement is in hand, it becomes highly unlikely that it will be reversed by added facts or information. New statements showing previously unnoted risks will probably be ignored. The idea of going back to resident experts within the organization for their opinion is not likely to occur. If their opinion is interjected, it probably will not have a substantial effect on the final outcome. If, however, the facts presented seem to bear out the consensus, they will be eagerly accepted and cited as evidence of the rightness of the decision. Most consensus decisions are not systematic, detailed, or logical, but are a summary of the feelings of the group members.

**10. Pride and tradition are vital in group decisions.** A large savings and loan company on the West Coast was in deep financial trouble. The founder had recently died, and after his demise the board often met to discuss remedial actions, but

---

[11] N. R. F. Maier and J. J. Hayes, *Creative Management*. Also, it has been shown that there is a discrepancy between values and behavior among group members. See H. Hartshorne and M. A. May, *Studies in Deceit* (New York: Macmillan, 1928).

never could bring itself to make basic changes in the ways the old man had done things. An oil painting of him looked down upon the board in the board room, and, as one director stated wryly, "Whenever we have to make a decision, we all seem to look up at the picture and ask 'I wonder what HE would have done?' and that is inevitably what we do. We don't run board meetings; we run seances."

In a large grocery firm, the founder was alive and fit and dominated all decisions by the board of directors. The process of decision making consisted of a highly refined and delicate sensing of what the founder would like to have happen, and the group always concurred. The pride they had in associating with him, the strong desire never to offend or oppose him, and the willingness to read carefully what he had done in the past as an indicator of his future desires left them with few independent decisions. On one occasion the director of finance researched the profits and losses of the company and found that one product line was a terrible drain on profits. Upon presenting this to the old man, he was scornfully told, "Young man, that product is the one upon which this company was built." Quickly the vice-president backed off, and agreed heartily that the company should never abandon that respected line of which they were all so proud. The line stayed in the company's sales catalogs for several years. It was only upon the death of the founder and the accession of a new president that it could be abandoned.

In contrast with this, at General Electric every product is scrutinized carefully and systematically by a strategic business unit annually to determine whether it should be continued. If it is a drain and there is no visible means of salvaging it, it will be abandoned. As one staff expert at GE described it, however, the process of dropping a line or a market is not easily done, for somebody will love it. "Pride is our most important impediment," reported one analyst after losing a management committee fight over dropping a loser.

## THE ROLE OF THE LEADER IN GROUP MANAGEMENT

Through all of this roster of possible shortcomings of the group process, however, it must be noted that the weakness is only a weakness if the leader allows it to be.[12] The assertive leader tries to claim the benefits of pooled experience, higher acceptance, and the creation of new options, all of which are implicit in group processes of decision making. At the same time he or she overcomes the stifling effects of group conformity by calling on each member of the group for criticism, making sure that silence and fellowship are not being used to cover up bad decisions. The creative leader also carefully withholds his or her own views until all those of the members have been heard in order to prevent an uncritical compliance. The leader also can overcome some of the worst effects of groupthink by systematically introducing outside opinions into the thinking of the group. Audits—internal and external—new ideas, and study groups to probe more deeply into areas for reporting

---

[12] R. Likert, *New Patterns of Management* (New York: McGraw-Hill, 1961); *see also* M. Mace, *Directors: Myth and Reality* (Cambridge: Harvard University, Graduate School of Business, 1971).

back to the group are all possible means of avoiding bad decisions and encouraging innovation. Outside directors, chosen for their independence and willingness to dissent, can be introduced into the structure of the group with a heartening effect upon the quality of its efforts. Finally, after the decision has been made, it can be deferred in implementation, time permitting, to allow time for thought and second-guessing to occur.

The scarcity of such leaders, and the difficulty of seasoning them through many years of experience and formal training, may be a cogent explanation of how groups within organizations serve more to prevent change and innovation than to make them happen. The importance of developing such leadership becomes apparent when we see how potent a group can be in resisting change. It would be nonsense to suggest that groups always resist change. As Maier's research has shown, groups are more likely to be innovative than individuals where risk is entailed. On the other hand, when the group is so disposed or so directed by its leader, it comprises a formidable resistance to change.

# sixteen

# Managing change in the world of change resisters

If the only conclusion from all of the foregoing array of forces against change, innovation, and planning were that change is impossible, it would hardly be worthwhile to attempt it. But it would also be a ridiculous conclusion, for obviously change has occurred, is occurring now, and will continue to occur in the future. The antidote proposed in the following chapters has a new theme: that change can be managed through strategic thinking. The ordinary approaches to overcoming resistance to change have limited effectiveness and are apt to be less and less productive as the force of change resistance gains momentum.

Strategic thinking and strategic *living*, or, if you are in charge, strategic managing, all require a special kind of human skill. You must live in an anticipatory state. You live events before they have occurred, not just after they have happened. Your mind projects into the future the events which will lie in your natural course and chooses from among those possible events. Further, you decide that if none of the natural events which lie in your course are acceptable or livable, or even desirable, you *invent a future* and make that future happen. Rather than being a passive recipient of the future that naturally lies in your course, you anticipate what that course holds in store and make active decisions about whether or not to accept it. As all of the foregoing chapters have demonstrated, this is not easy for humans. On the other hand, it is not impossible, and it lies within human capability. Furthermore, since natural acceptance of unanticipated events seems to be producing more disastrous consequences, it is more and more necessary that people like us work harder to sharpen our skills of anticipation and act to make the future better.

## LIVING STRATEGICALLY TO MANAGE CHANGE

If somebody promised you a sure-fire method of seeing and controlling the future, you would quite properly give that person a fast brushoff. Such a person, you would say, belongs in the category of snake-oil peddler, or hustler, and with good reason. Yet there is a way you can manage the future considerably better than you do. It is a six-part method that makes the unforeseen less harmful and more manageable.

The method in some ways resembles a course taught to automobile and truck drivers by automotive safety experts and called *defensive driving*. While it is used to train people who drive cars constantly in their job, in order to make them less likely to incur an accident, it can be expanded to fit social, personal, and business situations as well. By a more general application to living, this method shows some astonishing results in reducing life's accidents and reducing social and personal injury. To state the same thing more elegantly, the proposal here is that you live more strategically and less operationally. This is not just a plea for long-range planning, which is an academic exercise, frequently futile in purpose and result; it is a proposal that you change the character and direction of your thinking and behavior to be more effective. Strategic living for the individual or the organization produces some good effects:

- It presumes that you cannot control or change the world around you all by yourself, so therefore you must adapt your behavior to survive.

- It recognizes that most of the situations you see will be coming at you pretty fast, and that it is better to be ready to prevent injury and accident than to regret it later or explain how it was unavoidable.

- It treats things as they should be as well as how they will be.

- It permits the world to go along with its unexpected events, but allows you to have a greater measure of mastery and a lesser number of unpleasant surprises.

- You can improve your foresight to the extent that you will not be quite so powerless in the face of dynamic events and bad luck, influences more powerful than yourself that have the capability of ruining you. The six steps to strategic management are, in brief:

1. Keep your range of vision higher than you do now.
2. Get a bigger picture of the world than you now hold.
3. Do not stare at the world; scan it.
4. Make yourself visible to others and make your opinions known.
5. Always have alternative plans.
6. Practice your skill in managing your timing, for timing and positioning are the keys to survival.

We shall look at each of the six steps to social defensive driving in some detail, in the remainder of this chapter and in Chapters 17, 18, and 19.

## AIM HIGHER IN WATCHING THE WORLD

In a fast-moving world you really do not have all the information you need to see everything you need to see, and certainly not enough time to see everything. Most of us read a couple of papers daily, morning and evening. Perhaps we read the *New*

*York Times* or the *Wall Street Journal* for world news, the local weekly for community politics and school news, and a trade journal or two. Some professionals, such as engineers, keep up with the best of the journals in their field, catching things such as book reviews or think pieces along the way. Even so, we cannot really keep abreast of everything we would like to know.[1]

To see all of the things you might need to anticipate the blind-side event that will kill you, you should learn and practice some specific skills of seeing. People who live in the crater of a volcano, or in the valley just below a rather frail earth dam, puzzle us. We wonder how on earth they ever chose that kind of place for a residence. Actually, they fear the consequences less than most people because they have deliberately violated this first rule: they aim low in seeing things. This often fatal shortcoming is more widespread than you would suspect.

Take the case of the young college graduate who was offered a position in a small-town bank in New England. He was near the top of his class, a talented finance major, and with the kind of personal qualities that would have made him attractive to Chase Manhattan or Citibank and with good long-run career prospects with either. Yet he accepted the blandishments of the local banker. At age forty he found himself dead-ended, with an outsider coming in to become president of the bank. Obviously, if he lacked ability he should not have had the better job; but in his case it was a bad strategy that made all of his subsequent actions futile. Fifteen years of working below his best capabilities had in fact turned him into deadwood. A daily routine of dull and unchallenging tasks had stunted his personal growth and professional development. The directors really had little choice.

When General Arthur Wood was working for Montgomery Ward, on his own time he used to scrutinize—of all things—the statistical abstract of the United States. From it he learned that the American people were moving steadily from the country to the city. On the basis of this information he urged the top management of Montgomery Ward to expand into opening retail stores, and to locate them in the cities. He predicted that with both farm population and farm income declining, hard times would come to Montgomery Ward if it did not open stores in addition to keeping its successful catalog business. When Montgomery Ward refused, Wood moved over to Sears Roebuck, which bought his strategy and made him vice-president of its new retail stores division.[2] Within three years he was president of Sears. A West Pointer by education and a military officer by experience, Wood once said that "if you have the right strategy, you can afford a lot of small errors in tactics and still do all right."

Wood, like most successful executives—and leaders—aimed high in watching the world around him. Still another example was Tex Thornton, chairman of the giant Litton Industries. As a young man he joined Ford Motor Company, along with several of his friends from military service. Under the tutelage of Ernest

---

[1] L. Fahey and W. R. King, "Environmental Scanning for Corporate Planning," *Business Horizons*, 20, August 1977; *see also* R. Merritt, "Forecasting the Future Business Environment: The State of the Art," *Long Range Planning*, June 1974.

[2] A. Chandler, *Strategy and Structure* (Cambridge: MIT Press, 1962).

Breech, they assumed important positions throughout the Ford organization, and were known in the business press as the "Ford Whiz Kids." Thornton, however, could see that young Henry Ford II, heir to the family fortune, was coming along fast and that he, Thornton, would eventually end up in a number two post in the firm. While this would satisfy most ambitious people, Thornton knew that he could only survive in a firm where he was number one. So he quit and went to the West Coast. After an interval working for Howard Hughes, he launched out on his own. With some $26,000 of his own plus some borrowed money, he bought up a small firm known as Litton Industries from its founder. As the top man he built this tiny firm into a multi-billion-dollar electronics, shipbuilding, and office machinery conglomerate. His high aims steered him from what would have, for him, proved to be a frustrating future.

It would be foolish to assume that simply aiming high means instant success or even achievement of the first goals you establish for yourself. People who would like to become president of the United States are legion. One perennial candidate, former Governor Harold Stassen of Minnesota, became a stereotype of the person who aimed for something at which he would never succeed. People *can* possibly set goals of which they have not the slightest possibility of realization. Perhaps their education, their age, or their basic skills are not enough to make them even faintly qualified.

*Strategic scanning of the environment means finding goals that are tough but realistic, and aiming high may simply mean choosing an attainable plateau.*

Learning to aim high enough without aiming to achieve all at once is part of your social defensive living. Small businesses often err by expanding too fast and discovering that their receivables are eating them up, or that they have gone beyond the ability of the founder to manage what has been created. The higher the aim, the more important it becomes to have stages and plateaus that comprise the strategic scheme for getting there. The worker who would become president of the corporation must first please his or her immediate supervisor and get a recommendation from that person for the next promotion. The ultimate goal may be the executive suite, but affecting the manners of the executive right away, or trying to barge into the upper echelons' offices tomorrow morning, will merely invite an abrupt ejection. On the other hand, having high aspirations and a willingness to pay a price to attain them is a necessary first step.

Aiming high may mean doing things that surprise people, perhaps even yourself. The fact that something has not been done before is frequently the reason it never gets tried—except by those who aim high.

When Procter & Gamble (P&G) enters a new market with a new product, it succeeds more often than it fails because it has a marketing strategy that is aimed high. For example, P&G generally does not enter a new market to compete unless it has some kind of technical advantage in the product which will be discernible to buyers, unless it can take over a leading position in that market within a couple of years of entry, and unless it is entering a market that is substantial (over $100 million a year in added sales to P&G). This ordinarily means that it is entering an already established market in which excellent competition is already in place and doing well. All of which means that P&G has a strategy of aiming high on many fronts. Yet it has worked for them with such products as Crest toothpaste, Pampers diapers, Duncan Hines cake mixes, Folger's Coffee, Pringles potato snacks, and Charmin tissues, among others.

It is obvious that simply hanging out some wildly unrealistic goal and not having a well-thought-through—sometimes painfully detailed—strategy will not produce automatic success. More often it will only produce some foolish failures. But high goals coupled with some skillful execution are a great combination.

The island nation of Iceland provides a wonderful example of a people who have learned to live in a hostile world by aiming high in seeing the world around them. Iceland is located near the Arctic Circle in the Atlantic. A volcanic island, it sits atop constant earthquakes and volcanic eruptions. In one instance in the 1970's the town of Hemsley was the site of a giant eruption that wiped out the town. Yet, the people were prepared. They moved out until the eruption and the flow of lava stopped, and moved back to rebuild their town on the same site. There was no loss of life, and no major despair. They know they live on a volcanic island, that there may be another eruption, but they and their countrymen keep plans for evacuation, and for return to normal when the eruption ends.

Meanwhile, they capitalize upon their apparently tenuous existence. They have tapped deep into the crust of the island and tapped the hot water just below the surface. Every house gets a steady supply of hot water that heats it and provides *all of its energy needs* at a cost of $250 per year. This makes Icelanders immune to energy crises brought on by OPEC actions. People swim year-round in geothermally heated pools. They have built a thriving and prosperous nation of half a million people with no unemployment and no poverty. Fishing, farming, and light industry, based on an endless supply of low-cost energy, have turned this unlikely place into a flourishing society. The ground under them is so formed that an earthquake might occur or a volcano erupt, but this has not been the end of the world for them, but a way to prosperity. Millions of tourists visit Iceland yearly, marveling at the island, its natural features, and most especially its people, who have created their own island paradise of sorts by aiming high. They have even created their own airline to transport tourists from Europe and America to see the effects of their aiming high.

Aiming high means turning apparent disadvantages into opportunities and strengths. Aiming low means seeing disaster or inevitable doom in every shortcoming or hazard. The hazard is not itself the cause of the disaster; the response of the people confronted with it is.

New England provides many such examples, both good and bad. When the textile industry began to move south to be nearer its source of supply—cotton—many old New England mill towns died, overcome by change. Yet, the textile industry today in the South does not live on cotton but on chemistry, synthetic fibers, and the related industries. New England, with its universities, could have stayed alive in textiles if it had aimed higher.

# GETTING A WIDER PICTURE
# OF THE WORLD:
# THE SELF-FULFILLING PROPHECY

There is a special kind of character about prophecies: *They tend to fulfill themselves.* People who assume that things will go well for them are more apt to find that things do go well than people who assume that things will go poorly.

Teachers, in an experiment, who were told that they were teaching a class filled with students who had exceptionally high intelligence (not a fact by objective tests) produced a class of high learners. Teachers, on the other hand, who were told that their students were all tested and found to be of subnormal intelligence produced substandard learning from that class, even though objective tests showed both classes to be nearly identical in intelligence. This is an example of the self-fulfilling prophecy.

The prophecy that things will go well no matter what is far more likely to produce success than prophecies that things will not go well. The self-fulfilling prophecies in careers, in family planning, in business planning are not simply illusions, but realistic drawing upon the power of *expectations.* People who expect to be victimized will become victims in more cases than people who know that the world is filled with hazards but do not expect to be hurt. The latter will be better prepared to adapt, and their images will be those of winners rather than losers.

A few years ago, a large oil company operating gasoline and service stations on a major turnpike in the East became concerned over vastly differing levels of performance between different stations. It invited a consultant to study the situation, find causes, and make recommendations. The consultant drove along the turnpike like an ordinary tourist or customer and shopped in each station. In some stations he found that the attendants were quick, friendly, and pleasantly assertive in selling services. They caught evidences of needed windshield wipers, tires, and accessories and pointed them out to the driver. They serviced the car completely and wished the customers a safe trip upon departure. In other stations the attendants barely met the requirements of the job. They did not fill the tank, did not check the oil, more often than not washed the windshield or checked the car's radiator water only when asked, and then did so with a grumble. If asked about other products or services for sale, they muttered excuses and evaded providing information.

A subsequent study showed that the managers of the respective stations and their assumptions were distinctly different. The high-performing managers whose sales, service, and profits were highest told the consultant, "We have great people come in here. They are busy, friendly travelers and appreciate our good work." Those stations where profits and sales volume were lowest reported just the opposite: "The people who come in here are the most dishonest, conniving, and complaining bunch of people God ever put on the face of the earth. As a result I can't keep any good help, and I get the dregs of the labor market to work on the service islands. They are lazy and whining, and if you ask them to do an ounce of extra work, they quit."

Yet, it was the same population driving the same kinds of cars on the same kinds of journeys at the same times of day that shopped both the high-performing stations and the low-performing stations. The self-fulfilling prophecy is a powerful instrument.

Yet, we cannot fall into the trap of being a Pollyanna who looks at hard facts and distorts them. We aim high by making certain kinds of assumptions.

## GOOD ASSUMPTIONS AND BAD ASSUMPTIONS

One of the nice touches the most successful anticipators possess and the less successful anticipators lack is the skill of making the right assumptions. When a company, a government agency, or simply an individual tries to manage by anticipation, the key to distinguishing a wild dream from a shrewd objective often lies in the quality of the assumptions underlying the decision and the commitments made. People who assume that the price of real estate will rise rapidly and constantly seem to be sagacious investors will buy low and sell high some time later. Those who make such an assumption that proves false merely join a list of victims caught in a real estate bubble.

Clark Caskey, the management consultant, likes to point out that the word *assume* can be divided into three segments: ass/u/me. He explains that "if you assume the wrong things, such assumptions can make an Ass of U and Me." Yet, the art of assuming can be improved through applying some rules of common sense and experience. Odiorne's Law, "Things that do not change will remain the same," is one such rule for guiding assumptions. Here are some other practical guides to making assumptions that will assist you in aiming high.

1. **Assumptions should have grounds.** It is a bad idea to assume that an idea or proposition is true if there are no grounds at all for assuming that it is true. This proposal, when it was first advanced by Bertrand Russell, the British philosopher, caused a certain amount of polite scoffing from the anti-planners, for spontaneity and freewheeling seem to flourish on ungrounded assumptions. Young people often marry on the assumption that whatever visible shortcomings the proposed mate presently displays will be reduced or eliminated once the marriage is consummated. This produces numerous unsatisfactory marriages, and an alarming divorce rate. If the other person proposed as a mate were to display even an ounce of propensity to change for the better, there might be some grounds—however modest—for making an assumption of change.

Small businesses are often founded upon such groundless assumptions. The man who quits a good job to start a business growing mushrooms or raising chickens assumes that there is a market for his product, despite a complete absence of market studies, trend analysis, or even rumors that such a market will appear. He assumes that because more mushrooms will become available from his cellar-based production plant, demand will rise in proportion to the supply. Despite some vigorous effort and a heartwarming amount of hard work, he goes broke as soon as his original savings are gone. For several months our hero lives on an inordinate amount of mushrooms before throwing in the towel and returning to work for another firm as an employee, sadder but wiser.

Ads for small businesses for sale which cite the fact that there is "no competition" often make the same mistake. Negative grounds are somehow turned around into positive proof. The fact that there is no competition means to the buyer that a large market actually exists, when such an assumption is groundless.[3]

**2. When all evidence points in one direction, do not assume the opposite.** When a sizable majority of expert opinions point in a common direction, it is usually a pretty good idea not to make a contrary assumption and make an accordingly opposite commitment. If the assumption is mere idle speculation, then of course it becomes an interesting game of mental gymnastics to assume something unlikely will come true. If, however, the costs of failure and disaster are unbearable, then the only thing available as a rational assumption is the prevailing opinion. In short, unsubstantiated hunches have a very weak track record where they are based upon emotional binges, visceral rumblings, or the power of pure rationality at variance with reality.

In 1977, President Carter introduced a proposed energy program to the nation in a widely broadcast appeal for self-discipline, denial, and self-abnegation and called it the "moral equivalent of war." Since Congress saw no such assumptions in the minds of the people, the program ultimately enacted had substantially different assumptions.

The stock market as a phenomenon in human behavior is replete with examples of investors who have assumptions contrary to what the best evidence indicates. One such piece of esoteric upstream swimming occurred shortly after the United Mine Workers had negotiated a whopping wage increase for its members. One investor presumed that this would produce immediate automation of mining, and plunged heavily in the stock of one firm that manufactured automatic mining equipment. Shortly afterward, the benighted coal companies, faced with short-run profit pressures from the new settlement, cut back on all capital investment, and the equipment company's stock plunged. Logically, the assumption was pure brilliance, but it was ungrounded and flew directly in the face of several analysts' reports that had predicted the cutback.

Assumptions that fly in the face of prevailing evidence are more apt to be a product of emotional attachment to an abstraction, a social cause, a fervent wish, or an idea.

**3. When experts disagree, do not plunge.** Far more difficult in making high-flying assumptions is making choices between conflicting experts. Each has persuasive grounds for his or her position, and each would seek disciples for the truth. The temptation may be to go for broke, to buy the novel new idea and assume the best. This is solid fun when the consequences are trivial or at least affordable. When, however, the consequences of commitment are irrevocable and the downside possi-

---

[3] L. L. Allen, *How to Start and Succeed in Your Own Small Business* (Boston: Little Brown, 1973); *see also* T. Cochran, *200 Years of American Business* (New York: Basic Books, 1977).

bilities are great, better look around for another place to put your money, or your time.

The rate of small-business failure is notably very high. Most small firms start with a single assumption, that success is the only direction that can lie ahead, and do not seek out contrary opinion. In some instances, the contrary opinion is not really an expert opinion, but a negative demeanor generally, in which case it can be treated as any nonexpert opinion. When a large real estate developer in the West bought up an old factory section and laid out a wholly new concept of shops, theaters, stores, restaurants, and boutiques, local wiseacres scoffed. A survey of several such sites in similar places indicated success. The developer hired a professional organization to do a feasibility study, which showed that the project had a high chance of success if certain legal restrictions could be removed. Despite the uninformed scoffers, who lacked both optimism and information to make their judgment worthy, he proceeded and became very successful.

## DON'T STARE AT THE WORLD;
## SCAN IT

One of the modern techniques employed to pool expertise is known as the *delphi* method. This is a somewhat scientific system of polling experts about what the future holds. Named after the oracle at Delphi, whose predictions were notably accurate, the delphi panel consists of numerous experts who respond to several rounds of questionnaires. The first round is often productive of a wide range of differences. At this point, the surveyor runs a second round of the same question but with a significant addition: the second round includes the responses given by the same panel of experts on the first round. This summary seems to have a salubrious effect upon the subsequent opinions of the experts in honing their predictions. The end result of several rounds from the same experts is a far better set of predictions than could be obtained from a single expert, or from a single round of questioning. The delphi method has been used successfully in such diverse situations as picking horses and predicting the markets, social trends, technological changes, and social influences that lie ahead.[4]

Experts in bunches may not always be available, however, and other methods of anticipation are employed by the planning experts. Yet, the techniques of forecasting and strategic management are less important than the outlook of the individual who must make the commitment. Simply *persuading people to anticipate* may be a necessary first step before any of the extrapolation, trend analysis, and delphi methods can be brought to bear on seeing higher in planning.

## THE OVERLOOKED PLEASURES
## OF ANTICIPATION

The joys of anticipation, we are reminded, often exceed the pleasures of realization. Furthermore, the realization of a planned and consciously chosen objective

---

[4] "Forecasters Turn to Group Guesswork," *Business Week*, March 14, 1970.

will exceed that of the random or surprise success. While there may be fun in wing-ing it, there is also the risk of ignominious failure. This can not only be personally embarrassing to its author, but hurts many others who are dependent upon con-tinued successes. Stockholders, employees, and customers all have a deep interest in the continued successful operation of organizations and institutions.

Management by anticipation substitutes planned change for joy rides. It is the unanticipated disaster that generates personal stress for many managers and pro-fessionals. Management by anticipation is comprised of four elements: (1) Set forth clearly what you are trying to achieve and make some commitments to others for its achievement, (2) plan the route for getting there including the allocation of re-sources to accomplish the desired ends, (3) carry out the plan in a businesslike man-ner. This is where the majority of the time of most people will be spent, (4) check on actual results and make corrections as you go. Over the long haul, such a basic system produces numerous rewards. To name a few:

- Chaos and mistakes are reduced.
- Personal stress from unintended consequences is minimized.
- A sense of personal and organizational control is highly satisfactory to those who make such anticipation work for them.
- It provides a wider basis of subordinate participation in job-related decisions that affect them and their jobs.
- The rewards are multiple, for in addition to being psychologically paid off for ultimate success, subordinates are also paid off in advance by creative anticipation.
- As a means of preventing business or organizational failure it can prevent many of the failures.
- As a means of allaying unintended consequences, it can avert the most readily avoidable ones.
- As a general philosophy and concept of managing your affairs, it has some highly motivational effects on people who work in your organization.
- It is not an addition to your ordinary way of doing things, but is an approach which makes things work better.
- It suggests that it is better to decide what should happen and then make it happen than to wait until things have happened and then defensively respond.
- It starts with reality, not with dreams, fantasies, or what might have been, or what this "oughta be."
- It governs the release of resources, and the starting and continuance of activi-ties.
- It requires that people make things happen rather than respond to events.
- It is creative rather than routine and bureaucratic in character.
- It substantially increases the sense of power that people feel in their lives and jobs, which is a welcome and perhaps necessary reversal of the powerlessness that has been so widespread in modern society.

*Management by anticipation is not just a good idea; it is a survival skill that calls for some specific management practices.*

**We rely on the future** In all human experience we have learned to rely on the future.[5] We put our money in the bank and expect that the bank will have it when we go back to take it out. We pay small sums to an insurance company and rely upon its ability to pay our heirs large sums when we depart. We plant seeds in the spring with the faith that something like a flower or a vegetable will sprout in ten days and ultimately grow into something wholly new. The sun will come up tomorrow morning in the east, just as it has every other morning. We produce children with the expectation that they will grow into successful adults. We drive down strange roads at pell-mell paces with the full expectation that the road will not come to an abrupt end without notice.

**When all else fails, we rely on hope** Reliance on the future and hope that things to come will be better than situations as they are today is widespread in the human race. This is especially true for people whose present situation is most miserable. The people of an underdeveloped nation who have an income below $250 a year, a short life span, and a brutish life style are apt to live for the hope of better things. They cling to the church, which promises them heaven in the afterlife. They gamble with the hope that the future will bring them instant riches. They embrace political demagogues who offer nothing more than rosy portraits of the economy of the future when they have completed their revolution. For the prisoner and the peasant, the ill and the deprived, it is the hoped-for future that sustains them. The soldier in combat sees peace after victory, the spoils of victory, or discharge from service as something to make the present endurable. One of the most appealing features of communism for underdeveloped countries is the prospect it holds for the future and its promise of equalizing things with the giant landowner. Children are able to endure the mysterious ways of the adults who rule them with the assurances that they, too, will someday grow up and assume the roles of adulthood.

Anticipation, then, is the art of foreseeing the elements in our own being and the present situation that point the way from bondage to freedom. By helping us see the long-term consequences of our current behavior and actions, anticipation sets us free from the yokes of today's aggravations and suffering. It liberates certain energies within us that in ordinary circumstances we ignore in the light of present pleasures, habitual ways of doing things, and slavish adherence to procedures.

The purpose of anticipation is not to forecast or predict the future as the crystal-ball gazer or fortune teller does. Rather it is to create a better future through prediction and control. It is to presume that within us and our situation is contained the potential of better things in the future. D. T. Suzuki, writing about the sense of Zen, might have been describing the power and art of anticipation when he described the human body:[6]

*[It] is something like an electric battery in which a mysterious power latently*

---

[5] A. Toffler, *The Futurists* (New York: Random House, 1972).
[6] D. T. Suzuki, *Essays in Zen Buddhism* (New York: Grove Press, 1961).

*lies. When this power is not properly brought into operation, it either grows moldy and withers away and/or is warped and expresses itself abnormally.*

The person who wastes his or her health and physical vigor in dissolution is trapped by the present, and ignores the power of anticipation to make the deferral of present pleasure into a more fulfilling future. Much of the pain and struggle we see about us, the failures which dismay us, are the result of failures of someone to anticipate in the not so distant past. Anticipation means aiming high.

Beyond this there are some personal actions we can take to insert ourselves personally into the picture. We can make ourselves consciously visible, to our advantage. This is the subject of Chapter 17.

# seventeen

# Making yourself visible:
## putting yourself in the picture

Any competent farmer can set objectives and manage a farm by anticipation. The acres to be tilled and planted, the yields per acre, the costs of supplies and equipment, and the profitability of the farm can be budgeted with some precision. The intangible and unknown factors can also be named, and while they are risks of nature and cannot be controlled, the effects of their baleful influence are also predictable. The possibilities of tornadoes, hurricanes, freezes, and droughts can also be stated in probabilistic terms. The assumption that seeds, when planted, will grow into crops underlies it all.

In a production or sales management position, there are similar tangible outputs that can be stated as anticipated objectives. In fact, it would be abnormal for a manager in such a position not to be optimistic about the unit's output. We can count units, dollars, tons, pounds, and gallons. There is a discipline in *things* that brings a reality basis to such work, the reality of real things and the natural basis for finding tangible goals and realities. The building block is anticipation.

The rapid growth of modern occupations and life styles unfortunately has removed significant numbers of people from such realities. The conflict between human nature and society seems to be founded upon a loss of touch with nature, and the improbability of returning to the more simple life, where anticipation is easy. When people operate at a naturalistic level, specific things can be anticipated and can become the center of life's meaning, and life has some semblance of sanity.[1] People whose objectives can be expressed in tangibles enjoy the benefits of animal existence, for they are close to nature. Natural disasters may, of course, threaten them; steel fractures, and filaments burn out, but we are equipped to explain the facts of nature.

---

[1] H. Nearing and S. Nearing, *Continuing the Good Life: Half a Century of Homesteading* (New York: Schocken Books, 1979). Chronicles how one couple made such a retreat to Vermont. It is the essence of the counterculture.

Factory supervisors who can anticipate producing tons of copper or hundred-weights of flour are always characterized by higher morale than are managers who work in offices or deal with intangibles such as systems, policies, procedures, information strategies, technologies, and office politics. Yet, it is the latter environment where most people exist today. The new life of ambiguity places new requirements upon the people caught in it. Since outputs are not tangible, they are not easily seen, and the reliance upon animal abilities, even at the higher levels of behavior, is no longer suitable. Actions are no longer suitably determined by instinct or by adaptation to the laws of nature. Principles of physics and engineering, of gravity or inertia, are not of overriding moment in choosing one's actions. When humans transcend nature, they take on the new requirements of humanity, which has emancipated itself from nature, and become self-aware. They also fall into the anxieties of the activity trap, and their immediate activity in the postindustrial society becomes unrelated to life's objectives and loses meaning. The case studies of managers who were eminently successful in factories and sales territories but who failed miserably in offices and at executive levels are commonplace. The harmony of production and selling, from which behavior produces tangible results, is disrupted. Their outputs are now products like information and learning.

## SEEING THE BIGGER PICTURE
## IN AN INTANGIBLE WORLD

Modern humanity lives in fear of change because the world is ambiguous and uncontrolled. The new ambiguity has three facets:

1. For the manager, unlike the worker in touch with nature, experience may not be the best teacher. The eternal verities, the simple truths that tell the farmer to plant corn in May in the Temperate Zone, don't convert readily into professional-level work or managerial work.

2. The natural attributes that make us more successful in contact with nature are less useful. The physical requirements of the professional, technical, and managerial job are minimal. Being able to operate a ball point pen, a telephone, dictating equipment, and a self-service elevator comprise the extent of the physical demands made on us as animals in our new role.

3. The means of adaptation to life are now those of rational and emotional contact with others, rather than the adaptive skills of the man of nature, or the acquisitive skills of the industrial man, of the combative skills of the animal. We cannot return to the subhuman state and find security in harmony with nature; we must proceed to deal with affairs on an emotional and intellectual level to be productive.[2]

---

[2] C. Walker, *Toward the Automatic Factory* (New Haven, Conn.: Yale University Press, 1957). Proposes that in the factory tensions and mental effort have replaced muscular fatigue.

# WHEN HUMAN BEINGS
# FALL OUT OF NATURE

Because we have risen beyond the animal state to where we are only partly animal, we are all required to constantly find some new solutions to achieving unity with nature, with ourselves, and with our fellow human beings. The steel maker cannot be content if a blast furnace or continuous-casting plant turns out its daily tonnage, if in the process it was necessary to sever many relationships with other people and society. The executive and the professional produce no apparent tonnage, and accordingly can avoid being disciplined by goals but can lose the rewards of anticipation. They relapse into activity that is pursued relentlessly, even though the realization that all is not well continues to besiege them.

The reason for this discontent is that we retain the basic needs and drives that impel us at an animalistic level, yet cannot be satisfied by activity which is increasingly unrelated to purposes. At one level we find our kicks and our self-fulfillment in the details of work itself, and in the ego satisfactions, social satisfactions, and self-actualizing achievements. *The hitch in this model of human motivation is that it overlooks the constantly changing level of ego ideal which people generate.*[3]

Tevye, in *Fiddler on the Roof*, sings of his goals and ideals in his song, "If I Were a Rich Man." Being a victim of grinding poverty, he sees the rich man as one who would have a large house, surrounded by geese and ducks, and similar accoutrements of "riches." Yet, suppose some czar were to make Tevye rich, by merely presenting him with these tangible things? Tevye, like all of us, would be satisfied with these evidences of wealth for a while, but then *his aspiration level would rise,* and he would then have a higher level of needs. Satiated in his natural needs, Tevye would, we may safely predict, soon long for social and ego needs beyond his generous acreage. Or his needs might extend into his own personality to find greater psychological satisfactions in terms of his neighbors' views of him, his family's reputation and standing, or even a desire to create something in his own area of influence that does not yet exist.

Static existence will not work for us, because we are constantly raising our own ego ideals and are filled with inner contradictions for which we must find equilibrium. This search for equilibrium will keep us in a constant state of contradiction. The only possibility of living the satisfactory life, then, lies in a constant state of goal seeking. The attainment of meaning is the regular creation of goals that have meaning. In the process of pursuit, we find meaning in attainment.[4]

The major contribution of Maslow to motivation theory is not that he has described what the goals might be, but rather that he has described the tentative nature of all goals, which must be set again year after year. If people achieve their physical, social, and self-actualization needs and produce for themselves what Maslow describes as "peak experiences," their condition is such that they must

---

[3] A. Maslow, *Motivation and Personality,* 2nd ed. (New York: Harper & Row, Pub., 1970).
[4] J. W. Gardner, *Excellence* (New York: Harper & Brothers, 1961).

seek more. Our most pressing ego ideal is always an intermediate goal, for which full accomplishment is merely the means to raising our ego ideal.

The most damnable feature of the activity trap is that it permits this passion and striving of human beings to be blunted. The stunting of our appetite for attainment produces in the end a social neurosis that becomes self-feeding.

## THE NEED TO RELATE TO OTHERS IS THE BIGGER PICTURE

Unconnected with nature or the discipline of things and the reality of organic things, we live a life of ambiguity that can only be tolerated because we have the company of others. The absurd life of the commuter who lives in Connecticut and works at making intangible products all day in New York would be utter madness if the train weren't filled daily with others in the same condition. Our instinctual efforts are replaced by our relationships with others.

We sometimes find this relationship in *submission* to a company, boss, campaign, program, or an institution. In other cases we can relate to the world by *overpowering* other people, and transcend our own situation by dominating others. This does not, of course, free us, for the prisoner and the guard are both in jail.

Submissive persons cannot live by anticipation but find their satisfactions in identifying with something bigger than themselves. The singing of the company song or, as occurred in the older IBM under Thomas Watson, Sr., the following of the corporation's marching band provides a substitute kind of self-fulfillment.[5] Yet, as women especially have come to recognize lately, there is a void to be filled in such identification, for an individual cannot know whether one is expressing one's own basic ego ideal or piggybacking a ride on another's.

## LEADERS IN THE WORLD OF CHANGE

For the boss to desire submissive people is perhaps natural. It makes management less troublesome, for when the job and the boss provide the source of satisfaction, disagreements are less likely to erupt about goals and courses of action. Not unsurprisingly, then, the literature of management is replete with examples of how a boss can become the shaper and leader of a submissive group. The techniques of domination and manipulation by leaders require submissiveness in followers, and if they don't have such submissiveness naturally, then they can be directed, taught, coerced, persuaded, or "led" to be submissive. Over the long haul, say a lifetime, the truly submissive may find that their ability to generate anticipated ego ideals is blunted. Like the old-fashioned concept of conscience, an ego ideal may be beaten to death. Occasionally, however, a glimpse of the things that might have been emerges, and rebellion may flare up temporarily.

The process of managing subordinate workers, spouses, or children by

[5] W. Rodgers, *Think: A Biography of the Watsons and IBM* (Briarcliff Manor, N.Y.: Stein & Day, 1969).

counting on their submissiveness works only if they can be freed of frustration, which is to say freed of their own ego ideals. As long as the slightest trace of frustration remains, they might become rebellious. To make management by submissiveness work requires that every possible trace of troublesome optimism, anticipation, or assertive ego ideal be killed off on appearance.[6]

When the worker noted in Chapter 11 finally concludes that "I am Ford's man and Ford will take care of his men," he is stating the essentials of feudalism, except that Ford (or another surrogate) has taken the place of some feudal lord.

Similarly, persons who have attained domination over others have lost their own identity; their relationships are symbiotic, and they are less free. The movie star who seems financially able to quit the frantic pace and do his or her own thing but isn't because he or she has responsibilities to a retinue of followers, public relations writers, agents, secretaries, and the like, is no longer the boss but the servant. The corporation president who knows that the company would collapse after his or her exit and hangs on for that reason is a prisoner of that organization. The father whose children insist upon his solving their every problem has the joys of many offspring but can't walk away. Power-laden relationships bring ties, and absolute power brings absolute ties.

## BECOMING SOMEBODY IN THE AGE OF RELATIONSHIPS

The need to relate is not a need for bonds, but for union, which permits one to retain one's own integrity and wholeness. It is not a single leap from domination or submissiveness up to an anticipatory and reality-based relationship; the move is stepwise. The highest level is identified by some as a condition of *love*. It resembles the Christian *agape,* or in the aggregate a kind of statesmanship associated with Lincoln. Its thesis is that the other person is a human being made in God's image like oneself. Thus, it is probably a duty to assume that others can be better than they are and should be helped to become what they can be. It is the relationship which the most revered parents, the great teachers, the business statesmen, and the influential priests and rabbis have attained with others.

> *There can be no movement into the highest levels of anticipatory living without some highly personal and effective face-to-face relations, for such attitudes as care, respect, responsibility, and teaching are not impersonal but highly personal.*

## MAKING YOURSELF VISIBLE MEANS BEING RESPONSIBLE

One of the sad facts about the activity trap is that it has produced an epidemic of irresponsibility in its wake. The professional who is more concerned about prac-

---

[6] A. Zaleznik and M. F. R. K. de Vries, *The Dynamics of Interpersonal Behavior* (Boston: Houghton Mifflin, 1975).

ticing a profession at the expense of the purposes for which the profession was created behaves irresponsibly. He or she becomes more concerned with doing things right than with getting things done.

The research department in which scientists flatly refuse to be bound by any regulations is a phenomenon that many companies and agencies have been confronted with during the sixties and seventies. The rationale sounds like a logical sequence: "Since pure science includes serendipity, any attempt to suggest direction and commitment on our part is by definition antiscientific." More is involved, however. The scientists who refuse to make commitments to what they will try to achieve are saying in effect, "You must commit yourself to paying me, providing me with laboratory and equipment, plus travel and memberships and aides, but I in turn am not obliged to make a matching commitment to attempt to produce something. Whether you get anything depends on chance, and is your concern and not mine."

For the employer, of course, this is similar to the legal responsibility toward children and the obligation of parents to provide support and amenities without expecting compensatory returns. Teachers who refuse to propose outcomes of their work and the staff people who erect barriers to performance measurement are adult versions of the juvenile irresponsibles. The effects are predictable. The group flight into narcissism requires that educational administrators fend off queries from those who pay the bills, such as taxpayers, insisting that education is too complex for parents even to be entitled to opinions on it. Scientists fend off administrators with complex and often Byzantine kinds of intrigues and cliques that thwart all attempts to bring orderly, anticipatory goal-setting processes to bear upon their work. Behavior that originates in a desire to be free in the detailed operation of their tasks evolves into the deathly kind of irresponsibility that denies the rights of others to judge their outputs.[7]

The *professional irresponsible,* despite ample intelligence and imagination, suffers a loss of true identity where work is more important than the reason for its existence. We can become disoriented to the world and obsessed with activity. When we live in an illusory world, this wrong orientation satisfies only our narrowest need for a framework within which we may shape our activities. We have *lost our objectivity* and become almost wholly centered upon our own behavior and that of our immediate peers. Relationships become more convoluted, and the size of our office, the size of our chief competitor's office, the status symbols which each employs in his or her work, take on heightened significance as they all lose contact with objective reality. Golding's *Lord of the Flies* could take place in a modern research laboratory, a college faculty, the staff of a state board of higher education, or the department of social welfare of a large city. Without the development of objectivity, people lack the power to see the world around them, for reality is distorted by fears, desires, anxieties, and ambitions, all part of a tighter and tighter closed circle. The *intelligence* humans have in common with animals—albeit to a much greater degree—can thus be identified with the

[7]B. Barber, "Control and Responsibility in the Powerful Professions," *Political Science Quarterly*, 93, no. 4, Winter 1978.

procedures used by irresponsible researchers; whereas *anticipatory judgment* and reason are a product of living in a world and grasping its nature.[8]

This need to be reasonable or even wise, and to be in touch with the future, calls for objectivity, which requires effort and planning. It is more than a play on words to find a clear relationship between objectivity and objectives. Objectivity is an ability to see the world as it is. A commitment to anticipatory objectives requires that a person behave responsibly, and make commitments to others whose opinion is important. This commitment adds meaning to everything which transpires thereafter in that man's behavior. Anticipatory objectives are the best modes of rationalizing one's behavior, for the terms *orientation* and *disorientation* have meaning only in terms of the goals and objectives to which the person is committed.

Responsibility, then, means more than engaging in acts of pure motion. The pure motion of being a scientist, a worker, a doctor, or an engineer can be both intelligent and professional, but it lacks responsibility, for it has no anticipatory objective intention. The home in which the mechanics of living have taken the place of purposeful living breeds irresponsibility. Responsibility becomes thin and often meaningless when there are no objectives. To be committed makes sense only when it is commitment to an objective.

## OVERCOMING LIMITED TRUST

Being a responsible person means that you enjoy the trust of somebody else. That person relies upon you to take the actions which are under your own independent control to produce what you say you are going to produce and, if difficulties are encountered, to overcome them. The importance of trust in human affairs has been well spelled out. No number of police can make widely known laws work if people cannot be trusted to obey them. The Internal Revenue Service has pointed out numerous times how it relies on the desire of people to do the right thing, and that the IRS intelligence service would be vastly larger than it is if it were required to police every citizen rather than the small percentage who cannot be trusted and who cheat on their tax statements. Civilization is based upon our trust of other people. We trust engineers to build bridges that won't fall down rather than bridges that will. We speed along in our cars trusting complete strangers to stay on their own side of the road and not cross the line onto ours.

Beyond our own immediate associates there are more people than we can possibly have as deep personal acquaintances. Yet we are required to operate as if we had such a long, personal acquaintanceship—thus making their behavior predictable and worthy of trust—if the wildly absurd unrealities of the world are to be kept in check. The social chaos in American cities during the sixties and seventies, when addicts swarmed in the streets, apartments were looted, and muggings abounded, was both a product and a generator of limited trust. Chronic warfare, such as the war in Southeast Asia, the Arab-Israeli conflict, wars between

[8] C. E. Gregory, *The Management of Intelligence* (New York: McGraw-Hill, 1967).

India and Pakistan, and wars between rich and poor, is an extension and a natural concomitant of this limited trust.

There are some precepts that seem to be important in the development of trust, or, to state it in complementary terms, to reduce limited trust.

Precept 1. *Conformity and submissiveness are not desirable solutions.* One common pattern for solution seems to be that of enforcing likeness and similarity of behavior upon everyone.[9] If others or the masses of people cannot be extended unlimited trust, some propose, then more laws, rules and regulation will be needed. State legislatures have engaged in mad races to enact even more restrictive laws governing the intimate details of life. In the federal government, the number and size of the monstrous bureaucracies grows prodigiously. "In the public interest" we are governed increasingly by detailed rules. In our own interest we find airplane flights tortuous exercises in government scrutiny. Our luggage and persons are searched by marshalls, our seated posture governed upon takeoff and landing, and our preflight behavior scrutinized by trained observers who seek to note our profiles. Over a hundred small safety rules and procedures are applied to passengers on each flight because we cannot trust others not to highjack the plane. In recreation, in consumer affairs, in education, in highway and plant design, and in work procedures we are enmeshed increasingly in tighter rules designed to ensnare the person unworthy of unlimited trust.

The creators of the rules are not individuals we can see and argue with, or perhaps defy. They are the *faceless* authorities, for whom the local agents are mere executors of the veiled power, "fellows doing their job like everybody else." It becomes pointless to argue with the gate agent or the flight attendant who does not understand the reason for the rules any more than the passenger.

I recently asked cabin attendants on ten different flights *why* passengers' seat backs should be in an upright position for landing on commercial flights. Not a single one could go beyond a smiling disclaimer, "I just have to enforce the rules." When I explained that it was because in a crash a reclined seat could kill or injure the person in the seat behind it, they seemed interested, relieved, and grateful for the information. "Do you think, then," I asked, "that a person sitting *in the rear seat* should place his seat in an upright position?" Immediately the official mask went on. "I don't have any other instruction," they all stated.

The mechanism of making such faceless authority work is the widespread willingness of people to conform.[10] Such a willingness is inculcated from an early age in the teaching of *adjustment* in the school system and the home. Being one of

---

[9] A. P. Hare, "A Study of Interaction and Concerns in Different Sized Groups," *American Sociological Review*, 17, 1952; *see also* L. R. Hoffman, "Homogeneity of Member Personality and Its Effect on Group Problem Solving," *Journal of Abnormal and Social Psychology*, 58, 1959.

[10] J. W. Getzels and P. W. Jackson, *Creativity and Intelligence: Explorations with Gifted Students* (New York: John Wiley, 1962). Suggests that conformity and creativity are inversely related. *See also* S. E. Asch, "The Effects of Peer Group Pressure upon the Modification and Distortion of Judgments," in E. Maccoby, *Readings in Social Psychology* (New York: Holt, Rinehart, & Winston, 1958).

the crowd, whether by wearing one's hair the same length as others or by wearing the same clothes and engaging in the same behavior as one's peer group, is an integral part of the maturation process. People who fail to conform are considered mentally ill, or become misfits, outcasts, or exiles. Sensitivity training and, more recently, in business, Organization Development (OD) courses are powerful training instruments that have a tangible effect of producing conformity.

The idea that individualtiy, the cultivation of individual differences, and insistence upon personal privacy are socially undesirable is necessary to the enforcement of conformity. The rise of such influences, especially in educational philosophies, has been well noted elsewhere.

Precept 2. *If conformity and submissiveness to the group were means of overcoming limited trust, then the world would seem to be a sterile place to inhabit in the future.* For they deny the dignity of the individual, deny individual responsibility, deny our ability to anticipate, and substitute the true believer of Eric Hoffer for the whole man.[11] Being a true believer has many unfortunate aspects:

- The group-centered person is valueless, and the shifting norms of the group substitute for the values of each individual in it.

- It deracinates the individual, for there is no need for roots other than in the group itself.

- The group itself cannot be trusted, if it is uprooted from the values of the past and of the individuals constituting it.

- The bonds of the group, in which membership is more important than any other value, must be rooted in anxiety rather than wholeness and mental health. Guilt at being eccentric, however valuable it may be in enforcing conformity, is not especially conducive to individual development.

- More important than the other reasons, for the fully adjusted individual, group sickness becomes his or her own sickness. The platoon members at My Lai, the H-bomber crew in *Doctor Strangelove,* and the ten thousand screaming parents outside a Canarsie school being integrated with twenty-eight black children are all conforming ideally to a group norm.

Precept 3. *Frustration produces aggression.* Much of the behavior of people that produces limited trust is aggressive behavior.[12] People trapped in meaningless work may bear their frustration indefinitely, but some frustrated people smash out of their situation. The rioters in the ghettos of the sixties, in Watts, Newark, Harlem, and elsewhere, burned and destroyed because some small event triggered their rage. Usually in hot weather, in unbearable slums, younger people were set into violent motion by some trivial event.

This aggression started a chain of subsequent patterns of behavior. Those who hit hardest found that their tormentors moved to change things. The halls of the legislatures and the carpeted offices of the corporations were forced to alleviate

[11] E. Hoffer, *The True Believer* (New York: Harper & Row, Pub., 1951).
[12] G. Rochlin, *A Man's Aggression: The Defense of the Self* (New York: Dell Pub. Co., Inc., 1973).

the conditions after they were struck by the violence of the frustrated. The lesson to the aggressor was clear: Hit them and they move.

One form of motion in response was counterforce. Police forces around the country stocked up with Mace, a chemical used to stun rioters. Their arsenals were stocked with Stoner guns that could penetrate a brick wall. Riot training was introduced into law enforcement training. Civil disturbance intelligence required the maintenance of records and files on citizens of a wide range of professions, including members of Congress, ministers, professors, and others who might be secret sympathizers with the aggressors.

The growth of the counterriot sent many of the more militant aggressors into secret organizations of a guerillalike character. The Black Panthers, the Blackstone Rangers, the De Mau Mau Association, and similar groups clustered together for self-protection and sometimes became terrorists. This accelerated as the civil disturbance elements of the law enforcement agencies fastened upon the underground terrorists and dramatized and probably enlarged their significance.

The products of this frustration-aggression whirlpool also included increased lawlessness among individuals and small groups in the cities, and made violence a commonplace affair. The violence also produced the professional conciliator, identified by novelist Tom Wolfe as the "flak catcher." This was the professional frustration satisfier who took on great importance as a riot preventer. The university president who responded to threatened riots by opening admissions to all and the OEO program manager who threw millions of dollars into areas of discontent, often without regard for where it landed with respect to need, were flak catchers and aggression satisfiers. They had ample company in society. Parents responded to the generation gap by growing their own hair long, by abandoning standards, and by lavishing unlimited money, gifts, and privileges on their offspring to avoid frustration. Corporations provided buy-now-pay-later systems to avert the frustrations of deferred pleasures simply because one could not pay now. Early, casual, and shifting sexual gratification was accepted as superior to more lasting relationships.

The effect of this solution to the aggression-frustration pattern was a quantum leap upward in the number of people for whom life was a steady succession of desires and satisfactions. The cult of consumerism produced a new culture; "the beautiful people" being those who could consume freely. Work was not a life goal as in the past, but a means for gratification of unlimited desires. The only meaning to work lay in the paycheck, which was a magic key to the means of consumption, which is where the true meaning of life and happiness was to be found. As the purposes of work were increasingly denied, the activity trap's bite became deeper, the very idea of output became lost, and consumption as a goal heightened. Consumption was the ultimate satisfier of the frustration of work and its discontents.

Labor unions became less aggressive and increasingly sterile and irrelevant as they succeeded in obtaining more and more pay and benefits for their members. As they matured and their character emerged as increasingly centered in buck grabbing, their skills at mercenary pursuits led to their decline as frustration-aggression machines. More and more union members became conservative, and the elections of 1972 showed them increasingly sustaining the establishment party. Unable to devise strategies to remove the frustrations from work, they provided members with ample paychecks to vent their frustrations in consumer behavior. The auto worker saw a job at Ford and General Motors as a means of owning a camper, a boat, and a fine deer hunting rifle, not a means of growing and expressing his or her best capabilities as a human being.

The result is an increasing number of human beings who have resigned themselves to a life devoid of creative thinking, of the challenges of problem solving, and of the ambition and pride of personal achievement following the attainment of tough goals. The creation of working conditions which cramp the mental and emotional development of people is not made less crippling simply because it pays well enough to buy consumer goods.

## STEPS TO RESPONSIBILITY AND BEING THEREBY SOMEBODY

Reality is not to be found in either submission or aggression. It calls for mature relationships. What is maturity? It may be easier to define immaturity. The immature person is ordinarily considered not fully grown or developed, and thus is childlike in actions. Such a person is, for one thing, dependent on others and avoids independent actions, or actions that emerge from an inner consciousness. His or her behavior is more apt to be caused by the actions, words, or behests of others and is externally determined by things, people, or outside stimuli. If we are responsive to every stimulus regardless of source, we are said to be erratic, and therefore immature and childlike.[13]

Immature behavior is often destructive. It may turn into the destruction of property, one's own or others, and might even be destructive of other persons, or at least damaging to their interests. It is destructive because the immature person does not consider the full consequences of his or her own behavior. In the pathologically immature, it becomes a form of deliberate behavior, in which immaturity is sought out and practiced for the notoriety and attention it brings.

Selfishness is still another facet of immature persons. Their behavior is centered on their own pleasures or interests, and they are correspondingly disregardful of the effects of that behavior on the interests or pleasures of others. This pleasure-mindedness produces an excessive search for those things that are immediately satisfying and an avoidance of the less pleasurable things, even though the deferred pleasures might ultimately have greater long-run advantages and satisfactions. Immature behavior more often claims the kinds of rewards and pleasures that are visible and immediately tangible than those which are widely dispersed, slight in intensity, or interrupted in occurrence.

The widespread nature of immature behavior, especially among adults and modern professionals, has mutated this pattern of behavior from the seeking of sensual pleasures to other forms of behavior. The writer who insists upon throwing

[13]K. R. Sears, *Patterns of Child Rearing* (New York: Row, Peterson, 1957); *see also* A. B. Hollingshead and R. C. Redlich, *Social Class and Mental Illness: A Community Study* (New York: John Wiley, 1958).

verbal grenades in print and the scientist who would pursue fruitless but fascinating lines of investigation may also exhibit such immaturity. Immature professional behavior comes when an initial bargain is made to produce services in return for tangible rewards such as pay, status, or physical support from an employer or patron and the professional insists upon practicing his or her profession in such a way as to deliberately avoid those paths of behavior that meet the commitment.

*A dominant characteristic of mature anticipatory behavior is a willingness to commit oneself to other persons, and to enter into transactions and mature relationships to discover and execute behaviors that will meet the needs of others as well as one's own.*

The rap session has some cathartic value for the person doing the talking. It does much more for the quality of the relationships between people. Improving the quality and maturity of relationships means making commitments to others and keeping them.

The quality of these commitments is important. They comprise a *new maturity*. They ascend from the lowest and most revulsive form of relationship to the highest order. This stair-step path to maturity is represented both in a history of the human race and in a descriptive taxonomy of the present kinds of commitments between people, including bosses and subordinates, husbands and wives, parents and children, politicians and constituents, neighbor and neighbor, and salesperson and customer. From lowest to highest, human relationships fall into these classes:

1. *Barbarism*. People outside my own family or tribe are enemies who should be destroyed, for they are likely to view me in similar fashion. I must therefore commit myself to get them before they get me or mine.

2. *Enslavement*. The other person is an object, much like a chair, table, or disposable container. People may be considered with affection if they are useful, but basically they exist to serve my pleasure, and when that use is concluded they may be neglected, disposed of, or destroyed. If the other person is consumed in the process of serving me, the regrets to be felt are mainly due to personal inconvenience or expense, and they are certainly not based upon consideration of that person as a person like me.

3. *Contractual servitude*. The other person is committed to serving me for a consideration, which I will provide in return for his or her side of the bargain. The relationship is at arm's length, and when the other can no longer serve, my commitment is no longer necessary and shall stop.

4. *Social awareness for the other's welfare*. A somewhat higher level is that of welfare-mindedness. I recognize that I am part of a larger body of the human race, and when somebody falls I have an obligation to help him or her. Charity, kindness, and generosity for those less fortunate is part of my behavior, especially in considering people at large, if not any particular individual. I am thus committed to my fellow human beings at large, and will help them if they are down without asking them what caused them to get there, for I might find that the cause is my own behavior. It is better if such welfare can be reimbursed by gratitude on the part of the afflicted when they receive my munificence. Ingratitude or a suggestion

that I am the cause of the other's plight are, of course, justification for denying such charity. For the unfortunate recipient, my munificence, solicitude, pity, generosity, sympathy, charity, and awareness must be compensated through humility, gratitude, deference, and willingness to make token repayment through loyalty.

5. *Paternalism and familial grace.* Those in my actual blood family are deserving of my generosity, help, and assistance. This extends outward in concentric rings from my own immediate family to more distant relatives, and ultimately to those who accept my role *in loco parentis.* Children should be cared for, to the degree I decide, and providing of course that they are properly cognizant of my parental role and authority. Choosing to sever that parental relationship, they are, of course, no longer worthy of my favorable attentions.

6. *Participative management.* Although I have the power to make decisions and be arbitrary, I subjugate that power through a quiet kind of noblesse oblige and seek out the opinions of others. This is, in part, because the others have something to contribute and will be more likely to be enthusiastic about the goals we seek if they participate in setting them. This is best done by defining the purposes of the effort and allows them to choose their own means of getting them. This will instill in them a sense of freedom and self-expression, while at the same time it keeps them attached to my organization and moving toward my ultimate goals, and frees me from the onerous tasks of tight control in which puppet and master, prisoner and guard are equally tied to one another.

7. *The prudent trustee.* Even higher in the quality of relationships is that of the responsible trustee. I do not own that which I rule, nor do I administer it for personal benefit or gain, but direct its affairs and make decisions about its disposition for the benefit of others who have entrusted it to me. This lofty service purpose requires that I strictly limit my own desires to that of the group which trusts me, and execute their will in their absence, even when it might seem to them that I am thwarting some immediate desire to act differently.

8. *Love and statesmanship.* The other person has a potential of being even more godlike and great than at present, and my relationship with that person is one of assisting that growth. Because the other's growth is important to me, I consider his or her potential to be my responsibility. To diminish others diminishes myself, and to assist them in seeing their own ideals, to help them raise them, and to help them achieve them is to become fully functioning as a person myself.

The choice among these options is the life challenge of bosses, of husbands and wives, of parents, of neighbors, and of statesmen. To find the highest and best level is the ultimate goal of human relations.

## GETTING THE BIGGER PICTURE OF THE WORLD

You will not get a bigger picture of the world by traveling around it in a jet plane, or in seeing every documentary on TV. The big picture of the world will be found by improving the quantity and quality of human relationships. Getting in touch with people, anticipating the best, trusting more and being trusted more, and making commitments and getting them are the only avenue to finding the bigger picture and widening one's ambit or outlook. More technical knowledge, more mastery of science, and more definition in mathematical terms will not widen your picture but narrow it. To manage by anticipation in any worthwile way suggests, then, that you turn your attention toward mastering those relationships with people and groups and their interests.

# eighteen

# Managing change by keeping your options open

The purpose of this chapter is to explain a way of managing change. The massive forces spelled out in this book make it apparent that the most likely tendency of normal people is to be *noncommitters*. This tendency will become more prevalent as life becomes more complex, as people become more educated, and as profession-alism ensnarls more and more of our lives. A system for managing change means that we will produce change, but we won't do it by cramming it down the throats of people who are firmly attached to activity as it is being carried on now. Rather, the system of producing change must meet these requirements:

1. Management faces the fact that specialization produces the activity trap, and people will tend toward being noncommittal in decisions that might produce changes in their behavior.

2. Management needs to turn people from noncommitters into *reasonable* adventurers, to use a term coined by Roy Heath. This means that people cannot be expected to be plungers or blind risk takers, but that given a procedure accept-able to them and their professional cast of mind, they will make decisions that produce changes in an orderly fashion.[1]

3. The key to turning noncommitters into reasonable adventurers while avoiding wild plunges into a murky or concealed future lies in getting people to see the reasonableness and prefessionalism in *widening their options* when confronted with a decision.

## HOW TO NUDGE DECISIONS OVER INTO THE CHANGE-ACCEPTANCE MODE

People are more likely to change when they can see some advantages in changing and some more disadvantages in not changing. The presentation of a wider range of options can change decision making. The first step?

[1] R. Heath, *The Reasonable Adventurer* (Pittsburgh: University of Pittsburgh Press, 1964).

238

*Specify the problem in explicit terms as a deviation from a standard.*

It is not a statement of a problem to note ruefully that things are bad or to make some such vague statement. Even statements alleging that morale is bad or costs are too high is too general to be useful. The problem needs to be stated as the difference between what is and what should be.

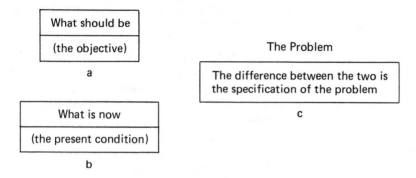

Thus the problem becomes one of differences in results presently being obtained and the desired condition or effect, perhaps something like the following:

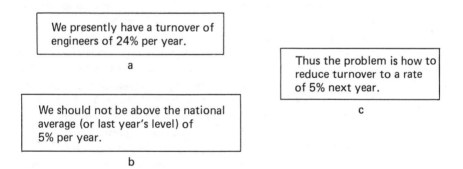

You now have turned the problem into an objective. While a 19-percent-point improvement will not produce perfection, it does bring things back to a satisfactory and livable level.[2]

At this point we are now ready to start seeking some options.

## SOME RULES FOR THE DEVELOPMENT OF OPTIONS

Getting good options onto the menu before the decision is made will improve the quality of choice. Here are some guidelines to help you in developing options. Simply having a bull session or a general brainstorm conference to wing it freely

---

[2] H. A. Simon, *The New Science of Management Decision* (New York: Harper & Row, Pub., 1960); *see also* R. Kepner and B. Tregoe, *The Rational Manager* (New York: McGraw-Hill, 1961). The goal is not perfection but improvement.

may have some advantages in stimulating the people taking part. But it does not do the complete job. Nor can we always rely upon genius management, or rely wholly upon specialists and experts to think up everything that needs thinking. Four rules will make options work:

1. *Take enough time to explain the problem.* This usually means involving as many people as necessary to get all of the available opinions and options. The common process of participative management suggests getting "input" from all concerned. This choice, however, is too general. The input should be founded upon fully acquainting everyone who is making a contribution of options with the definition of the problem as the top management, board of directors, or decision maker sees it. Orville Beal, one-time president of the giant Prudential Insurance Company, is reported to have said that while "the purposes of the company flow down, the methods of getting to those purposes should flow upward." Without the crystal-clear definition of the problem in people's minds, their options may be irrelevant or contradictory.[3] They will press personal hobbies and immediate causes rather than presenting options that deal with possible solutions to the specific problem.

2. *Build acceptance into the process early.* As Norman R. F. Maier points out, the final decision must have attributes of both quality and acceptance.[4] There may be people in the organization who are chronic and even pathological resisters to any change whatsoever, but most people will go along with decisions that they have themselves assisted in creating. Seek agreement on the problem, even when it is no more than stating the problem and ensuring that it is clearly understood by all involved. For most problems this means doing a fair share of listening as well as directing. Have a clear idea of what you are planning to communicate before you start transmitting. Be sure that the means and media are suitable to the audience to which you are communicating. Finally, allow feedback from the listeners to be sure the intent of your message is understood. Ask them to restate your ideas in their own words, and correct any misconceptions you yourself might have created in the telling. Listen to that feedback, not merely for the words, but for the apparent feelings that surround them:

> *I understand that you feel we should make our own valves in this division and not buy them from outside, and you are apparently strongly in favor of such a policy. I understand what you have said, and I know your reasoning.*

This is not necessarily acceptance of every opposing view, but it demonstrates that you have sought and obtained feedback and attended upon it carefully. Even when the suggestion must be denied or rejected, the proof of understanding on your part will help in ultimate acceptance of the final decision. Be willing to make small compromises easily, and be lenient in the choice of means toward the necessary end if such moderation will increase the likelihood of final acceptance:

> *The decision on policy on buying valves from outside has already been made*

[3] R. Likert, *New Patterns of Management* (New York: McGraw-Hill, 1961).
[4] N. R. F. Maier and J. J. Hayes, *Creative Management* (New York: John Wiley, 1962).

*at the corporate level, but I see no reason we cannot have some skilled people inside the house who work closely with our suppliers, and perhaps a small program of modifications and design changes. Even with the given policy we can use our own expertise by specifying such design, and testing their performance against our standards. I think we can find some unity of opinion here.*

The objective of acceptance in decision making is to produce a *unity of effort* among people whose collaboration is needed to make the final choice work.

3. *Take enough time to hear the details of every option.* For many people at work the major question to be asked of the boss is *What do you really want?* Once that has been spelled out, they are willing to go along and cooperate. For others, perhaps a minority of one, a diametrically opposing position may be taken. Before the person is cuffed down and subdued, take time to hear the whole story with its reasoning, and learn what interests lie behind the reasoning and what the outcome would be of that option for the rest of the organization. Using an interrogatory style of discussion and avoiding sharp put-downs will help you understand that dissident viewpoint.[5] Once stated, its existence can be acknowledged, even if it is not accepted. Do not express approval or disapproval of any suggested option until the whole story has been told. Invite position papers from people who have conflicting views if time permits.

4. *Take enough time to arrive at a consensus.* If the boss or leader takes the time to listen to all views before deciding, he or she may find that consensus can be shaped. Often the conflicting viewpoint can be described as a *constraint* rather than a conflicting viewpoint:

*As Bill has pointed out, we need to have tight quality control over both design and manufacture of these purchase products, and we should devise such a scheme as part of our acquisition plans.*

## THE CATEGORIES OF
## A GOOD OPTIONS LIST

The major effort in decision making is often the early adoption of an attractive option, or an option presented by an impassioned advocate. The function of the decision maker should be to press for more options, until the best emerges.

Good options are as valuable in personal decision making as they are in managerial. For you, this means that making personal decisions—in personal affairs— is a sound practice field for making managerial decisions. You press yourself for options, taking sufficient time to get the full array before you decide. If you are the boss you press your subordinates to widen their options before they—or you— make the decision. A study of the decisions managers make shows that options can be divided into classes, which are likely to appear when you have wrestled with the problem long enough and gotten a full range of choices in front of you. Options

<hr>

[5] R. Back, *Communication: The Art of Understanding and Being Understood* (New York: Hastings House, 1963).

can be of one of the following types, or of some combination of them. Some options are *defensive* in nature, others offensive.

**Option 1. Do nothing different** Doing nothing different is a perfectly sound defensive option that should be explored before all others. If after a waiting period the problem will resolve itself, then it is pointless to spend a lot of time and money to jiggle with it. Apply first the old Georgia maxim, *If it ain't broke don't fix it*. If things are working, leave them alone. This option, at first, may seem weak or vacillating, but in truth it is a prime means of checking to see if there really is a problem. Our irresistible impulse toward activity sometimes prompts us to fiddle around with things that are going OK simply because we are activists in temperament. Vince Lombardi often advised, "Don't change a winning game," and if you have a good game plan and it is working basically well, don't let minor misfortune and ordinary vicissitudes tempt you into throwing away the plan. Be sure that the need for change is real before you start restructuring things.

On the other hand, this choice should be examined with considerable caution lest it be a cover for inaction. Hiding one's head in the sand from a real problem may be comforting to an ostrich, but in times of real danger this is an ineffectual defensive posture and a terrible plan of offense.

The right question to ask here might be something like this: *If we didn't do anything other than what we are doing right now, what would the consequences be? What is the probability that that outcome would occur?* If the answer to that question is that disaster lies in our natural course, then this do-nothing option should, of course, be rejected. If, on the other hand, the chances are high that the threat will go away of its own accord, or if the risk is minimal or acceptable, the option should be seriously considered.

The test of whether or not to stand still and wait things out is in the amount and kind of *risk*. We live in a risk-laden world, and minimal risks have to be accepted because we haven't any real choice.[6]

If the risk we are taking is reasonably high or is based upon the assumption or fond hope that others will overlook their own main chance, we must reject the option to do nothing. It should be assumed that the world is filled with others who might easily see their own best interest and won't be gulled into error. The opposite assumption isn't a sensible idea when we are engaged in risky behavior or are faced by a frightening problem. It's wise to ask ourselves, What are our downside loss possibilities? Suppose we get caught at what we are doing now; What would the losses be?

The Boston Consulting Group, a leading consulting firm in strategic management, classifies some businesses as "cash cows." This condition exists when the firm has a leading market share in a stable market and, without pressing heavily with aggressive advertising, it "milks" the market. Perhaps someday the cow will dry up, but for the foreseeable future, the best strategy is to *do nothing differently*.

This highlights an important distinction: the difference between doing

---

[6]P. F. Drucker, *Management: Tasks, Responsibilities, Practices* (New York: Harper & Row, Pub., 1973). Asks, "Is a decision really necessary?"

nothing and doing nothing differently. To do nothing differently may be to keep up the same pace as in the past. The racing driver who holds the lead at 120 miles per hour does not stop because he is ahead, but he does not need to do more than retain his present behavior until somebody else changes pace and tries to capture the lead.

There are times when it is apparent that this option should be rejected. In the beer business, when Philip Morris entered the field with heavy outlays of advertising and new light beer products and began to capture a large share of the market during the late seventies, those firms that hung onto old ways did not survive.

The small business located in the central business district that learns plans are afoot for a large shopping mall on the outskirts of town cannot count upon its many years of past success downtown to carry it through the forthcoming competition. Studies show that thirty percent of the shoppers' dollars will move out to the new mall in the first quarter after it opens. Such is not the time to do nothing differently. The mall won't go away, and the dollars will move, and actions to restore buyers' preferences for downtown shopping, such as improving the parking, training the sales force in better sales methods, and using more progressive design to highlight the unique features of the downtown shopping areas, are called for, not inaction. Yet, most old downtown merchants adopt this option and often go broke.

**Option 2. Find (and fire) a scapegoat** One of the common defensive options in the time of a change that threatens an organization is to try to find someone *who is wrong* to fire or displace. The late mayor of Chicago, Richard Daley, was noted for using this option. If his administration was caught in some flagrant misdeed, he promptly chose a department head and publicly relieved him of duties. This had a number of salubrious effects. First, it protected the entire organization, while expending one visible victim. Usually the realities of the situation were explained to the victim, and some mollifying act, such as giving him an inconspicuous job to ease the blow, accompanied the action. Firing or removing some individual has the same effect in some cases as sealing off one compartment and the sailors trapped therein in order to save the ship and the remainder of the crew.

Such an execution is, of course, different from an ordinary firing. It is not a run-of-the-mill discharge for an offense like stealing, drinking on the job, or similar peccadilloes. Rather, it is entailed when the entire organization looks bad, which is a problem for the whole top management. That is when the therapeutic firing must occur, and it should always be noted as an option.[7]

In addition to the external effects of quieting the pressure of the public or the stockholders for action, scapegoating has some fine internal effects as well. When a person departs abruptly, the effect is often to unload a whole burden of guilt and blame at the same time. When somebody departs, immediately everyone left behind discovers a whole rash of problems that can be attributed to "the late

[7]G. S. Odiorne, *How Managers Make Things Happen* (Englewood Cliffs, N.J.: Prentice-Hall, 1961).

Joe Smith," the fired or separated person. Every blunder, every oversight, every malfeasance or nonfeasance that rears its head in the coming quarter now has a handy alibi: "It's Smith's fault."

The option, while not morally admirable, is especially likely to appear when something political in character is involved. The politics may be community relations for the local plant, the recall of a product for defects, or a widely heralded scandal such as bribes to get business, or other hanky-panky. The rule is easy to remember and, for those not overly fainthearted in their dedication to the organization, simple to execute:

1. Find a scapegoat.
2. Sack him or her.

The fruit of such an option may be highly beneficial to the organization, to the persons whose sense of righteous justification will carry them through, and to everyone else, with the possible exception of the hapless victim. As a means of completely solving problems, of course, it has some shortcomings, for after the sacking, the causes of the problem probably still remain, but it does ease the worst pangs of anguish and worry and defers things for a bit. It also has been known to produce pangs of regret if not conscience for the humanistic type.

**Option 3. Reorganize the company** *A major reorganization of the company or bureau* is a defensive option. Business reporters and the media are especially enthralled by such an option: "Mr. Jones, newly appointed president and chief executive officer of Horseless Carriage Motors has announced sweeping reorganization of the president's office." This has an air of command decision about it, with grand moves and dramatic charges and countercharges against apathy and inertia, without necessarily having a great deal of effect upon the way the trucks roll and the goods get sold. It does, however, hush the critics, the dissident stockholders, or the creditors for a while. "After all, you must give this new organization a chance to settle in and the dust to settle." Such a delay may give the new chief a chance to quietly dig in and find out what is really wrong and fix it.

Several large firms over the years have employed this game skillfully. If the firm was centralized and ran into problems, they decentralized.[8] Decentralization is an especially fine option for delaying decisions, for it is soberly asserted that "it often takes five years before decentralization really takes full effect." If, on the other hand, the firm was already decentralized and ran into problems, it could centralize. This is especially attractive to business and financial reporters, who write down soberly about the reported reorganization, "President Jones assumes tighter command to cut losses and improve efficiency." The idea of centralizing means that everybody in the entire organization reports to one person. The janitor in Omaha cannot buy a new mop without getting an OK from the corporate office in Cleveland. In time, all risk taking stops and all decisions get delayed, but time has been bought to straighten out what was really wrong.

[8] J. Dearden, "Limits on Decentralized Profit Responsibility," *Harvard Business Review,* November-December, 1961.

Delay as a defense mechanism, of course, can be achieved by other means, and there will be perfectly suitable occasions to use delay. It may be the delay needed to get a second opinion on the one strongly recommended by local doctors. It might be that a delay is needed to let some kind of statute of limitations take over, as occurs when highly placed politicians are discovered with their hands in the public cookie jar. In other cases, it may be a delay needed to await a desired retirement a couple of years hence. Or it may be a delay with an eye toward the possibility of a well-placed funeral in the upper echelons. It may be necessary to delay some human-resources plans until after the union contract expires and the union can be decertified or a tougher contract language can be negotiated. These are all seemingly prudent reasons for delay.

If, however, the reorganization or other delay tactic is done for one of the following reasons, it is probably time for somebody to simply press over the opposition and make tough and even unpopular decisions to proceed.

- If the decision to delay is rooted simply in natural timidity and hesitancy, then, as with the rookie paratrooper standing in the door of the plane, a firm bit of assistance out the door may be just the ticket.

- If the delay is founded on the opposition of people whose professional status and functions might be greatly reduced and they are a sufficiently small group that their perfectly understandable wishes cannot be allowed to stand in the way of great gains, then overruling and suppressing such delay is needed.

- If the delay is rooted in any of the other temperamental, philosophical, or theoretical arguments against change that fall within the substance of the change-resister phenomenon, then overrule of dissidents may be the order of the day.

The point is not, of course, that all delays are bad, or that all movement is good. The trick is to know when reasonable change is clearly needed and to make it, and defining this option does not increase the likelihood of delay. Rather, it shows those opposed to change and those seeking delay and status quo management of the affairs of the organization that they have been understood fully but that change will proceed nonetheless.

The three options outlined so far, which of course also permit numerous variations, are not proposed as action plans to be adopted universally, but as options which should be considered and either accepted or consciously rejected in every major decision. They are, of course, all defensive options. They prevent losses. They keep us or our organizations from sliding backward. They are often related to problems and threats that surround us. They might apply as well to the problem of a marriage as to those of a corporation. If your marriage is creaky, all too often one or both of the partners think too quickly about "firing" the other. In still other cases the matter is settled when one of the partners decides to bear with the situation and hope that it improves. Lincoln was reported to have adopted such a solution in his marriage to Mary Todd. When advised to get her out of Washington, where she was a source of gossip and even scandal, Lincoln rejected the option of sending her to Illinois. "If you make a bad bargain, sometimes if you hug it tight, it will work out," he is reported to have told his counselors.

*Defensive options are most useful when the situation calls for defense. When the organization is under attack—or when you are—then defensiveness isn't a weakness but a virtue.*

But there are more options to be considered which are more assertive and compelling in character and in some cases are offensive in direction, if not in manner. What are *options on the offensive*?

**Option 4.  Define something noble about a proposed change** When President Carter, in his famous speech on energy, suggested that "the moral equivalent of war" was embedded in his request to people to quit driving their cars everywhere they went and to conserve energy in all forms, he was relying upon this option. Such rhetoric, despite the scoffers, has a genuine human purpose of placing the change within some sort of philosophical framework, which is often necessary.[9] A war on poverty has an air of nobility lacking in a dole, a handout, or a welfare program. A war against godless communism is better than ruthless invasion of a helpless small country. Being a tough competitor has a nicer air to it than being a cornercutting chiseler. Husbands who abandon their families to run off with a mistress can feel better about it if they can couch their act in terms of attempting to find true happiness in a life which has grown pointless.

All of this, of course, is not to suggest that noble goals are either cynical or deceitful stuff. There is instead a need in almost all of us to find some kind of larger meaning in what we are doing. As an often invited speaker at conferences and conventions of various professional and trade groups, I have learned that almost without fail I can win the accolades and appreciation of the audience if my message can be summarized, "There is a larger meaning to what you do for a living, and I am here to tell you what that meaning is." I find myself applauded and personally thanked with sincerest gratitude, for so many people never hear such ennobling statements where they work. The undertaker, the plumber, the traffic manager, the retail clerk, the police officer, and the production worker in the factory all hold within themselves some hope that they can find a larger meaning to what often seems mundane and occasionally demeaning.

Insurance clerks are providing life-long security to people, garbage collectors are protecting the public health, and teachers are molding the character of future generations. Often the bureaucratic world or the mean-spirited environment in which these people work stifles any such ennobling and uplifting descriptions. On the contrary, the systems and the supervision and even the training teach them that they are nobodies and not really necessary in many instances. The boss who has the wisdom and the ability to hang out a higher meaning of work to subordinates will be loved and appreciated, and incidentally will be rewarded by more productivity and greater willingness to follow the paths of change he or she suggests.

---

[9] J. W. Gardner, *Excellence* (New York: Harper & Brothers, 1961; *see also* D. C. McClelland and D. G. Winters, *Motivating Economic Achievement* (New York: Free Press, 1969).

Here are some ways you can define noble options that place you in an initiating posture rather than a defensive stance:

- You can start a crusade.
- You can stamp out something evil.
- You can raise the level of the human condition.
- You can make people more godlike.
- You can prove to people that they are better than they think.
- You can be generous, giving, kind, charitable, and self-denying.
- You can show people how they can be lofty, splendid, and shining.
- You can hold out new possibilities that people have never grasped before.
- You can stress the high moral qualities of some proposed action.
- You can make the choices that are noble rather than those which are ignoble or base in the way you do things.
- You can join the select few who are noble, great, enlightened, and uplifted by their own actions.
- You can dare to be great and rise to great challenges.

All of these kinds of phrases are characteristic of the kinds of noble options that you can hold forth for yourself. If you are responsible for others, you can likewise raise their behavior from rutlike, mechanistic, bureaucratic, and change-resisting by appealing to a higher motivation.

The ennobling motive, when presented as an option, is best put forth in polar-opposite terms. While hanging up such lofty possibilities for others (or for yourself), you must at the same time destroy by scorn and satire the ignoble things that comprise the undesired behaviors. These include such horrors as being slothful, lazy in body or mind, sneaky, corrupt, deceitful, tricky, and cynical. The higher is endorsed by destroying the lower.

Sadly enough, the effectiveness of the noble option has fallen on hard times for many leaders today. The higher level of education of the people, their sad experience with demagogues, their distrust of politicians, and a host of other influences have made hortatory and inspirational speeches less effective than they used to be. The examples of Hitler and Mussolini, whose oratory roused the emotional fervor of their followers, gave public speaking a bad name for many of the more intelligent. For many intellectuals, the very ability to deliver a masterful and compelling lecture or address is itself a cause of suspicion. Despite this, for the majority of us, the person who moves us in new directions is the one who can present to us a new vision—a new option—which seems noble and uplifting in character.

**Option 5. Being creative and self-actualizing** Perhaps the best option for managing change is to propose that people move up to the highest level of human potentiality, that of prompting others and ourselves to live at a level of our highest potentialities. While all of us, suggests psychologist Abraham Maslow, have certain physical needs of an animal nature, when such needs are fulfilled, we move immediately to a new order of priorities.[10] For one thing, we raise the levels of our aspirations for higher amounts of ego satisfaction, social prestige, and acclaim, and ultimately, when all of these seem reasonably satiated, we aspire to the highest level of all. That highest level of motivation, says Maslow, is that of *self-actualization*. This is the mature state of successful people when they *have attained all that is possible for them to have attained*. They have employed their talents to the utmost; they have created, faced, and overcome important challenges they might not have dreamed possible. They arrive at what Freud described as their own "ego ideal." They measure up to or exceed their most exemplary performer in the world that surrounds them.

In some cases this may center around competence and improvement of personal skills and abilities: "You could learn to be the best programmer in data processing." Or perhaps, "With your skills and personality you could eaily become an executive secretary to a major officer of the firm."

In other cases it may be that a person who is trapped in mundane and boring kinds of work could be motivated to shift attention to innovative work at the frontier of the field.

The creative option is a change-inducing option. It is faced in an affirmative direction, not a negative way ("Oh, you stick-in-the-mud").

Maslow's research discovered that the healthiest people, the most creative, strongest, wisest and saintliest of us often comprise what he called "biological assays." Such a model person is a form of advanced scout and keen perceiver of what it is that the rest of us value.

Thomas Gilbert, in his recent work *Human Competence,* makes an eloquent statement for the use of exemplary performers as a means of engineering worthy performance.[11] He would apparently agree with Aristotle, who proposed that "what the superior man thinks is good . . . is really good." Maslow calls this a theory of "metamotivation," which means taking superior people, who are at the same time superior perceivers of facts and values, and using their choices of ultimate values for the whole species.

The assumption here is one that could help us reverse the world dominated by change resisters. If the gloomy list of reasons presented in this book as to why we have become change resisters were based upon something in the species genetically and culturally founded, then there would be no hope of producing and managing change. As long as there are exemplary people who do indeed manage change and flourish in the process, the change indeed can be produced without rending society to shreds.

*The thrust of this book has been that resistance to change is the big problem*

---

[10] A. Maslow, *Motivation and Personality*, 2nd ed. (New York: Harper & Row, Pub., 1970).
[11] T. Gilbert, *Human Competence: Engineering Worthy Performance* (New York: McGraw-Hill, 1978).

*of humans and of societies. Managing change means solving the big problem by making the good person and thereby the good society.*

In such a solution to the problem of change resistance, managers become teachers, as do parents, administrators, and other authority figures. The ideal is to produce the good person. This is not to be done by biological advances such as cloning, but rather by starting with the raw clay we have at hand, ordinary people who can be taught to do extraordinary things. This teaching is not done by didactic means (lectures and sermons) but by policies and supervisory practices that reinforce those things that demonstrate self-evolution and self-creation and avoid the reduction of people into narrow hacks, professional slaves, and robots to procedures without meaning.

People can also teach themselves. Every time we take an action we reinforce the motive that caused us to take it in the first place. Thus, if we find ourselves relating to the world by overpowering it, we will find reinforcement in the behavior of being exacting, hostile, judgmental, and punitive of others. The sight of others cringing is what reinforces the bully. When we see in everyone including ourselves a potentiality of the exemplary performer, the good person, the self-actualizing person, we reinforce the behavior that caused us to produce such self-fulfilling actions.

What are some of the specific things that we as parent, boss, or teacher can do to elicit the innovative and creative behavior to produce orderly and satisfying change?

- We can state explicitly that we desire to see such creative behavior.
- We can ask for commitments to innovation and change.
- We can arrange our systems in such a way that rewards and reinforcements flow to people who are self-actualizing and are denied to those who are stifling their own and others' best qualities.
- We can inform people when we observe that they are moving toward exemplary behavior, and reinforce it by our praise.
- We can demand that effort at less than one's best level be redone at a higher level. This higher level is that of the exemplary performer, or the highest potential of the person as he or she now stands.
- We can use the skills of interrogation to help people find where their highest potential might be.
- We can remove the obstacles that bar people from fulfilling their potential for growth and change.
- We can use the tools of recognition and achievement motivation to make exemplars of those who are fulfilling their highest potentials.
- We can speak the language of success rather than the dour words of failure.
- We can organize people into groups to reinforce one another on their path.
- We can leave people alone while they are working on their goals and give them freedom to fail or succeed, and to reward and punish themselves.

## WITHOUT GOOD OPTIONS THERE
## ARE NO SUPERIOR DECISIONS

In this chapter the emphasis has been upon a key means of introducing change in a world of change resisters. The bureaucrat, the professional, the conservative, and the traditionalist all fuel the anti-change, anti-planning behavior of society. Exhorting such people is useless, and ordering them autocratically will merely produce resistance, for without their acceptance no change will be implemented, even when it is directed.

Lincoln once said that a mind stretched by a new idea never returns to its original dimension. Herein lies much of the power of the option. It is a possible route for introducing a new idea, teasing and eliciting it from the mind of its maker. This causes the idea to originate in the person who must implement it, which is perhaps the only way in the world of professionals for such change resistance to be overcome. Methods of aggressive selling or authoritarian directives to produce change will merely stiffen the level of resistance.

*The best option for change is one created by the people who must implement it, or one for which the implementers can claim ownership.*

# nineteen

# Toward surprise-free management: the ideal
## in managing change

Organizations and people who plan on a regular, systematic, formal basis outperform those who don't. Professors S. S. Thune and Robert House studied thirty-six firms from six different industries and found that companies that engaged in such comprehensive planning for the future consistently outperformed companies that confined themselves to informal or short-range peeks into the future.[1] The advantage of such planning was most apparent in industries with a rapidly changing external environment, such as the electronics and drug industries. In sales volume, earnings per share, stock price, earnings on equity, and earnings on total capital, the formal planners outstripped the informal planners. Not only were there differences between companies, but within individual companies tested on a before-and-after basis, there was a clear-cut advantage of planned management over informal planning. In sales, earnings per share, and stock price, there was substantial improvement after a firm switched from informal to formal planning. In a subsequent check on the same thirty-six firms two years later, David Herold found that the trend was no isolated exception. The same firms showed continued superiority in sales and profit.[2]

In the beginning much planning is defensive in nature. Competitors, laws, and cultural influences press upon the firm to change, and the company learns to respond. But it learns more than that. It eventually learns the value of planning and starts to create changes, to which other people and organizations must now respond.

---

[1] S. S. Thune and R. R. House, "Where Long Range Planning Pays Off," *Business Horizons,* 13, no. 4, October 1970.
[2] D. M. Herold, "Long Range Planning and Organization Performance," *Academy of Management Journal*, 15, no. 1, March 1972.

# THE NEED FOR CLEAR GOALS IN THE FACE OF THE SPORADIC NATURE OF CHANGE

As we scan events back over time we might, like Darwin, assume that change is not only inevitable, but due to some kind of universal cause such as survival. We might also assume, as Darwin did, that change is gradual. If we get hung up on that assumption we presume that change is an invisible wave seen only by periodic measuring to take stock. Modern biology now has adopted the assumption that change is not really gradual but occurs in leaps and jumps, fits and starts. Change in nature, they conclude, is more episodic and discontinuous. Mathematician Rene Thom is even designing a mathematical model capable of predicting random events.

Since change is not gradual but arrives in leaps and jumps, it is not surprising that change resisters are often surprised by change, especially if they have assumed that change is nonexistent or always gradual. This sporadic nature of change is a sufficient reason for many to conclude that managing change is impossible and that all change and its management requires nothing more or less than being speedy in response time. The rest is fate. Being orderly and careful in doing things right is enough until we discover that a leap has occurred. Then we can scramble. So reasons the change resister.

Many change resisters, in the light of this erratic rate of change, have become unconscious existentialists. The existentialist philosophy denies the value or even the truth of systems. All that counts is luck, guilt, situationality, and death. If nothing is sure but death and taxes, what value is there, then, in even trying to plan? Yet, the evidence is clearer every year that planning helps us attain our purposes. *How can we succeed in the world of sporadic change*? A few commonsensical ideas present themselves.

1. We can define goals and objectives for ourselves and our lives. One of the characteristics of those modern organizations that do better than others is that the organization and its people are clearer on their purposes than less well-run and less successful organizations.[3]

2. When people find out what is expected of them in specific form, their behavior changes and they are more responsive to change.[4] Many of the professional irresponsibles are often merely people who have lost sight of their purposes.

3. To succeed in a world of change, it is necessary to have both long-run and immediate plans, with the longer-range plans being the governing criteria for the merit of the short-run. If you don't know where you are going, any road will get you there. The purported pleasures of winging it in life, of living the unplanned and unexamined life, are immature pleasures, which are best left behind when adulthood comes.

---

[3]C. Barnard, *The Functions of the Executive* (Cambridge, Mass.: Harvard University Press, 1938).

[4]B. H. Raven and J. Reitsema, "The Effects of Varied Clarity of Group Path and Goal Both Upon the Individual and His Relationship to the Group," *Human Relations*, 10, no. 1, February 1957.

4. The process of defining goals and plans for attaining them contains most of the ennobling, self-fulfilling, success-producing processes of living. It is quite true that getting there is *half* the pleasure. Setting the goal is half the pleasure. Getting there and realizing achievement is the other half.[5]

5. Goals as the symbolic form of success have the capacity of igniting the human spirit in a way that nothing else can do. If we have people in our sphere of influence who have no goals and we can provide some by any means that they can feel responsibility for, we have enriched their lives.[6]

6. Sporadic changes are not catastrophic for people who have clear goals and visions in mind of what condition will exist when those goals are attained. The *oops effect* becomes an ordinary part of living for change resisters, for their goals remain the same when conditions change.

7. Success need not be unavailable because of bad luck. It is possible to manage bad luck when one's goals are skillfully defined. In management and in life there are the risks of mismanagement and there are the risks of nature.[7] Evidence of the failures of businesses indicates that over 90% of such failures are due to mismanagement and God must take the rap for only the other ten percent. This suggests that there is considerable room for human management of change, and considerable hope that we can respond with some aplomb to the leaps and starts of nature if our purposes are firmly held.

## SURPRISE-FREE MANAGEMENT HAS NINE ELEMENTS

The well-managed company operates under a system of surprise-free management. This doesn't mean that the giant firm does not have the same downturns in business that every organization faces. Nor is it immune to the vagaries of luck and the changing tastes of customers. Yet, its considerable growth in sales and profit is undoubtedly due to being better prepared to respond quickly to change. Even more important, it learns to create the changes that will give it a competitive advantage. There are some nine elements to surprise-free management that, my studies reveal, make up its practice:

- An above-average knowledge of the present situation
- A systematic way of preparing long-run strategic goals
- A willingness to shift resources to their highest-yield uses
- Skillful use of timing and positioning
- Giving and getting commitments to goals on the part of all hands
- A sound system of management information

---

[5] D. McClelland, *The Achieving Society* (Princeton, N.J.: D. Van Nostrand, 1961).
[6] G. H. Litwin and J. A. Ciarlo, "Achievement Motivation and Risk Taking in a Business Setting," technical report, Behavioral Research Service, General Electric Co., New York, 1959.
[7] J. Milnor, "Games Against Nature," in Thrall et al., *Decision Processes* (New York: John Wiley, 1954).

- An optimistic view of the future and a willingness to make it happen
- A strong commitment to developing human potential
- A relentless feedback of the facts of the situation as it emerges

Let's look at each of these in a little more detail.

**Facing the present situation** Many people would rather hide from bad news than come out and face the truth. We often live our lives on illusions about our condition, our resources, our actions. Once in a while, then, it's valuable to have an honest auditor come look at things as they are and report what really is.

The modern practice of organizational audits that extend far beyond financial audits has been a characteristic of surprise-free management. Corporate staffs, rather than interfering in operations, serve more often today as auditors and reviewers of the performance of divisions and departments of the organization.[8] The new product of staff work is a clear view of the strengths, weaknesses, and problems inside the firm. These open up opportunities for the prevention and cure of ills while they are still manageable. The strongest universities are those which are reviewed periodically by outside visitation teams and accreditation bodies. Rather than being defensive against such intrusions into their affairs, they welcome such reviews, for they bring the sanitizing light of objectivity to programs that might have become ingrown. For some organizations, the audits are self-audits. For others, it requires external observers without a personal stake in the outcome to bring objectivity and fresh viewpoints to bear on the organizational posture and character. More than that, audits by the world outside are rising in significance. As boards of directors come under increasing scrutiny and are subject to more government and stockholder suits for malfeasance, they adopt more energetic audit practices, both inside and outside.[9] Surveys, interviews, investigations, and systematic organizational scanning are all part of this drive to face the present situation more thoroughly. Historian Charles Beard noted that "when the sun goes down the stars come out," which suggests for organizations and for individuals that the surprises which become disastrous usually have been present for some time but unobserved. The audit and review of the present includes some history to show how the firm got where it is, from which trends can be noted and imminent threats averted while · they are still merely threats.

Such a practice suits individual career planning and life planning as well.[10] A thorough self-assessment, perhaps with advice from outside counselors, is a sensible start to avoiding some of the surprises that are sometimes unpleasant and often personally disastrous. The seeds of much personal trauma lie in an unwillingness or inability to face oneself fully. A majority of people avoid annual physical checkups. They resent the intrusion of an audit. They resist looking in the unflattering mirror.

---

[8]H. I. Ansoff, *Corporate Strategy: An Analytic Approach to Business Policy for Growth and Expansion* (New York: McGraw-Hill, 1965).

[9]C. C. Abt, *The Social Audit for Management* (New York: AMACOM, 1977.

[10]J. Aplin, "Issues and Problems in Developing Managerial Careers and Potential," *Business Quarterly*, 43, no. 2, Summer 1978; *see also* E. H. Schein, *Career Dynamics: Matching Individual and Organizational Needs* (Reading, Mass.: Addison-Wesley, 1978).

Yet, without such a first step, no sound strategy for the future is possible. For the organization or the individual, managing the future means knowing oneself and being used to oneself before thinking about improvements or changes.

**Systematic preparation of long-run strategies** The money-tree companies, the ones that regularly produce growth in sales and profits and the like, are almost unanimously engaged in systematic planning that stretches into the distant future, with strong emphasis upon the coming five years. Such firms as General Electric, IBM, Ford, General Motors, and Procter & Gamble have a firm grasp of the present situation and trends that emerge from it. They are then ready to define some missions and strategies for attaining success. Typical of such strategies would be the following:

- Exploit some technical advantage
- Use your financial power
- Move more quickly than others
- Turn the other person's strength into a weakness
- Surround the competition
- Penetrate the competition's area of strength
- Flank the competition
- Overpower a major competitor by collaboration
- Hire away the opposition's best people
- Tie up the opposition's strongest weapons
- Play your own strength strongly
- Play upon the weakness of the competition
- Exploit a single cash cow to finance new growth areas
- Use good staff work to produce surprises for the others
- Execute everything better than anybody
- Turn small innovations into a major edge
- Wait out your competition with patience

These and other familiar strategies are combined to gain market advantage, develop your human resources, or make maximum value of your technical lead. Most important, all of these strategic ploys call for a prior change in the attitude of top management and the rest of the organization as well.

*An organization must be taught to think and act strategically until the culture is one that encourages change and innovation.*

Waiting for the light to flash, or for the *eureka effect*, to produce money-tree organizations is a chancy business, usually doomed to failure. However dramatic such startling triumphs might be, they do not produce surprise-free management. Management by surprise sometimes produces pleasant surprises, for which there will be ample numbers of people to claim credit. On the other side of that coin are those surprises that are unpleasant or even disastrous. Coaching and training your managers to face reality and to reach out for better things does not insure against all unpleasant surprises, but it improves the ratio. The more people are trying for strategic gains, the more likely that happy events will occur.[11]

Once again, the same principles that work for corporations will work for career planning or life planning at a strategic level. The student who has a good five-year plan will do better in choices of classes, targets for part-time jobs, satisfaction of financial needs, and even recreation. Not that it is always advisable to close all of one's options too early. Nonetheless, having a strategic life plan can reduce one's likelihood of ending up in one of life's cul-de-sacs by accident.

**A willingness to shift resources to higher yield uses**  Organizations that become overly committed to being tied to one product, or to the production of goods from a fixed plant, are more apt to be surprised than those who will move to higher yield ventures. When R. J. Reynolds was confronted with an opinion of the Surgeon General of the United States that tobacco and cigarette smoking was the cause of lung cancer, they systematically changed their strategy. Rather than plowing back earnings into this high risk area, they reinvested instead in other products that were less risky, such as liquor, theme parks, and shipping.

A heavy investment in one line of product, one kind of equipment, or one technology often produces resistance to change on the part of the top management. They often lack the strategic insight to take their losses from a dying line and move on to more productive opportunities. When flour consumption declined in this country, General Mills moved its resources into packaged grocery products, toys, games, and restaurants. In this manner they averted the disasters that come when a firm suddenly wakes up one day to discover that its markets have dried up, leaving it with a hopeless product. Identifying and distinguishing between products and markets that are rising stars, or presently profitable but heading for a decline, or already dead, and ones that have potential but aren't yet fully developed is part and parcel of surprise-free management.

**Skillful use of timing and positioning**  Most management development courses these days have a session on the management of time. Such sessions have apparently struck a responsive chord, not only with executives, but also with show business personalities, homemakers, and athletes, because they deal with getting more done without wasting time doing it. All of which is perfectly useful in the hurly-burly of everyday life. Yet, more important than overtime management over the long haul is the management of *timing*. The dramatic extra base hit is less dramatic if it happens when the batter's team is behind 10-0 with nobody on base. Surprise-free management often means that the *order in which things are done* is orchestrated better than in other organizations. Several guidelines to manage timing seem to characterize people who have grasped these elements of doing the right thing when its impact is highest:

• The longer the lead time you take in planning, the less likely you are to be surprised by the event itself.

[11] T. Naylor, *Corporate Planning Models* (Reading, Mass.: Addison-Wesley, 1979).

• Having an end in sight before you start will give you a better fix on what kinds of lead time and lag time are permissible and necessary.

• Having some kind of model of the entire situation in your mind will help you see the relationships clearly. Timing is as much a matter of seeing positioning and relationships between events as it is being a skilled seer of future events.

• The practice of *patience,* of knowing when to simply sit and wait, is a personal skill of timing that is often learned late in life when its value will be least. Showing patience as a virtue to the young is God's work, and it should qualify the mentor who teaches it for a special crown. No matter how well trained the obstetrician, it still takes nine months to have a baby. If someone pressures you to "snap it up now or it will be gone tomorrow," forget the whole idea.

• Don't rush to judgment and action upon the urgings of unreliable informants. The unreliable informant may not be an immoral person, but may simply be somebody you don't know well enough. If your father-in-law's dear friend's spouse is suggested as a reliable source of good counsel, listen to the counsel and promptly ignore it. People you admire and cherish for their lovability may not always be paragons of wisdom in things beyond their competence. Be kind, but evade the action they espouse.

• Don't confuse the time-bound decision with the non-time-bound decision; running for the last train home at night may be sensible, whereas running for the 4:45 P.M. is senseless if there is another departing at 5:00 P.M. Walk calmly; save your heart.

• Think sequentially about the future, like a chess or tennis player, and your positioning will make your timing right. If the whole sequence of what should happen and can happen isn't clear in your mind, retreat until you get better intelligence, more complete scouting reports, or more facts.

• Stay far enough ahead of followers that they can look to you for leadership, but not so far ahead that you are invisible. Likewise, if you are a follower, the fine art of timing and positioning lies in following your blockers as you run; but don't run up their backs.

• Blind leaps in the dark are great stuff in escape movies, for stunt artists or for the pathologically reckless, but not for responsible managers of organizations or for people who care about their own careers.

• Managers who learn to manage timing and positioning are apt to find that life consists of some fairly long stretches of routine boredom, interspersed with momentary bursts of change. If we realize this, we can be tolerant of some boredom without lashing out in frustration to break its hold on us.

• The personal skill that is most worth practicing is learning when to talk and when to shut up.

• A tentative fix or a partial solution made in order to conserve time is the worst enemy in the world of perfection and self-fulfillment.

• In managing your portfolio of stocks, risks, opportunities, and skills, follow the advice of the old poker player: Learn to "know when to hold, and when to fold."

• When things seem icebound and impossible to change, wait for the big event that *unfreezes* the situation and then take action. If a spouse, lover, or friend is locked into a wrong course and pigheadedly refuses to listen, wait until something traumatic happens and then make your move to persuade him or her to change.

• The last few minutes of a battle are when victory and defeat are determined. John L. Lewis, the labor leader, used to have a jingle: "When you are an anvil, stand you very still. When you are a hammer, strike with all your will." Timing means knowing when you are a hammer and when you are an anvil and never mixing the two.

• Good timing means knowing what the consequences of an act may be before you take it. If your information is complete and it feels right, strike.

• Never enter the battle without a contingency plan. Know the possible downside losses, and don't count on somebody else's foolishness to match your own. On the other hand, don't presume that everyone you compete with will be perfectly rational at all times. Pure chance governs much of the behavior of many people, and their emotional attachment to some irrelevancy may be your undoing.

• Take the time to find collaborators and seek useful coalitions to manage both timing and positioning.

• The old infantry adage "take the high ground and hold it" is sound strategy for the executive suite, the professional practice, or even the career-advancement game. First, you must identify the high ground for you, which isn't always easily determined if you are viewing things from below.

• When you make a move or release an initiative, have not only a plan for dealing with the counterattack, but also have a second-level offense of your own ready. This means positioning yourself with some reserves held back in every contest and only entering the competition without reserves if your last move is one of desperation.

• Many of the best strategies have been based upon finding a crack or a seam into which you can rush. These are the sites where small, early gains are turned into major victories.

• The middle ground generally is a better position than the extremes if you wish to protect your position and keep your options flexible.

**Giving and getting commitments with other people is good risk insurance**
Being able to predict the behavior of others is the most difficult aspect of producing surprise-free management. People don't do the things you believe they should do; their early efforts become bogged down; their momentum slows; or they engage in wholly unprecedented fits and starts. Surprise-free management is more likely if you get the people under your direction, or those who serve you in any way, to make commitments in advance. These commitments ask people to be responsible for the consequences of their own behavior, by asking for promises,

which for normal people means that they are practically obliged to do something about what they have promised.[12]

There are some well-used practices in those well-run organizations that operate by some variety of management by commitment, such as management by objectives. There are four basic truths about getting people committed that are important to both subordinate and boss:

1. Left to their own bureaucratic devices, the average manager and subordinate will more likely fail to agree on the subordinate's responsibilities than agree. Research shows that the average manager and subordinate, queried independently of one another, will produce statements of objectives for the subordinate's job that differ from one another at an average frequency of thirty percent. This gap between what the boss expects and what the subordinate thinks is expected to produce all kinds of mischief. For one thing, it builds failure into the job. It demotivates the subordinate, produces a loss of confidence by the boss, and means that raises, promotions, and recognition will be slow in coming or withheld altogether.

2. When a person finds out what is expected of him or her in advance, that increases the likelihood of achieving it, exactly to the extent that he or she has such expectations firmly in mind. Most people are not saboteurs or slackers and want to succeed, but such success at work is often denied by the boss's failure to present them with clear statements of expectations in advance.

3. When people find out what is expected of them, their performance shows an immediate improvement and is likely to persist in that improved state.

4. A characteristic of the best-run organization is that most of the people in it are clearer on what is expected of them than in less well-run organizations. Furthermore, in well-run organizations the boss is more apt to be in clear agreement on those expectations, and this mutuality of understanding improves the relationship and produces a greater likelihood of surprise-free management. The employee in the organization where expectations are known is under a simple but powerful kind of control, the self-control of a responsible person, which is the tightest and most perfect form of control possible in an imperfect world. It beats top-down autocratic and dictatorial control hands down. It requires that the boss have a clear fix on where the overall organization is going, and what criteria would be present if it got there. The subordinate is able to exercise diligence and responsibility if five conditions are present for him or her pursuant to those organization goals:

- Let me know what is expected of me in advance.
- Tell where the help and resources will come from.
- Leave me alone while I am working to wield my own skills.
- Arrange for me to learn how well I am doing in my work while that work is going on, and allow me time to amend my ways if needed.

---

[12] J. W. Atkinson and W. R. Reitman, "Performance as a Function of Motive Strength and Expectancy of Goal Attainment,' *Journal of Abnormal and Social Psychology*, 53, 1956.

- Reward my achievements of goals I have agreed on and not something extraneous.

This calls for a systematic plan for every boss and subordinate to sit down face to face at the beginning of each year or shorter time period in which results are sought to discuss expectations and objectives. The outcome of these discussions should be confirmed in writing. The boss then is available to help and round up the necessary tools, money, and assistance to do the job. Beyond this, the employee is left alone while working, unless he or she requests assistance, or is clearly failing to deliver on expectations. When the day, the quarter, the season, or the year is done, the rewards are dished out according to the contributions made.[13]

While management by objectives is orthodoxy in the *Fortune* 500 largest corporations, its uses are not limited to them. Small firms, offices, and work teams and families can benefit from applying this five-step plan to their relationships. The family in which every member knows what is expected and how well he or she is doing will avoid some of the trauma that affects the families where bloody war is an everyday occurrence. If you would deal effectively with a spouse, a colleague, or anyone who serves you or whom you serve, mutually define expectations and get a commitment to work for the building of the relationship.

**Sound management information systems produce surprise-free management**
Daniel Bell suggests that we have arrived in a new age: the postindustrial society. This society has supplanted in large part, he proposes, an industrial society, just as the industrial society supplanted an agrarian society. The distinctive feature of the postindustrial society is what it produces. Rather than simply producing goods like flour and cars, which it of course still does, it becomes more concerned with producing knowledge, information, and relationships. The growth of the computer and automated data processing systems, and the computer industry which fuels them, is evidence of the growth of an information-based society.[14] *Data banks* collect great inventories of information, which can be retrieved from their memory in an instant by a skilled user of computer technology. To produce information quickly and properly will substantially enhance the likelihood of producing surprise-free management.

1. Information about the present condition is necessary to make any kinds of forecasts and projections. Not only is a still photo of the present needed, but a dynamic picture of what has happened in the past will assist in seeing what lies in the natural course ahead.

2. Information can be too voluminous or so poorly organized that it hides the truth more than it reveals it. Many bosses labor under the illusion, suggests Professor Russell Ackoff, that getting more information than they now receive will unfailingly produce better decisions. This has not been the case, especially when the information is unorganized or unclearly seen. Ackoff suggests that the manager

---

[13] G. S. Odiorne, *MBO II: A System of Managerial Leadership for the Eighties* (Belmont, Calif.: Fearon, 1979).

[14] R. Ackoff, *A Concept of Corporate Planning* (New York: John Wiley, 1970).

who has one kind of conceptual model will be best equipped to use the information available to improve things.

3. The uses of information can be divided into two categories. The first are those actions based on information where the purpose is to produce *control*. The organization that has standards and then obtains information showing that the standards are not being met can make adjustments continually and periodically to get things back on course. But, as Professor Joseph Juran points out, a second use of information is to produce *change* and creativity. Ample information and knowledge is needed to arrive at new combinations that will stick through the vicissitudes of a competitive world.[15]

4. A distinctive and highly fragile kind of information system is that which flows between two individual human beings. People talk, write, and behave in ways that transmit information. There is more to the information here than the binary numbers and the bytes of the computer. It rests upon a definition of behavior that suggests that communication is behavior that results in an exchange of meaning.

5. Surprise-free management requires, then, that all four elements of information be present and grow in sophistication and skill. There must be banks of data previously prepared and ready for use when needed. There must be standards and controls that tell when things are off the track and need immediate or periodic correction. There is a need for information that can be combined into new and unique ways of doing things and into the creation of new and beautiful products. Finally, there is a need for face-to-face, person-to-person communication, which blends into a human organization, not simply a mechanized network of one person's answering service talking to another person's answering service.

Surprise-free management information systems will thus be more than technically sound; they will also be humanistic. The system will tell people that they are important, that they are growing, that they have done well or poorly, that they are somebody. The system that is only technically sound but not humanistic will fail. Equally apparent is how often humanistic relationships that are unsystematic and chaotic produce more misery than happiness, despite their noble objectives. The organization that ignores technical systems will often be surprised by the blow that blindsides and wrecks its best-laid plans.

The organization that ignores its information systems' human aspects will be even more sadly surprised. The eruptions that come when employees quit at the worst possible time or join a union or protest strongly against what apparently was considered in their best interests won't come from outside. They will emerge right out of the organization, which, on its surface, was calm and serene until finally the dehumanizing and depersonalized nature of its information systems became intolerable. "Why, I thought people liked me," protested one plant manager. "We saw each other every day, and I presumed our relations were good until the union election came up and ninety percent of them voted for a militant union. What could we have done wrong?"

---

[15] J. Juran, *Managerial Breakthrough* (New York: McGraw-Hill, 1964).

**An optimistic view of the future will produce fewer unpleasant surprises**
Surprise-free organizations do not really operate without surprises. Some organizations are graced with a steady stream of pleasant surprises. Their people rise to challenges, their markets respond to their products, and their suppliers make every effort to deliver on time, above and beyond the call of business. Few bosses really enjoy bad surprises, but almost without exception they cherish pleasant ones. This outlook resembles the old army game of "let's go to town and get into a fight," an off-hours pastime of infantrymen in my old outfit. This, however, was really a code language for *Let's go downtown and find somebody we can lick and beat them up.* Seldom did they pick on a ranger or a paratrooper; rather, they preferred a clerk, a quartermaster, or a sailor (spirited but not tough). Similarly, surprise-free management aims merely at limiting unpleasant surprises; but even these can be borne with some aplomb and equanimity if there is a counterbalance of pleasant surprises flowing in.

Surprise-free management, then, means systems of control over unpleasant surprises, but it must go beyond that and produce some pleasant ones to outweigh the few unpleasant ones that erupt through even the best-laid safeguards of controllers. While there is no guarantee of pleasant surprises in well-organized programs of innovation, they are most likely to occur when the climate of the organization greets them warmly. In recent years, optimism has had a rather bad name in some quarters. The drying up of optimism in human affairs produces surprises that are almost wholly bad news.

The optimistic outlook is one which presumes that the world of tomorrow will be better than the world of today. As America grew toward the west, it was characterized by such optimism. People no sooner crossed the Mississippi than they began to dream dreams and make plans they never would have imagined possible in a dingy flat in a dark and crowded eastern city.

Optimism has the dimension of being a self-fulfilling prophecy when it permeates an organization.[16] If people believe that things will be better, they take those steps and think those thoughts that make them better. The pioneer Mormons who dragged pushcarts with their possessions from Illinois 1500 miles across the Plains and the Rocky Mountains to settle the Salt Lake Valley were motivated by the optimistic belief that beyond the mountains lay a new Zion, where they would make a paradise on earth. When Jim Bridger wagered them that they couldn't make a single ear of corn grow in the barren salt flats, he couldn't have imagined the optimism that would impel them to do just that.

Nicholas Murray Butler, one-time president of Columbia University, is reported to have said that you can classify people into three categories. There are a small group of people who make things happen, a little larger group of people who watch what is going on, and the overwhelming majority, who haven't the slightest idea of what is happening. It is the first class who make the world move into new and better ways of doing things. Whether Butler's taxonomy of the human race is accurate or not is not the point. There are people who make things happen and

---

[16] L. Tiger, *Optimism: The Biology of Hope* (New York: Simon & Schuster, 1979).

those who don't, and the reasons for failure are seldom rooted in the obstacles. The same obstacles that stop one person are overcome without hesitation by another, which would indicate that obstacles don't stop people as much as people stop themselves.

In achieving surprise-free management, then, the best insurance against unpleasant surprises, and perhaps a fair bet that some favorable ones will emerge, lies in the caliber of persons chosen to do the jobs. This isn't, as Butler's statement might imply, something genetic. More likely it is an organizational and cultural climate that generates motivated behavior.

David McClelland, the Harvard psychologist, calls this tendency toward making things happen "achievement motivation." Using a test of his own devising he tested leaders in numerous nations and cultures. He found that the achieving society was one in which the people in charge of things were more likely to have a high score on his achievement motivation tests.[17] McClelland concluded that the development of people with a high motivation to achieve will have tangible economic effects for the nation that produces such people. This, of course, implies that there is adequate investment and opportunity to achieve. This forward-looking outlook, the mental set that things will be better in the future, tends to produce more favorable surprises than unfavorable. The people in the optimistic achievement-centered society are more likely to set goals, speak the language of success, have systems that reward success, and reinforce one another in their efforts to succeed and achieve.

How, then, can you as a manager apply this to making your organization optimistic and achievement-centered?

- *Concentrate on the future* rather than the past. Don't be *exclusively* forward-looking, for there are uses for the past. But the major emphasis in management affairs lies in making a better future rather than in ruing and lamenting a depressing or unsuccessful past.

- *Imagine and create the future* rather than simply waiting for it. This requires goal setting—the statement of missions, dreams, aspirations, and hopes. These, in turn, are converted into specific commitments on the part of responsible people.

- *Use the desire of people* to take part in decisions to get their commitment to these future goals.

- In watching and reviewing progress, *speak the language of success* rather than the language of failure.

- *Build systems that recognize and reward achievement* rather than systems which catch and punish failure.

- *Organize the members of the organization into teams* where their efforts can be mutually supported and reinforced.

- *Provide opportunity* for people to make the future better for themselves and the organization.

[17] D. McClelland, *The Achieving Society*.

• Spend more time in *seeking out resources and assistance* to people in their pursuits than in checking and correcting their efforts. Judge people by their attainments, not their activity.

**A strong commitment to developing human potential** At the end of World War II, because of work force distortions from the war and great growth, the American industrial scene was caught by a great shortage of experienced managers. The average age of managers was high enough that a majority of them were due for retirement within five years, and in some firms eighty percent of the management team retired in a five-year period. The result was a burst of management development programs at universities and in trade and professional associations and a rash of consultants serving this demand. The effort continued through the sixties and seventies. The growth of decentralized firms meant that more general managers were needed. Economic growth and the larger work force meant more supervisory jobs were created for which manager training was needed.

By the end of the seventies, it was apparent that the money-tree firms, the ones which grew fastest with the highest levels of profit, were also those which paid the greatest attention to training and were committed most strongly to the growth of human potential within their ranks. IBM, it was reported in 1977, had 42,000 full-time-equivalent people in training for the year. Their bill for training and development, not only of employees but of customers and service people, ran well over half a billion dollars. General Motors owned its own accredited college (General Motors Institute of Flint, Michigan), with 2500 degree candidates in engineering and management. Xerox built a giant training campus in Leesburg, Virginia, reported to be over $50 million in cost. Eastman Kodak constructed and operated a giant training and education center outside Rochester, New York, said to have cost over $40 million. Likewise, in other major firms, it became apparent that the development of human potential through formal educational efforts inside the firm was a vital part of the strategy of growing business for the future.

Despite its size and expense, this effort didn't comprise the main site for the development of human potential inside the corporate and government organization. Such development is most likely to occur on the job itself, most experts agreed. People learn by doing, learn by working for a boss who teaches them or arranges for learning to occur.

*Surprise-free management requires that people be delegated responsibilities and given the chance to acquire skills to do the job. The rate at which companies can delegate important jobs is a function of how well and how fast they can teach people to do things right.*

As one president of a large office machinery firm told me, "The rate at which this company can grow in sales and profits is the rate at which we can grow people to operate the new businesses." Thus, when IBM grows at $2.5 billion in a single year, its major problems are not the financial or technical ones, although these are important concerns, but growing enough qualified people to operate the proposed and hoped-for new $2.5 billion business. Further, these new people must operate the newly created organization and its business at the same level of competence as the old employees who built the business to begin with or at a still higher level. General Motors grew in sales by $15 billion over a three-year period in the late seventies. This is larger than the volume of many whole industries, yet because of sound development the company had the people ready to staff every new plant, office, and managerial position.

Management development and employee development, well executed, are a vital element in surprise-free management. Without such development, the growth can become a nightmare of incompetence, errors of omission, bloopers of inexperience, and a loss of control.

**Unremitting feedback of information into the situation as it evolves** The cycle of management control is one that starts with standards, specifications, expectations, plans, and goals. It proceeds to action, doing things and executing processes. Finally, it requires periodic review and feedback of the actual results against the standards and goals. This feedback can be instantaneous and continuous like the wall thermostat measuring temperature and controlling the furnace, or it can be like the periodic review of the controller, who checks actual financial outcomes against a budget.[18] Beyond these controlling types of feedback are other kinds of feedback, which are less planned but nonetheless significant.

1. *There are signals from nature,* which has its own inscrutable and sometimes concealed standards, which it imposes on the rest of us. Your car may drop into a hidden pothole in the road. The lack of notification doesn't change the law of gravity, which can break your suspension system. Nature's feedback can be very unforgiving of bad memories of its laws. If you don't maintain your plant and equipment, they will break down.

2. *We can get feedback from other people.* They respond to our behavior according to how they view our behavior. They may have interests that are hurt by what we do and they will inform us of that fact. Or they might respond by reciprocal damage to our own interests as a means of letting us know. They may find that what we do is pleasing and satisfactory and reciprocate by doing us a favor in return.

3. *We all have selective systems for handling signals.* As I sit writing, my hi-fi set is playing and it doesn't interfere with my thought processes, for I selectively receive the music (by Borodin). A dog is barking on the next block, but it is filtered out. This filtering system seems to work for some kinds of feedback but not for others; such selectivity is apparently something most people have, or we would be driven to distraction constantly. This means that feedback is usually selective as a result of some internal reception process.

4. *We are constantly giving out signals* which for us comprise only ordinary behavior but which for other people comprise incoming signals that may be physical (I blow cigar smoke in your direction), social (my crowd ignores you at a party),

[18]T. Connellan, *How to Improve Human Performance* (New York: Harper & Row, Pub., 1978).

or psychological (I use sexist language). Recognition of our own signals is as selective as our receiving ability.

All of this has a great deal to do with surprise-free management and the generation of change, or overcoming resistance. Here's how.

• Surprise-free management is not really surprise-free; it is just that we get a series of tiny surprises at more frequent intervals and therefore can make continual corrections in our situation. This prevents the surprise from becoming big and painful when it arrives, and it allows us to prevent its growth.

• Widespread feedback serves us well, for it spreads the tiny surprises among a great many more people who are closer to the point of action and change. If, in sitting here writing, I were to overhear in the background the trumpeting of a charging bull elephant, not common in residential Amherst, Massachusetts, I would be surprised. If, rather than rain on the roof, which I filter out of my hearing, I were to hear an even softer sound of something gnawing at the foundation of the house, I would drop the filter in my mind and investigate, before the house collapsed around me, I would hope. Small signals are a continual safeguard mechanism by means of which surprise-free management can occur.

• We can develop an awareness of and sensitivity to the feedback we are receiving. In some cases the feedback foretells something favorable, and in other cases we can note impending unfavorable consequences. When the pattern is predictive of something unfavorable, we will take actions to avoid it. When it projects something we see as favorable, we will take actions to have the situation continue.

• We can teach other people to respond to feedback and then arrange feedback for favorable and unfavorable behavior in order to keep them on track.

*Change occurs when people receive favorable feedback for changing, and no unfavorable feedback. Resistance occurs when the messages received are that such change will have more unfavorable consequences than favorable.*

Here lies the sum and substance of the change resisters in our world. If change and its management are to be accomplished without producing earthquake-like consequences for everyone, we must arrange our affairs so that we eliminate the unfavorable consequences of change for most people and offer more favorable consequences to more people for changing.

Lamentably, we live in a world that increasingly provides too many unfavorable consequences for people who do the right things and too many favorable consequences for people who do the wrong, the weak, and the cowardly things. It may explain our malaise in a time of plenty.

# twenty

# Notes and suggestions for further study or reading

This is a very short finale to the brief presented in this book. You may perhaps be interested in knowing more about the change resisters and the anti-planners, and what others have said can be done about them. The following is a brief, almost cryptic list of books a manager or other individual desiring to study the subject of change might read to gain new insights.

1. ERIC HOFFER. *The Ordeal of Change.* (New York: Harper & Row, Pub., Perennial Library, 1963. Paper, 120 pages).

> This short paperback by the noted longshoreman-philospher is filled with original thoughts on change and its difficulties. Within sixteen brief chapters, Hoffer deals with drastic change and its pains, how imitation and fanaticism arise, the role of intellectuals in the process, the unnaturalness of human nature, and the role of the misfits and undesirables in society.

2. JOHN W. GARDNER. *No Easy Victories.* (New York: Harper & Row, Pub., 1968. 172 pages).

> John Gardner, shortly after leaving government, where he ran the giant Department of Health, Education, and Welfare, issued this book of his collected essays. They deal with tasks for the tough-minded and confront the resistant character of institutions to constructive change. In this book, he deals with specific issues of the public mood, building a just society, and other key issues, including a stirring chapter on change. Institutions which are not innovating are dying, he proposes. He covers equality, health, schools, the universities, leadership, aging, and the individual and society. A reflective and thought-provoking work you should read.

3. PETER F. DRUCKER. *Landmarks of Tomorrow.* (New York: Harper & Row, Pub., 1957. 270 pages).

> The noted management consultant ranges over the future in an original book. Like Hoffer and Gardner, Drucker thinks for himself and deals with change as

267

a major problem. Of especial interest is his "new world view," in which he says we have moved from progress to innovation, beyond collectivism and individualism to new frontiers. He ends by warning us that the human situation rests upon the fact that the meaning of man is changing. Because of our knowledge we can now easily destroy ourselves, and "there is no danger that man will ever run out of ignorance. We try to steer by old landmarks while sailing new seas."

4. DANIEL BELL. *The Coming of The Post Industrial Society*. (New York: Basic Books, 1973).

This is a germinal book by a Harvard sociologist generally credited with the discovery and perhaps invention of the idea of the postindustrial society. We can already see tangible evidence of the characteristics he describes: the knowledge society, the rising influence of the knowledge industry and the university, and increasing government. A thought-provoking and important part of your further reading.

It would be easy to add dozens, or even hundreds, of other books on the management of change. Many of them are research studies on the mechanisms of change, or the psychology of change. These four, however, comprise my recommendations for your next stage. Many others noted in the chapter footnotes will do if your persistence and interest wax. I suspect that these will be a sound beginning.

# Index